Caesars, Saviours and Suckers

The good, bad and ugly of football's foreign owners

Caesars, Saviours and Suckers

The good, bad and ugly of football's foreign owners

BOB HOLMES

© Bob Holmes, 2016

Published by Bob Holmes

A CIP catalogue record for this book is available from the British Library.

ISBN 978-0-9955666-0-6

Book layout and cover design by Clare Brayshaw

Cover image © Svitlana Zakharevich | Dreamstime.com

Prepared and printed by:

York Publishing Services Ltd
64 Hallfield Road
Layerthorpe
York YO31 7ZQ

Tel: 01904 431213

Website: www.yps-publishing.co.uk

Dedication

To Gerv Leyden and Geoff Bennett, thinking football men, who dispensed enough wisdom, passion and what might be called pearls of bias to last several lifetimes. Alas, both of theirs were tragically cut short just months apart while I was writing this book. Giving you an honorable mention is the least I could do, young men. As someone said, be good.

About the Author

Bob Holmes was raised in Nottingham, where his Derby-supporting dad nurtured his love of the game on both sides of the Trent. A few early deadlines were missed by taking a 'gap decade' to see the world, but stints with the Observer, London Evening Standard and Telegraph convinced him that watching sport beat working for a living. He wrote books on athletics, cricket, football and rugby union before joining the Sun-Herald in Sydney. He ended up in Kuala Lumpur but has never taken his eye of English football.

Contents

Acknowledgements

Tackling a subject like foreign ownership from a distance was always going to be pushing the phrase 'on a wing and a prayer' beyond reasonable limits. Whether it would even get off the ground would depend as much on football people's willingness to talk to an ex-pat scribbler as my own sacrifice of precious annual leave in places like Blackburn, Portsmouth and the West Midlands. The background is out there but, in many cases, the stories and perspectives of those involved remained untold. I am deeply grateful, therefore, to those that did agree to talk as well as those that gave permission to reproduce previously published comments. I am also indebted to the media outlets listed below where I may have peppered the boundaries of Fair Usage. The upshot has enabled me to stitch together tales of 10 takeovers that altered the course of each club's history. I hope I've done you justice and that the result is a small contribution to the debate on football ownership. I would also hope that it makes for an interesting read for fans in general and not just those of the clubs involved. My heartfelt thanks to those listed here as well as those who preferred to remain anonymous. This was never meant to be a definitive study as the level of scrutiny has inevitably varied. Indeed, the margin for error is wider than some opinion polls we could mention and any judgements are purely personal. Last but not least, thanks go to my long-suffering wife, Jane, who, despite my best – and worst – efforts, steadfastly remains a football atheist.

On the Aston Villa story, I particularly thank Bill Howell who provided an instant recall of his days covering the Randy Lerner takeover for the *Birmingham Mail*. Thanks also to that paper's current football editor Mat Kendrick, and Dave Woodhall of *Heroes and Villains*. Blackburn Rovers die-hards John Pittard, Jim Wilkinson, Dave Rose, Brian Haworth and Ian Battersby gave me a real insight into the Venky's debacle as did, from a somewhat different perspective, Shebby Singh. Chelsea fanzine editor David Johnstone was an invaluable help in penetrating the impenetrable

Roman Abramovich. Manchester City's former head honcho Garry Cook could not have been more helpful or enthusiastic while supporters-cum–scribes Simon Hattenstone, David Conn and Colin Shindler allowed me to include their own fascinating and divergent views on the Abu Dhabi takeover. And then there are former City stars Peter Barnes, Tommy Booth and Didi Hamman. At Hearts, there were politicians involved: former chairman Lord George Foulkes of Cumnock found time to give me chapter and verse on Vladimir Romanov's tumultuous reign while Ian Murray MP modestly downplayed his own heroic role in the rescue. No one has more vivid memories than broadcaster Charlie Mann who was 'the mad Russian's' spokesman and lived to tell the tale. Long-term fans Iain Mcleod, Andrew Donaldson and Ross Pilcher were fulsome with their views, Donaldson even fact-checking the story. And I'm not forgetting Myles Edwards whose contacts made this unforgettable chapter possible. Forest long-term devotees Clive Dearden and Andrew Cotton were invaluable on the recent shenanigans on the Trent. On the other side of the river, Notts County's *Trillion Dollar Con* led me to China where Sven-Goran Eriksson still struggled to believe what happened as he talked fondly of his early months there as well as offering widely differing appraisals of Blackburn's Jack Walker and City's Thaksin Shinawatra. Thanks also to ex-CEO Peter Trembling, former chairmen Steve Thompson and John Armstrong-Holmes, former supporters trust secretary John Collin and Paul Fallon whose own tome on the Munto saga, *Political Football*, came from the vantage point of being a lawyer working on the case. At Portsmouth, chairman Iain McInnes managed to find some gallows humour in a tale that if it had been fiction, would have been too far-fetched. Pompey officials Colin Farmery, Ashley Brown and administrator Trevor Birch were at pains to confirm it was for real. QPR supporters trust's Neil Jackson has been a continued source of information, not forgetting *Loft for Words*' Clive Whittingham and *The Guardian's* Michael Hann. At Wolves, the former *Express & Star* trio John Dee, Dave Harrison and Steve Gordos recalled the Bhattis reign, Harrison giving a blow-by-blow account of the takeover and subsequent debacle. Roger Hipkiss and Doug Hope offered their perspective on it as ex-board members.

As for publications and broadcasters, I would like to thank the BBC, Sky News, Daily Express, Daily Mail, Daily Mirror, Daily Record, Daily Star, Daily Telegraph, The Guardian, The Independent, News of the World, The Observer, The Scotsman, The Sun, The Spectator, The Times, Birmingham Mail, Evening Standard, Lancashire Telegraph, Manchester Evening News, Nottingham Post, Portsmouth Evening News, Wolverhampton Express & Star. Mention must also be made of Football365.com, The Four Year Plan documentary and books Richer Than God, The Terminal Spy, Manchester United Ruined My Life, Manchester City Ruined My Life, Running with Wolves, The Doog, Deadly Doug and Sven: My Story.

Introduction

Foreign ownership has been an incendiary topic ever since Roman Abramovich bestowed the spoils of the aluminium wars on Chelsea in 2003. "He parked his Russian tanks on our lawn and started firing £50 notes at us," is how Arsenal director David Dein described it. The barrage would intensify and smash the burgeoning duopoly of Arsenal and Manchester United. With over £1 billion's worth of rounds fired, the Blues plundered a dozen major trophies in as many years. But Abramovich's arrival would prove a game-changer in an even wider sense: he became an unlikely Pied Piper for a procession of foreign zillionaires wanting to park on English lawns.

Well over half the 44 clubs in the Premier League and Championship are now owned by non-UK citizens and the landscape has changed forever. Without their investment the top flight would not be the El Dorado of football it is today. That said, several British clubs would not have been taken to oblivion and back by absentee shysters either. For every Chelsea and Man City, there's a Portsmouth and Blackburn Rovers, not to mention in Scotland where Heart of Midlothian's oligarch experience held far more terrors than trophies.

It's long been a source of fascination as to why the super rich from abroad should regard a British football club as the ultimate fashion accessory when the locals can't be arsed. And when some of them don't know the offside rule! Fenway Sports Group's John Henry admitted "Liverpool were a mystery to me", Flavio Briatore thought QPR was a "barbecue restaurant", while Blackburn's Mrs Desai famously said: "I've watched cricket, yes, and hockey, sometimes, but never football". This book is an attempt to assess the impact of these takeovers by looking at a cross-section while relating their colourful stories. It is neither a xenophobic exercise nor a hatchet job, but examines the reasons behind them and makes a stab at evaluation.

Those that followed Abramovich are a disparate bunch and have come from some unlikely corners: among them are American tycoons and Middle Eastern royalty, a Thai duty-free king, Indian poultry magnates, a Soviet sub-mariner and a Hong Kong hairdresser. Portsmouth endured five different owners in little over a year. And always you have to ask: why football? And why, in particular, English football? The answers you get invariably mention the unmentionable – the dreaded words 'brand' and 'franchise'. Others want a plaything or to put their country on the map; occasionally there is even a love of football. But mostly they have been drawn by the television riches that have turned the Premier League into the new Klondyke. Not only is there an £8.3 billion mother lode from broadcasting rights, the values of the clubs themselves have more than doubled in just over a decade. Six of the top eight are owned from outside the UK including the four richest – and the Premier League is by far the wealthiest, most watched league on the planet. By the end of the 2016-17 season, all 20 clubs will be among the 30 richest in the world. It is has not been dubbed "The Greed is Good League" for nothing. Yet none of this could have happened without paying the king's ransom wages that top players demand – and which mostly comes from abroad.

In terms of how they have been perceived, the owners divide into three categories which I've called Caesars, Saviours and Suckers – although there are several overlaps. Indeed, Hearts' Vladimir Romanov qualifies for all three having saved the club, milked the adulation and dropped £50m. The Venky's have lost more than double that at Blackburn, the Al Hasawis are fast catching up at Forest. No one has ever called Tony Fernandes a sucker but his venture into the transfer market at QPR has been likened to "lowering a hunk of meat into a tank full of piranhas". The theory that intelligent men leave their brains in the car park when it comes to football still has its believers.

They never leave their egos behind, though, and "many want to be Caesar." So says a man who knows what it's like to be a senator. "Sitting up there in the directors' box is a bit like being in the Coliseum," he told me. "There can be no doubt that ego is behind a lot of football takeovers." Yet Henry and Desai are largely absentee landlords as are the Glazers, while inviting Sheikh Mansour has been compared to inviting the Queen. The richest and arguably best owner of all, he has pumped

£1.5 billion into Manchester City but attended only one game. Even Abramovich himself, you feel, could be jealous of Howard Hughes. So, clearly, adulation only works for some. The Glazers are vulture capitalists while the Sheikh is doing it for the glory of Abu Dhabi. Whatever the reason, few appreciate that to the faithful, football is not just a game but a religion whose mores and rituals might be observed by cardinals. Nor are they necessarily compatible with a return on investment.

Yet nothing shakes or stirs the febrile imaginations of fans more than an impending takeover. The last thing they think of is where the money is coming from; the first is where it might be going. If a fantasy troika of Al Capone, Bernie Madoff and Ivan the Terrible pumped a billion into their beloved club, bygones could very soon be bygones if they delivered a 20 goals-a-season striker. That said, the guardians of our game still have a responsibility to ensure that the new mob are kosher.

All that stands between a prospective buyer and a place at sport's most exclusive trough is something called the 'owners and directors' test. You could call it an 'A' level to the oft-derided 'fit and proper' person's 'O' level, but one which, to a savvy zillionaire, appears no more a stumbling block than the two times table was to Stephen Hawking. Even Leeds' Massimo Cellino found a way around it. Dodgy or doolally, home-grown or foreign, football's new breed of owner invariably sails through to become either messiah or pariah – depending on their fancies, fan perceptions and the bounce of the ball.

Ian Battersby, who has tried to help the hapless Venky's at his beloved Blackburn, feels strongly there should be more protection from such people: "What we can't have is foreign owners coming into the game – a game that's worth billions a year to this country and globally – where they pick up a toy and leave it with huge debt piles around its neck when they go." The Venky's haven't – yet – but it's already happened at Portsmouth and Hearts where the fans had to wrestle with the albatross and pick up the mess. At Notts County in 2009, fans were already in charge but got duped by con men who pretended to be "mystery Middle Eastern royalty". They were a mystery alright – they were deemed 'fit and proper' without showing their faces or revealing their names!

Indeed, when it comes to being unfit and improper, home-grown owners have so far surpassed anything the invaders have come up with.

Ken Richardson tried to burn down the Doncaster ground in a doomed attempt to claim the insurance – and did four years. Safe-cracker George Reynolds built a 25,000 capacity stadium for Darlington's 4,000 fans and ushered the club into oblivion. Asset-stripper John Batchelor, who snaffled a sponsor's cash at York City, admitted: "This is what I do for a living: I fuck companies". Nor have the big clubs escaped: think of Peter Ridsdale, Ken Bates, Mike Ashley and Craig Whyte, whose respective reigns at Leeds, Leeds again, Newcastle and Rangers never suggested they were auditioning to become Chancellor.

The 10 clubs I've looked at are a diverse bunch and range from the ill-fated Bhatti brothers at Wolves through the *Trillion Dollar Con* at Notts County to the mega-rich reboots at Chelsea and Man City. In the cases of Blackburn and Forest, comparisons are made with their local predecessors; at City and QPR with foreign predecessors. Like British owners, there's the good, the bad, the ugly and the bonkers. Vladimir Romanov, an ex- Soviet sub-mariner who sailed in British waters with nukes locked on our cities during the Cold War, took Hearts for the ride of their life when he came to the surface. Pompey were like a hand grenade being tossed between five owners in a year before they were saved by the fans. At Villa, Randy Lerner went from walking on water to hate figure.

The verdicts are as mixed as their motives and the jury is still out in some cases. Overall, the successes far outweigh the crackpot moments and the Premier League would not be a must-see for a sizable chunk of mankind without them. But what is becoming increasingly apparent is the widening disconnect between owners and fans. Successes on the field and on the balance sheet are not always in tandem, and sometimes the very DNA of the club will feel tampered with. The more distant from the action, the less likely an owner is to appreciate the peccadilloes of a particular fandom. Both Premier League and Football League hierarchies are concerned that should a foreign majority of owners get together to form a united block, the structure itself might change. Another reason that some fear colonisation is that only 31 per cent of Premier League players are available to the England manager. But Wales, with barely 3 per cent, put that into perspective with their performance at Euro 2016. For the traditionalist, it is a trend that is as worrying as it can be exciting. Clubs want stability but they often find themselves on the big dipper. Some have soared to heights they hadn't dreamed of but the downers, as Portsmouth and Hearts fans will testify, can be near-death experiences. Either way, they have cracking stories to tell.

Aston Villa

ASTON VILLA

1

"There are two things in life you cannot choose. The first is your enemies; the second your family. Sometimes the difference between them is hard to see, but in the end time will show you that the cards you have been dealt could always have been worse."

Carlos Ruiz Zafón, The Midnight Palace

Football fans might add a third thing: the owners of their club. Take Villa fans during the 2015-16 season. Doomed to relegation since January, they had a lame duck manager and players who didn't seem to care. Off the field they were just as big a shambles: executives were quitting, fans were rebelling and even the match-day receptionist resigned in protest. The owner? A conspicuous absentee that was desperate to sell. But it could have been worse: when he'd bought the club, Randy Lerner had been preferred to one of the cowboys who bought Liverpool.

All that stopped a deal going through was chairman Doug Ellis realising George Gillett didn't have the cash. He writes in *Deadly Doug*: "Gillett badly wanted the club, and was willing to meet the new asking price." Ellis had dropped it by £20m, he said, "because I thought I was on my deathbed." 'Deadly' could be deadpan too. But when told by Rothschilds that all but one of the interested parties would have to borrow the money to buy him out, Ellis was instantly drawn to the one who didn't. "I was impressed by Lerner's demeanour and by his record," he wrote. "I believed Randy was the right man and so far I have been proved right."

Eventually, Ellis would criticise Lerner for trying to run the club from the other side of the Atlantic, but for the first half of the American's tenure he had no reason to question his decision: and certainly not after Gillett had roped in Tom Hicks to buy Liverpool.

No Villa fan would be surprised to find the most important box Lerner ticked for Ellis was the cashbox. As notorious for his thrift as for his profligacy with managers, the old man was determined to ensure that his legacy would not be a mountain of debt. What he and his beloved club got was an awful lot more than a man of ample means.

A rich man's son, Lerner was in the billionaire league yet of modest demeanour, quietly spoken and cultured. He had inherited his father's credit card company, MBNA, as well as the Cleveland Browns American Football team, and had been a capable operator both as a lawyer and a businessman. He had studied at Clare College, Cambridge where he had acquired a keen interest in football, watching Arsenal and Fulham as well as Villa. He made all the right noises but softly – yes, there would be money for new players and the aim, he said, was for Villa to "compete at the highest level within the Premiership and in Europe". He admitted: "This isn't a lifelong thing. It'd be dishonest and disingenuous to suggest it was. But it seems the opportunity to make a difference. Martin O'Neill is great. He's got the record, the history and the makings for a steady, long-term commitment to Villa. That's the plan."

Bill Howell covered Villa for the *Birmingham Evening Mail* back then and has the takeover on instant recall. "Doug told me that as soon as Randy came to the table, he knew he was the man," he remembers. "He could just tell; there was never any doubt after that. Talks went on for a few weeks – months even – but he was always going to get it. Randy said at the time he was a Villa fan and had become close to them in their great era – of their European Championship. But I've met him a few times and I'm not convinced by that story, to be honest. He was at college over here and Villa were big at the time. I've got no doubt that there was interest, but Villa were a huge club, had fallen on hard times, needed investment and had a huge fan base. And he got it for £62m. It looked a good investment.

"Everything was right for that takeover and Lerner had clearly got the money. He was only 44 and had something about him. It was like royalty when he was introduced to the media that first day. He was softly spoken and intelligent. There was nothing brash about him. And for four years everything went right. He'd done his homework and brought a big team with him – all the top jobs went to his people. Paul Faulkner was a relative junior in his credit card company and became CEO."

Lerner's homework would have told him he was taking over at a good time. Villa had done little since winning the European Cup in 1982, apart from two League Cup triumphs, and the fans were restless. Says Howell: "The club was on its knees after a few bad seasons. Lerner talked to fans' groups privately to try to find out where he could take Villa, what the expectations were. In 1987 they were relegated from the top flight but managed to return in time to be founder members of the Premier League in 1992. There had been some terrible decisions – Josef Venglos might have been a big name on the continent but he was a disaster, as was Billy McNeill, and the £15m from the NTL [sponsorship] deal was wasted. John Gregory knew he'd taken the club as far as he could and, although Graham Taylor brought a bit of stability, David O'Leary was another terrible appointment. He talked too much about his "babies" at Leeds and when he called the fans "fickle" that was the end for him. At one point Villa had been pushing Arsenal but in the 1990s, when Arsenal brought in Arsene Wenger and rebuilt to become the huge club they are today, Villa slipped backwards under Gregory and have never recovered."

As for Ellis, Howell says: "There's no doubt he's very egotistical – his ego has a mind of its own – but in terms of criticising his running of the club where you try and look after every single penny … well, that's surely doing your job. When Lerner took over everything was rosy. It was a phenomenal time. There had been talk that he would bring Jurgen Klinsmann in as the new manager, but when Martin O'Neill came to the fore a few weeks later there was huge excitement because of what he'd done at Leicester and Celtic. He was *the man* at the time and Lerner knew this. To unveil him just after the takeover… Randy did all the right things."

Even the one box Lerner left empty – living *in situ* – he circumnavigated with a flourish. Unable to shift to Birmingham, he upgraded and completed the training ground at Bodymoor Heath – a project on which Ellis had pulled the plug – and bought a nearby farmhouse to stay in when he came to watch Villa play.

Bodymoor Heath was just one of many moves Lerner made that would have ensured him first place had there been a popularity poll for owners. *Football365.com* named him the top Premier League chairman, stating: "Lerner purchased Aston Villa a little more than a year before two other American financiers with their fingers in sporting pies took over Liverpool, but they have offered lessons in how to and how not to carefully run a football club. If nothing else, Lerner is a PR expert."

The training ground cost £10m, was four times the size of the original complex and one of the best facilities of its kind in the country. If that was appreciated by the players, what warmed the hearts of fans was his £1m restoration of the Holte pub, an historic building that had stood derelict for years behind Villa Park's famous Holte End.

Lerner also commissioned a statue to William McGregor, the Scottish draper who became Villa chairman and founded the Football League. A visionary of his time, McGregor had long been neglected but he stands tall in bronze at Villa Park today – clutching the letter that would change the game. A more contemporary gesture was the parade and all-expenses paid reception for the 1982 European champions at a home game with Sheffield United. Once again, the only return on investment for Lerner was goodwill which the cavernous stands could barely contain. "The fans worship the ground Randy walks on," said Dave Woodhall of fanzine *Heroes & Villains* at the time. "He can't do anything wrong. He's got the common touch. He and his staff have tapped into the fans' mentality. Free scarves, free coaches to Chelsea, refurbishing the Holte pub – and it seems like he genuinely cares."

The lauding of the 1982 team was long overdue. The European Cup had been won during a brief gap in Ellis's long reign which, in some eyes, was why the chairman had not made more of it. For an American owner to make up was all the more damning for 'Deadly'. Besides being a sports fan, Lerner was an art lover and philanthropist, and donated £5m to the National Gallery as well as a similar amount for a new accommodation block at his alma mater in Cambridge.

As if all that were not enough, for two years he eschewed the big bucks of shirt sponsorship in favour of a local children's hospice, Acorns. Following the lead of Barcelona with Unicef, the seven-figure magnanimity won universal approval and gave a serious boost to the charity. It also appeared to lift what some saw as a curse. According to the *Financial Times*, no less than six of the previous nine shirt sponsors had subsequently abandoned production, entered administration or both. However – and this is perhaps a metaphor for Lerner's reign – he would eventually succumb: first to a currency trader and then to a casino operator.

Gaining all these brownie points from a distance showed Ellis that a hands-off chairman didn't have to mean switched-off. Indeed, the ideal owner is one who doesn't meddle as long as there's someone to fill the void. And into that role with no lack of enthusiasm, stepped the new manager. Says Howell: "Martin O'Neill is a control freak. He grabbed the club and did everything – the stuff Graham Taylor had wanted to do years earlier – by being in control of every decision made at the club on and off the pitch that he was able to. He would have made it clear through his agent that he wanted that job and it wouldn't have taken too long for a naïve American billionaire to know that this was the man he needed. And for two years it worked brilliantly.

"As a partnership O'Neill and Lerner was a dream. They wanted European football, they had their goals and ambitions agreed, they were working beautifully together. Lerner was still living in the US, looking after the Cleveland Browns and his business interests there. He'd come over to the odd game. He very rarely met the media after the first burst of interviews, but he didn't need to – and you can't criticise him for that. He was moving the club forward, running it well, spending money – on some of the wrong players as it turns out! Not stellar names but Martin was getting them to play. At that time there was a euphoria about the club, they had the right man in – Martin was terrific for those first two years."

In truth, playing performances didn't match the gestures off the field, but there was a clear sign of progress. O'Neill was accused of overpaying for Ashley Young, a £9m recruit from Watford, but Manchester United would pay double that for him four years later. That first season (2006-07) Villa finished 11th, just five places but several ozone layers of optimism above O'Leary's 16th. In the summer transfer window of 2007, the major signings were Nigel Reo-Coker and Zat Knight for a combined

£12m. Once again, the names were less than stellar but throughout his career O'Neill had operated on limited budgets – mostly shoestring – and he favoured players of character who would work for him. Both players would eventually be sold off at a considerable loss, but no one at Villa was complaining about a sixth place finish. The top four and the Champions League were in sight.

A £40m splurge in the 2008 summer transfer window was meant to hasten the club's return to the competition they had won in 1982, but the amounts paid and the names signed did not quite tally for some observers. Curtis Davies came for almost £10m, Steve Sidwell for £5m, Luke Young for £6m, James Milner for £12m and Carlos Cuellar for £7.8m. And there was Emile Heskey for £3.5m in January 2009 – deemed a good deal at the time but not quite so good when Radamel Falcao was the rumoured alternative.

It was also in January that the *Daily Mail* dubbed Lerner: "The right sort of American," and contrasted the Villa owner with his compatriots at Liverpool. O'Neill was quoted as saying of his boss: "He knows the game well enough to have a full enjoyment of it. But I think it's better the chairman doesn't have too much knowledge. I'd prefer him just to stay with a basic knowledge, if you get my meaning." As a breathing space between them, the Atlantic Ocean was ideal.

Looking back, early 2009 was one of the high water marks of the Lerner/O'Neill regime. Villa were back in the UEFA Cup for the first time in six years, four points above Arsenal in the league and pushing hard for third. Too hard, as it turned out. Asked when the regime first stumbled, Howell does not hesitate: "It all started to go wrong one night in Moscow in the UEFA Cup," he says. Having had the better of a 1-1 draw with CSKA in the home leg, Villa fans felt they would still go through and some 300 booked the long trip to Russia for the return. Howell also saw the debacle first hand.

He says: "Martin played the reserves in the second leg because they had a home game against Stoke on the Sunday. And they got KO'd." The *Birmingham Evening Mail* sports desk was swamped with angry messages from fans, the vast majority feeling Villa could have advanced with a full-strength side. A few had been placated by O'Neill going to the back of the plane on the way home and explaining his prioritising of the League game. And Howell still feels: "He may have got away with it if they'd beaten Stoke. They were winning 2-0 with five minutes to go and 2-1 in injury time. Then Glenn Whelan put one into the top corner from 30 yards and they drew 2-2.

"The whole atmosphere around the club changed from that moment. For the first time fans started to criticise Martin. He doesn't take criticism from fans and he didn't take it well. He held a dinner for those who had gone to Russia as a sort of thankyou gesture but it backfired. Someone said something and he retorted with words to the effect of: 'Don't tell me what to do'. It was totally the wrong thing to say. These fans had spent hundreds of pounds flying out to watch this team of reserves and he bit – he said something like that. The club were trying desperately to finish in the top four and looking good for two-thirds of the season, but they fell away. They'd overspent and brought in players who just weren't good enough at the end of the day. They had Martin motivating them but at this point you'd got the relationship between Martin and Lerner falling apart. It coincided with Randy having personal troubles as well – his marriage ended – and that great relationship, during which Randy had given Martin loads of money for whatever players he wanted, ended as well."

ASTON VILLA

2

"It's the cautionary tale. To me, English football is not philanthropy."

Randy Lerner.

Neither the surrender in Russia nor the slip-up with Stoke is likely to feature in the *History Channel's* Turning Points, but the two matches marked a watershed in O'Neill's relationship with the fans. Paul McGrath, in his column in the *Birmingham Mail*, accused O'Neill of "making a mockery of a competition that still holds special memories for myself and thousands of Villa fans." Howell recalls: "There was outright anger now. Fans were criticising the players he'd bought, the style of play and the fact that he was now admitting that Villa were not interested in winning silverware, but only in finishing in the top four. The fans wanted trophies; they'd had nothing for a long time. So they were desperate for ambition and Martin was no longer giving them ambition – he was interested only in bringing money to the club. Having said that, I'm sure he would have laughed at his critics if Whelan's shot had not gone in. But he put all his eggs in finishing in the top four.

"Unfortunately for Randy, whilst he was taking Villa up a level, his rivals were going up five levels. A sheikh arrived at Man City, Leeds fell away, Arsenal sold a ground for tens of millions and corporate money went through the roof. Chelsea had had a takeover and continued to dominate, United had a takeover on endless debt and Villa just couldn't match it. Roman Abramovich had changed the landscape and the initial excitement among Villa fans was that Randy Lerner would do for Villa exactly what Abramovich had done at Chelsea."

After the retreat from Moscow, Villa failed to win any of their 10 remaining league games in 2008-09 and had to be content with sixth place for the second season in a row. In June, O'Neill suffered a blow when he lost his skipper Gareth Barry to Manchester City for £12m – City's new-found wealth being hard for either club or player to refuse. It was one of many "never the same since" moments.

Villa spent relatively big again in the summer of 2009 but the recruits were again pretty much B-listers. Richard Dunne came from Man City, a move that was now regarded as a step down instead of a step up, along with James Collins from West Ham for a combined £11m. The biggest buy was Stewart Downing for £10m from Middlesbrough and probably the smartest, Fabian Delph, a £5m snip from Leeds. The outlay was less than the previous year but substantial for a relationship that had supposedly broken down.

Still, whatever was going on off the pitch, Villa started solidly in the league and reached Wembley twice in early 2010 – for the final of the League Cup and the semi-final of the FA Cup. They lost both games – to Manchester United and Chelsea respectively – but at least the fans had a sniff of the rarified realms to which the club aspired. And the narrow 2-1 loss to United is still regarded as another 'what if?' moment. When Nemanja Vidic felled Gabby Agbonlahor in the box after just five minutes, Milner scored from the penalty. It was a blatant sending off offence but, as officials sometimes do on showpiece occasions, referee Phil Dowd kept his cards in his pocket. Just what difference it would have made to the match, the manager and his relationship with the owner as well as a few wantaway players had the trophy been won, we can only speculate.

At the end of a season that had promised so much they were again nearly men, nearly reaching the top four and nearly winning silverware. Their signings were mostly nearly men too. For all its size, Villa was no longer a massive club – it was nearly massive. O'Neill had never managed one of the Big Boys in England – neither establishment nor nouveau riche – and had never won the League or FA Cup. He'd won the League Cup twice with Leicester and a clutch of Scottish domestic honours with Celtic, where he'd been runner-up to Jose Mourinho's Porto in the UEFA Cup. Dare it be asked: Was he nearly a top manager?

Whether Lerner felt Villa were hitting a glass ceiling or that he was feeling the pinch – the financial crash of 2008 was still hurting – he decided he would no longer be a bottomless pit for O'Neill to plunder. After a third successive sixth-place finish, he had yet to sanction a single summer signing. He hadn't bought anyone in the winter either, but with Man City offering £24m for Milner, it was thought players would be bought with the proceeds.

With just five days to go before the start of the 2010-11 season, there were still no arrivals, but one sensational departure: on August 9, O'Neill resigned. For the club, any club, the timing could not have been worse. Pre-season had been done, plans had been laid, season tickets sold, and all the best managers snapped up. Yet now the club was suddenly rudderless and it was only days before the best player went too.

It was not entirely out of character for the Northern Irishman to suddenly walk: impulsive and always his own man, he'd clearly come to the end of his tether with the lack of funds, and being denied the Milner money was the last straw. He put out a simple statement paying tribute to players, staff and fans. Lerner responded, saying he and O'Neill "no longer shared a common view as to how to move forward, but the two remain good friends."

If this was the first real jolt to the regime and the first time doubts about the owner's commitment were raised, Lerner still had a huge credit balance of goodwill at Villa – even though he was an infrequent visitor. "I'm not going for the sake of it," he would say, having sequestered himself away in The Hamptons, a billionaire's row on Long Island, New York. But he was not so travel-shy about his American sporting interest. According to *The Wall Street Journal*, Cleveland Browns Transportation was the No.1 frequent flyer out of East Hampton Airport with 390 trips logged between 2007 and 2011. His reign as owner of the club he inherited from his father Al was one of failure and misfortune, and he had far more of what might be called Brownie points with Villa than with Cleveland. For a lifelong fan who had slept in the Browns' orange and brown pyjamas as a kid, it was yet another heartbreaker. Yet, as Matt Slater wrote in his *BBC* blog in May, 2010: "At a time when American owners of British businesses are about as popular as Icelandic volcanoes, Lerner is a shining exception."

With no obvious candidate for the succession, the enormity of the hole O'Neill had left began to sink in. Lerner didn't want someone who'd spent too long on the managerial merry-go-round; nor did he want an unknown or a rookie. So in the end, he was relieved to get... Gerard Houllier. Out of work for three years and with a dicky heart, the 63-year-old Frenchman represented a huge risk. But at least he had some pedigree and might be able to attract a player or two. Faulkner expressed his chairman's delight at the capture: "Gerard Houllier stands out as a football man who understands the ethos of our club and shares our core values."

But that didn't seem the case when Houllier claimed Villa "belonged between seventh and 12th place in the Premier League." His remarks after the 3-0 defeat at Liverpool in December were even more damning. "If I was going to lose 3-0 to anyone it would be Liverpool," he said. Like O'Leary before him, he seemed to be wishing he was somewhere else. He would not endear himself to the players either, being nicknamed "Joe Le Tactics", and was undermined throughout his tenure. But his greatest problem was his heart and in April, after a scare similar to the one he suffered at Liverpool in 2001, he was hospitalised. He recovered but accepted the job was over.

Aided by goals from Darren Bent, for whom Lerner had stumped up £18m in the January window, Villa ended up ninth. But an apt postscript on a divisive season was the drunken row between central defenders Collins and Dunne – during a team bonding exercise.

If Houllier was a gamble that failed, Lerner's next choice was a racing certainty for a DNF. Alex McLeish is an experienced international manager, a gentleman and came with the recommendation of Sir Alex Ferguson: but he also came from Birmingham City. No one ever comes from the hated "Blose" and not even the back-handed "credit" he got for taking them down twice in three years could cut him any slack. The protests broke out even before the Scot was under starter's orders and continued throughout a wretched season. "I would have had to win the Treble to win some of them over," he said. The size of the hole that O'Neill left behind was growing by the day. The only signings were Charles N'Zogbia, Alan Hutton and Shay Given for a total of £15m while wings were more than clipped with the sale of Stewart Downing and Ashley Young for close to £40m. Things got even worse when popular skipper Stilyan Petrov was diagnosed with leukemia. It was a season to expunge from the memory. McLeish's appointment had been botched from the outset. Initially, Steve McClaren had been invited for an interview until the fans' screeching protests convinced the club to think again.

The removal of Big Eck in May 2012 was, cynics noted, the first decision Lerner had got right in a couple of years, a couple of years when he'd hardly shown up. But he could point to major distractions. In 2011, there was a messy divorce from his wife Lara, with whom he had four children, and he ended up as a virtual single parent to his son. In an effort to keep some of his house in order, he sold the Browns the following year. Oh, and the family business wasn't doing too well either. Not that the fans would look at it this way, but with the turmoil this private man was going through, Villa was the distraction.

At the time he kept his counsel but in a rare interview with *The Times* in May 2015, he acknowledged his errors. "I don't disagree with the criticism," he said. "And what I should have done several years back was bring in a chairman." He had planned to shift to the UK, where he owned a property in London as well as Bodymoor Heath, but said: "The responsibilities that I have at home, in the US, both personal and professional come first. If I lived and worked in England, it would be an entirely different matter." Not since the days of Deadly Doug had the manager's job been such an interim affair while *The Mirror's* Brian Reade wrote: "For the past few years, Villa has been a ghost ship, drifting towards the rocks." Attempting to steer it to safety in the 2012-13 campaign was Paul Lambert, who had led Norwich to two successive promotions on a small budget. He did not get much more at Villa but showed his eye for a bargain by snapping up Ron Vlaar and Christian Benteke for a total of £10m. His brief was to root out the slackers and high earners. Two seasons of 15th place finishes followed. Was this the new norm? Villa fans wondered. At least under O'Neill it used to be sixth every year...

On May 12, 2014, Lerner announced "with a heavy heart" that he'd finally put the club up for sale. "Fates are fickle in the business of English football," his statement read. "And I feel I have pushed mine well past the limit." He'd always said: "To me, English football is not philanthropy." The sale announcement came six months after he'd converted £90m in loans to equity.

The belt was tightening and, to help identify any wasters he might miss, Lambert brought in none other than Roy Keane as his assistant. Faulkner was replaced as CEO by Tom Fox, erstwhile commercial director at Arsenal. When Fox's salary of £1.25m a year was later revealed, fans felt Keane's remit should have been widened. Lambert was given a new contract, but the Keane experiment hadn't worked – the Irishman left after six months and yet another bust-up with players. His unrelenting 'bad cop' persona had darkened the mood and, after a 1-0 home defeat by Leyton Orient in the League Cup, he told the goal-shy squad: "If I gave you ten grand, you couldn't score in a brothel!"

In January, Villa were still celibate and the goal drought lasted 659 minutes. By February, Fox felt only a change of manager could avert relegation. Lambert, worn down by trying to run a big club on a small budget, was replaced by Tim Sherwood. It smacked of panic but, as a short-term fix, it worked. A lively presence on the training ground, the ex-Spurs boss lifted the mood. The new manager bounce carried them not just to safety but twice to Wembley and a FA Cup semi-final thrashing of Liverpool. Could this be another turning point?

ASTON VILLA

3

"He's a decent man, a giving man and a simple man – one who had no business owning a pro sports franchise, let alone two."

Cleveland.com writer Tom Reed on Lerner's stewardship of Aston Villa and the Cleveland Browns.

Making a rare trip across the pond, Lerner showed up for the 2015 FA Cup final with genuine hopes he might enjoy a last hurrah. But it was not to be as Villa were outclassed by Arsenal in a one-sided affair. With the club still for sale and wanting to insure against a repeat of the relegation battle they'd survived with only a game to spare, he sanctioned £52.5million's worth of summer signings but over £40m was recouped with the sales of Benteke and Delph.

Says Howell: "Villa were very unlucky to lose their two best players. It was unseemly the way it happened and left a really bad taste. But they started the season off with a win and you thought they'd grow together. They had a manager who'd instilled a lot of confidence in them at the end of last season and now had a lot of French players. You thought 'this is it' and they were going to build and challenge again. But they were unfortunate in a couple of early games and then the team just totally and utterly imploded. They bought Joleon Lescott from West Brom but it didn't come off. And the French players didn't come off. There's definitely something to be said for team spirit – Leicester are a terrific example – but when you haven't got that and haven't got strong leadership at the top of the club, which was certainly the case, you've got problems. There was poor management and certainly a very weak board."

Sherwood did not have control of the budget and blamed Sporting Director, Hendrik Almstadt, and Director of Recruitment, Paddy Riley, for buying players such as Jordan Amavi and Jordan Veretout who, he believed, were not cut out for the Premier League. Unable to halt the slide, the ex-Spurs boss was sacked in October, 2015 and replaced by Remi Garde. The logic appeared to be that a French boss might get more out of the French players, but the cerebral Garde was not the kind of firefighting butt-kicker a dire situation demanded (as Sherwood had been the previous season). Denied the funds that he'd been promised in January, Villa couldn't buy a point and there could be only one outcome. The fans turned their fury on Lerner once again.

Having refused to strengthen the team, the owner then brought in stellar names ...to the board. Former Governor of the Bank of England, lifelong Villa fan and lord of the realm, Mervyn King, arrived in March along with former FA and Manchester City chairman, David Bernstein. Club legend, Brian Little, was appointed advisor. Had he bought players of equivalent stature they might have been saved. The irony was not lost on Howell. "The problem at Villa has been five, six, seven, eight years of poor buying," he told me. "O'Neill didn't buy brilliantly – he bought well for two years and badly for the next two. I thought Lerner had realised his mistakes and was now going to turn things around. And that negativity wouldn't be there with good results on the pitch. But it has been the total and utter opposite. To defend him, he did spend very heavily in the summer but replaced his best players really badly."

Garde was yet another Villa manager who never had a chance. A success at Lyon, he was once considered a possible heir to Arsene Wenger at Arsenal where he'd had a brief spell as a player. At Villa he lasted just 147 days that ended in a bitter wrangle over compensation. *BBC Sport's* Pat Murphy said there was "mutual antipathy" with "both sides fed up of each other. Lerner turned the tap off and Garde felt badly let down. He's looked more and more downcast. His body language has been graphic."

Garde, who had consulted Wenger before accepting the job, ended with the worst record of any Villa manager in Premier League history – two wins in 20 games. But without doubt he had been handed the shortest straw, and followed Fox and Almstadt out of the club. If it was a belated clearout, fans wished the players had been included.

Ex-Villa and England manager Graham Taylor told *BBC Sport*: "I have never known it so low at Aston Villa. Both the club and its supporters are at such a low ebb. Somewhere along the line the feeling around the club, with the owner wanting to sell and not being able to, has crept into the dressing room. It is like a slow death in football terms. For me there are too many non-football people running football clubs in this country and one of those is Aston Villa."

Adding to the desperation was the £5.1 billion TV deal. As *Heroes & Villains* pointed out: "Only Villa could find the worst possible season to go down in." Under the new contract, the bottom club in the 2016-17 season will receive £99m – 71% more than Villa got. Premier League clubs are set to dominate the Rich List's top 30 in the world. Aston Villa, founder members of the Football and Premier Leagues and winners of the European Cup, will not be among them.

Not that it would have been much consolation to Garde, but the fans didn't blame him for the debacle – they reserved their wrath for Lerner. The group behind 'Out The Door On 74' described the Frenchman as "a sacrificial lamb" and asked: "How many more times must we cycle through managers, players and board members before Mr Lerner finds the winning combination? In our view he has had long enough. The Aston Villa job is a poisoned chalice because of one man's inability to provide either consistent support, vision or, in Remi Garde's case, simply be true to his word. Randy Lerner, bow your head once again in shame."

As with dud players, Lerner had shelled out fortunes to failed managers and was now trying to cut back. It made the story of Elaine Rose, the match-day receptionist who resigned in February, even more poignant. "They have cut back so much they are even sending members of staff home at half-time to save money," she told the *Daily Mail*. "They must save £20 on each person." Among several complaints, Rose said she'd seen players laughing after defeats and that Fox, who hired bodyguards, had voluble critics removed from the ground. The 6-0 humiliation by Liverpool saw thousands leave on their own accord during another abject surrender. Their mood was further soured soon afterwards when Lescott tweeted a photo to show off his latest toy – a luxury Merc. He claimed the tweet was "an accident" but the impression was that a senior player – and perhaps others – had been less than devastated to lose 6-0 at home. In contrast, Deadly Doug felt "heartbroken".

Howell summed it up: "Randy Lerner is now seen as having gone full circle. Up to 2011 he was the dream owner but he went from saviour to No.1 villain. His marriage break-up and the financial crisis had a lot to do with funding drying up. The two things combined to hit him hard. He had got the appointment of O'Neill right, but then it backfired spectacularly. After that he could not get it more wrong with Houllier and McLeish. Then there was anger as the owner was seen as not interested. He started to spend a bit of money again just to ensure safety. The day after the announcement of the £5 billion TV deal, he said he was staying on. But it was too little too late.

"He wanted to be liked. I think the Premier League offered him a chance at Villa to put a warm face and build up a persona that he didn't have in America." I ask: 'Is he a Caesar, Saviour or Sucker?' Howell: "He's definitely not a sucker. Did he get anything back? Yes, he got a huge amount of kudos for a number of years. The criticism he got in the lean years at Villa is nothing compared to what he was getting at Cleveland Browns. They were glancing over from American shores and wondering what on earth he was doing at Villa. He had some bad luck, he made some bad appointments. He was Caesar for four years and the following five he's been more of a sucker, but not entirely. He could have been a bit more open – he was almost reclusive – and the media were irritated by his lack of words. He never resorted to social media sites and just carried on building the club. In style, if Hicks and Gillett were David Gower, Randy Lerner was Geoffrey Boycott."

His innings at Villa did seem to have lasted as long as one of the Yorkshireman's, and it seemed apt in a sad sort of way that his club should end the season messing around with their badge. Cynics wondered if Lerner would alter the one he'd had tattooed on his ankle and if removing the word "Prepared" was an admission they were anything but.

Disillusionment was rife and extended from players to boardroom. Forty-eight hours after relegation was confirmed, Lord King and Bernstein resigned, claiming their positions had become untenable. Skipper Agbonlahor's certainly was after the so-called 'Mr Villa' had gone on a laughing gas bender. It was symptomatic of the disarray in a dying empire – while millionaire players posted pictures of luxury Mercs and white Lamborghinis on social media, job cuts were being made in the hundreds.

At long last, Lerner, who accepted that "the blame lies at my feet and no one else's", managed to sell to a Chinese consortium headed by Dr Tony Xia's Recon Group. He got more than the £62.5m he paid for it, but he had dropped at least £300m during his eight-year reign. And so ended what had begun as one of the most enlightened regimes of the modern era. But like a marriage, no matter how much good will is stored from the blissful early days, it can melt like butter once things go awry. In Lerner's case, it was nothing sinister – simply that he didn't have time for Villa any more amid the upheavals in the rest of his life.

To sum up, Mat Kendrick, Football Editor of the *Birmingham Mail* who covers Villa now, said: "His reign as a whole has been a game of two halves... I think Randy Lerner lost interest in Villa around the same time that there was the financial crash and then Martin O'Neill walked out..." He added: "I'm Mr Cynical with Randy Lerner. The message I got from his statement was 'it has cost me quite a few quid so don't you forget that. I might have messed up a lot of things but my kids' inheritance has taken a bit of a battering because of it'. It's just sad. Lerner is somebody who has been forced by circumstance to cling on too long after he should have gone."

Doug Ellis was more sympathetic. "He hasn't done anything terribly wrong," he said. "I would complain about the lack of times he's come over to Aston Villa. That's what our loyal fans wanted to see – the owner."

I asked Dave Woodhall of *Heroes & Villains*, who had once eulogised Lerner, to explain how he could go from the best owner to one of the worst – at least in the eyes of Villa fans. He wrote: "He arrived in August 2006 and seemed the answer to a prayer. Not only was he wealthy enough in his own right to bankroll success but he wanted nothing more than to enjoy himself while he was doing it. For four years money was no object and just as importantly he seemed to have an intuitive ability to know what supporters wanted. Then, it all went wrong. No-one knows why he lost interest – global crash, divorce, personal circumstances, a feeling of betrayal by successive managers. Lerner either made or allowed a series of appalling appointments in key roles and the result was eventual relegation. It's a sobering lesson about what happens when too much power is put into the hands of one man, and a man at that who is rich enough to be able to ignore a quarter of a billion pound investment simply because he doesn't want to play with it anymore."

Cleveland.com writer Tom Reed saw stark parallels in Lerner's stewardship of Aston Villa and the NFL Browns: "He's a decent man, a giving man and a simple man – one who had no business owning a pro sports franchise, let alone two."

Sadness is the prevailing sentiment as one asks: How did it come to this? Lerner had even used Leeds United as a prime example of what not to do, and insisted his executives read all they could about that classic of the genre. He said: "If you do not study and get a triple first in Leeds United, case study No 1, underline, bold, super-big font, then you are living a very dangerous game. It goes right to the issue of how you spend. It's the cautionary tale." Tragically, and for very different reasons, any future owner of a football club would be advised to study Aston Villa as well – and the font would be pretty big here too.

Blackburn Rovers

BLACKBURN ROVERS

1

I read the news today oh boy
Four thousand holes in Blackburn, Lancashire
And though the holes were rather small
They had to count them all

From A Day in the Life, The Beatles

Even if the pot holes were filled in, the streets paved with yellow metal and the River Darwen overflowed with Thwaites' Original, Blackburn would never challenge Venice for tourist arrivals. Nor does it feature in those league tables of liveable cities: boasting a football club that's the only founder member and champion of both Football and Premier leagues doesn't do much for the quality of life. Not the way they rate them anyway. Blackburn is a bit like Uruguay, about which a coach once said: "Other countries have their history, Uruguay has its football." Blackburn has its football.

It has a bit of history too, but of the grimy, industrial revolution kind, and today it's a skint, old mill town whose better days were a lifetime ago. Once a spinning, weaving, happening place, it is now a hotchpotch of moribund mills, shut-down shops and grim estates. No one has ever tried to build a New Jerusalem here but a fan-cum-steel magnate-cum-benefactor tried the next best thing – Jack Walker built a new football team that won the Premier League. But it couldn't, and didn't, last. A proper look at his tenure, however, is necessary to appreciate why, under his hapless successors, even football seems to belong to Blackburn's past.

Uncle Jack, as he became known, set up a trust to maintain his legacy, but knew his home town would never be a magnet for the game's glitterati. After he'd persuaded Sven-Goran Eriksson to become manager in 1997 – a signing conducted in Walker's daughter's house and a discreet distance from the centre – the Swede fancied a gander at his future base. Eriksson, then one of the most coveted coaches in Europe, recalls: "Jack was flying me to his home in Jersey and then back to Italy. We had a couple of hours to spare so I said: 'Can't we have a look at the city centre?' Jack said: 'It's better if you don't, Sven.'"

John Lennon never saw it either, but was inspired to write his weird lyric about potholes by a prosaic news item in a January 1967 edition of the *Daily Mail*. Such towns are sitting ducks for disparagement and one columnist wrote: "Not even Maradona could make Blackburn sexy." On the list of Premier League champions before Leicester arrived, Blackburn was the plain Jane in pinny and curlers among the glamour pusses: older sirens, Manchester United and Arsenal, and the strutting, nouveau riche Botoxed supermodels, Chelsea and Manchester City. Its 105,000 population is only one and a half times United's perennial home gate – give or take a prawn sandwich nibbler. The place is too close to Manchester for comfort, too far from London for convenience. At least that's how it may seem to a sheikh or an oligarch, weighing up whether to go for another yacht or the dubious privilege of owning an English football club.

Walker was not looking for a toy or fashion accessory when he bought Rovers. Neither did he seek an additional franchise for his sporting portfolio nor a global repositioning for his brand. In the wake of the overseas billionaire influx, Walker has become a case study for the hometown boy who bought the club he'd always supported. Simple as that. He didn't want to be Caesar and had repositioned his brand by flogging it. Now he could spend his cash on players. In terms of football ownership, no one has ever been more 'fit and proper' than Jack Walker was for Blackburn Rovers.

It is a supreme irony that after he'd sold his Walkersteel business to British Steel for £360 million in 1990, he was feared by the football establishment. There were no foreign owners then and Walker, a graduate of the 'where there's muck there's brass' school of business and a blunt-speaking Northerner who'd failed his eleven plus, put the wind up the big boys: he had more brass. Long before Roman Abramovich and Sheikh Mansour altered the landscape forever, Walker was indulging his boyhood fantasies at Blackburn. He was like a kid in a sweet shop. A rich kid in a small sweet shop.

After he'd signed a cheque or two, it became commonplace for rival clubs to say: "Yes, we're interested [in a player] – but we won't be doing a Blackburn". 'Doing a Blackburn' became a byword for spending with which the gilded elite of the English game could not compete. And Blackburn were still in the Second Division. For a brief period, they were not the Chelsea, Manchester City or PSG of the early 1990s, but the Anzhi Makhachkala before the potash price crashed.

Walker said he wanted to make Manchester United "look cheap" – and he did. He outbid them for Alan Shearer, the most sought-after player of the day, yet Walker was a mere multi-millionaire. Rich enough to go and live in Jersey and buy an airline, but with roots in the cobbled streets of working class Little Harwood. His dad had founded the family business after the war with £80. At the end of the 1980s, Walker was paying Steve Archibald £4,000 a week to move from Barcelona on loan. It was more than his dad ever made in a year. Ossie Ardiles, Kevin Moran and Frank Stapleton also came. The bandwagon was rolling.

Jack and his brother Fred had taken over their dad's sheet metal business and built it up from a 1956 turnover of £46,000 to profits of £48m in 1988. A lifelong Rovers fan, Jack could now fulfil those childhood dreams and buy who he wanted. And it was not just his money that was persuasive: lifers were easier to extract from Alcatraz than Kenny Dalglish was from the golf course, but Walker's silver tongue managed it. Just seven months after quitting Liverpool following the trauma of Hillsborough, King Kenny's arrival confirmed that Uncle Jack was serious.

The truth is that Rovers had not given Walker a lot to shout about in his lifetime of loyalty to them. Much of it was spent in the Second Division, with brief spells in the top flight in the 1960s and the third in the early 1970s. As Walker became rich, Rovers remained poor. In 1979, then manager Howard Kendall was asked to cut costs by putting less milk in the players' tea and sending his mail second class.

Rovers' glory days had been in the ancient past. The five cup wins when "Manchester United" were still clad in the green and gold of Newton Heath seemed as relevant as Roma fans regarding the Coliseum as a fortress. But thanks to Walker, Blackburn were the only club outside the cabal of billionaires to have won the Premier League (1994-5) – until Leicester's miracle. Besides, 13 years after Kendall had to cut the milk bill, Rovers broke the British transfer record with a £3.5m swoop for Shearer and smashed it again the following year by paying £5m for Chris Sutton. Thus united, the famed SAS partnership went on to spearhead Rovers to the title. Sutton's wages of 10 grand a week were another landmark on the road to the unsustainable finances of today's game. In some quarters, Walker still gets blamed.

Landing the title for the first time since 1914 would be the zenith. As Rovers' fanatic and writer Jim Wilkinson put it: "Without Jack we might have gone up but wouldn't have won it. If there hadn't been sugar daddies in football, we wouldn't have had a sniff." But what followed would be a sad twilight for Walker and his best-laid plans.

With Dalglish gone upstairs as director of football and his assistant Ray Harford put in charge, Rovers couldn't follow on. Early Brexiteers in Europe, they finished seventh, 13th, sixth and 19th under four different managers (including caretaker, Tony Parkes) over the next four seasons. It was not what Walker had envisaged when the title had been won. Harford had seemed a sensible choice, but was stymied first by constant rumours about Shearer going to Man United – and then by his departure to Newcastle.

Even vehement denials didn't stem the ill-feeling and when Shearer did eventually leave, not even a world record fee of £15m could make up for his weight of goals – 112 in 138 games. He had once been a much-loved figure: during one of Shearer's injury absences, a Rovers' mate told me his mother had sent him a get-well card – for a groin strain. For Rovers fans there was immense relief that he hadn't gone to Old Trafford. "There was no way that Rovers would let him come here," explained United chairman Martin Edwards to their disappointed faithful.

Walker was behind that just as he was the next big decision – to hire Eriksson. "Not only do I want us to be a top club in this country, I want European football to be the norm for us," he said. Walker was still thinking big and they didn't come much bigger – in name, salary and silverware – than the Sampdoria boss who had won titles in Sweden,

Portugal and Italy. Eriksson would have been quite a coup for Rovers but it was not to be. The Swede told me: "I signed a contract to take over at the start of the following season. But when I left for home [Italy], I got a call from Lazio owner Sergio Cragnotti. He said: 'You've never won the league in Italy: do you want to do it now?'" Cragnotti was 'doing a Jack Walker' with the Rome club and would buy the likes of Christian Vieri, Marcello Salas and Pavel Nedved. It was the Eternal City vs the mill town. "After a couple of meetings with Jack," Eriksson recalled, "he understood [my dilemma]. At the time Roy Hodgson was sacked from Inter so [when I pulled out] Jack took Hodgson instead."

Hodgson got Rovers back to sixth and into Europe in his first season, but was sacked in November of the next. He was still paid for the remainder of his contract. This time it was Hodgson who was struck by Walker's "honour" in dealing with managers. Not that every decision he made – or even idea he had – would turn to gold. When Dalglish had wanted Zinedine Zidane, Walker responded: "Who needs Zidane when we have Tim Sherwood?" He made another error when he gave untested Brian Kidd the top job and Rovers were relegated. It was the sort of denouement that Hollywood would have hesitated to script, but television showed in graphic detail. On the night the bottom dropped out of Rovers' world, fans still sang: 'There's only one Jack Walker.' As the cameras zoomed in, the self-made, steel-tough multi-millionaire had tears running down his face.

Not even a mid-seventies shift to the sunny south tax haven of Jersey could sever the umbilical cord between Walker and Blackburn. He would always say: "If they don't win then I am bloody miserable on a Sunday." He had bought Jersey European Airways, it is widely believed, so he could fly back for home games. Kidd was replaced the following season – with Rovers alarmingly close to an unthinkable second successive drop. They had begun the season as favourites for promotion. Walker, who had driven a Morris 8 until it fell apart in his early years, was not about to watch a similar fate befall his beloved Rovers. He had redeveloped Ewood Park, established a trust and then he hired Graeme Souness. Tragically, Uncle Jack would not see the encore the Scot delivered.

Diagnosed with prostate cancer in early 2000, Walker died in August of that year. The season Rovers returned to the Premier League had barely kicked off. The club dedicated their success to his memory, but he would not see them play in the top flight again. Still, they were in it, had a fine ground, a state-of-the-art training facility and were well-funded thanks to the trust he had set up. Local MP and former Justice Minister Jack Straw summed it up: "Jack Walker did more than any other individual in the last century to enhance the self-confidence and the prosperity of his home town. He was completely committed to the town and its people. Blackburn Rovers was in many ways the love of his life." There was only one Jack Walker indeed.

BLACKBURN ROVERS

2

"I don't know a thing about football. I've never seen a football match in my life. Cricket, yes, and hockey, sometimes, but never football."

Mrs Anuradha Desai

Even by the grossly incompatible standards of modern football, Blackburn Rovers FC, founder members of the Football League and essentially blue-collar, north of England club, getting hitched to Venkateshwara Hatcheries, Pune, India, will always be one of the game's more unlikely marriages. It certainly wasn't about love. "I don't know a thing about football," announced Mrs Anuradha Desai, the firm's head honcho and matriarch. "I've never seen a football match in my life. Cricket, yes, and hockey, sometimes, but never football." When they heard that, half of east Lancashire felt a tremor – many thought it was Jack Walker turning in his grave.

The naivety was stunning, the innocence almost virginal. In comparison, any customary faux allegiance claim might have seemed reassuring. But there was none. Not even any pretence about having supported the club while growing up – where was Robbie Keane when you needed him? No new-age claptrap about synergies, not even an old-fashioned soft spot that had been in hibernation since some half-remembered televised highlight of long ago. Of affinity, there wasn't the proverbial sniff. Not by any stretch would Walker have sold his beloved Rovers to someone who didn't "know a thing about football".

It was just over a decade since he had died. Rovers had not done badly since without reaching the same extraordinary heights. They went back up to the Premier League at the end of the first post-Walker season and stayed there. They had won the League Cup and been in Europe twice, but sixth was their best league finish. It wasn't quite the nineties but they were a solid top-flight team with decent crowds, and any description of

Rovers as a club would always contain the words "well-run". Walker's money was still funding them and John Williams was still running the show.

Four months before he died, Uncle Jack reassured supporters that he had provided for the club. "A number of years ago I put in place a family trust structure to own my various business interests, including Blackburn Rovers," he announced. Although the club was run by chairman, Robert Coar, and chief executive, Williams, five trustees had the final say. Walker, who was married three times, left four children but none had his passion for football or Rovers. Indeed, it was his son-in-law, Richard Matthewman, who represented his family's interests on the club's board of directors. But even from the grave, Walker was making sure Rovers got preferential treatment from his businesses. The trust funded the club from profits from those other companies and if Rovers made an operating loss, it was covered. Well, as long as the trust was prepared to keep robbing Peter to pay Paul.

In the second season after Walker's death, Rovers had paid a club record £8m for Andy Cole and were rewarded when he scored the winner in the League Cup final of 2002. At such times, it was almost as if Uncle Jack was still there, but the fans were not fooled into thinking everything in his memorial garden was lovely – however well-tended. In the previous financial year, losses had been £30m, and £19m the season before that – even with the £10m sale of Sutton to Chelsea. And when relegation loomed in 2003/4, there was a growing unease about how long their privileged status could last. The fear was that if Rovers were to go down again, the trustees might turn off the life support. Unlike their founder, these men were so publicity-shy they made the Illuminati look like Paris Hilton. And fans could be assured that when Rovers lost, the trustees' Sundays were some way short of miserable.

Jim Wilkinson told me: "I know with the utmost certainty that members of Jack's family wanted to get rid. By the mid 2000s, it became well known they wanted to sell it under Mark Hughes. I heard that one family member had said he was sick of his phone ringing and there being a problem with the football club. He said: 'We have airlines, pilots and professional people in other businesses and they're not ringing us with problems over divorces and such. But the football club is different. They ring up about little things.' After a 2-0 loss to Bolton, the family met up in a restaurant. No sooner had they sat down than a waiter came over to introduce two lads who told them: 'We're big Rovers fans and it's a shambles – we wish your family would step in.' The Walker lad told the waiter not to do that again. The family were more into motor racing and wanted to wash their hands of the club."

In the summer of 2007, they decided enough was enough and appointed the Rothschild bank to find a buyer. For all the angst their decision caused, the trustees might have acted sooner. The world was about to experience the biggest economic crash since 1928 although there would always be sheikhs and oligarchs eyeing up the big boys. But Blackburn? With competition even in its small catchment area and significantly lower match day revenues than most Premiership clubs, it was difficult to see a return on investment in the short to medium term. But it did have a well-appointed stadium, a superb training ground and relatively little debt. And they were in the top half of the most watched football league on the planet. Take off the pinny and curlers and it wasn't a bad catch – for a suitable buyer.

After a couple of unlikely flirtations came an even more left-field candidate. Indeed, can there ever have been a more improbable paramour for a founder member of the Football League than the Venky's? To have and to hold, and take the club forward beyond the Walker dynasty? Or from a more unlikely corner? Mail-order brides can seem like soul mates in comparison.

Venkatash Hatcheries was founded in 1971 with just 500 chickens on a seven-acre plot near Hyderabad. The business had grown to become the largest poultry company in India, being the preferred supplier to McDonald's and KFC, and venturing into health care and pet foods. Established by Dr B.V. Rao and his wife Uttaradevi, it was now run by their daughter, Anuradha Desai, and two sons, Balaji and Venkatash.

Doubts about their suitability were hardly banished by confusion over the size of the company. The *Daily Mail* called them "Bollywood billionaires" but others put their turnover at just north of £100m. Forbes had them at 67th in the top 100 "global small companies". It turned out they *were* in the billionaire league and three times richer than Uncle Jack. Calling them chicken farmers was like calling him a scrap dealer.

If they'd been oligarchs or sheikhs, it is hard to see a problem. Their appearance offered no clue. Madam was matronly in an Angela Merkel kind of way, the younger pony-tailed Balaji did at least sport a 1970s rocker look whereas the more studious Venkatash could pass for a ticket inspector on Indian railways. The nature of the business didn't help, either – oil, minerals, phones, tech, yes, but poultry? It stretched the 'where there's muck there's brass' theory beyond reasonable limits. Muck, certainly, but thanks to the *Mail's* Nick Harris visiting the inner sanctum in January, 2011, we learned there was also bling and fast cars.

The brothers had no less than 74 motors between them including several classics. Balaji, who was a bit of a medallion man at home besides wearing a pistol, owned the bulk, including the obligatory Rolls, Bentley and Hummer. They also shared six bodyguards. Balaji had a genuine interest in football as well as revealing that it was SEM Kentaro who introduced them to Blackburn.

Why did they buy? The answer was not what Rovers' fans wanted to hear. "People are crazy about football," Mrs Desai said. "In all these markets I'm talking about, south-east (Asia) market, Middle East market and even in the European market, it is a very famous game and I feel that the Venky's brand will get an immediate recognition if we take over this club. This is the main reason we are doing this." So they very much belonged to the 'it's not what we can do for your club, but what your club can do for us' school of ownership.

Mark Ashworth of the Rovers Trust was one fan who was singularly unimpressed. One afternoon in the Postal Order pub in the centre of Blackburn, he told me: "They've gone into this blindfolded. They've no interest in football so why come and buy a football club? They've never run one, don't know what it's like to run one, don't know what it's like to own one so why buy one? If I applied for a job but had no experience, they'd say 'no' to me. So why should it be any different for owners? They should have some experience. Jack Walker was Blackburn born and raised, he bled blue and white, he was Blackburn through and through. We, the fans, bleed blue but these people don't – do they really care?"

But back then, when the Venky's emerged as preferred bidders upon whom the Walker Trust had settled to offload their unwanted burden, not even Ashworth could foresee the tragicomic events that have unfolded. At least Rovers appeared to have landed an international conglomerate with pockets deep enough for them to compete with other similarly-funded fat cats. And the attitude among most fans, said Wilkinson, was: "Wow! These people are rich – get 'em in! But if the authorities had vetted them, these same fans would have been up in arms about the delay."

Despite their ignorance, the Venky's had been persuaded to come in by a mainstream sports, media and entertainment company. SEM-Kentaro had also been tasked by the trust with finding a buyer and SEM's founder, Jerome Anderson, was a well-known name in the football industry, having had an advisory role at Manchester City when Thaksin Shinawatra took over. He had since linked up with Switzerland-based Kentaro, a major player in Brazil among other places.

The Jack Walker trust had taken months to satisfy themselves about the Venky's financial health, and managed to persuade fans that they were people they could do business with. In a *Lancashire Telegraph* poll, 60% were in favour of the takeover. Crucially for the dreamers, they suggested it was the only way Rovers could again challenge the big boys.

Now big in Indian industry, Venky's expansion had been masterminded by Mrs Desai. Diversification was her watchword but by far the biggest detour the company had ever taken was buying Rovers. "I'm very excited to be the first Indian owner of a Premier League club," she announced. "And in a few days I'll know the basics of the game." Blackburn and the rest of football watched and waited.

The new owners agreed to keep the statue of the great benefactor and not to rename the Jack Walker stand. But, as no high-flyer seems able to, Mrs Desai could not resist indulging in more tiresome corporate cant that included the 'b' word. "We plan to focus on leveraging the global influence in establishing Blackburn Rovers as a truly global brand," she said. "We will absolutely respect the Jack Walker legacy and will be actively supporting the organisation to ensure that Blackburn Rovers remain one of the best-run clubs within the Premier League."

There were less reassuring noises about recruitment. A modest £5m for the January transfer window was mentioned while names like

Beckham, Ronaldinho and Maradona (as manager, presumably, but you never know) were bandied about. As none of that trio would get out of bed for less than £5m, Rovers' fans didn't quite know what to make of it all. They would not have to wait long.

For someone who knew "nothing about football", Desai proved a remarkably fast learner. On November 26, she had said of Big Sam: "He deserves a chance. To this end, the group has promised manager Allardyce funds to spend in the January transfer window." On December 13, she sacked him. "We want good football and Blackburn to be fourth or fifth in the league or even better," she declared. She had already grasped one of the basics of the game: that promises are made to be broken.

The players and senior figures were aghast. Skipper Ryan Nelsen spoke for many when he said: "I didn't see it coming at all. Sam did an incredible job with limited resources. I don't know what the owners felt, but in the world we live in – the real world – he did incredibly well." Allardyce divides opinion over his style, but there was unanimity in the game that a gross injustice had been done. Richard Bevan, the chief executive of the League Managers' Association, called the decision "extremely difficult to understand." He added: "It is ironic that one minute Sam can be proposed as the next England manager and the next, he finds himself out of work."

Mrs Desai made it worse with a feeble attempt to explain the inexplicable: "We had been talking to Sam in the past few weeks but he did not fit in with our vision for the club's future. We wanted good football, wanted the games to be interesting and of course wanted to win and to have good players… This is a major step but it was needed. We thought: Why delay?" Mrs Desai was proving a star pupil on the Beginners Course for Football Club Owners – she was already contradicting herself, employing classic euphemisms and speaking in code.

Fans were similarly outraged, a poll in the *LT* revealing 76% of respondents felt it was the wrong decision. That the wider football world, by now accustomed to the annual pre-Christmas managerial cull, still managed to be shocked said it all. Big Sam was the wily old elephant that had dodged the big game hunter's best efforts only to be brought down by an errant shot from a tourist using a rifle for the first time.

Sir Alex Ferguson, who had just surpassed Sir Matt Busby as Manchester United's longest-serving manager, felt Mrs Desai was getting the wrong advice. He said: "I think it's very difficult these days [to build a club] with the life we're in now. There's intense pressure on managers. You've got that issue at Blackburn of an agent involved and deciding the future of the club, Jerome Anderson, he couldn't pick his nose. It's baffling and it's a serious threat to how clubs get run and how they conduct themselves."

When I asked Ashworth what he thought was the first turning point in Rovers' Venky-induced decline, he was in no doubt: "It was when they started talking about Champions League football – and spending £5m apiece on Ronaldinho and Beckham. You thought, hang on a minute… these guys are cuckoo. Then Sam departed and I thought it's really getting bad." Long-standing fan and local historian, Brian Haworth, agrees. "It was the first of the daft decisions. We were safe with Sam. He'll keep you in the top division. When he signed I wasn't overly impressed. But he delivered." Former Tottenham chairman Alan Sugar was equally sceptical. He tweeted: "Blackburn Rovers has just been sold to the Indian family, another PL club in foreign hands. I hope they know what they are doing."

BLACKBURN ROVERS

3

"He is a thinking manager and we are very impressed with him and we are confident going forward."

Mrs Desai on Steve Kean.

Contrary to popular perception, the 'marriage' was neither a shotgun nor a sham – the courtship took a while and it has survived relegation and five anniversaries. It was also anything but a union of convenience – the Venky's have shown up all too rarely, never stayed the night and, on one infamous occasion, were pelted with snowballs. It would be a struggle to call it a domestic.

Allardyce's successor Steve Kean, meanwhile, was summoned no less than 14 times to India during his 22 excruciating months as manager. The Venky's HQ is in Pune, once a favourite hill station of the British Raj, whose haughty bureaucrats and bored memsahibs would seek respite from the enervating heat of old Bombay. Kean went there to take the heat.

Today, Mumbai is an eight-hour flight from London and the road trip to Pune is no longer an all-day obstacle course of lackadaisical rickshaws and recalcitrant cattle. Thanks to India's first expressway, it is a mere four-hour, hindrance-free drive – well, apart from the odd stray elephant. But once there, unlike his predecessors in those cooler, re-energising days of empire, Kean would face a grilling. Along with the heads of the other 28 branches of the Venky's empire, he had to report in on a regular basis. If minutes were taken, what a dispiriting tale they would tell of this divergent outpost.

Whether a click or two away on a hard drive or on mouldering sheets of longhand in some fusty cupboard, the account of Kean's reign would not just chronicle the decline of a venerable football institution, it would provide a template for anyone wishing to write *How Not to Run a Football*

Club – A Dummies Guide. Whatever spin or brave face was put on it, that fractious first period of the Venky's tenure marked an inexorable shift from lofty aspirations to survival scuffle. Bouts of ineptitude alternated with moments of sheer battiness to confirm Sugar's suspicions. No malevolent Burnley sleeper cell could have done it better.

But back in those early, expectant days, you have to wonder what thoughts Kean, an eager and "thinking" young manager getting his first big break, had on those long flights to and from Mumbai; each time he was summoned, each time the plane settled at its cruising altitude and dinner was served, what hopes he harboured before he descended into fitful sleep; what dreams he had and what fears the trip would bring.

At Venky HQ there would be so much to talk about that he (sometimes accompanied by his wife, Margaret) would stay an extra night for further debriefing the following day, occasionally having to scramble to make the last flight home. Three days training would be missed but that was deemed of little consequence by his inquisitors compared to having Kean appear before them in the flesh. Skype and video conferencing were never considered, nor was the inconvenience to the manager and disruption to team preparations. Often he was called when vital matches were coming up. Under the Venky's, every match would soon become vital.

Asked about his trips when he took the team out in October 2011, he said: "We always have a sit down and a talk. I come here once a month to sit down with the family and talk about all aspects of the club and the games, the development of the younger players, the integration of the new players, what we want to do in the next transfer window, the funding of that. We speak about all aspects and what I will be doing is exactly what I normally do – going through all that." In January, 2011, he told the *Daily Mail*: "I don't mind going out there once a month. It's not as bad as it sounds and I'd prefer to meet the owners face-to-face."

Despite my repeated attempts to contact him, Kean never responded. Not to texts, calls or e-mails, even when trusted third parties were mentioned. So I never did get to ask whether discussions centred on David Dunn being deployed in a slightly deeper role or an increase in the percentage of hatchlings in Uttar Pradesh.

Besides Maradona, names mentioned to succeed Allardyce had included the less fanciful Martin Jol and Stuart Pearce, but with assistant manager Neil McDonald having also been removed, Kean was catapulted into pole position. The Scot had never made it as a player but had gone to Portugal, learned Portuguese, and was becoming known for his coaching. In 2009, the then 41-year-old was appointed Blackburn's new first team coach under Allardyce, replacing Karl Robinson. At the time Allardyce said: "Kean stood out above the rest through his personality, experience and knowledge of football at the highest level."

Seven months later, when he found himself in charge of the first team, it did not seem that he was regarded as a long-term successor. Mrs Desai said: "Right now we are going to have a study and put a lot of thought into who the next manager of Blackburn Rovers will be. We don't want to make a hasty decision and we are in a good position to take our time because Steve is quite capable."

On December 22, nine days after Big Sam was sacked and following just a single game – an unconvincing 1-1 home draw with West Ham – studies were completed: Kean was appointed manager until the end of the season. Mrs Desai said: "We have been studying him and have been very impressed. He works long hours and is talented at his job. He also works well with our very skilful young players and that is important." Without having seen the team play or train, without having listened to a team talk or met the players – skilful, young or otherwise – there was widespread wonderment as to how she had arrived at her evaluation.

A month later, after just two wins in six league games, Kean was given a three-year contract. One might say, never in the history of football has a manager with so little experience owed so much to someone who knew so little. After his first six games, Cloughie was still painting the stands at Hartlepool; after his, Fergie was wondering if he'd have to play in goal at East Stirling. They, the Busbys, the Shanklys, the Paisleys and the Steins did not get three-year contracts until their trophy cabinets were creaking and their open-top bus parades were on the timetable. However you looked at it, Kean's apprenticeship was never going to be confused with Pep Guardiola's, yet he was rewarded as if he was the next big thing. And Mrs Desai had still not seen Rovers play.

That didn't stop her insisting: "The manager [Kean] is very good. He is a thinking manager and we are confident going forward." On the vexed question of the SEM-Kentaro agency's involvement with the club, she added: "Jerome [Anderson] has helped us, but I want to be very clear that he does not run the club. We will be working with anybody and any agents to make this club successful, but we are not controlled by his company. His role will now diminish." Well, not entirely – Anderson was Kean's agent.

Amid the growing December gloom, chairman John Williams had issued a rallying cry: "We do not want negativity around the club. That could work to our disadvantage by playing into the hands of our upcoming opponents. We need solidarity in every area. Football is a precarious business, fuelled by opinion, but I repeat that this is a time for everyone with a love for Blackburn Rovers to really show their support. This is not about individuals, either. It is about the club – first, second and third." It was typical of the man – Jack Walker's man – who had handled the difficult post-Walker decade with dignity and aplomb.

What could have won back a few sceptics was activity in the January transfer window. It turned out the Ronaldinho idea was not as daft as it had sounded. Balaji had a friend who knew the superstar and Kentaro, through their Brazilian affiliations, had contacts with him. But nothing happened and it was as hard to see Ronny banging his bongo drums around Brockhall as it was to imagine Victoria Beckham strutting along Darwen Street with the paparazzi in tow. With such names being bandied about, there were hopes that at least some recognisable B-lister would join. But with rookie owners and a rookie manager, just who would be driving the search?

Despite what Fergie said about Anderson, he was a 20-year veteran of the industry and several of his Manchester City recruits were good value. He spent so much of that January on Rovers' case that he practically lived at the club. Still, the only permanent arrivals were Ruben Rochina and Mauro Formica. It wasn't just Mrs Desai that hadn't heard of them.

In a marked ratcheting up of the concern expressed by Williams just three weeks earlier, the chairman, managing director Tom Finn and finance director Martin Goodman, wrote to Mrs Desai on 4 January,

2011 of their deep fears about being overlooked on both managerial appointments and transfers. Their sentiments were echoed by the Rovers Trust. Ashworth said: "I would have been happy with stability and security. When they first came in, I thought I can take a few chicken jokes as long as we're still comfortable, safe and secure. Keep it running as it is. Yet in the years since, everything has been turned upside down. Sometimes I ask myself whether this is the same football club I started supporting when I was a kid? It's a completely different entity now."

Underwhelming, under-used and, eventually in certain eyes, under suspicion. Judging by the comments section in the *LT* and on numerous websites, that's how fans came to view the January signings. As the window slammed shut, the prevailing sentiment was frustration – concerns would arise later. Instead of Maradona, Ronaldinho and Beckham they had Kean, Formica and Rochina. And Roque Santa Cruz came back on loan along with Jermaine Jones. Rochina oozed talent but Kean seldom played him, and it was not the modest fee they paid Barcelona that would raise eyebrows, but the immodest amount that went to his agent. According to the *Daily Mail*, Blackburn paid just £400,00 to the club but a staggering £1.65 million to one Manuel Salamanca Ferrer, an associate of Anderson's who had worked on the deal. A shade over a couple of million for Rochina? He might even have been worth it if he'd been given a few more games. But that was not the main issue. With Formica's deal also including massive agency fees and rumours of a previous third party ownership, fans smelt something rotten in the state of Denmark. The feeling festered through a terrible year before reaching a climax in January 2012. The forums were full of vitriol and Anderson put out a statement to clear his name.

From Jerome Anderson, Chief Executive of The SEM Group

To all Blackburn Rovers Fans.

I am taking this opportunity to write to all Blackburn Rovers fans regarding the many comments that have been posted online at both the Lancashire Evening Telegraph & through social network sites.

I wish to assure all fans at Blackburn Rovers Football Club that despite the contents of many posting's that have appeared, I do not have any role or involvement with the club.

At the request of the Trustees, I was asked to assist them to find a buyer for their club. I was able to introduce a number of potential buyers to the Trustees and the Trustees chose the Venky's Group as their preferred purchasers.

In January 2011 I was requested by the Owners to assist the club during that transfer window. I or SEM did not receive any payment whatsoever for any extended contracts for the players & neither have I or SEM ever received any payment whatsoever for the transfer of Ruben Rochina.

At the conclusion of the January 2011 transfer window I ceased to assist Blackburn Rovers Football Club in any capacity and I can confirm that I have not had any role or influence in their transfer policy or any other business of the club whatsoever since that date.

Unfortunately, within the last few months I & members of my family & staff have received abusive messages and threats that are unjustified and without foundation.

As a result of the abuse and threats that have been made, I have been left with no alternative but to consult my lawyers however, I remain of the opinion that those football fans that genuinely care for the club will ensure that such abuse and threats to both me and my family will now stop.

During the past few days, I have been privileged to have spoken directly with many Blackburn Rovers fans, who have totally understood, appreciated & respected any work that I have been involved with at the club & I would like to thank them personally for their ongoing support & I naturally wish Blackburn Rovers FC, its players, its Manager & its fans every success for the future.

13th January 2012

This statement is submitted upon the condition that it is published in its entirety & is not edited in any way whatsoever.

Anderson also maintained that he'd done a good job when he spoke about his involvement at Blackburn in a *Sky TV* interview. He said: "We entered last year's January transfer window and I received a call from the owner of the club saying: 'We have one or two issues causing us concern. Would you be kind enough to help us through this difficult period?' So I basically slept at the training ground for the month of January and helped the club in so many areas. First and foremost, trying to bring in players. We were very, very successful in that area. When I left the training ground at the end of January the place was absolutely rocking."

That wasn't how Rovers fans saw it. The stellar names might have been unrealistic but all they got were unknowns. It was the beginning of an era when mere disgruntlement would have been a welcome relief, while watching an Allardyce team eke out a 0-0 draw would seem like a rheumy-eyed glimpse of a lost golden age.

If supporters felt Allardyce had been a safe pair of hands, they would have trusted John Williams with the Crown Jewels in a rucksack. One of the most respected chairmen in the game, he was the man they looked to during troubled times and considered a paragon of steadfastness and decency. Few behind-the-scenes suits become legends but he did. Neither born nor bred in Blackburn, Williams was the umbilical cord with those heady days. But just two days after the window closed on February 2, Williams was gone too.

It got fewer headlines than Big Sam's axing but to many in Blackburn it was a bigger loss. Dismayed by the sacking of Allardyce – a deed he would have performed through gritted teeth – and marginalised by the increasing influence of Anderson, Williams' departure was inevitable. In the end, he couldn't take the transformation of the model club that he loved into Fred Karno's circus any longer. And the circus didn't want this straightest of straight men hanging around. Long-time sponsor Crown Paints terminated their contract the next day. Less than three months after Desai had admitted: "I know nothing about football," many were wondering if she knew anything about running a business either.

BLACKBURN ROVERS

4

"Time to go Steve! Saturday's humiliating home defeat to West Bromwich Albion was the last straw following a disastrous run of results stretching back months. The club is now waist-deep in the relegation mire."

Lancashire Telegraph

The spring of 2011 held scant optimism for followers of Blackburn Rovers. They were stuck with a manager they couldn't abide and owners they didn't want: there had been no honeymoon and all they wanted now was a divorce. Rovers' descent from Premier League's higher reaches was not precipitous: more an undignified and wholly unnecessary slither. From the sure-footedness of Big Sam's crampons, ropes and safety precautions, it was as if they had suddenly switched to flip-flops. Losing their footing, they careered south in mini-avalanches of their own making. Occasionally, the brakes would be applied with a half-decent performance, but their momentum was unstoppable as was the gravitational pull of a relegation battle. But what angered Rovers' fans even more than inconsistency on the field was the Venky's refusal to countenance that their hastily appointed, ridiculously-trumped up, long-term manager should cop even a scintilla of blame. Kean was staying come what may, they insisted. It was a depressing outlook with which to enter the last three games of the season just three points clear of the drop.

Rovers did survive with a 3-2 win over Wolves, but relief was tempered by the fear that it may only be a pit-stop on a downward spiral to oblivion. They knew they would have the same manager and owners next season, didn't expect to spend and would flog their best players. Not even a fee of £16.5m from Manchester United for Phil Jones could temper the anger at losing one of their best assets. To the game at large, the sale seemed both routine and inevitable, but to Rovers' fans, it was much more than that. Wilkinson wrote plaintively on his blog: "It was felt by many that Jones' departure was the true end of the Walker Era, it was the final poke in the eye to Jack Walker's legacy; the feeling being that Rovers had now become nothing more than a finishing school for Manchester United."

That summer, there were other departures that did not make the national headlines but added to a sense the ship was being abandoned. Tom Finn left in May after more than a decade and, within days of each other, two long-serving doctors also quit. They were followed by the physio and the finance director.

The Venky's denied they were about to put the club up for sale, while the pre-season trip to India was postponed after a bomb blast in Mumbai. It didn't stop Kean, though, and this time he spent five days in India and was promised 'a sizable budget' in the transfer window. For once they kept their word and no less than eight players arrived with Yakubu and Scott Dann the most notable. They had reinvested the Jones money, but any optimism would soon be dashed: Rovers endured their worst start for 60 years. Not even Kean getting banned for drink driving could lift the gloom: the first protest took place on September 17.

Before that, however, a chance meeting occurred at the Everton game in August (2011) between Anderson and prominent local businessman and Rovers' fan, Ian Battersby, who I met at Blackburn station three years later. He tells the story.

"I'd met him [Jerome Anderson] before, around 2000, and saw him coming out of the ground after we lost one-nil having missed two penalties. The animosity was beginning to build and cracks were appearing. I asked him: 'What's going on?' We had a quick cup of coffee and he told me broadly what the Venky's had in mind. He was working alongside and on behalf of the owners and said to me it looks as though they are making a few fundamental mistakes that need to be rectified. I told him they haven't bought a London West End club, they've bought a north west mill town club with a finite population where the whole thing up here is glass half empty as it's a hard existence. I said I don't think they appreciate the connection between the club and the community that the club has always had. This is a club that sits at the heart of the local community and quite a lot of what happens locally hinges on the success of the club. He said: 'From what you've said, I think you ought to meet the Venky's and tell them.'" Battersby ended up meeting Balaji at The Lowry hotel in Manchester when he came over for the next home game.

"I had two hours with him of absolute fist-pumping. I told him: 'This is Blackburn Rovers. You need to understand the dynamic, the heritage and the part it has played in the lives of generations of many families for 130 years. You mustn't get this wrong. These are the principles we've lived by for 100 years; this is what it means in a town like this, you have to understand the connection. You have to understand it's hard for people to afford to buy tickets. Employment is difficult; it is not a generally prosperous area of the country. He sat in total silence for two hours in this private room. I must have sounded almost Churchillian at times as he then said: 'This is absolutely fantastic. I had no idea that this is what it was all about. But you have to come and meet the family with your business partner. The team are coming to Pune in two or three weeks. Come then.' I said 'I'd be delighted.'"

Following the path of Kean, Battersby and business partner Ian Currie landed in Mumbai and were whisked by Mercedes for the four-hour trip along the highway to Pune. "We were going to put the same points to Mrs Desai that I'd put to Balaji," he explained. "There was no agenda as such. We were put up in the Marriott – a 6-star hotel – and the next morning we were woken by reception, telling us: 'Your driver's here. Want [sic] to take you to the Venky's temple.' So we went – we'd come to see the Venky's not their temple, but it probably would have been rude to turn it down. Then it was back to hotel. But still there was no contact with Mrs Desai. Another day passed. On Thursday, there was a junior tournament Rovers were involved in and Balaji said only a brief hello. We thought it a bit strange. 'Big event for us tomorrow,' he said. It was the first time an English Premier League club had played in India and it was live on TV. Rovers won 3-0 and Balaji was telling everyone what a brilliant manager Kean was. It didn't stop a 'Kean Out' banner from appearing though.

"That night there was a gala dinner. We'd seen Madame at the game but it was only a quick hello. She seemed a quiet, soft-spoken lady who looked almost uncomfortable in public. She certainly didn't want to be the centre of attention like, perhaps, Balaji did. Then we had to attend a reception in another magnificent hotel. Everyone was there – Kean, directors, wives. People were saying 'you're going on the board, you two', and we said 'no, we're not – we haven't met anybody yet.' We spent most of the time enquiring of Balaji why we had been here for five days on the premise of meeting formally with Madam and had so far encountered radio silence.

"Another day went by and it was now Sunday – we'd been here since Tuesday and we hadn't had any contact from anybody. We were losing the will to live. So we got hold of the driver and asked him to inform the family. The upshot was a meeting at 4pm at the Venky's' house. We were flying at 11pm from Mumbai which was four hours away so it didn't give us much time. On the journey to the Rao family home our escort informed us: 'You'll have five minutes with Madam. If she likes what you have to say she'll invite you to stay, if she doesn't, you can leave.' We said 'five minutes! We've been here six days at outrageous cost.' Even that comment made you wonder how much regard they were putting behind this visit.

"As it happened, we had two and a half hours, so something was going well. We sat in a big, square room and put every point that I'd put to Balaji before, and Madam sat there and asked all the questions. She said: 'This is absolutely fantastic – it's told us everything we want to know and given us a real insight into how we should run this club. How we should approach everything we need to do.' Crucially, these were the factors which will be essential in getting some unity back into the club. She seemed a really bright and logical lady – certainly in a business sense – and she'd obviously done a lot of prep work. There were even bogus attempts at understanding players' career histories etc. Finally, she said: 'What I'd like to do is to bring you back in 15 days and have you present to the advisory group we have working around the Venky's Group.' Fifteen days sticks in my mind as it's neither one thing nor the other. She wanted photos with Ian and I, and Balaji, on the steps and we were waved off. On the face of it, it was great – we finally felt that we'd got through to her. She made all the right noises. We never heard from her again.

"But that pattern, though strange to accept at the time, has occurred before with other people who've made contact and then it all just falls away. So it was all quite strange, bizarre even. I started emailing, ringing, texting to find out what had happened. Had something gone wrong?

"We definitely felt that somebody, somewhere on the inside, had got to them and said, 'you don't want these guys around', as if we were a threat to someone in the inner sanctum. Maybe we were a threat to someone on a cushy existence who was having his pocket lined. It did appear at the end of that meeting as if there was a possibility of boardroom representation. But we didn't go with that intention. Nor to buy the club – far from it. What we did say was that we'd be prepared to get involved in order to try to act as a bridge between the ownership in India and the football club which needs day to day operational support on the ground in Blackburn. The notion of absentee landlords with no local empowerment was failing miserably. One of the problems they were having was that they were 6,000 miles away from Ewood Park and had no connection. There was a huge disconnect between them, Ewood – what the fans see – and the training ground at Brockhall where the players are. We said we're not taking anything away. We just want to explain what's going on." We were basically offering to manage the Venky's plan, within reason, on a local basis. It would appear some four years later that there never has been a plan."

For all Battersby's criticism of the regime, he dismissed two popular perceptions: he felt that the Venky's not knowing about relegation was "an urban myth" and didn't agree that Anderson had taken them for a ride. "If you look at it now, with the benefit of hindsight, I don't think that's the case at all," he told me. "That's not to say agents and possibly Jerome, too, haven't done very well out of Blackburn Rovers. It happens at every club. I don't think it looked very pretty to the outside world. Jerome Anderson was a prime target. Fans heaped a lot of blame on him but I don't think there was anything illegal at all. Opportunistic, maybe, but this has been allowed to run away with itself because there has never been any denial from anyone inside the club nor any explanation of anything. Can anyone substantiate anything? No, it's never come out."

Asked what Madam is like, he said: "She came across really well. She seemed very genuine and straightforward, she's fluent in English and an educated woman. The way they've gone about it has been completely and utterly unfathomable in terms of what's happened: that a lady with that much business acumen has let a situation develop where a subsidiary of the VH Group has absorbed £100m of their money and trashed their commercial reputation. And they've done very little about putting it right."

As Battersby and Currie waited in vain for the Venky's to invite them back to India – or even to reply to their emails and calls – protests against the owners and Kean reached new levels – quite literally. A group of supporters raised £1,000 to pay for a plane to fly a protest banner over Ewood during the Chelsea game. The plane circled above during the first half with the message 'Steve Kean Out' fluttering behind it. Fans also held a protest on terra firma before the kick-off, and organised 'human banners' where lines of supporters wore matching T-shirts. This was in response to a dire start to the season that saw Rovers in the relegation zone with one win in their first 10 games.

By the end of the year, the writing was on the wall as well as in the sky. And it was in a giant headline in the front page of the *Lancashire Telegraph*. "Time to go" it screamed at Kean. "Saturday's humiliating home defeat to West Bromwich Albion was the last straw following a disastrous run of results stretching back months," it explained. "The club is now waist-deep in the relegation mire." It went on to catalogue the cock-ups of a reign that had seen only seven wins in 37 games and called on the Venky's to take decisive action. The paper blamed the owners "for much of the chaos". Also in December, Wayne Wild, of main sponsors WEC Group, met with senior Rovers officials over his fears about the direction the club was taking. Local council leaders added their frustrations as did local MP and former Foreign Secretary Jack Straw, also a Rovers' fan. The message was deafening but Mrs Desai chose not to hear it. But then Kean said he never saw the plane despite photographic evidence of him peering up at it.

BLACKBURN ROVERS

5

*"We are desperate to do something about it because there is a legacy
of generations to protect here. Blackburn is a northern mill town
and the club is at the heart of that community, but the picture just
gets worse and worse under the current regime."*

Ian Battersby.

It was almost Christmas but there was absolutely no goodwill among
Blackburn fans in late December, 2011. The team were languishing,
the manager hapless, the club in free fall, the owners beyond parody.
It was not funny anymore. No football manager – and certainly not
with his wife in attendance – should have had to endure what befell
Kean during the wretched defeat to Bolton on a wet Tuesday night at
Ewood. The vitriol came in torrents, the rage as relentless as the rain:
chant after despicable chant, verse after repulsive verse. "It created
the worst atmosphere we've ever seen in the ground," said Brian
Haworth. "Even pensioners were shouting." And amid it all, Kean stood
steadfast, maintaining his dignity. Bald pate soaked from the downpour
and glistening in the floodlights, he remained in his technical area,
expressionless, almost Buddha-like.

Few despots would have deserved such vilification and the media laid
into Rovers fans as if they were a baying, uncontrollable mob. But they
were only words – angry and unprintable some of the time – and there
was no violence. It was a year now since they'd had this regime forced
upon them and the club was already unrecognisable from the Europe-
contending, full-working-order outfit it had been under Sam Allardyce
and John Williams. The fans had warned the owners time and again,
formed groups to protest, written letters, visited India, made sensible
proposals to stop the rot and even offered guidance. They'd tried demos,
protests, flown banners, sung songs and released chickens. Local civic

leaders had spoken, the local paper had shouted from the front page, the esteemed local MP had the ear of the Minister of Sport. All to no avail. Kean was only half the problem but became the fall guy. He was taking it on the chin for the Venky's who, back in the Pune hills of India, were the principal objects of the anger and ridicule.

The way the owners had treated the club, you worry about the state of their chickens. It was simply beneath contempt. There had been no communication whether it was ignoring messages from people they'd already met (Battersby and Currie) or with the fans who kept the turnstiles clicking. Some would say clucking, but such lines were wearing thin after 12 months of unmitigated torment. From the unjustifiable sacking of Big Sam, his mystifying replacement, the claptrap about Maradona, sticking with Kean no matter how bad things got, the reliance on an agent, the departures of grandees like Williams and Finn, to being forced by Barclays' Bank to deposit the players' wages in December to make sure they were paid on time... the list was endless, the cock-ups relentless.

When the media gathered for the post-match press conference (after the Bolton defeat), there was admiration for Kean's fortitude. And the mere fact that he hadn't ducked this inquisition after such an ordeal was more than commendable. But much of the sympathy waned when he assumed full denial mode. Asked, with genuine concern, whether it was really all worth it and whether his family should have to suffer through his own misery, he was unmoved, reeling off the casualty list he felt had caused the crisis.

At least the new CEO Paul Hunt was still in touch with reality. The next day he wrote to the Venky's in a dutiful, thorough and well-intentioned attempt to alert his bosses to the danger, inform them where the faults lay and suggested what might be done to avert the looming disaster. The letter was ignored until it was leaked in May whereupon he was sacked.

Even the leader of Blackburn with Darwen Borough Council, Kate Hollern, waded in. "Fans are just rightly frustrated and angry at how the club is currently being run," she stated. "We simply want greater transparency from the owners, better communication, a visible presence from them in Blackburn and proper leadership to sort this mess out..."

Wilkinson commented: "That kind of behaviour [at the Bolton game] went beyond normal limits, but on the other hand I can understand it. The Kean situation damaged the club incalculably. His lack of competence – he was almost wilfully defiant about the performances and where we were heading."

The team continued to struggle – and disintegrate. In the transfer window, stalwarts Ryan Nelsen and Jason Roberts were allowed to leave along with Chris Samba who went to Anzhi in February. Many felt they were just the kind of characters needed to wage a relegation battle, and Nelsen had gone for nothing without explanation. At least they got £12 million for Samba and this fee, when added to that for Phil Jones, meant the Venky's had more than recouped their initial £23m outlay to buy Rovers. Of course, they had spent an awful lot more than that – mainly in wages – and were making losses at an unsustainable rate to add to the debt they had already taken on board. As a telling footnote to their epic mismanagement, the club confirmed that they paid £4,679,349.22 in fees to agents during the financial year ending September 30, 2011.

The inevitable came against Wigan, when a late goal meant Rovers were relegated from the top flight for the first time since 2001. Back then Jack Walker had shed tears; this time Ewood erupted with tears of rage. "There was a lot of hate around," says Haworth, "and elements of racism. There were some who just didn't want the club owned by what they called 'Pakis'. It was an awful time and there was a danger fans could be turned off for life." It was the nightmare scenario: the chickens – one more was released in the game with Wigan – really had come home to roost. A week later, a video emerged of a Rovers pre-season tour to Hong Kong in 2011 showing a drunken Kean branding Allardyce "a fucking crook" among other outrageous boasts to fans. He ended up having to pay significant damages to Big Sam. The own goals kept on coming.

As Rovers faced up to the reality of the Championship, Battersby had still not given up hope of persuading the Venky's to see reason. After relegation, he approached Mrs Desai again, telling the *Daily Telegraph*: "We are desperate to do something about it because there is a legacy of generations to protect here. Blackburn is a northern mill town and the club is at the heart of that community, but the picture just gets worse and worse under the current regime."

But that Olympic summer of 2012, a strange thing happened: the Venky's listened to advice. Not from Battersby and Currie, but from erstwhile Asian TV pundit, Serbegeth 'Shebby' Singh. Having been spotted on the box for his forthright views on the Premier League, the former Malaysian international defender was hired by the Venky's to look after 'Asian football development'. But belatedly realising they needed someone on the ground in Blackburn, they appointed him as their eyes and ears at Ewood, bestowing upon him the ludicrous title of global advisor. Asian viewers hoped they paid more attention to what he said now than when he was taking aim from the pundit's chair: from that safe distance his favourite whipping boy had been... Steve Kean.

Whoever or whatever was behind it, there was suddenly a sea change in the Venky's approach to spending. Armed with the first tranche of parachute money, they coughed up £12.5m in the summer transfer window, culminating in a club record £8m on striker Jordan Rhodes. Rovers' fans could scarcely believe what they were reading. Leon Best at £3m and Dickson Etuhu at £1.5m made up the total with no less than seven other recruits joining for free or nominal fees.

When Rovers were unbeaten after six games and Shebby told fans he would sack Kean if he lost three in a row, there was the first glimmer of optimism around the club since the heady days of the takeover. Thanks to the Venky's finally opening the purse strings, they had in Rhodes a striker with an impressive scoring record, albeit in a division below. And in Shebby there was a long-awaited link to the owners actually in Blackburn. Says Wilkinson: "We hadn't had any communication from the owners until Shebby appeared. He came and pandered to the fans at first, accepting every invitation to meet people in every pub and club." Haworth remembers: "He was popular – for about five minutes."

Rhodes started scoring and Shebby couldn't stop talking, but it would soon be said that he'd arrived with his foot in his mouth. He immediately followed his threat to Kean by dubbing Morten Gamst Pedersen 'a pensioner'. Unfortunately for Shebby, Pedersen was a fan favourite. The global advisor had to apologise to both manager and player, but a trend was set. He even defended the indefensible – his moniker. "Madam chose it," he said, "as I was working in both Europe and Asia – two continents." Geographically justified it may have been, but Madam could never have imagined the ammunition it would give her GA's critics. "If he was promoted, he'd be Galactic Advisor", wrote one columnist. Another wondered: "If I could quiz him on Mitt Romney's choice of running mate for the US Presidential election or ask about forest fires in Spain – he's supposed to be on top of these things as a Global Advisor." The jokes had begun and never stopped.

Crowds were down by nearly 10,000 from the previous season's highs but Rovers made a bright start. However, Wilkinson wasn't fooled. He said: "We were getting away with murder. We got 14 points from six games. We won three that we had no business winning. People were saying we're gonna walk this league, but I said we're not going to get away with this."

He was right but no one foresaw the next development. With the team third in the table and yet to lose three games in a row, Steve Kean finally spared Blackburn fans further torture and resigned. It was almost anti-climactic. It was a Friday (September 28), the day before a game at Charlton, and after his pre-match press conference in London. This was not how anyone thought it would happen and there appeared no trigger for it. Indeed, after almost two years resisting a football version of the Hadron Collider, the timing seemed odd. His statement read: "For reasons I cannot discuss on legal advice, it is with deep regret, given my hard work and service for the club for a number of years that I have been forced to resign as manager with immediate effect due to my position as team manager becoming untenable." *Becoming* untenable? In most people's eyes it had been untenable for 18 months. The bigger question was: why did they wait so long? Ashworth said: "If anyone has an answer to that question, I'd love them to give me a call."

BLACKBURN ROVERS

6

"He may be a lovely guy but in terms of his credentials for running a football club and being a global advisor, it's nonsense. It was ridiculous, a weird choice. You're basically letting King Herod take charge of the nursery."

Ian Battersby on Shebby Singh.

Kean had had the owners' patronage but not their support. Like wealthy, distant relatives, they paid the school fees but didn't meet the kid at the gate. He had to go to great lengths to meet them and those monthly get-togethers were no substitute for a day-to-day, on-site presence. He might still have a career in management in British football once he's completed his stint in the Far East. But it is difficult to find anything positive about his stay at Blackburn beyond his stoicism, and that only prolonged the agony. His legacy is one of bitterness and failure, of protests and relegation. He looked a certainty to be remembered as the worst Rovers manager of all time – until we saw the next two. The day after he quit, the verdict was unanimous: he had to go. Rovers legend Simon Garner said: "He was never going to win the fans over," while Mark Fish, secretary of the Blackburn Rovers Action Group, noted: "It has taken 10,000 people making the painful decision to turn their backs on the club to make this happen."

Predictably, leading ex-players were among the names mentioned as possible successors. Tim Sherwood, former midfield dynamo in the title-winning side and then coaching at Spurs, was the early favourite. Alan Shearer, superstar of the 95 champions, was in the mix although he was thought unlikely to swap the *BBC* sofa for the bed of nettles that Ewood Park had become. Kean's assistant, Eric Black, took charge at Charlton. Black had to wait four games for his first win and, as the Venky's dithered, Rovers took a month to find a new manager.

But at least they now had a global advisor. Many believe it was Shebby who sacked Kean – something he defers to those in Pune – but he was responsible for appointing his successor. And that wasn't straightforward either. I did not meet Shebby until he'd left the scene and was in Kuala Lumpur in late 2013. He told me he had been hired "to get promotion" and given the brief, "do what you have to do" by Mrs Desai. He understood it to include spending millions and sacking managers. He showed me a motto on his mobile that read: *Promotion or die trying.*

It was never going to be easy and his son Sonuljit told him: "You've walked into the most impossible [sic] job in the world." I added that his title, the nature of the Venky's business and Madam's ignorance of football hardly helped. Shebby disagreed: "You've got to be stronger than that," he said. "It doesn't mean I have to commit *hari kiri* because someone in the press doesn't know the meaning of global advisor. You have to laugh about it. But I thrive in this situation. Let the critics keep on barking: like dogs, they'll get tired in the end." It was typical Shebby – unrepentant, indefatigable and, some would say, incorrigible. However, he does go some way to acknowledging: "It's very difficult because fans believe what's written out there."

He was referring mainly to the drip, drip, and occasional flood, of leaks to certain newspapers, adding: "Everybody and his dog has had a go at Shebby Singh. I knew I had enemies from day one. I arrived and there was a spillover of hostilities, a lot of friction. Relegation is not easy, the fans were hurting." But there was also his unique place outside the pecking order: "I am not employed by Blackburn Rovers but by the Venky's," he made very clear. Already in situ were managing director Derek Shaw and operations director Paul Agnew, both board members. And suddenly parachuted in came this pundit from Asia. A recipe for a right old chicken jalfrezi, then, and so it proved.

"I was very excited by the challenge," he said. But there would be times when his reported £400k a year salary was hard-earned. A battle that soon became a standoff ensued between Shebby and Shaw and Agnew or "Shagnew" as Rovers humourists dubbed them. Shebby wanted Henning Berg to take over from Kean, while Shaw and Agnew favoured Ian Holloway. Harry Redknapp was considered but said: "It's not for me," to the disappointment of many. A Harry & Shebby (Shabby perhaps?) double act would have been irresistible viewing. Once the butt of humour, it's hard to be taken seriously and the word 'farce' was used to describe the level to which the search had descended. It would not be the last time. Holloway got as far as an interview but walked out in disgust. In the end, Shebby won and so Norway's Berg, a doughty defender in Rovers' 95 side, but whose managerial pedigree was on the slim side of modest, took the reins.

One-nil to Shebby, but it soon turned into a disaster. Rovers won only one game under the Norwegian, but even in his homeland his win ratio had been a mere 31% before he was sacked by mighty Lillestrom. Berg made Kean look like Mourinho, and Shebby ended the agony after just 57 days. Berg's win ratio at Rovers was 10%. "Better to do that than disappear into oblivion," the GA said. But with a boardroom split and dressing room unrest, Rovers were in danger of doing just that.

They were plunging down the table – false dawn long since forgotten – which was why the players were unhappy. Seniors, dismayed by the drop in status, had been told to hold on to see if they could bounce straight back up. But the way things were going, if they were to play in a different division the following season, the third was more likely than the top flight. Rovers were in an even worse state than under Kean and £12.5m had been spent.

The situation prompted Shaw, a former chairman of Preston and an experienced football administrator, to fly to India and have it out with the Venky's. More precisely, to have Shebby out. Adding to the sense that Brian Rix was giving way to Monty Python, *The Sun* reported that Rovers had offered former Arsenal trainee and sometime actor, Judan Ali, a place in their coaching set-up – even though they had yet to decide on Berg's successor. London-born Ali, 39, had acted as a footballer in the 2007 Bollywood feature film *'Dhan Dhana Dhan Goal'*, and did turn up at Brockhall. Some Indian papers claimed he would be picking the team but Shebby was quick to deny that, saying Ali was just a friend.

But the exodus continued with assistant manager Black, first team coach Iain Brunskill and goalkeeping coach Bobby Mimms all departing with immediate effect. Shebby asked reserve team coach Gary Bowyer to take temporary charge of the first team. To outside observers, it looked like the circus had stuck around. On the *BBC 6-0-6* live show hosted by Darren Fletcher and Robbie Savage, Shebby provided a half hour that will live forever in the podcasts of car-crash radio. If there were any doubts about his suitability for the role the Venky's had chosen for him, a slew of off-the-cuff remarks and rants to the nation's listeners would have removed them. Despite the clear distinction between the voices of the two hosts and Fletcher asking as many questions as Savage, every single blurt from Shebby's motormouth began, "Yes, Robbie…" It was a performance so crass and clueless it left you seriously questioning not only Shebby's, but the Venky's judgment, and with grave fears for Rovers' future.

But Shebby survived both the programme and Shaw's mercy mission. He never did restore diplomatic relations with his 'enemies', even sitting in a different box at games. "I had nothing to do with them," he said, citing the example of "Andy Cole and Teddy Sheringham [who] hated each other – but they got the job done on the field." But the job was not being done at Blackburn where there was now a state of open hostility among the hierarchy. The fans? Their attitude was summed up in January when the Venky's, making one of their Halley's Comet frequency visits, had been met by a protest before the home game with Charlton. As the party stepped out of a fleet of Rolls Royces, a volley of 'Venky's Out' abuse was not the only thing they had to duck. Mrs Desai's husband, Jitendra, didn't and was hit on the head by a snowball. The incident was captured on a mobile and went viral. Completing a day of discontent, after 65 minutes, the party departed to more derision from the crowd. Rovers slid to a 2-1 defeat.

That visit came on a cold winter's day but spring hardly brought a thaw in relations. The prevailing climate was of rumour, falsehoods and intrigue. A leak to the *Daily Mail* about young Portuguese players being signed with mysteriously high fees going to agents caused Shebby to issue a statement saying he had had nothing to do with their recruitment. "It was absolute rubbish and part of a concerted effort from within the club to try and disgrace me," he said. "I was NOT responsible for negotiating contracts, but identifying the talent was part of my job." It emerged that an agent admitted to making more than £1m on the deals. And Shebby left it to me to guess from where the leak came.

There had, however, been a subtle shift in the balance of power. When it came to the next manager, it was Shaw, in alliance with Agnew, who made the running. Shebby was surprisingly hands-off. In fact, he was unaware 'Shagnew' had given the job to Michael Appleton when it was announced. The score in the Cold War was now one-all. How did you allow that to happen? I asked. "I decided to take a step back. I can't carry the can for people. As a global advisor I report to my bosses and speak to my bosses."

It seemed a curious contradiction for a hands-on man, but that is Shebby, impulsive and very much his own man. He added: "As a player I got abuse from between 30,000 and 40,000 people and as a pundit I polarised opinion. I grew up in a tough area and my philosophy in life is I don't give a damn about the world." During the near two hours of our chat, he said he 'didn't care' often enough to suggest that he did. And to be fair, he did care about Blackburn. Appleton's reign also turned sour and despite a sensational FA Cup win over Arsenal, Rovers were heading south in the table. Seeing the danger, Shebby renounced his ceasefire and resumed hostilities. He warned the Venky's they could be heading for League One and sacked Appleton by letter, which he famously delivered to reception 15 minutes before the manager was due in. "No, I never met him – I took a back seat as people were beginning to say I was interfering," was his explanation for why he hadn't waited to tell his unfortunate victim to his face.

The news of Appleton's dismissal was met with predictable disbelief. "Madness," was how former Blackburn and Real Madrid defender Michel Salgado described it. "When you ask me to tell the truth I don't even know it, I don't know who is making decisions," he tweeted. Former Blackburn striker Jason Roberts added. "I've never been more concerned for the club."

Appleton had outlasted Berg by just 10 days. He had not done much better but the decision was the latest salvo in the power struggle between Shebby and 'Shagnew'. It also came as the club prepared for a harrowing day in court – Berg's claim for compensation was about to be heard.

Judges are renowned for their restraint when passing their verdicts on all but the more extraordinary cases. But sitting at Manchester

High Court, Judge Mark Pilling described Rovers' behaviour as "utterly unforgivable". Not only did he order them to pay Berg the rest of his contract, he expressed serious reservations about Blackburn's handling of the case. He reserved a special disdain for owner Mrs Desai, her brothers and their 'global advisor'. Not only had they failed to produce evidence to support their claims about Shaw or Berg's contract, not one of them had turned up. Rovers' own lawyers made the extraordinary admission in court that the club was 'out of control'. As for Shebby, he was stuck somewhere else in the globe. The global advisor was having visa problems.

Wherever they were, neither he nor the Venky's could escape the barrage of criticism that was launched in their direction. Players, judges, everyone – even 'Dr Who' – was to have their say. Dr Who actor and Blackburn fan Matt Smith declared: "It's an absolute farce, a joke. It's being run by complete numpties. Great players, great team, great club and those berks have ruined it."

At least Rovers had stopped leaking as many goals in the final month of the season. And Bowyer was turning the team around. Eventually, he was given the job on a permanent basis and made a success of it. What's more, Shebby even talked to him. Another sign that he appeared to be outlasting his enemies was the abrupt dismissal of Agnew at the end of the 2012-13 season. But as it turned out, Agnew had outlasted him – he was not seen in Blackburn after the Appleton sacking.

After visiting Blackburn and talking to the fans, the feeling I got was that Shebby was perceived as more a clown than a villain. Indeed, when he first arrived, he won a few over. Ashworth said: "When Shebby said he'd sack Kean, he got the biggest ovation since Yakubu scored a hattrick." In the eyes of the Rovers faithful, there was no doubt that Kean was the No.1 villain of the piece and Shebby might be disappointed to learn that he was never higher than No.2.

Sadly for Shebby, he would never go back to Blackburn. There was no announcement, no fanfare, not even a brief press release... just a deafening silence. I had tried many times to contact him but e-mails, phone calls and messages were ignored. But as the weeks drew into months, the feeling grew that he had been quietly dropped. Eventually, he answered one of my calls. Bullish as ever, he said: "I am still employed by the Venky's, still global advisor, nothing's changed." Oh, but everything had. He was no longer there, no longer sitting in a different box to the directors, no longer putting his foot in his mouth. He maintained he was still the Venky's Development Officer for Asia and may even have been collecting the second year of his £400k a year contract. If so, good luck to him. He tried but, like Kean, found the going too hard. And like Kean, there was no lack of effort or thinness of skin. But neither should have been chosen – both were several leagues out of their depth.

Rovers Trust's Duncan Miller said of Shebby: "You've only to be in his company for 30 seconds to know he's a moron." Ashworth agreed: "I wouldn't be able to look him in the eye. All these divisions occurred after he came in. You've had Kean vs Shebby, Agnew vs Shebby, Shaw vs Shebby, Morten Gamst Pedersen vs Shebby. He's just come in and made enemies."

Ian Battersby is in no doubt. "We've floundered from one situation to another when you start looking at Shebby [Singh]. For crying out loud! If he was an attempt by the Venky's to be their link, he was an absolutely ludicrous choice. After what we've said about the need for links to the community, the history, the ethos, to bring him from Malaysian TV to be the man to deal with it was self-serving nonsense from start to finish. I've nothing against him personally but the guy is a complete buffoon. He may be a lovely guy but in terms of his credentials for running a football club and being a global advisor is nonsense. It was ridiculous, a weird choice. You're basically letting King Herod take charge of the nursery."

BLACKBURN ROVERS

7

"Of all the takeovers, they knew the least and it arguably makes the least sense to anyone. I don't think there is one Rovers fan anywhere who could tell you why they bought the club, what they are doing with it and more importantly what they intend do with it from here, £100million later."

Ian Battersby

At first, they were only rumours and whispered in hushed tones: the first green shoots of sanity restoration had been discerned. The global advisor had been quietly removed and the manager given a contract. As for the transfer policy, it was to buy cheap and off-load the high earners. Fans didn't call it progress but felt it might just be a slowing of the alarming regression that had taken place since the Venky's had changed their world. Even then there were hiccups but with its principal clown gone, Blackburn Rovers were perceived as slightly less of a circus. They spent much of the 2013-14 season well down the table but hiccups were a big improvement on cock-ups. And they even made a late run for the playoffs, going 12 games unbeaten, but had to settle for eighth place in the end.

None of this amounted to much for Ian Battersby, however, when we met just as the 2014-15 campaign got under way or whenever we have exchanged views since. The first part of the conversation had been about his trip to Pune and attempt to salvage the dire situation as related in chapter 4; the second was more of a review of what had happened since and a stark warning about the future.

Ian Battersby: "It's been an absolute car crash. And it's happened because there was no process of approval for the capability and substance required for running a football club – especially not from thousands of miles away. Getting rid of Sam Allardyce and the entire board of experienced professionals within the early weeks struck fear and alarm in the minds of most supporters. I think there would have been a public outcry if it had been Liverpool or Spurs. Because it's little old Blackburn in the north west of England – the fans have made noise – it's been largely ignored.

"Blackburn is a football town, a one-club town, and it means a massive amount. When we got relegated all these cottage industries around the club that were depending on match days just disappeared overnight. It was killed in that respect. They may be feeding 5,000 people a week in Pune [as they've claimed] but they've shown nothing but a major disregard for the community over here. It's extremely sad and extremely difficult to get that back. Ian [Currie] and I offered them a potential way out. But we got no response from that. The next thing that happened was the appointment of Shebby Singh, which was laughable to be honest, and with the lasting legacy he left behind, the thing is toxic now as a business proposition. 'Champions league within five years,' they said when they took over. Of all the takeovers, they knew the least, and arguably it makes the least sense to anyone. I don't think there is one Rovers fan anywhere who could tell you why they bought the club, what they are doing with it and, more importantly, what they intend do with it from here, £100million later.

"Venky's put in £23m cash plus £18m to cover the debt. People said it was a good deal. Brockhall [training complex] and a Premier League club for just over £40m didn't sound such a bad deal. If you stack that up against the TV revenues for PL clubs now, you'd say, come hell or high water, the important thing is to stay in the Premiership. So what's the first thing they do? Fire the manager and dispense with the board. Why? I have no idea."

Barely containing his frustration, he continued: "There's an awful lot of hard yards to go as we deal with FFP and the legacy of Shebby Singh. Shebby and I had had run-ins and I'd referred to him as an imbecile on local radio. He took great exception to it. But that guy set us back years. We're still picking up the pieces. There were a raft of Portuguese players – all arrived from nowhere that no one had ever heard of and anecdotally – and this has come from someone within the club – the agents' fees paid for this bunch of Portuguese were more than the transfer fee for [Rudy] Gestede. Ridiculous!

"One of them, Edinho Jr, played 45 minutes against Leicester and he ended up playing for Whitehawk in the Conference South League on loan. We were flying him down to Brighton on a Friday and back. They sent him back after three games – his attitude stank. Leon Best is supposedly on 27 grand a week but has been loaned to Sheffield Wednesday, and more latterly Derby and Brighton, teams in the same league as us whilst we pick up the bulk of his wages. It's absolutely crass.

"I remember Danny Murphy saying that when Etuhu came from Fulham, where the two had played together, he was offered a two-year deal and he told Murphy: 'I don't really want two – I want three.' So Murphy said: 'Go and see him and ask for three if that's what you want.' Shebby gave him four! When you're spending someone else's money it's very easy to dish out ridiculous contracts without realising the longer term implications. There's no accountability and this was after I'd been writing to Madam and saying: 'This is going to cost you millions – it doesn't need to operate like this.'"

But aren't there signs they might be coming to their senses? I ask. "Losses of £42m and £38m are about to be followed by something around the £25m mark for the year to 30 June 2015 – and that is supposed to represent progress. So in that context, I wouldn't be wanting to describe cumulative losses of over £100m in the last three years under the heading of stability! Venky's have little option but to carry on paying for the largesse of the Shebby Singh reign of terror and we are still shelling out for the likes of Murphy, Etuhu, Pedersen and Orr. So this arguably could get worse rather than better."

Indeed it has. Rovers had a payroll of £35m before Bowyer's attack on it yet losses of just £8m were permitted under Financial Fair Play. With Rovers' income from both season tickets and sponsorship off a cliff, the club's plight was encapsulated by what might be called 'the Jordan Rhodes dilemma' – and Battersby warned of dire consequences whatever the outcome. If a wage bill of £10m a year was realistic under FFP, Rhodes would be picking up a ridiculous 20% of it. But the Scot was scoring goals as Battersby acknowledged: "Rhodes and Gestede's 40 goals would be a massive issue for us."

When the FFP embargo was finally imposed in January, 2015 it left Rovers with no option but to sell their stars. The line from the club had been that if a top club came along with the right offer and a player wanted to leave, the club would not stand in his way. The fans would not like it, but knew they'd have to lump it. They did not, of course, want anyone sold to a rival club. But that is exactly what Rovers, contrary to the last, did at the end of June when they let midfielder Tom Cairney go to Fulham, who had finished eight places below them the previous season. Overnight, the Cottagers' were strengthened and Rovers weakened. And the £3m fee wasn't enough to have the embargo lifted anyway.

Next month they sold Gestede to Aston Villa for £6m and began the season in the drop zone. They rallied but only stayed in the top half for a fortnight and Bowyer was relieved of his duties in November. Paul Lambert replaced him but was soon made aware of the realities when Rhodes, after some hesitation, joined Middlesbrough on February 1, 2016 for a fee that rose to £11m when Boro sealed promotion. At least, by then, the embargo had been lifted. But other signs that stability was still a distant dream came when long-serving managing director, Derek Shaw, who had somehow survived since the pre-Shebby days, finally threw in the towel in February. He was followed in March by communications director, Alan Myers. Lambert left at the end of the season. Gestede had cost Rovers just £200,000 while Rhodes had been a record £8m buy, so there was a handsome profit on both strikers. But Rovers really did miss their goals. Lambert struggled, and with the playoffs out of reach, he left, disillusioned at the end of the campaign. All that and the Venky's were still looking at losses beyond £100m.

It is the end of the 2015-16 season and Battersby writes: "It's now difficult to stop it. It's not sellable as a club with its current overheads. The only thing they could do to stop their losses is to run – and that's what frightens a lot of fans. No one knows whether it's hard capital or whether it's stacked up as debt somewhere in the background. So we're now faced with a situation where although a lot of fans are against the Venky's, they fear if they left it would bring the house of cards down."

Battersby, along with business partner Currie, had made another approach to the Venky's, offering a joint-ownership proposal. Nothing if not concerned about the plight of their beloved club, the pair had secured sufficient backing from High Net Worth individuals and medium-sized businesses through their company, Seneca Partners, to buy a 51% share in exchange for a capital investment. But the proposal once again fell on deaf ears.

Meanwhile, the Venky's went on running the club in their own idiosyncratic way. If selling one of your best players to a rival club in the same division was one thing, appointing a former Burnley manager was quite another. But the owners did that, too, when they announced Owen Coyle as the new boss on June 3. The hashtag 'Venky's Out' was already trending in the Twitter top 10 and the fan behind it, Josh Boswell, told the *Lancashire Telegraph*: "It's got to the point now where it's hard to muster the energy to get angry; it's just another big sigh. The appointment of Owen Coyle is hardly inspiring and unfortunately it brings back memories of the Steve Kean era."

Mate, journalist, blogger and lifelong Rovers fan, Dave Rose, who managed to see 23 games of the title-winning season while living mostly in Sydney(!), still mustered the energy to be angry. He raged on his blog: "In 2010 the lunatics, in the form of the Venky family, came out of nowhere to create a madhouse that now resides at Ewood Park. Since then it's been one painful and depressing figurative blow to the head after another for the fans. And just as you thought the crackpot owners could not do anything more bafflingly deranged, they do. They appoint Owen Coyle as manager."

Gazing dreamily back at that 1994-95 season, he goes on: "From the halcyon days of the Jack Walker regime when we were all in heaven and things could not get any better, to the equally unbelievable Venkys' rag-tag regime of self-destruction. It's been a barmy ride. Presently, it's as if Masterspy and friend Zarin have got together with the cybermen, the daleks, all the Batman baddies and anyone evil in particular to create the Venkys. Mission: to 'white ant' the very foundations of Blackburn Rovers Football Club and send it into a bottomless black hole from which it can never return."

So dire is the situation and such is the scale of the owners' incompetence, assessment of their tenure is inevitably skewed. I ask Battersby if he has yet discovered why they bought the club in the first place. He says: "The answer we were given was enhancing the Venky's brand in the West. They were launching Venky's Express fast food outlets all over India and wanted to bring them to the West. I said at that meeting, 'The way this is going, you're going to suffer major brand damage not enhancement'. This is now way beyond the water mark of what they were trying to do – the cumulative losses added to the initial consideration plus ongoing losses probably mean they could not leave the club now without dropping £120m."

I ask if he ever had the feeling they were even interested in football? He said: "Balaji is the front end of it and seemingly quite likes the idea of owning a football club though the novelty must be wearing off and they are very much absentee landlords these days. Significantly, he did none of the talking [when we met in India] – it was all Madam when we were in the room. And it seemed very much to us as if Balaji had wanted to buy Rovers and it was going to be his plan going forward. I would think Madam would have been pretty cautious about such a venture and I would imagine there have been a lot of family arguments about it since.

"It's a self-destruct button that has taken us in five years from mid table in the Premier League to where we are now and it's the self inflicted nature of it that hurts most. At no time has there been a strategy nor has there been much, if any, logic to what has happened, and sequence after sequence of mind-numbing decisions have disconnected lots of fans of long standing. From a fan's point of view, you always need to have something to hang on to. However small it is, you need that glimmer of hope, something to cling to. That's been a problem and the reason we've lost so many fans. Look at the crowd now. As much as 10,000 down on when they [the Venky's] came in. We've got the cheapest tickets in the game. Football is much more affordable at this level than anywhere else in the UK. But people just got completely disillusioned with the entire regime."

By now, the Venky's themselves must be pretty disillusioned and the family arguments might be a little heated. They've demonstrated an uncanny knack of getting almost every major decision wrong, every manager wrong, and now the kindest interpretation of events is that they do not know what to do. But doing nothing is not an option either, unless they are comfortable with losses of £20m plus a year with the already-slim chance of being able to sell becoming positively anorexic. From naively believing it would boost their brand, they have become the biggest laughing stock in football – and it is a crowded field. Tommy Docherty might rearrange his Oxo cubes but it's beyond a joke now. That an otherwise astute businesswoman, Mrs Desai, can flounder so hopelessly only underlines the case that football really is unique, but then her ignorance and decision-making were a bit special too. Sacking Big Sam who has gone on to take West Ham up, keep them up and then, in almost impossible circumstances, keep Sunderland up before getting the England job is just where it kicks off. On his lack of continental cool, Big Sam once quipped: "I won't ever be going to a top-four club because I'm not called Allardici, just Allardyce." If the Venky's thought he played cave man football, he might have been better off being Aladdin.

Their stubbornness in sticking with Kean, the joke appointment of Shebby Singh, dispensing with the heart and soul of both office and playing staff, the refusal to even respond to offers of help and advice from within or without the club amount to prima facie evidence for the charge sheet. The list is endless, the failure is epic, the culpability absolute. Their sheer haplessness and wanton disregard for not just a club, but a community, earns them a special place in this book – in wilfully destroying a great sporting institution they have done themselves irrevocable harm too. And to think they followed Jack Walker. The Venky's have made a sizable chunk of East Lancashire "bloody miserable" every day of the week. Four thousand holes? They've fallen into every one of them.

Chelsea

CHELSEA

1

"I wasn't totally convinced he was the real thing."
Chelsea CEO Trevor Birch on meeting Roman Abramovich
in 2003.

He was so ordinary; so, so ordinary. He never looked you in the eye, wore jeans and had a wet-fish handshake. Charisma? He hadn't just had a bypass, he'd had the M25. Graeme Souness couldn't get a word out of him in the car, and Trevor Birch "wasn't totally convinced he was the real thing." He wasn't just underwhelming, he was what you might call a Russian diffident. How on earth, then, had half the Soviet oil wealth landed in his lap?

"He'd been in the right place at the right time," was the official line. That was what they said about the best strikers. Do nothing all game but hang about and then, when the moment comes, wham, bam. It was the mother of all euphemisms. But dig a little and there are tales of diverted oil tankers, forged documents and billions paid in *krysha* (protection). Surely enough to have been flagged offside and what of the assist? Messrs Glasnost and Perestroika had changed the rules, Boris Yeltsin kept his flag down and Roman Arkadyevich Abramovich had done the rest.

He was real, alright – Forbes List real and it wasn't fantasy football he was playing. In the Premiership of the world's richest, he was just below the Buffets and Gateses but pushing for a Europa League place. And he had the trappings – the Bond villain trappings of yacht, dream boltholes and customised Boeing. His bodyguards would out-bodyguard the KGB.

He had come out of nowhere when no one was looking; the ultimate nowhere man. None of the famous Russians – and you can throw in some of their marquee names, Tchaikovsky, Trotsky, Dostoyevsky, Tolstoy, who had either written masterpieces or tried to change the world – had made £23 billion in their thirties. And that was after being orphaned at three and dropping out of college. His first business venture? Flogging plastic ducks from a market stall.

How he'd got into football was less far-fetched. The puff – and widely accepted – version is that it was a love affair: love at first sight at a match without the remotest connection to him or Chelsea. It was the magical night at Old Trafford in November 2002 when Manchester United beat Real Madrid 4-3 (but lost 6-5 on aggregate) and the Brazilian Ronaldo scored a hat-trick. There was a two-goal cameo from David Beckham, but it was the intensity of the game and the atmosphere that awakened in Abramovich a dormant love of football. It was one of the great European occasions: a storied ground, a full house, a Champions League classic between two fabled clubs. Besides Ronaldo and Becks there were other stellar names like Zidane, Luis Figo and Roberto Carlos, lots of goals and refulgent football. Even the quadrants were quaking. To witness such gigs in the flesh, the European winter seems worth enduring. And to a Russian, Manchester in November would have seemed like Marbella.

Souness, in the unaccustomed role of chauffeur, remembers it well. Super agent Pini Zahavi had asked him to give a lift to 'a Russian who had landed his jet at Manchester airport'. He recalls: "Roman sat in the front seat and there were three other people in the back. He didn't know who I was. I tried to talk to him but I got this distinct vibe from him and the message was, 'You just get on with the driving'." Souness could never have imagined how much noise his silent passenger would be about to make in the English game.

No one told Abramovich it's not always like this – he was smitten and wanted more. According to Avram Grant, who was one of the trio in the back, he had not even needed a goal. "He went there, watched the game start and within 10 minutes said: 'I want to buy a team,'" said Grant. "He was almost in shock at the atmosphere, the theatre. He then needed to find the team he wanted to buy." It was the first live game he'd ever seen.

An alternative version is rather less romantic. It is that his main reason for buying Chelsea was *Krysha,* a word which cropped up many times during the 2012 trial with his erstwhile mentor-turned-enemy, the late Boris Berezovksy. *Krysha* literally means "roof" but in the world of Russian business equates to a combination of access, protection, and generally making sure the necessary things happen and the unwelcome things don't. At the time of the purchase, cynics felt that there had to be more to it than the roar of the crowd. For a Russian with no previous in football to suddenly buy a prominent Western club smacked of bets being hedged. Back home, post-Soviet scores were still being settled, Putin was in power and Opposition leader Mikhail Khodorkovsky, who was even more loaded than Abramovich, would soon be rotting in Siberia. Getting cash out of Russia and owning something as high-profile as an English Premier League club in the centre of London was surely a prudent step towards self-preservation.

If that was the driving force, 10 goalless minutes at Old Trafford had convinced him that football ownership could provide some fun as well. Indeed, even as a neutral, he could sense an excitement his other toys simply couldn't match. Not even a yacht half the size of the QE2, a room full of Rembrandts or a Caribbean island: they all paled to Ronaldo going through the gears and ripping the far corner. If things should go awry in Russia, this looked to be win-win all the way.

An investment bank was tasked with finding the club and came up with five, three of which were Manchester United, Chelsea and Spurs. United might have been the number one choice but the ownership was complicated and Abramovich preferred London anyway. Sir Alex Ferguson was already several furlongs into his bitter dispute with the race horse owners JP McManus and John Magnier, who were the club's biggest shareholders, while the Glazers were starting to build up their stake. Spurs were seriously considered but their location did not appeal. According to David Johnstone, the Chelsea fanzine editor and among those who know him best, the Russian was flying over London in his helicopter, saw Stamford Bridge and said: "I'll have that". Its proximity to London's West End landmarks couldn't have gone amiss. From the air, Big Ben and Buck House vs Broadwater Farm estate isn't much of a contest. The absence of an adjacent tube station may also have been a factor although he was never likely to do 'a Christian Gross'. White Hart Lane wasn't ideal if you were creating a superclub. But the clincher was that Chelsea were in the Champions League and Spurs were not. So Chelsea it was.

Birch recalls the deal was done in about 20 minutes in one of the Millennium boxes. Chairman Ken Bates came to the Dorchester later, doing a pretty good job of concealing his relief. Chelsea were in a bigger financial mess than the wider world realised. The July payment on a £75m Eurobond was unlikely to have been met and the only signing in the previous summer transfer window had been a free one for Quique de Lucas, recently of Biggleswade Town.

Hearing that the deal had been done was a JFK moment for Blues. "I remember where I was and exactly what I was doing when I heard," says Frank Lampard. "I was in America on holiday, in LA, in a shoe-shop buying sandals. And my dad rang and told me." John Terry told Chelsea's official magazine: "I remember being at home and seeing it on the news. I didn't really know what to make of it at the time, but it is one of those days that I look back on now and realise the significance of. That first pre-season we were all texting each other about what players were going to come in and stuff like that; I think that was probably the first thing the fans thought of. However, from our point of view, it was a case of, 'Who are they going to bring in and is your place in jeopardy?'"

It was a Wednesday and Tim Henman was preparing for a Wimbledon quarter-final. The biggest sports story was that Beckham had signed for Real Madrid. But both would be unceremoniously dumped from the back-page lead by an unknown Russian businessman. No one knew how many future headlines he would hog or how much he would change the face of English football. Keith Harris, the banker who was advising Chelsea at that time, remembers the moment well. "I was in the City of London having lunch on a Friday when I received a call from Ken Bates saying: 'I need you here. At Stamford Bridge. Now!'"

Bates was not the only one who couldn't believe his luck: Chelsea fans spent the summer in a state of euphoric incredulity. Just as the owner had known hard times, they had. This was not Arsenal, not MU, those two grand dames of English football who were turning the Premier League into an either or affair. As his homework would have told Abramovich, it was a club Bates had bought for a quid and nearly went down to the third division but for a last minute Clive Walker goal from 25 yards at Bolton in the penultimate game of 1982-83. It was a club Marler Estates had owned – the same Marler Estates that wanted to merge QPR and Fulham. Cabra Estates, who bought out Marler, also wanted to shift them to Loftus Road until they went bust in 1992. It was a club massively in debt and had had hooligan fans so violent they were banned from away games. They'd been bad enough at home where they would sing 'It's a long way to Fulham Broadway' or 'You're Going Home In A Wooden Overcoat' to away fans to warn them of the ambush as they left the ground. They drove Bates to distraction and he infamously erected electrified fences although they were never switched on. Those were dark days: the ground was a tip and had a team and support to match.

Back then it was so different, so, so different. Ray Wilkins even had hair. I remember seeing Forest beat them 6-0 at the City Ground in 1979 with a Martin O'Neill hat-trick. I actually felt sorry for the bus load of Chelsea fans that had witnessed the slaughter. A decade earlier they had Charlie Cooke and Peter Osgood and a King's Road swagger. Had anyone been hovering over London in a helicopter circa 1980, they wouldn't have picked Chelsea. This was the club's own plastic duck era, but thanks to a feisty rearguard campaign by Bates, who treated property predators and hooligans just the same, they survived.

They were boosted by cash from multi-millionaire fan Matthew Harding with whom Bates had an increasingly rancorous relationship. Bates described Harding as "evil" even after the benefactor had died, but their split didn't prevent Chelsea from beginning a mid 90s revival. Ruud Gullit and Mark Hughes joined in the summer of 1995 and a year later came the Italian trio of Gianfranco Zola, Gianluca Vialli and Roberto Di Matteo. Uruguay's Gus Poyet and Norway's Tor Andre Flo followed. But in October 1996, Harding, who had become vice-chairman, died in a helicopter crash on the way home from a game at Bolton. The tragedy might have overshadowed the season but the Blues ended it in style winning the FA Cup and finishing sixth in the league. Even when Gullit was sacked in February 1998, the trophies kept coming. His successor Vialli picked up the League Cup and Cup Winners Cup inside two months and capped those with victory over Real Madrid in the Super Cup.

In 1999, 44 years after being denied entry to the European Cup as champions, Chelsea finally entered what is now the Champions League from fourth place. They were seven minutes away from the semi-final before eventually falling to Barcelona in the Nou Camp. In 2000, they won the FA Cup again and there was a sophisticated, cosmopolitan feel to the team. The club, whose hooligan fans had neo-Nazi leanings a decade ago, were the first to field an entirely non-English side. It was multi-racial and oozed continental stardust. Entering the new millennium, the second tier, the Headhunters, Marler, Cabra, crumbling terraces and electrified fences were long forgotten. But Bates was still there and the club owed gazillions.

Vialli was sacked just five games into the 2000-01 season, Bates handing the reins to another Italian, Claudio Ranieri, despite his lack of English. Ranieri made Lampard his major signing and introduced Terry from the youth setup – if he'd done nothing else, those two decisions make him worthy of a special mention. But he had also concluded the transfers of Petr Cech and Arjen Robben, and laid the groundwork for Didier Drogba's arrival. And he qualified for the Champions League. It was a goal from Jesper Gronkjaer that clinched it via a 2-1 win over Liverpool. Chuffed as they were at the time, Chelsea had no idea just how much that goal would be worth.

But before the new owner was able to start throwing his financial weight around, he received a rebuff – from the most popular player at the club. A telltale illustration of oligarch thinking came with Zola. The little Italian was Chelsea's Player of the Year, Player of All Time and all-round good egg, but he was leaving. Abramovich didn't want to lose him and tried everything to keep him. I asked Zola: Is it true that he tried to buy you back? And when that didn't work he tried to buy Cagliari?

"That was the story told to me by the chairman of Cagliari," he replied. "I think he did try to buy me back from Cagliari but the chairman didn't want to [let me go]. Whether it is true or not, I don't know. He [Abramovich] did want me to be part of the club [Chelsea] as when he bought it he wasn't aware that I was leaving. He thought I was part of the package. I hadn't actually signed for Cagliari when he bought Chelsea. I remember getting a phone call from Ken Bates saying 'please don't sign anything because somebody is buying the club and it could be very good for you. But it [ending his career in Sardinia] was something I wanted to do at the end of the day and this was the last opportunity. So although it was very painful it turned out to be a fantastic experience.

I had been tempted to stay not just because of Abramovich but because Chelsea really was an important part of my career. I wanted to have that experience there and I didn't. I had given my word. Professionally it wasn't very wise to leave the Champions League to go to Serie B, but sometimes you do things for other reasons and I think for me it was a very strong reason." Abramovich had to accept it. There was no truth in the rumour that he tried to buy Sardinia.

One thing about the Russian, he didn't dilly-dally. After 10 minutes of watching football and 20 of negotiating, he was not going to gaze too long out of the transfer window. He bought the club for £140m and, as Arsenal director David Dein put it: "He parked his tanks on our lawn and started firing £50 notes at us." His ammunition would be much higher calibre than that. First in was Glen Johnson for £6m from West Ham. Then came Geremi from Real Madrid for £7m the next day. Wayne Bridge soon followed for £7m. It looked as if they were shoring up the back first when you'd have expected a Fancy Dan striker. But this seemed sensible in an insane sort of way. Chelsea fans spent the summer counting the days until the new season kicked off – and the signings. Like kids on Christmas morning, they would wake to see what Santa had brought them. A dozen came in a few weeks for a total spend of £130m. Wages took it to £200m and there were strikers – Hernan Crespo and Adrian Mutu. Most interesting of all was Seba Veron, the languid Argentine who was supposed to take Manchester United to the next level in Europe, but who just hadn't clicked at Old Trafford. If some of the recruits were less than stellar, bids were made for Ronaldinho and Alessandro Nesta while even Fergie, himself, was considered.

The most controversial arrival *was* from Old Trafford. When Peter Kenyon, the chief executive, joined, Ferguson said he was "intensely disappointed" by the defection to a club that was shaping up as United's biggest rival both on and off the field. Abramovich more than doubled Kenyon's salary to £1.5m – and told him to turn Chelsea into the biggest club in the world. Credited with being the mastermind of United's expanded empire, he was well qualified for the post. And he had the thick skin too – his brashness was well-known in the game and some Chelsea fans even booed him.

As the season got under way a camera would be trained on the Russian mystery man throughout each televised game. Viewers would get glimpses of the kind of deadpan expression that a poker player would die for. Even when Chelsea scored. Occasionally he would clap, very occasionally he would stand up and maybe twice a season he would smile – but even that was a half-smile soon to vanish as he turned to his companions with a self-effacing shrug. It was impossible to say whether he thought he was getting his several hundred millions' worth. Indeed, *The Independent's* James Lawton, in an open letter, wondered just that: "...with all the bodyguards and that expression of yours which mostly suggests that on balance you would rather be somewhere else, even a Siberian snowdrift..."

The public image was, however, very different to the one the players saw. Marcel Desailly, who just missed out on the Mourinho years, was still at Chelsea when Abramovich took over, and he told me how it felt to be part of a club when one of the world's richest men buys it. He said: "For us players money didn't count really. You know I had [Silvio] Berlusconi before [at Milan]. Abramovich to Berlusconi was like CocaCola to PepsiCola. And there was Bernard Tapie [at Marseille]. For us what was important was whether the chairman had the passion for the game. Whether he was able to bring a real unity internally. Abramovich did. I asked him why he was so passionate and he said to me, 'My reason for life is football'. A business deal does not give him the same excitement as when Chelsea win.

"It's really something special. It's not an ego thing. He's never given an interview to any journalist. He sees the game, he takes his plane to wherever the team goes. He goes to the African Cup of Nations and watches other matches that nobody knows about. He's a real passionate man when it comes to football and that's why Chelsea have succeeded. And he also brought luck with his passion. You remove Andre Villas-Boas or Carlo Ancelotti that nobody is expecting – and you bring in Roberto Di Matteo and you win the Champions League. And you remove him and everybody says 'no' and you bring in a different face that nobody likes [Rafa Benitez] and you win the Europa League. He studied the game very well and no journalist has noticed."

Not long after the takeover, none other than England boss Sven-Goran Eriksson was spotted at Abramovich's door in Mayfair and the rumour mill nearly came off its axis. But assumptions that the Swede would become the next Chelsea boss were denied although such stories would haunt the rest of Ranieri's reign – even though he was given over £100m to spend on players. He spent some of it wisely, some of it wastefully, but still piloted Chelsea to their highest finish since they won the title in 1955. And it was the Arsenal Invincibles who were above them. Kenyon said of Ranieri: "I didn't think he was up to the job," but what really did for the Tinkerman was his madcap tinkering in the Champions League semi-final against Monaco. An eminently winnable tie which, if safely negotiated, would have seen a £130m side facing Jose Mourinho's Porto. But he mucked up spectacularly – going for broke with his substitutions when the home side were reduced to 10 men. Chelsea ended up losing 3-1.

He would put his brainstorm down to the speculation about his job, claiming: "It came to my knowledge that, while we had been preparing for the Monte Carlo match, Chelsea had a meeting with representatives of Mourinho. I had put up with a lot but this was really hard to take. It showed a lack of respect not just for me but for the players and the effort we were putting in." In his biography *Proud Man Walking*, Ranieri admitted: "I let myself be affected by anger over the meeting and wanted the win as a way of retaliating." He would not be the last to blow a bundle in Monte Carlo. After Mourinho had won the Cup, he was duly appointed Chelsea boss. Abramovich had seen a man he could do business with in the ambitious, charismatic Portuguese and even if the Tinkerman had not tried too hard to prove himself, he would still have been a dead man walking. "Abramovich's sword is in me," the Italian wrote.

CHELSEA

2

"I've got a present for you. This is for you, from me."

Boris Berezovsky serving a lawsuit in Sloane Street to
Roman Abramovich.

For a man unaccustomed to taking *niet* for an answer, Abramovich
suffered a surprising number of rebuffs in the world of football. Sven
had stuck with England, Zola with Cagliari and Cagliari with Zola. But
his charm offensive had managed to pull Kenyon and he now had his
sights set on bringing the next big thing in management to Stamford
Bridge. And this time he got his man.

Mourinho could truthfully say he had taken Porto as far as he could –
they'd won everything – and he fancied a new challenge. A fluent English-
speaker, the Premier League appealed and he was ready to rattle the
cages of the European football establishment. If he could get his hands
on Abramovich's booty, there was no telling what he might achieve.

After showing interest in Liverpool and initially dubbing Chelsea
"an uncertain project", the Portuguese finally chose London over
Merseyside, and Abramovich was delighted. In Mourinho, the Russian
saw the chutzpah he so admires in others but lacks in himself – except
in business. He would have seen the manic run along the Old Trafford
touchline when Porto knocked out United; he would have noted him
standing up to Fergie; and he would have seen his record – in Portugal,
and now Europe, he was a serial winner. To have overcome Mourinho's
doubts, it may have needed more than the obligatory once over on his
yacht. The owner's enthusiasm and a salary of £4m a year sealed the
deal. But even Abramovich would have been amazed by the subsequent
unveiling.

Fleet Street's finest could hardly believe what they were hearing.
"Please don't call me arrogant," Mourinho told them, "but I'm European

champion and I think I'm a special one." Had he been hired solely to divert attention from the owner, he had already accomplished his mission. Special, indeed, he ensured the cameras switched from flogging the dead horse of waiting for Abramovich to blink to a gift horse that kept on giving. If the Russian made the Sleeping Buddha look animated, Mourinho was the incorrigible jack in his technical box. He was also more successful on the field than anyone dared hope. He had spent close to £100m and did a better job of fitting in the new boys than Ranieri had. There was a predictable Portuguese core in Ricardo Carvalho, Paolo Ferreira and Tiago along with Ivorian Drogba, his biggest signing at £24m from Marseille. Cech and Robben had joined late in the Ranieri reign but did not make their debuts until Mourinho took over. Under his brash new management, they chased Arsenal down and caught them to sit top of the Premier League before Christmas. In the Champions League, they sailed through the group stage. But this was nothing to what was to come. Victories over Barcelona and Bayern took them into the semi-finals albeit not without controversy. The Portuguese was nothing if not a man o' war.

Seasoned Norwegian referee Anders Frisk was hounded to hang up his whistle following death threats after Mourinho accused him of inviting Frank Rijkaard into his room in Barcelona. UEFA's referee chief Volker Roth branded the Chelsea boss "an enemy of football" and banned him for two games. He descended to slapstick by allegedly hiding in a laundry basket and having fitness coach Rui Faria wear a woolly hat to cover an ear-piece that received his instructions. While he could be charming, there were no limits to what he would do to gain an edge. Nor was he a graceful loser, never ceasing to complain – albeit with some justification – about Liverpool's "ghost goal" that knocked Chelsea out of the semi-final and ended his hopes of winning back-to-back Champions League titles.

Publicly, Abramovich maintained a thundering silence but privately he was said to be less than impressed. By now though critics felt the owner was carrying on with Chelsea where he had left off in Russia – riding unashamedly roughshod over what may have passed for rules. Chelsea gave them ammunition by tapping up players under contract to their rivals. In January 2005, there was the Ashley Cole restaurant rendezvous with Kenyon, agent Zahavi and Mourinho for which the club and manager were heavily fined. Weeks later the nocturnal Kenyon, Zahavi and Rio Ferdinand were spotted together in what they described as "a chance" encounter. Arsene Wenger had been predictably incandescent about his player being targeted and when he heard about Ferdinand, he quipped: "It's like watching the same movie twice." Wenger had dismissed the Russian's largesse as "financial doping". He would be further outraged by a £50m bid for Thierry Henry.

All Chelsea were doing was what every club does – sounding out potential signings – but they were caught. Later that year they went toe to curling toe with United for Jon Obi Mikel whom Chelsea were accused of kidnapping. The player received death threats and although Chelsea won in court, the cost was sizable fees to both United and Mikel's Norwegian club Lyn, while the ferocity of the pursuit did nothing to change the perception of how the Blues were now doing business. Nor United, for that matter.

None of these shenanigans were allowed to interfere with their progress on the field, Mourinho's first trophy coming against Liverpool in the League Cup. Three months later he delivered the club's first league championship for 50 years. By any stretch, it was an extraordinary achievement and for all the peccadilloes, confirmed the smouldering, young Portuguese as the hottest manager in the game. For the owner, to pick up two trophies in his second season was total vindication for his investment. Now the challenge was to maintain the momentum and win in Europe. Kenyon raised the stakes and a few hackles when he insisted: "The winner of the Premier League will come from a small bunch – of one."

To fast-track his understanding of the game, the owner sought the wisdom of veteran Dutch football guru, Piet de Visser, whom he hired as a scout-cum-mentor. Besides acting as a tutor, de Visser recommended the well-connected former Danish international, Frank Arnesen, as head of recruitment. Abramovich was assembling his own coterie of advisors so that he was not solely dependent on his brilliant but headstrong manager. There were differences of opinion which Mourinho would later acknowledge. "In my first period, my personal relationship [with Abramovich] was very good [but] professionally we had some interferences and a bit of a disagreement with some ideas," he revealed on his return in 2013.

If Mourinho had grabbed the limelight, Abramovich's omerta maintained his own mystique. A flat refusal to give interviews only added to the public curiosity and all we were fed were scraps from players and his inner circle. "He's a nice guy," we were told. "You'd like him if you got to know him," said Bruce Buck. But no one could get near him. The only person outside his cabal that could was David Johnstone, who backs up the Desailly view of the Russian. "He's one of the nicest, coolest guys you'd ever want to meet and he loves his football," he told me. "Because of his business, he doesn't come to every game but he watches on TV, watches the kids, the reserves. People moan about him and say he never says anything but why should he? He doesn't have to say anything. We wouldn't be here now without him. He saved us from extinction." Johnstone is known to the owner as the only man who sued Bates – and won. He told me: "I was given permission to shake his hand in the main office when he first arrived. Eugene Tenenbaum was translating and I rattled off my CV and told him: 'You've got more business acumen than Ken Bates, more money and you're a lot nicer person.' He said: 'The dog is nicer than Ken Bates.'"

While the owner was making friends, the manager carried on amassing enemies. He called Lionel Messi 'a cheat' and Arsene Wenger 'a voyeur' – the latter coming perilously close to a damaging court case. He blamed the ambulance crew for a slow response when Petr Cech broke his skull at Reading. All allegations were unfounded. But there was no second season syndrome where he was concerned and he retained the league title by an eight-point margin over Manchester United. More content with the squad at his disposal, spending was less in the summer with dynamic Ghanaian midfielder Michael Essien from Lyon the major purchase. Chelsea were the fifth English team to win back-to-back league championships since the Second World War.

Off the field, however, manager and owner had been at loggerheads for more than a year. The football never reached the heights of the 'Ronaldo night', while fuelling the discord was the ongoing power struggle with Arnesen. Then there was the constant badgering to buy new players yet a reluctance to play the owner's favourite. Andrei Shevchenko was a

£30m 'gift' for his third season, Abramovich believing the Ukrainian was still the same lethal weapon that won the *Ballon d'Or* two years earlier. But Mourinho barely concealed his disdain for having foisted upon him a player that he knew was past it. It was perhaps no coincidence that transfer funds dried up after that. All in all, it adds up to a lengthy charge sheet, and we also have to remember why Abramovich sank his billion into Chelsea in the first place. Self-preservation may have been a factor, but it was also for the love of football and to give him the respectability he craved. But the upshot was bitter-sweet – the price he was paying for success on the field was almost constant controversy, litigation and bad blood.

In Mourinho's third season (2006-07) Chelsea surrendered the title but won both the League Cup and FA Cup. In the Champions League they had lost on penalties to Liverpool in a titanic semi-final which saw Mourinho's feud with Rafa Benitez worsen, the Spaniard chiding Chelsea about laying out plastic flags. It would be something the fans would not forget. At that time, Abramovich had other things on his mind. Irina, his wife of 19 years, had seen enough of his association with Daria Zhukova, glamorous daughter of a fellow oligarch, to sue for divorce. They settled matters in Russia so he could keep the majority of his stash and avoid the paparazzi. Irina had to make do with £1 billion, two London houses, a Sussex country pad, a holiday home in the Caribbean and a yacht.

There had been speculation that he might have to sell Chelsea to pay off his wife – a theory given legs by his disgust at media intrusion. Although disgusted, he was totally committed to Chelsea – an unequivocal sign being the completion of the £20m new training ground at Cobham. Chelsea had moved from windswept Harlington under a Heathrow flight path to the sequestered Surrey vale in 2005 while construction was going on. The state-of-the-art facility was on a par with those at Manchester United and Arsenal and a clear signal the Russian was here for the long haul. But was Mourinho?

Avram Grant had joined as director of football with a place on the board – and despite his mild mannered approach was inevitably seen as a threat by Mourinho as was the similarly affable Arnesen. If his antics early on in his reign and in the middle of a period of great success sowed the seeds for the subsequent rift, his departure would still register as a shock.

When Abramovich left his seat before the end of a 2-0 defeat at Aston Villa, easing past 'Deadly' Doug Ellis as he did so, it was seen by many as the thumbs down moment. It was one of several but he was hesitating over how to deliver it so Mourinho hung on. There would be a forgettable home draw with Blackburn yet still time for one of the manager's most memorable quotes. Prior to what would be his final match in charge in 2007, Mourinho found a novel way to air an old theme, saying: "Omelettes, eggs. No eggs, no omelettes. And it depends on the quality of the eggs in the supermarket. They are class one, two or three, and some are more expensive than others and some give you better omelettes. When the class one eggs are not available, you have a problem."

In the end, his eggs were scrambled. Failure to beat Norwegian minnows Rosenborg in front of a half-empty Bridge appeared to seal his fate. But it took a chance meeting in the corridor after the game for the deed to be done. It had been reported that Abramovich said the team had to "do better", a remark to which Mourinho took offence and dared the owner to sack him. It was a measure of how low their relations had sunk that he did.

Supporters were still coming to terms with the loss of the best and best-loved manager in Chelsea's history when Grant was appointed in the Special One's place four days later. Mourinho had given them the ride of their lives and they would be forever grateful. He was quite simply irreplaceable – especially as the owner could not get the replacement he wanted. Guus Hiddink was managing Russia at the time and Abramovich had to tread carefully in Russian football. So he opted for a safe pair of hands. Grant, of morose countenance and pedestrian speech, was the antithesis of the Special One and, according to former Chelsea player Pat Nevin, "as welcome as Camilla at Diana's memorial".

The fans demonstrated at Chelsea's next home game and a few even sank to anti-Semitism to protest the switch. The morons were presumably unaware that Abramovich is half-Jewish and Grant's mother was a holocaust survivor. Back in Israel, Grant was known as a lucky manager so perhaps Abramovich was following Napoleon's lead when choosing his generals. We shall never know but Grant was the *Prozac* to Mourinho's EPO. No one outside of the owner gave the Dull One a chance.

As Grant was getting to know the players, Abramovich was suddenly reacquainted with an all-too-familiar face. It was none other than once-close friend but now sworn enemy Boris Berezovsky who literally bumped into him in Sloane Street as the two were out shopping. According to Alan Cowell's account in *The Terminal Spy*, as Abramovich entered Hermes, the high-end boutique, he was spotted by his former mentor's bodyguards who alerted their boss as he was about to go into Dolce & Gabbana two doors away. Berezovsky, who travelled with legal papers just in case such an opportunity arose, retrieved them from his £300,000 Maybach limo and the rival bodyguards became embroiled in a brief scrummage. Amid the confusion and in front of astonished shoppers, Berezovsky, then 61, managed to evade Abramovich's flankers to serve the suit on his former protege. An onlooker told the *Mail* he'd heard Berezovsky say: "I've got a present for you. This is for you, from me." Abramovich spread his arms and the papers fell to the floor, but the contact was enough for the two to appear in court four years later. It would be the biggest lawsuit in British history.

By now Chelsea was a smooth-running machine. The players knew what to do and, recovering from a poor start, they gave Manchester United a run in the League. Grant had the sense to leave well alone and they also reached the final of the League Cup but for once Spurs got the better of them. They gained revenge on Liverpool to reach the Champions League final for the first time where they met United – in Abramovich's home town of Moscow. It would be a crowning moment for the 'boy done good' and in the build-up, he made a couple of expensive signings. Lucien Freud and Francis Bacon were not names to excite the Shed but a combined fee of £60m for one each of their paintings was more than he'd paid for any player. West Stand wits noted they wouldn't be the first that did little but hang around. But Freud's *Benefits Supervisor Sleeping* and Bacon's *Tryptich* were gifts for Daria and, for a man who had just been through an expensive divorce and now faced a suit of £3.5billion, their purchase allayed fears he would be selling the family silver.

For the grand homecoming, Abramovich booked hundreds of hotel rooms and many restaurants in Moscow so his friends and cohorts would be able to celebrate a first European Cup win in the style Russians expected. An entire floor of the Ritz Carlton was booked for the club as was GQ, the city's hottest nightspot within a grenade toss of the Kremlin, for the party. Then football took over. The first and only all-English European Cup final was predictably short of a feast and Chelsea took a while to get going. Once they did they bossed the game only to have Drogba harshly sent off and get taken to penalties. Then came the fateful slip by John Terry and it was all over. Fergie's boys won and it had been another 'football bloody hell' moment. According to Johnstone: "Mr Abramovich was devastated, absolutely devastated." He paid off his friend soon afterwards and Grant's tenure ended trophyless. But he'd taken Chelsea further than Mourinho and had an almost identical win-loss ratio. As stopgaps go, he wasn't half bad.

July revealed the contrasting sides of Abramovich. *The Times* reported that he'd admitted paying billions of dollars for political favours and protection fees for a large slice of Russia's oil and aluminium assets as shown by court papers obtained by the newspaper. Also that month he resigned as Governor of Chukotka where he'd ploughed his own cash in to raise the living standards of Russia's poorest region nine time zones east of Moscow. He'd slashed unemployment, brought in industry and saved the reindeer. He was now free to concentrate on living the life of an oligarch and owning Chelsea.

CHELSEA

3

"The owner didn't pay €15m to get me out of Porto only to pay me another fortune just to let me go again."

Andre Villas-Boas

Like many owners, Abramovich swung like a pendulum when it came to managers. The laid-back yin of Ranieri was followed by the hands-on yang of Mourinho and then back to the leave-well-alone yin of Grant. Now it was back to another Portuguese speaker, who admires General Pinochet and changed his mind about the England job because the paparazzi parked their long lenses on his lawn. But Luis Felipe Scolari was a World Cup winner, had taken Portugal to the final of the Euros and won nine titles in Brazil. Very much his own man, he had defied 180 million Brazilians by leaving out Romario for the 2002 finals. A modest player himself, he'd grown up in cowboy country and had used the tactics of the Wild West in charge of Gremio. Known as Big Phil, his formative years made Mourinho look like Little Lord Fauntleroy. But pushing 60, there was just a chance he had mellowed. And he had the decency to admit that the money was part of the attraction. "Yes, that is one of the reasons. I'm 59 and I don't want to work as a coach until I'm 70," he said.

After the splurge on art, Abramovich spent little in the transfer window but Scolari made a positive start. With his two main signings, Deco and Jose Bosingwa, blending in and a third of the season gone, Chelsea were topping the table. But that was as good as it got. Two defeats in early November – to the disparate football powers of Roma and Burnley – jolted confidence and rumours emerged of dressing room unrest. Drogba was often left out and by February, Chelsea were fourth in the league. Fergie had warned about an aging squad but Scolari's tactics – primarily 4-3-3 – revealed an unexpected naivety. He was finding it difficult to cope with the pace of the Premier League and an opinionated squad. During a 0-0 draw with Hull, the fans chanted, 'You don't know what you're doing' and booed the players off at the end. And then there was the training. In De Visser's opinion, it was so bad he had to tell Abramovich. "I died of shock," said the Dutchman. "It was so weak, it made the entire squad lack sharpness in matches. I did not need a lot of time to conclude things were really bad with Chelsea."

Scolari hadn't been helped by allowing assistant boss Steve Clarke to leave for West Ham and the axe fell on February 9. Ray Wilkins, who had replaced Clarke, was put in temporary charge but Abramovich had managed to persuade Hiddink to come and salvage his club's season on a short-term deal. Yet again the pendulum swung – replacing the naivety and halting English of one manager with the nous of one of the best foreign communicators the Premier League has seen. It was also a measure of Abramovich's new standing in football that for a second time he had been able to turn to a mate to manage his club in a time of need.

For the Brazilian it was a brutal anti-climax but the turnaround was instant. With Drogba restored and Essien fit, Chelsea were their old selves again and stormed to the later stages of both the FA Cup and Champions League. They even knocked out their old nemesis Liverpool in the latter and were only denied a place in the final by another Norwegian referee, Tom Henning Ovrebo, who refused three stone-wall penalty claims against Barcelona in the semi-final. This was a Barca side close to its zenith and besides being one of modern football's great acts of larceny, it was one of Chelsea's finest performances. But they had to be content with the FA Cup, beating Everton in the final, third place in the Premier League and a glorious failure against the best team on the planet. Hiddink had done magnificently and Abramovich was fully justified in making the switch. But despite his appeals and those of the appreciative players, the Dutchman wasn't for turning and went back to Russia.

In came Carlo Ancelotti, who was vastly more experienced than Big Phil in European club football and had won the trophy that Abramovich craved – the European Cup – both as player and manager. He too made a flying start. An amiable man, the Italian was liked and respected by all and his English was coming along. He ushered Chelsea safely through to the knockout stage of the Champions League but in the round of 16 came up against Mourinho's Inter. Ignoring the Special One's mind games, Ancelotti was subjected to a Mourinho masterclass in both legs and went out. The luck had been with Inter, but many felt he would never recover in the owner's eyes. Only the League and FA Cup double kept him in the job. But Abramovich's frustration was apparent the following January (2011) when he splashed £72m – surpassing the cost of those paintings – on David Luiz and Fernando Torres. Neither were on Ancelotti's wanted list and Torres had Shevchenko 2.0 written all over him – the owner's vanity purchase that the manager was obliged to fit in. Unfortunately for them, he didn't. As Chelsea fell out of contention, Torres cut an increasingly forlorn figure. His goal drought would last 903 minutes – until late April.

The end for Ancelotti was inevitable but the manner – a brief word in a Goodison Park corridor – suggested the owner still needed to polish his PR skills. For his successor Abramovich turned to a younger man. He had tried hard but failed to woo Pep Guardiola who was intent on a sabbatical. It was as if the owner was fed up with the rebuffs as well as the constant chopping and changing so he decided to go long-term. In Andre Villas-Boas, the Russian thought he'd found the new Mourinho. Besides being Portuguese, AVB was a Mourinho disciple having worked under him at Stamford Bridge before leading Porto to a similar monopoly of trophies at an even younger age. Villas-Boas was just 33 when Porto lifted the Europa League title, having romped away with the domestic league, cup and Supercup. Abramovich had to pay over £13m in compensation to Porto for breaking AVB's contract and clearly thought he'd finally got his man for years to come. Younger, speaking better English and without the attitude, could this Portugueezer be a newer and nicer version? No one was privy to their conversations but the assumption was that AVB's brief was to change the style and the personnel – i.e. play more attractive football and weed out the older heads. And the owner would back him.

It would have been a tall order for Fergie, let alone a 33-year-old. At least AVB had medals to show, but was barely older than the senior players and had not been much of a one, himself. To the gnarled veterans there was something of the eager schoolboy about the young tyro and for all the homework he was putting in – all day most days according to some – it wasn't working. He had steered them safely through the group phase of the Champions League but in February they dropped out of the top four in the Premier League amid dressing room discontent.

After defeat to Liverpool in November, the under-pressure manager had said: "The owner didn't pay €15m to get me out of Porto only to pay me another fortune just to let me go again." A loss at Everton on February 12 led to an inquest in which senior players spoke out in front of Abramovich. On February 21, Lampard, Essien and Cole were left on the bench in the Champions League away tie at Napoli which was lost 3-1. There's an old saying 'See Naples and die'; the team AVB pinned on the wall would be his suicide note.

After a defeat to West Brom, Abramovich lost his nerve – and another small fortune in compensation – by not sticking by his chosen one. AVB was supposed to build a dynasty and he lasted barely longer than Big Phil. Portuguese sports daily *O Jogo* blamed player-power: "Roman Abramovich had two options. He either fired 25 players, or the coach." The coach is understood to have left in tears after being sacked – despite the prospect of a £10million pay-off. AVB had looked long-term but the short-term had got in the way.

A couple of years later when he paid a visit to Kuala Lumpur as a Laureus ambassador, I asked AVB which had been the greater shock: getting axed at Chelsea or Spurs? Without a hint of bitterness, he said: "Obviously, at Spurs it was a mutual agreement but at Chelsea it was a shock. It was difficult for me at the time as I took the step to leave Porto and a very good team to go to Chelsea. But I understand that the results weren't there and in football results are requested on an immediate basis. That is the reality of life for a football manager." Were you given enough time? I ventured. "Well, definitely not at Chelsea but in the end I respected the decision that was taken. And in the end it did have the desired effect and they won the biggest trophy of all."

He would later tell Portuguese TV that he paid the price for Abramovich being distracted by the court case with Berezovsky which had begun in October 2011. Villas-Boas said: "Of course we never know what will happen and what I found at Chelsea was not what I wanted. I arrived at a difficult time in the private life of the owner, who was rarely present. This clearly had an effect. Then I was surprised and I am still surprised that the owner's intentions changed. When I went there the idea was to rebuild the team." Also in 2014, Ashley Cole told *ESPN*: "There were some players who didn't want to work hard for Villas-Boas. But as soon as [Roberto] Di Matteo arrived, that all changed."

The Italian, who had been AVB's assistant, was put in temporary charge and engineered a turnaround that would have had Lazarus asking for the manual. Chelsea would beat Liverpool in the FA Cup final and, incredibly, Barcelona when down to 10 men en route to the final of the Champions League. Torres scored a memorable goal. Taking on Bayern in the final in their very own Allianz Arena seemed a step too far even for a rejuvenated Chelsea, but their reversal of fortune was complete when they won on penalties, Drogba scoring the clincher. Di Matteo was dubbed the greatest caretaker manager of all time.

The irony – or was it karma? – was not lost on anyone. After several near-misses, the owner had finally achieved his ambition, the culmination of his £1billion investment, almost by default. He is known to feel luck played a huge part. He'd done it with a temp he didn't really know and, according to reports, didn't even like. It was a great shame as Di Matteo had engendered a magnificent defiance in Chelsea that owed much to the players' respect for him. But his achievements as a player which led to cult status with the fans had been before Abramovich had pitched up and were lost on the owner. All he knew was that as a coach RDM had been at MK Dons before being sacked by West Brom. With Guardiola still unobtainable, Abramovich had wanted Rafa Benitez to take over but had been persuaded to choose a former player to reconnect with the fans. Now he was stuck with him, it seemed, but even in the moment of celebration, RDM did not impress his boss. Walking up the steps to receive the congratulations of the owner, he couldn't resist saying: "I did it." It wasn't what Abramovich wanted to hear. The Russian's reaction convinced the Italian that he would not be there long. Scarcely believing that his team had pulled off this unlikely triumph, Abramovich gave a dressing room speech to the effect that it was just the beginning. But to Di Matteo, it felt like the end.

As it turned out, he was given a two-year contract and lasted six months. As all Chelsea managers seemed to do, he started the season well. Bolstered by £80m of new players, he carried on where he'd left off in the spring. With Eden Hazard, Juan Mata and Oscar irresistible in the opening weeks, he got Chelsea playing some of the best football seen since the owner had bought the club. But playing those Three Amigos, scoring in three cup finals, winning two trophies including the Holy Grail would not be enough. After a poor run, a 3-0 defeat by Juventus was the final straw. The Italian was given the bad news by chief executive Ron Gourlay and chairman Bruce Buck upon returning to his office at 4 o'clock on a misty November morning. He may as well have come back from Turin in a shroud.

Chelsea fans reacted badly. "But what did everybody's head in," says Johnstone, "was getting Rafa Benitez." The Chelsea hierarchy – the owner was advised by Eugene Tennenbaum, Eugene Schvidler and Bruce Buck – knew there was antipathy to the Spaniard but thought it would fade once Rafa had started to turn Chelsea around. It did not – to Chelsea fans, he would always be: "Rafa Beneath Us." It was also another swing of the pendulum – from the freedom RDM afforded the players – especially attackers – to putting them on a tight leash. Benitez was a renowned organiser and after splashing £80m in the summer, Abramovich was impatient to get the best out of them. Ditto Torres – Benitez had been his manager during his Anfield heyday – and he thought he might be able to reboot the £50m folly.

That task would be beyond Benitez as was keeping the club in the Champions League. The 3-0 deficit proved too much so Chelsea, defending champions, bowed out at the group phase. But at least Benitez salvaged something by winning the Europa League. Johnstone says: "They got the wrong man. It was one example of Mr Abramovich – or the people who work for him – not reading it right."

Meanwhile off the field, there had been good news and bad news. In July, Chelsea's £300m bid to build a 60,000 seat stadium on the old Battersea Power Station site lost out to a Malaysian property developer who had offered £400m. And with it went the chance to build an iconic stadium with a unique backdrop. But that was about mere hundreds of millions: in August, Abramovich won his £3.5 billion case against

Berezovsky. After a four-month trial, Judge Elizabeth Gloster announced her verdict in favour of the Chelsea owner, dismissing Berezovsky's claims "in their entirety". The judgment was damning of the older man and stated that his evidence was "vague, internally inconsistent and, at times, incredible." She even called him an unreliable witness but in contrast, praised Abramovich's "careful and thoughtful answers, and described him as "meticulous" and "frank." One report said: "There was a sad, Shakespearian feel to the whole trial, with the unmistakable sense of an apprentice outpacing his onetime master."

CHELSEA

4

"The largest single heist in corporate history and a lasting emblem of the corruption of modern Russia."

Economist, Paul Gregory.

Never go back, they say, but Mourinho was happy to return to Stamford Bridge and Abramovich was just as happy to have him. After a fractious third season at Real Madrid, the manager craved the adulation he'd had in England. As for the owner, he'd just removed his seventh manager since the Portuguese in six tumultuous years. And he'd tried all sorts – a World Cup winner, two European Cup winners, the next Big Thing, two mates as caretakers and one ex-player who had won the Holy Grail. But he thought that was a fluke and never rated the man. He now knew he'd been a tad hasty in removing Mourinho in the first place.

Time flies and it also heals. Yes, there'd been acrimony but it was his five trophies in three seasons that were remembered. Even so, there was an element of second best about the reconciliation. Abramovich's first choice was Guardiola whom he'd been courting for years; Mourinho's was Manchester United. But Pep had opted for Bayern and United for David Moyes. If the remarriage wasn't made in heaven, it made an awful lot of sense on both sides. They were both older and wiser – and they needed each other. Looking at the eligible clubs, there was nowhere else for Mourinho to go just as, surveying the equally small field of eligible bosses, it came down to "a bunch of one" for Abramovich too.

So when Mourinho reintroduced himself to the media as "the Happy One" in June, 2013, there was no reason to doubt him. He was back where he was loved, where he belonged, and there was still a core of his former players to welcome him. The fans were beyond happy – they still sang his name all these years after he'd left. And there was a challenge ahead. Chelsea had finished third under Benitez the previous season besides winning the Europa League and reaching the semi-finals of both League Cup and FA Cup – all 'achievements' he – Special or Happy – would come to disparage. It had been a nearly season and nearly for him or the owner had never been good enough.

There were two other areas where Abramovich demanded an improvement on the previous reign – more attacking on the field and less off it. And after three seasons of sulphurous conflict in Madrid, Mourinho was well aware of the need to soften his tone. If he was truly the Happy One, he could no longer be "an enemy of football".

July saw the 10th anniversary of the Abramovich takeover to which the papers devoted vast, albeit varied, tracts of approval. All agreed he had changed the game forever but not necessarily for the better. Chelsea, though, may not have existed without him. And their rise prevented Arsenal and Manchester United from turning the Premier League into a La Liga-like duopoly. It also opened the floodgates to any Tom, Dick or Mansour bin Zayed Al Nahyan with a couple of billion to rub together.

For Mourinho there was another important difference with 2004 – the size of the budget. Abramovich had spent lavishly the previous year but now Financial Fair Play was coming into being. Surprising some mindful of the way he'd made his pile, the owner wanted to play within the new rules. Mourinho had to largely make do with the existing squad and if he wanted to buy, he'd have to sell. The other problem for the manager was that the players he knew were those with sell-by dates fast approaching. He was happy but did not peer into a cloudless sky. As for the opposition, Manchester City had emerged as a major force, Liverpool had Luis Suarez, but Arsenal were Arsenal and United no longer had Ferguson.

He tried hard but failed to prise Wayne Rooney away from Old Trafford and would go through the season a striker short. And when the two sides met there in August, he parked the bus, content to take a 0-0 draw. When Chelsea snatched Willian from Spurs' grasp after he'd had a medical at White Hart Lane, it was the owner who swung it, Abramovich calling his Russian counterparts at Anzhi. Like those oil tankers, the player was duly diverted. Samuel Eto'o was a late stopgap in the absence of Rooney.

The season began well and it was not until November and a lame loss at Newcastle that Mourinho had his first major outburst. "I am angry, because I don't understand why after a fantastic run of matches, we lose this game," he fumed. He was dubbed 'The Angry One' the next day. But it was not until the New Year that he reverted to his true confrontational colours.

It had not gone unnoticed that before Mourino's return the owner had overseen the arrival of several attack-minded players. "He's gone for a certain type," an insider told the *Mail*. "Mata, Oscar, Hazard, Willian, Schurrle. Even Luiz and [Cesar] Azpilicueta. These are players who want to play." But in January, Mourinho sold Mata, along with Kevin de Bruyne, to fund his own type. "It's almost as if he is fighting against the philosophy Roman has tried to instill," noted the insider.

By now Abramovich knew that it was the same old Mourinho. As keen on the cheap shot as the expensive sale, the Portuguese eased into adversarial mode by dubbing old foe Arsene Wenger "a specialist in failure" while mischievously mispronouncing the City boss's name as 'Pellegrino'. He also came up with one of his more memorable, self-deprecatory quotes: "The title race is between two horses and a little horse that needs milk and needs to learn how to jump. Maybe next season we can race." By the end of February, the little horse had galloped to the top, having done the double over City. In March, Spurs were thrashed 4-0, Arsenal eviscerated 6-0 and the manager looked to be ahead of schedule when they went seven points clear. He couldn't, could he?

Mourinho lost his fabled unbeaten home record after 77 games against Sunderland and, in a disappointing denouement, Chelsea were knocked out of the Champions League by Atletico Madrid and ended up third in the Premier League. It was the same position Benitez had achieved, but there was a sense that the manager was inexorably building another title-winning team.

Before the second season kicked off, Cole and Lampard left along with Luiz but Drogba came back. His biggest signings were Ces Fabregas and Diego Costa but he also added Felipe Luis and Loic Remy. It was excellent business and, looking back now, the end of 2014 appears the closest Stamford Bridge has come to tranquility since Abramovich's helicopter whirled into SW6. The books not only balanced but were showing a profit of £20m and they were top of the league. The owner had eased in his right-hand woman, Marina Granovskaia, as a de facto replacement for departing CEO Ron Gourlay. Meanwhile, Mourinho's biggest contretemps of the season saw Wenger as the aggressor. There was also a distinct softening of Chelsea's corporate tone from the braggadocio of Kenyon, but peace couldn't last. Before the end of the year, Mourinho was claiming a conspiracy against his club after being denied a penalty at Southampton. Sluggish ball boys incurred his wrath in a defeat at Newcastle. Still, despite a couple of wobbles, Chelsea's grown-up horse cantered to the title by eight points.

At the start of the 2015-16 season, the Blues were everyone's favourites for the title even though they hadn't strengthened significantly in the transfer window. And absolutely no one could foresee the unravelling that would begin in the dying minutes of the very first game. The now-infamous "doctor incident' at the end of the 2-2 draw with Swansea would turn out to be the most catastrophic blunder of Mourinho's career. His criticism of Dr Eva Carneiro and physio Jon Fearn for rushing on to attend to Eden Hazard at the referee's request was not merely a misjudgement, it undermined his standing with the players and everyone at the club. The sexist, expletive-laden rant at Carneiro in the heat of the moment might have been forgiven if he'd apologised. But his refusal saw respect drain away and he never regained it. It would cost him his job and the club a fortune in an out-of-court settlement.

Coming on top of a late start to pre-season training, a lack of transfer activity, the departure of Cech and a continuing shortage of strikers, it contributed to Chelsea making the worst start to a defence of the title in Premier League history. That, along with speculation about Mourinho's future, became the story of the first half of the season.

Mindful that he may have been premature in removing Mourinho in 2007, Abramovich took his time. There had been a huge desire from everyone – from the owner down – for the appointment to work out and for the manager, to whom he'd just awarded a new four-year contract, to build a real legacy. Abramovich had been belatedly trying to improve Chelsea's image. He was hurt when, in 2013, Chelsea were voted the most hated club in the Premier League, claiming the unwanted title from Manchester United. Before that *The Independent's* James Lawton warned the club was "becoming the leading representative of all that is cheap and despicable in English football," before adding "but there is growing evidence that you don't really give a damn." Honouring a promise to Cech suggested he did.

To Mourino, allowing one of his two top keepers to go to Arsenal was helping their bitter rivals solve one of their biggest problems as well as depriving Chelsea of cover in that position. And he could say 'I told you so' when the other, Thibaut Courtois, got injured early on. But Abramovich had given his word to one of the club's greatest servants and even Mourinho would later say: "I understood the good thing about the decision the club made. I think it brings the club into a different dimension. It makes every player understand what this club is. Our owner is saying to everybody that human relationships and loyalty are more important than football."

Such sentiments marked a sea change for Chelsea and it was doubly frustrating for the owner that Mourinho had turned back the tide almost before they'd been noticed. But it was not until the December defeat at Leicester that Abramovich decided to act and old pal Hiddink was swiftly installed as caretaker. Incredibly, Chelsea were not entirely safe from the drop but the Dutchman steered them to mid-table without quite having the impact he'd had almost six years earlier. Even so, the suspicion that Sod had had a hand in their season was not allayed when Leicester, of all people, arrived at Stamford Bridge for the final game. Chelsea were looking at their lowest finish of the Abramovich era and giving the newly crowned champions a guard of honour might have felt like the ultimate humiliation. But the ex-champions provided a classy pre-match salute with Abramovich offering a warm handshake to Ranieri, whom he'd fired almost 12 years earlier.

By then, he'd chosen Antonio Conte to lead them in the 2016-17 campaign. The Italian would be the eighth permanent manager since the Russian took over with Mourinho having two stints, Hiddink two as a caretaker and Benitez one as 'interim'. That's a lot of upheaval in 13 years. But in that time Chelsea won 14 trophies – just ask Arsenal fans what stability has done for them. Although some sackings were justified, Mourino (I), Ancelotti and Di Matteo were undoubtedly premature and

Chelsea owed their success to a resilient core of seasoned internationals who won in spite of the chaos, not because of it. Avram Grant's win-loss record was almost identical to Mourinho's first term.

Understandably, Chelsea fans regard Abramovich's arrival as the best thing that's ever happened to the club and are loath to criticise. Those sackings are their major quibble, but a major disappointment is that no academy player has established himself in the first team since Terry. Here, at least some blame can be laid at the owner's trigger finger as no manager with a thought for self-preservation can afford to give youth a chance. Overall, recruitment has been scattergun and occasionally whim-driven – Messrs Shevchenko and Torres being exhibits A and B of the latter.

In summing up his reign, mention must be made of how he made his money – *The Times*' Matthew Syed calls it "not just the elephant in the room, but a festering pile of manure." Yet for the most part, football has turned a blocked nostril to it. When in October 2014, Crystal Palace fans unveiled a banner that read: 'Roman's dirty money is a disease that has plagued our game', it made news because of its rarity. Even when many of the gory details emerged during the Berezovsky trial, it was left to people outside the game to question his exalted place in it and even in society. Fit and Proper? The economist, Paul Gregory, called it "the largest single heist in corporate history and a lasting emblem of the corruption of modern Russia," while Mikhail Gorbachev dubbed Abramovich a symbol of Russia's rich debauchery". Even his own QC, Jonathan Sumption, acknowledged there was "an agreement to sell media support to the president of Russia in return for privileged access to state-owned assets". He added that the whole arrangement was "easy to rig and was in fact rigged". Nor did it do much for the owner's image when Chris Hutchins, a biographer of Vladimir Putin, described the relationship between the Russian president and Abramovich as like that between a father and a favourite son.

Sifting through all this as we look at his 13-year reign, what we see is an enigma not unlike the old Soviet Union itself. Abramovich had been ruthless in acquiring his stash in the Wild East yet craved respectability in the West; he was labelled both passionate and dispassionate, inherently shy yet materially ostentatious. Like him or not, he has not been a mere game-changer, he has changed the sport – his intervention made the top flight of English football more competitive and led to the gold rush of foreign players, managers and owners all wanting a share of the broadcasting mother lode. Yet for all that, his public relations could be clumsy or non-existent – he never gave interviews and could treat managers as an 18th century Czar might have treated his serfs. After the dismissal of Di Matteo, Henry Winter, then of the *Telegraph*, noted: "There is a darkness at the very heart of Abramovich's Chelsea empire, a soullessness seeing employees treated like pawns, moved around or moved out."

If that first night at Old Trafford had shone a shaft of light into that darkness, it had not changed his modus operandi. To even begin to understand that, we have to look at the culture he came from and the clique to which he belongs. *The Independent* owner and former KGB officer, Alexander Lebdev, is perhaps best placed to explain what being an oligarch is about. He said: "I think material wealth for them is a highly emotional and spiritual thing. They spend a lot of money on their own personal consumption. They don't read books, they don't have time. They don't go to exhibitions. They think the only way to impress anyone is to buy a yacht." Abramovich already had enough for Cowes week so bought a football club.

Throwing money around then is, itself, the goal and the Berezovsky trial showed just how much there was to throw: the £70m or so that Abramovich has wasted on compo for sacked managers is, give a kopek or two, one tenth of one percent of his total wealth. As for certain strange signings, even some of those can be seen as originating in the Russian system of favours or *blat* – a likely example of which was the "parking" of a patently unfit Pato in January, 2016 and the same day sale of fringe player Ramirez for an inflated fee from China – both handled by the same agent.

It is a curiosity, perhaps, that as he sits up there, in front of his £1million-a-season suite in the middle tier of the West Stand, surrounded by a coterie of advisors, he has largely retained his mystique. It says much about us that the club in general and "captain, leader, legend" Terry, in particular, have copped more flak. An affair with a mate's girlfriend, parking in a wheelchair space, flogging tours of the ground and racism is a substantial charge sheet but compared to "the biggest heist in corporate history"..?

Maintaining his omerta has much to do with it – and the perfect antidote to the 'in yer face' perception of his club. Chelsea were not widely popular before he arrived – mainly because of their fans. And what they've achieved since can be said to have been bought. But for a club that 'ain't got no histry', they've certainly been making up fast over the last 13 years. And it has all been down to one diffident Russian.

Heart of Midlothian

HEART OF MIDLOTHIAN

1

"I went home and told my wife I'd met a Lithuanian banker who might buy Hearts. She had to check the calendar to make sure it wasn't April 1st."

Former Hearts chairman Leslie Deans.

Submariner, high-flyer; banker, bootlegger; dictator, dreamer; saviour, megalomaniac; soap-dodger, money-launderer. Had Winston Churchill known Vladimir Nikolayevich Romanov, he may well have applied his famous description of the Soviet Union to Hearts' most infamous owner. After all who, among football's 'fit and proper persons', is more deserving of the moniker "a riddle wrapped in a mystery inside an enigma"?

As a survivor of hard times, Romanov boasted the pedigree of a thoroughbred. His father was a major in the Battle of Berlin and his mother survived the Siege of Leningrad. He himself had endured three years' national service in a ticking sardine-tin of a Soviet nuclear submarine. It's only when we hear how he won and lost his £260 million fortune that traits of the mongrel appear. But when it came to Heart of Midlothian, he exhibited all the wild-eyed hallmarks of a mad dog on heat.

As an oligarch, he may have been a Roman Abramovich-lite, a few divisions lower on the Forbes List, but he was also several rock-concerts louder, loonier and more controversial. He did not suffer fools, and with managers it was shoot-to-kill. He soon went from saviour to certifiable. Hearts were top of the table, unbeaten after 10 games – their best start since 1914 – and playing superbly. Tynecastle throbbed and the Old Firm looked uneasily over its shoulder. What could possibly go wrong? Well, everything if you get rid of the manager. Of the 11 sackings that Romanov made, none were as mad cap as George Burley's. Two of his successors didn't speak English and there were several dispensable caretakers, but Burley had masterminded a brilliant dawn to what had the makings of a golden era. Not good enough for this owner though. Romanov liked to pick the team, picked his son as chairman and even tried to pick himself to play – when pushing 60. It was only a friendly though – against Barcelona.

Reputations and performances were no guarantee of job security. After Burley went, inspirational skipper Steven 'Elvis' Pressley was next – for leading a dressing room revolt. Romanov would launch tirades about 'criminals', 'the mafia', referees, Scottish football in general and the Old Firm in particular. He compared the media to monkeys and served bananas in the press room. Eventually he went broke and his bank went with him. Hearts were left teetering on the brink.

'Mad Vlad' they called him among a salty lexicon. But early doors the insults were few and he was hailed by many as a messiah of sorts. He was. His *perestroika*-begotten gains saved Hearts' much-loved and hugely atmospheric home of Tynecastle from the bulldozers. And he saved the club from becoming a downstairs lodger at the upstairs rugby mecca of Murrayfield. Or, if that 'solution' had not panned out, there may have been a shift to a DIY stadium in some suburban wasteland of the developer's choice. Or even of oblivion. Or a fate worse than oblivion: sharing with Hibs.

These were the options that Heart of Midlothian, of the highfalutin Sir Walter Scott title but blue-collar Gorgie roots, fourth oldest club in Scotland and storied Edinburgh institution, had been staring at before the Russian-Lithuanian ex-submariner turned his periscope onto Scottish football. He, too, had a name he didn't live up to – sharing it with the last Czar no less – for he was no more than a bog-standard bootlegger-to-banker opportunist when he rode to the rescue. Not on a white charger, alas, and via Dundee, Dundee United and Dunfermline. All three clubs were close enough to the knacker's yard to have been sorely tempted by his roubles, but one by one they knocked him back. Three Duns but none dusted. They'd sniffed a sizable rodent.

Undeterred and back-pocket bulging with Yeltsin-enabled riches – he bought shares in a Belarussian club, MTZ-Ripo Minsk – his main target was the Scottish Premier League (SPL). He knew the Old Firm were out of reach – if only he'd waited a few years! But Hearts were in the capital, had a fan base, history and really were skint.

Romanov, whose parents had moved to Lithuania when he was nine, had been alerted to the parlous state of Scottish football after Lithuania were beaten 1-0 in a European Championship qualifier at Hampden Park in October, 2003. Lithuanian FA president, Liutaurus Varanavicius, and his opposite number, John McBeth, discussed the idea of Lithuanian players being introduced to the hard-up Scottish game and it was this conversation that led to Romanov's quest to buy a Scottish club. Almost any club would have been considered thriving by Lithuanian standards where football is a minority sport. Romanov owned the biggest – FBK Kaunas – and their gates were 400.

But by the time he arrived at Tynecastle, where Hearts have played since 1886, the ground's, if not the club's, fate was all but sealed. Documents had been signed and the wrecking crew was poised. Hearts' chief executive, Chris Robinson, had agreed to sell a site that should have been protected by Unesco to a property company, Cala Homes. Hardly softening the blow, he'd signed with the Scottish Rugby Union for the club to play home games at Murrayfield. Robinson saw selling Tynecastle as the only way of saving the club who were £20m in debt and counting. To the dispassionate, actuarial mind for which Edinburgh is famous, it might have made economic sense. But to anyone with a football pulse, it was vandalism – the pillaging of a beloved institution. To former chairman, Leslie Deans, it was "a death knell". To Jambos, as Hearts fans are known, it was war and it had to be won.

Leading activist among them was Iain Mcleod who was sure the figures did not add up. He told me: "We were a club making a loss of £3m a year. There's no way we could have traded our way out of that. Our average gates were 12,000 and the debt was secured against Tynecastle which Chris Robinson wanted to sell for about £20m. Under his plan we were going to get liquidated."

Fans were aghast at the prospect of being sprinkled around Murrayfield's 68,000 seats, their raucous backing reduced to a whimper – and that would depend on which way the wind was blowing. The supporters mobilised. They formed the Save Our Hearts fund, met in pubs, most purposefully in the Tynecastle Arms, an old Victorian boozer near the ground that would become the command centre of their campaign. They raised money, rattled buckets, emptied piggy-banks, got favourable acreage in the media and brought MPs on board. But what they really needed was a white knight.

Early in 2004, Steve Cardownie, the Deputy Lord Provost of Edinburgh and a Hearts fan, met Romanov and introduced him to Deans, still a substantial shareholder in the club. As Deans told Brian Viner of *The Independent*: "I went home and told my wife I'd met a Lithuanian banker who might buy Hearts. She had to check the calendar to make sure it wasn't April 1st."

Romanov may have been in the Soviet navy, but the timing of his arrival belonged to the US cavalry, Hollywood version. Hearts had been supposed to sell Tynecastle and shift to Murrayfield for the start of the 2005-6 season. Auditors PricewaterhouseCoopers described the club as being technically insolvent, while the Hearts supporters trust said: "We were heading for the abyss." But they were a public limited company and no individual shareholder owned more than 20% of the club. It allowed minority shareholders to bolster their holdings and block the plan. And the deal with Cala Homes had an escape clause that wouldn't have troubled Houdini: Hearts could back out before January 31, 2005 as long as a viable alternative could be found. It was through this unbolted door that Romanov drove his coach and horses.

He offered to buy the club and his trump card was the promise to keep it at Tynecastle. He stumped up the money and provided the guarantees – given by his own bank. "When Romanov appeared," remembers Mcleod, "he was literally the only show in town. To be honest, no one knew much about him, but we welcomed him with open arms! Beggars can't be choosers and we were definitely beggars at the time. And 2004 was the 90th anniversary of McCrae's battalion going to the Somme and we had a memorial ceremony at Contalmaison. Romanov sent his right-hand man, Sergeijus Fedotovus, over there to speak about the history of the club and how important the traditions were. Romanov even wrote a poem about it so we thought, 'Wow, this guy really does care.'"

By the end of September, Robinson, under siege from angry fans and sensing defeat, had agreed to sell his 19.6% stake to Romanov at 35p a share – a third of the 1997 stock market valuation. In January 2005, the Russian called an EGM to invoke the escape clause and with the backing of chairman, George Foulkes, and major shareholders, Hearts was his, more than 70% supporting his motion. Tynecastle was saved.

You just couldn't have imagined it not being. Well, only in Jambos' worst nightmares. Trendy townhouses where proud Maroons once took centre stage. Forcibly evicted and grudgingly granted squatters' rights on the other side of the Western Approach Road. The books might have briefly balanced, but the soul of the club would have been destroyed. As Foulkes put it: "If Chris Robinson was still there, we'd probably be in the First Division and playing in front of 5,000 people at Murrayfield." The Tynecastle roar? It would have been stifled in all those scattered larynxes. Back in Gorgie, the hallowed turf, on which Dave Mackay and Alan Gilzean, Gary Mackay and John Robertson used to stride, would have been sold off in souvenir slices – the rest tarmacked. If they were lucky, they might have got a cul-de-sac named after them.

But thanks to Romanov, in a couple or three bounds, they were saved. As Hearts die-hard Andrew Donaldson put it: "There were protests after every home match and constant anti-board chanting during games. At this point in time, such was the hatred for Chris Robinson and his plan that Saddam Hussein himself could probably have put forward an interest in buying Hearts and it would have been welcomed."

Abhorrent though the Murrayfield option was, it had a ring of sanity compared to some suggestions. One of Robinson's early brainwaves had been to store the steep-sided stands in a secret location until a suitable site was found. The thought of dragging the Wheatfield Stand on a trailer along Princes Street belonged in the same Cuckoo land as playing a match with Celtic in Australia to tap into ex-pat support down under. Another was to share with... Hibs. At some presumably steep-sided new plot at Straiton retail park.

Even that, though, wasn't as daft as what had been proposed more than a decade earlier – disbandment of both Hearts and Hibs to form a single united Edinburgh club! This was what might be called the hare-brainwave of the late Wallace Mercer. We talk of crackpot ideas and foreign owners riding roughshod over local sensitivities, but in all of Romanov's reign, he never came up with anything to match the lunacy of Mercer and Robinson.

So in early 2005, the villain of the piece had been routed. And the 'villain' was a local. The saviour was a foreigner, a man who, four decades earlier, had been a conscript on a boat that patrolled below the North Sea and had doomsday warheads locked on British cities. It could have blown Hearts and Hibs, Rangers and Celtic, Arsenal and Auchtermuchty to kingdom come. Back in the late 1960s, the Cuban missile crisis was a recent memory and oblivion a more likely prospect than *glasnost* or *perestroika*. Less than four decades later, this erstwhile enemy combatant was not just 'fit and proper', he was strolling on Duddingston Loch.

Sub-mariners are a special breed and regard themselves as the elite of the navy. As they're not slow to tell you, the surface is for wimps. It takes a special kind of temperament to tolerate life in conditions that would have battery hens complaining to *The Telegraph*. Devoid of all distractions, it affords a rare opportunity for introspection. In Romanov's case, an armchair Freud might say it was an incubator for narcissism, but the man himself described it as "character building". Just to make sure they weren't getting too comfortable, every six months he and his comrades were locked into torpedo tubes that were then flooded with water – "to toughen them up". Romanov had time to dream, even to write poetry – something he still did between cutting deals, making millions and sacking managers. Businessman-cum poet, dreamer-cum-ass-kicker, romantic-cum-Alan Sugar… you can't get much more of a riddle than that.

Arriving less than two years after Abramovich had descended from nowhere to dispense his largesse on Stamford Bridge, comparisons were inevitable. Besides being Russian and rich, both had humble beginnings and lost parents at an early age. And both were winners in the aluminium wars. For the Chelsea owner, an orphan at three, it had been rubber ducks that first kept him afloat in a Moscow apartment – he sold them; for the Hearts man it had been black market LPs of the Beatles, Rolling Stones and Elvis. He sold them from the boot of his taxi, incurring scrutiny but escaping censure from the KGB. Even in this tale the entrepreneurial spirit was wrapped in an enigma. His dad had paid 25 roubles for a box of 30 records for him to sell to his friends. Young Romanov charged them five roubles each but donated his first profits to a local theatre company to buy puppets. Only when his father died of a heart attack did necessity force him to keep the proceeds. He was 16 and had to support his mother and sister. But he would retain a fondness for puppets – he appointed a few as managers.

National service also taught him how to cope with fear. During his charm offensive in 2005, he told fans: "Around 30-35 years ago I was serving in a submarine and we carried out a lot of assignments off the coast of Britain. It was an atomic vessel with 16 missiles and 10 warheads, and I still have pictures of it in my wallet. In those days people feared there would be a real disaster, and now there are many people thinking the same thing here in a different way. But we are going to develop this club to a better quality, so why should they be afraid?"

When he came out of the navy, he got his land legs in business as the Soviet Union began to unravel. And by the time the old Communist infrastructure came apart, he, like Abramovich, ensured he was standing near the juiciest joints at the carvery. He would make his pile in textiles, property, television and investment banking as well as aluminium. He made £260m – not too shabby for a former cab-driver and enough for him to buy a foreign football club. Not a Chelsea but a respectable B-lister with a decent fan-base, a history and a bit of cachet.

But he was far from what might be called oligarchetypal. A bodyguard-free zone, Romanov's demeanour was more benign than we have come to expect from his ilk. When he first came to Scotland, he stayed at the likes of The Radisson, The Balmoral and The Caledonian. Hardly 'man of the people' but at least he didn't demand Holyrood Palace for his entourage. All this gave rise to hopes that there might be more to him than being just another mega-rich Russian flaunting his new-found wealth.

2

"Our goal has to be champions of Europe. I want us to be at the stage where to do anything else, to come back without the trophy, would be shameful. I think we're looking at three years."

Vladimir Romanov, October 15, 2005.

When he breezed into Tynecastle promising the football conquest of Europe, there was as much mystery about Vladimir Romanov the man as his motives. There was a vague notion of newly-minted roubles washing up on former Soviet shores. Beyond that there was only what dim light the media had been able to shed on his chequered past. His ascent from ocean depths to high flyer raised more questions than it answered: just what did a multi-millionaire who ran a vast business empire from a yacht in the Med want from Hearts, from football and from Scotland? If he wanted to be Caesar, why pick an old, run-down ground in an old, run-down suburb like Gorgie? Did he not know what he was letting himself in for? Besides runaway debt and clamorous fans, there was a football hierarchy that was not just Old and Firm in name but as ancient and immovable as Arthur's Seat in nature? Did he need the hassle? And how much of a football man was he anyway?

Few were better placed to answer than Hearts' former chairman and Labour peer*, Lord George Foulkes, who had helped usher Romanov into this hottest of seats. He invited me to the Royal Scots Club in Edinburgh, where I asked him how it started and what he made of Vladimir Romanov.

"Hearts were in a very difficult position and the fans were up in arms," he began. "There were riots and Chris Robinson claims his life was threatened. The Bank of Scotland wanted someone to come in and try and resolve this as most of the money was owed to them. A Tory councillor had asked him 'why don't you ask George?' I was in Mexico at the time on a House of Commons delegation and got this call from Robinson. He asked if I would like to join the board, then if I'd like to become chairman. I said I'd have to think about it. I asked friends, several of whom said: 'Don't touch it with a barge pole'. However, I accepted. I managed to get Cala Homes to pull out without any compensation at all so we could stay at Tynecastle. The Scottish Rugby Union were also very good – we'd signed a contract with them but they said we won't push it so the first day I was brought in I managed to keep us at Tynecastle.

"But then the problem was: what are we going to do with the club? We were in debt and losing a million a year or more. Robinson had brought in players we couldn't afford and the ground hadn't been developed. There were major problems so we had to bring in a new owner or major investor. I started looking around, using all the contacts I could. A guy came over from Nigeria who had his Caesar moment at Tynecastle. There was a local plumber who kept emerging. All sorts of other people, but nothing came of them. Meantime, this Lithuanian had been showing interest in Scottish football and I arranged to meet him at the Houses of Parliament.

"He seemed perfectly OK – very friendly, liked to joke a bit but I thought a little eccentric. He was not very tall, about 5'6", but very fit-looking. My wife thought he had a Napoleon complex. We agreed to meet again as he really was the only option we had. Basically, what he had to do was buy the shares from the two main shareholders, Robinson and Deans. He did that and in those early days at the time he was the largest shareholder, he was still very friendly and I got on quite well with him. It was the best time – before he owned it outright. Then he seemed to change his character." I asked if it was all an act. He said: "I think it was. He was lauded, had pictures taken with everybody and was absolutely charming at the beginning. The players liked him and he'd even have a kickabout with them. But once he got control he had a personality change and this authoritarian Napoleon complex came out."

Asked how good his English was, Foulkes said: "Not very good, but not as bad as he claimed. And in some ways I don't blame him – I think he knew more than he let on. He had an interpreter. But he never seemed to have the trappings of wealth that Abramovich and [Boris] Berezovsky had. Or many Russians in London have. He seemed to be reasonably well off. He had a chauffeur-driven car while he was here and stayed in a good suite in the hotel. But he didn't fly in on private jets – just the normal scheduled airline. There was always something uncertain about his finances though. He bought this building in St Andrew's Square, costing a huge amount, and then he put in a planning application for it to be altered. It was refused. It was still empty when he went bankrupt. Hearts were just a very small part of his empire. He had an aluminium smelter in the Balkans and other investments. He had really diversified but wasn't on the scale of Abramovich. He didn't flaunt it, but was never short."

I asked if his plan for Hearts seemed sound. "It was a perfectly valid idea to bring in and showcase Lithuanian players, and if he'd done that systematically and sensibly, he could have built up quite a lot of money for the club. But he spent stupidly. He brought in players that successive managers didn't want – some at huge salaries. Afterwards, some people told me: 'You didn't do due diligence on Romanov'. It's very difficult to do on someone coming from abroad but, having been a minister for national development and shadow minister on foreign affairs, what I did do was phone around and there was a guy – a Celtic fan – who said 'leave it with me'. He checked with the then ambassador to Lithuania and said: 'They don't know much about him but what they do know is that he's no worse than any other oligarch'. So, what do you do? It's not an endorsement but if there'd been something really awful they'd have known. When I get people saying you are the guy who brought Romanov in, I say, 'yes, but it was Hobson's choice. He was the only one after a long time of searching who showed any real interest.'

"I've been out a few times to Lithuania and at a party at the British embassy I introduced him to our ambassador. His ownership of Hearts made him big in Lithuania. He went on to buy the national stadium in Vilnius, he owned the basketball club, a Belorussian club, went on [the Lithuanian equivalent of] *Strictly Come Dancing*. He became a huge personality – at one time he was thinking of running for president but got ruled out because he wasn't born there."

Romanov had other delusions – and checked in vain to see if he was related to the last Czar. His vanity knew no political bounds: he would host business and church leaders at his summer retreat in Nida, yet super-imposed a photo of himself onto one of Lenin and hung it on his office wall. It was made to look as if he was rubbing shoulders with the communist leader. Never mind that Lenin was in his tomb long before Romanov was even a twinkle.

For another opinion on the man and his motives, I asked PR consultant and BBC reporter, Charlie Mann, who had the dubious privilege of acting as Romanov's spokesman for four and a half tumultuous years. 'Why do you think he bought Hearts?' I asked. "That was absolutely clear," said Mann. "He was the owner of Ukios Bankas in Lithuania and wanted to establish his bank in the UK. There are probably five major European financial capitals and he could see that Edinburgh was the cheapest in which to establish a foothold. And he had used football to good effect to establish his businesses in other parts of Europe."

I asked if Romanov was a genuine football fan. After a giveaway moment's hesitation, Mann answered: "He certainly had an interest in it, was actively involved with Lithuanian FA. Showcasing Lithuanian players was part of the philosophy for getting involved in football in Scotland but banking was the primary one."

The more I delved, the more doubtful I became about Romanov's football credentials. After all, he was from a country where it was a minority sport and finance always seemed to come first until his ego took over. I asked Iain Mcleod what he thought of the players he brought in.

"Some were good, some not so good. But none were of the calibre of the English Premier League and that's where the money would have been. Then we would have been quite happy. But sometimes we'd look at a player and think 'how's he getting' a game? Oh, he's Lithuanian'. So I definitely think certain managers were under pressure to play them. But we had some good ones. [Marius] Zaliukas was a gem but for every Zaliukas there were 10 guys whose names escape me."

The fans' view of Romanov's arrival had been summed up by Hearts Supporters Trust chairman Martin Laidlaw who said in 2005: "For the last year, being a Hearts fan has been like being on a rollercoaster. We have looked at it now and said that we can either go back to our ambitions of finishing third and getting into Europe occasionally, or make the jump with this new regime and maybe go somewhere we have never been before. It might be hazardous and bumpy at times, but we are going to take the ride." No one could have known then that it wasn't the Big Dipper they were stepping onto but the launch pad at Cape Canaveral.

The first butterflies were felt when John Robertson, a Hearts icon with over 200 goals in 500 games, became Romanov's first manager-victim at the end of the 2004-05 season. Robbo had been appointed by the previous regime and the dismissal itself – harsh and unjustified – was one thing; that it followed not just a vote of confidence, more a eulogy, was quite another.

Many had thought that, as a new broom, the owner would sweep clean immediately and appoint his own man. But he had allayed those fears by declaring: "From my first meeting with John I noticed he is clear in his own mind about what he wants for himself, the team and Hearts as a whole. I like that certainty in a man. It's what I have in terms of my ambitions for the club."

Even so, Romanov still appointed a director of football, the veteran Russian Anatoly Byshovets, to keep an eye on him. And at the end of the season, despite all his 'certainty' and 'thought', despite doing well in Europe, reaching two cup semifinals and finishing fifth in the league, Robbo was dumped. He was offered a coaching role but declined. It was a foretaste of the owners' ruthlessness but, more worryingly, his caprice. It would be the first of many brutal dismissals albeit nowhere near his most controversial. That dubious privilege would not be long in coming.

*On 16 June 2005 George Foulkes became Baron Foulkes of Cumnock, in East Ayrshire.

HEART OF MIDLOTHIAN

3

"We could have won the Premier League – an almighty achievement. But Burley was getting too much positive praise and Mr Romanov wasn't very comfortable with that and wanted some for himself."

Gary Mackay.

The term 'Old Firm' has always struck outsiders as a misnomer. It has an implicit commercial ring, but one of a trusted family business, passed down the generations. It could be a high-class grocer's gallantly resisting the encroachment of franchises on the high street of a well-heeled market town. But to Romanov it was a euphemism – for "the mafia". At its sectarian worst, Old Firm can mean bullets-in-the-post, bottle-barrages, safe houses and rivalry of medieval intensity. But above all else it means a Rangers/Celtic stranglehold on the Scottish game that had not been challenged since Alex Ferguson was at Aberdeen and Jim McLean led Dundee United. Or since Rangers went bust. Not that it came about through sinister means – although Romanov believed it did – but simply through having two Goliaths dominating the landscape. Even towns with teams in the Scottish Premier League would dispatch coach loads to Glasgow to watch the Bears or the Bhoys rather than their own Davids. It was an all-encompassing hegemony but in the late summer/early autumn of 2005, it again came under threat.

Robertson's successor was George Burley. Appointed on June 30, he took Hearts to the top of the table, winning their first eight games and leaving them undefeated after 10. They looked the part, too, and Romanov's claim that they would challenge the Old Firm did not sound so fanciful. Recalls Hearts' legend Gary Mackay: "We were watching a team with parallels to Rangers and Celtic. We were going to half-time and winning three-nothing. That had not been done for 50 or 100 years. George Burley was threatening to do what Fergie did at Aberdeen. He had Hearts playing a type football that was so pleasing on the eye – that was the most disappointing thing [about his sacking]."

Mcleod remembers: "We had never seriously threatened Rangers and Celtic but finally in 2005 we were briefly ahead of both. And even after George Burley was sacked we overtook one but not the other. With players like [Rudi] Skacel, [Steven] Pressley, [Paul] Hartley and [Craig] Gordon, if ever we were going to do it, you sensed it was then. It was a tragedy we didn't build on the success of that team."

Donaldson concurs: "I don't think there has ever been a more exciting summer to be a Hearts fan. We saw this manager and all these great players coming into a squad which had only finished fifth in the league the season before. Besides bringing in Burley, Romanov oversaw the signing of quality players such as Skacel, Edgaras Jankauskas and Roman Bednar amongst others." Four months into the job, Burley was gone – and things would never be the same again.

The former Scottish international full-back had cut an instantly impressive figure. He had managed both north and south of the border and was blending Hearts' old and new, foreign and native, with the mastery of a fusion chef. It was during this period that Romanov had begun to bring over players from his Lithuanian club, FBK Kaunas. The best – Jankauskas – Burley had no problem in picking alongside Czech internationals Skacel and Bednar, and Greece defender and a hero of Euro 2004, Takis Fyssas. This was it, Jambos sensed: Romanov was delivering, Tynecastle was buzzing and the best run since World War 1 was under way.

It would be the high point of his reign. And people began to whisper that there might be the makings of a genuine threat to the balance of power in Scottish football – the first since the rise of the New Firm in the 1980s. Back then there was no multi-millionaire backer at Pittodrie or Tannadice and once Fergie left for Old Trafford, the threat from the east petered out. But this looked as if it might be different: Hearts had a sugar daddy.

But to those with ears to the ground and eyes for body language, all was not as it seemed: despite the success, owner and manager were not getting along. Romanov wanted more imports in the team and Burley would have no truck with what would be famously dubbed the "fax machine" selections. To him, managers pick the team like Cardinals pick the Pope and he bridled against having the line-up delivered electronically from Lithuania on a Friday afternoon.

The two were Caledonian chalk and Baltic cheese. Burley was a proper football man, Romanov an impulsive empire-builder. "I'm investing money so it's my right to buy players," the latter insisted. "Not ideal," was Burley's understated response. Burley liked a drink but couldn't enjoy one with Romanov, the strictest of teetotallers. Burley demanded to run things his way and saw Romanov as an interfering busybody. After the flying start, though, the entire football world – including the few who had noticed the strain between the two men – assumed the manager was bullet-proof. They had reckoned without a Romanov scorned.

The day after he'd upped his stake in the club to 55.5 per cent, he fired Burley. The manager, who had masterminded the best start to a season in almost a century, the man responsible for the owner's current popularity, his handpicked recruit, was gone. It was a decision that still makes it on to lists of '10 Biggest Shock Sackings'. Inexplicable to the wider world and an own goal of a magnitude that Romanov failed to appreciate at the time (and probably still doesn't), it was the precise moment he went from cracking it to crackpot. "It was the beginning of the end," says Mcleod.

Foulkes remembers it like a painful war wound: "The way Romanov had dealt with John Robertson showed how ruthless he could be with managers, but all seemed to be going well under George Burley," he said. "We'd also appointed Phil Anderton from the Scottish Rugby Union as chief executive and he was brilliant. We were on a roll and it was Anderton who'd done all the commercial stuff and Burley had done it with the team, yet Romanov was getting some of the credit! The fans were singing *La Donna Immobile* to him and he loved it. So I thought: 'This is great – everything is going well.' Then I made a fatal mistake – I got fed up with Chris Robinson. He'd been undermining me and I wanted him off the board. While he was there, Scots had a majority but I wanted rid of him and Romanov nominated this very attractive lady, Julija Goncharov, his niece, to take Robinson's place. She was probably the nicest of his people that we dealt with. So it meant that he now had a majority. But the door would have opened sooner or later anyway."

As it turned out, guttural renditions of Verdi were nowhere near enough to satisfy an egotist like Romanov – he felt Burley was getting all the glory! Foulkes said at the time: "George Burley was getting a lot of the credit, and rightly so. The media were giving him the credit, and the supporters were giving him the credit. Of course they were – he was doing a good job. However, Vladimir Romanov has a problem with anyone who is in the limelight at the expense of him. He does not like it at all."

Mackay agreed: "We could have won the Premier League – an almighty achievement. But Burley was getting too much positive praise and Mr Romanov wasn't very comfortable with that and wanted some for himself. Why try to fix somethin' if it's no' broke?" Indeed, if Romanov was Hearts' Abramovich, Burley should have been their Mourinho. Foulkes said: "He used the board meeting to say Burley wasn't doing the job properly because of drink which was outrageous. George liked a drink but so do a lot of others. I went out to the training ground after being out with George and Phil [Anderton] the night before, having a drink till about 1am. The next day I was at Riccarton at about 10am. George had been there an hour taking training and all was perfectly well. It hadn't affected him in any way. He was really respected by the players.

"Romanov tried to persuade Phil Anderton to sack Burley but Phil refused. Romanov then contacted me and wanted to sack Anderton. I then had the awful job of announcing George Burley's sacking on the Saturday after the match. It was really dreadful. There was huge TV coverage and I said he'd gone through mutual agreement. I should have resigned then. I wondered why?

"What Romanov used to do – and I remember sitting with him in his room in the Caledonian and he had all the Hearts players' names on a list on a piece of paper – was mark them all. He thought he knew better than Burley or anyone else who should be picked, when the substitutions should be made etc. And even when he wasn't present he'd be watching on TV somewhere and phone up to say 'you must take so and so off'. Burley wouldn't hear of Romanov choosing the team or making the substitutions and that was clearly one of the reasons [for the sacking]. The other was that he was jealous."

The gloom around Tynecastle intensified after Hearts lost their very next game – and unbeaten record – to Hibs, of all people, and Celtic took over at the top with a 4-2 win over Dundee United. Donaldson will never forget it. "Everyone was completely stunned," he recalls, "and it was probably the darkest day in the club's history since Dens Park in 1986 [when two late Dundee goals denied Hearts the title]."

As outrage at the decision grew, Romanov belatedly realised he needed Foulkes' support and took the trouble to visit his Ayrshire home. "Romanov came to see me on the following Sunday," Foulkes recalls. "It was pouring with rain and he'd brought flowers and red wine – the sort you buy at a BP station. My wife isn't mad about football and it didn't charm her in any way. So he sat down and tried to persuade me to sack Anderton but I refused. He went away in high dudgeon. He'd come with his factotum Sergei Fedotovus, who I felt sorry for as Sergei was a real nice guy and would become the last man standing [in Romanov's reign]. I saw him age. When you worked for Romanov you had to do what you were told.

"After he left I had a funny feeling that he was going to do something on the Monday when I was due to fly down to London. I phoned up first thing to be told that he'd called an EGM. Without my knowledge he'd brought over all the Lithuanians on the board and they'd requested a board meeting. I chaired it and had a stand-up row with him. I said 'I won't be chairman for long, but as long as I am you're not going to deal with people in this club like that. Get out!' His son had never heard anyone speak to his father like that. But when I said 'Get out' he did. They moved the sacking of Phil Anderton. I said: 'Well, I'm intimating my resignation so there's going to be a vacancy.' I had assumed that if they had been clever enough to have organised the board meeting behind my back they would have found some patsy [as a replacement]. So I said: 'Do you care to nominate a successor?' And they nominated his son, Roman. He was useless. He showed all the traits of a son of a rich dictator.

"But then he said he wanted me to stay which surprised me and others, too, because I was standing up to him. But then I realised he wanted a fall guy. I'd been the fall guy for Burley's sacking and was going to be the fall guy for Anderton's sacking and any other decision he was going to make. So there was a delay in announcing the sacking of Anderton. When they announced it I said I disagreed with it and resigned. But I wish I'd resigned straightaway."

Mcleod was in no doubt what was behind the Burley sacking. "It looked like he was taking out people who were more popular than him," he said. "And George [Foulkes] was in an impossible position – you can't be chairman and justify the actions of a raving lunatic – which is what it looked like to everybody. It was a great shame that George left as he had brought warmth back into the club and was doing it without remuneration."

After maintaining a seven-year silence – until Romanov was gone – former Jambos star Saulius Mikoliunas told the *Daily Mirror*: "Romanov has an ego. When we were top of the league under Burley he was jealous that the fans were talking about George rather than him. That is why he kicked him out. Romanov liked to be at the centre of everything."

So, however you look at it – and the armchair shrinks did in microscopic detail – it really came down to a personality defect in the little man. He would become a serial sacker of managers, but this one still beggared belief. When the news broke, most thought it a wind-up. In the Tynecastle Arms before the game, the landlord remembers: "About 150 mobiles rang at the same time," and the talk boards went into meltdown. Trigger-happy? This was the Lone Ranger shooting Tonto.

Foulkes told *BBC Radio Five Live*: "Romanov is behaving like a dictator and if he continues there will be a revolution against him. I brought him in and very much regret that now. Now that he is the majority shareholder he seems to be acting like a megalomaniac and I really do find it astonishing."

Nothing hints more darkly at tin-pot dictatorship than nepotism and here Romanov did not disappoint: his replacement of the esteemed Labour politician and lifelong Hearts fan, with his own son was a shameless classic of its kind. Roman Romanov was just 29, had attended a few games and been seen around the place, but prior to the Burley sacking, there had never been any suggestion that he would be taking over. His father said he'd had plenty of experience in the family business and pointed to his academic qualifications – from Moscow University, Marietta College, Ohio, and 18 months at Pace University in New York. When a check was done at Pace, a spokesman said there was "no record" of a Romanov having attended. At least Roman spoke decent English – and had a sense of humour. When asked about his dad's poor grasp of the language, he quipped: "He has all the words he needs: 'Yes, 'No' and 'You're fired'."

HEART OF MIDLOTHIAN

4

"I'm very glad that you finally got down from the trees and found a worthy place for yourself – a safari park. It shows you have both the habits and instincts of monkeys."

Vladimir Romanov to the media.

Among the names bandied about as Burley's successor were Bobby Robson, Ottmar Hitzfeld, Claudio Ranieri, Nevo Scali and Gianluca Vialli, and the illustrious quality of the field did provide Jambos with a sliver of comfort during their post traumatic stress. All but Hitzfeld were interviewed but none impressed enough to get the job. Indeed, Romanov called Ranieri, of all people, "a pillock". So the eventual choice was... Graham Rix.

Had he not been a convicted sex offender, the former Arsenal midfielder might have been an acceptable choice... as a cone carrier. He had been an excellent player, winning 17 caps for England, but his managerial aspirations were a good deal more modest – he had failed at Portsmouth and recently applied for the job at Crawley Town then in the Conference. It is said that Vialli put in a word for him and Romanov, losing patience with the process and just wanting a 'yes' man anyway, opted for someone who could hardly say 'no'.

The fans' reaction was predictable: instead of a manager who had briefly displayed the Midas touch they had one who hadn't been able to keep his hands off a 15-year-old girl – and whom many thought should still be behind bars. Laidlaw said: "We are absolutely gobsmacked and pretty disappointed. We expressed our concern before this appointment was made and our feelings have not changed." You wondered how much more smacking their gobs would have to take. Foulkes believed the dismissal of Burley, who was one of Robson's star pupils at Ipswich, may have led to the former England boss thinking twice about taking the job. Robson was also said to have been "insulted" by the salary offered – another sign the owner just wanted someone to do his bidding.

The sacking of Burley and hiring of Rix were combination punches from which Romanov never recovered. It showed him in the worst possible light – meddling in team matters and displaying appalling judgment. Donaldson says: "If the sacking of Burley hadn't got the alarm bells ringing, now they definitely were. It's an understatement to say that the supporters were unimpressed with the appointment of a manager who had last been in charge of Oxford United for one season (not to mention he was a convicted sex offender – which really didn't go down well!)"

Romanov had arrived as a knight in shining armour but now that armour was pierced, the shield had fallen and the horse was on the verge of bolting. When questioned about Rix's past, he quoted a Russian proverb: 'The man who'd been in trouble was twice the man once he'd served his punishment'. In the Scotland of 2005, it simply wasn't good enough. Rix, dour and out of his depth, admitted to the team that Romanov was picking it yet somehow survived until March.

Although Hearts had already surrendered their lofty perch to Celtic, they clung to second place. The top two met on New Year's Day, 2006, and when Pressley headed Hearts into a 2-0 lead, hopes were high that they would close the gap to a single point. Celtic pulled a goal back and then added two more at the death after the controversial sending off of Hearts' defensive pillar, Fyssas. It was one of the most agonising defeats in the home side's history and Romanov, who had by now increased his stake in the club to 80 percent, demanded a replay. He also wanted previous games against Rangers and Hibernian replayed after claiming his team had been "beaten up". The SFA rejected his demands but did overturn Fyssas's red card.

But Romanov's novel idea of replays was overshadowed by his even more manic diatribe at the media. "I'm very glad that you finally got down from the trees," he told them, "and found a worthy place for yourself – a safari park. It shows you have both the habits and instincts of monkeys. I'll visit the director of the safari park and ask for a personal cage for each of you. One thing is very important. First you have to pass the quarantine rules and the vet will vaccinate you against rabies." By way of a follow-up, he ordered that bananas be laid out in the press room and his statement was accompanied by a picture of a monkey sitting at a computer, pen in hand and wearing a *Sun* t-shirt. *The Sun* cartoonist responded by suggesting Queen Elizabeth might want to pick the team. The caption read:

The Queen – "Oh please Mr Romanov let me pick the team this week!"

Vladimir Romanov – "Rather you Ma'm, than any monkey journalist."

After this, Romanov decided enough was enough with British managers, sacked Rix and turned to one from home. Enter Valdas Ivanauskas, who had been running FBK Kaunas and was well aware that, under Romanov, picking the team was not the inviolable duty of the manager. Remarkably, in spite of all the rancour and upheavals, the team that Burley built finished second in the league and landed the club's first silverware since 1998 by winning the Scottish Cup. Rangers' slump (after Alex McLeish's premature announcement he would quit at the end of the season) may have helped but, 16 months after taking over, Romanov was delivering. Kind of.

No matter that mighty hard work was made of the final – a nail-biter won on penalties against third-tier Gretna, whose story was as romantic as some of its marriages – the triumph still goes down as one of Hearts' greatest moments of the modern era. In the unique Nelsonian way football fans have of viewing a game, not to mention history, Jambos ignore the near-embarrassment and look back with one misty eye at the memory of a packed Hampden reverberating to the voices of 35,000 maroon-clad fans.

As befits a true showman, the owner was always going to milk the big occasion and invited the crew of his old submarine to the game. It was not any old submarine, but the K19, nicknamed 'Hiroshima' and immortalised in the Hollywood movie *Widowmaker*, starring Harrison Ford and Liam Neeson. In 1961, years before Romanov and his mates went on board, the boat had suffered a radiation leak that cost 23 lives. Living up to its nickname, eight years later it collided with a US sub and, in 1971, suffered a fire in which 28 sailors died. Mikhail Gorbachev suggested the crew that repaired the reactor should be posthumously awarded the Nobel Peace prize. It was finally decommissioned in 1991 and more than a decade later bought by Romanov who wanted to turn it into a Moscow-based meeting place "to build links between submarine veterans from Russia and other countries". But even that attempt at fostering harmony ended in discord as many of the survivors objected. Knowing Romanov's Napoleonic tendencies, it's a bit of a surprise that back in the 1960s, he hadn't led a mutiny, fired the missiles and started World War III.

Far more impressive than the Cup win had been Hearts' league performance. Second may be nowhere to some people but it was the first time since 1995 that any club outside the Old Firm had finished in the top two. And by doing so, Hearts had earned a place in the qualifying rounds of the Champions League. Ivanauskas was rewarded with a permanent contract in the summer when a period of relative calm ensued. Well, for a few weeks anyway.

Despite the outrages, Romanov still had the majority of Jambos onside. Mann explains: "You have to have lived in Scotland and understand how Scottish football has been in recent years and that's why some of the Hearts fans will still look back at his time with high regard. The fans were singing 'we are unbeatable' even when they played Rangers and Celtic. That's never happened before and hasn't happened since. I've been involved with football for 50 years and can say with some authority that that was a spell when the momentum was as great as it's ever been, or certainly since the New Firm days, in terms of challenging Rangers and Celtic. That's why there's still that degree of admiration for what he did."

Still, Donaldson can't help but wonder if it might have been even better. He says: "The question that every Hearts supporter will be forever asking is, 'what could have been?' Like many others, I have no doubt that if George Burley had been retained as manager and allowed to strengthen the squad in January with one or two more quality players (instead, we signed about 11 players in that window, some of whom *were* good but it was still overkill) we would have won the league. No doubt."

Former Hearts media man Ross Pilcher concurs: "We had a quality manager and squad that seemed to instantly click with a good mix of youth and experience. Rangers were comparatively weaker than previous years and I think that squad could have pushed Celtic all the way. I'm not saying we would have won the league, but I think we'd have gone closer than at any time since '86."

As every Hearts fan knows, there was a poignant parallel to this false dawn a century earlier. It will remain the most tragic of 'what ifs' not just for the club and Scottish football but for the lives that would be cut down in their prime on the Somme. When it comes to team tragedies, everyone in Britain knows about Manchester United's Munich air crash of 1958; a few are also aware of Torino's similar tragedy nine years earlier and of Zambia's national team in 1997, but the story of the Hearts players' supreme sacrifice tends to be lost in the mists beyond Edinburgh.

The lamps may have been going out all over Europe in August, 1914, but football carried on in Britain, both north and south of the border. Hearts chose that season to assemble one of their greatest ever sides and won their first eight games. Sound familiar? By November they still topped the Scottish table and had beaten reigning champions Celtic. But there was a mounting public disapproval of football being played when soldiers were dying on the front – incredibly, there was no conscription, Lord Kitchener's pointed finger doing the rest. In Edinburgh the charismatic lieutenant colonel, George McCrae, did the recruiting and no volunteers assembled more enthusiastically than the 16 players and some 500 fans of Hearts. Supporters of Hibs and Raith Rovers joined in and in six days a battalion of 1,350 had mustered. They were called the McCrae battalion or 16th Royal Scots. The players played on but the extra burden of military training took its toll. Hearts went unbeaten between October and March but exercises and all-night marches before a league game were not the best preparation, and Celtic were able to overtake them and clinch the title.

Footballers' battalions were formed all over Britain and the McCrae battalion found itself on the Somme on July 1, 1916. In the worst carnage ever suffered by the British army, three Hearts' first team players were among 20,000 British soldiers who perished on the first day of battle. Four more died before the end of hostilities in 1918. Their sacrifice may be hard for the pampered millionaires of today to get their heads around, but at least they are not forgotten – a clock tower memorial to them stands at Haymarket and a 40-tonne Scottish sandstone cairn memorial at the French village of Contalmaison was unveiled in 2004. Pilgrimages by Hearts fans are made to France every year.

5

"Celtic and Rangers? Even Kaunas are a match for them on the pitch. They have turned football into a type of showbusiness with their underhand games. They buy off players and referees. When it comes to weaker teams then nobody can help."

Vladimir Romanov, 2008.

Despite the turmoil of his first full season, Romanov's roubles had transformed Hearts from also-rans to Scottish Cup winners and Champions League qualifiers. With one trophy already stashed away, the SPL runners-up took the first formative steps toward those European glory nights about which all fans and owners fantasise. The date – late July – was unseemly early. Tiger Woods had only just won the Open and it was barely a fortnight since Zidane's head-butt in the World Cup final; the Edinburgh Festival had yet to begin. The opponents were Siroki Brijeg of Bosnia-Herzogovina, who, in European football, were not even on the fringe of the Fringe. Yet interest and UEFA requirements demanded that the home leg be switched to Murrayfield. Chris Robinson would have appreciated the irony.

With 28,486 fans enlivening the vast rugby temple, Hearts did the business, winning 3-0 and, after a goalless draw in the return, faced the more familiar name of AEK Athens in the second round. Another expectant crowd (32, 459) turned up but a 10-man Hearts went down to an agonising 2-1 defeat, conceding two goals in the last minute, before a 3-0 away loss consigned them to a summertime exit. Had they won, there would have been another two-legged hurdle before the group stage. Still, at a half-full Murrayfield, those were two of the club's biggest nights in recent memory; alas, it was the closest they would get to the tournament proper.

But if the team were faltering – they would also make an unconvincing start to the domestic season – the club still hogged the headlines. PT

Barnum couldn't straddle the high wire if his trapeze artist was sick and Don King couldn't answer the bell if his boxer went AWOL, but when Vladimir Romanov's team were sliding into mid-table mediocrity, he would ensure that Hearts still stole the show. As Donaldson puts it: "The 2006-07 and 2007-08 seasons were when he went into full crazy mode."

The uncharacteristically logical promotion of Ivanauskas to permanent boss had again raised hopes for a period of calm and stability. It was like asking for a minute's silence in a hen house. When the Lithuanian manager cracked under the pressure and a disaffected dressing room cried out for some rallying oratory, Romanov opted for a Russian who couldn't speak English. Eduard Malofeyev got the job after a 2-0 loss at home to Kilmarnock. Romanov hardly spoke it either but he and his translator shared a hairdryer that was locked onto the SFA. It was soon switched on again.

"Last season," he roared, "you didn't manage to protect the Scottish Cup and gave it to Hearts, despite all the referees' efforts and intrigues." He would be fined £10,000 for his pains. Then he vented his anger on his own players, telling them that if they didn't beat Dunfermline in their next game, they would all be transfer-listed.

With Romanov stuffing the starting XI with imports, the threat sparked a rebellion by a trio of senior Scottish players, none of whom were natural bedfellows of Che Guevara. Skipper Steven Pressley, flanked by Craig Gordon and Paul Hartley, read out a statement to the media, who had assembled at the club's Riccarton training ground. "I have tried," Pressley began in apologetic monotone, "along with the coaching staff and certain colleagues, to implement the correct values and discipline, but it has become an impossible task." He ended by saying: "However, due to circumstances, morale understandably is not good and there is significant unrest in the dressing-room."

Thoughtful and measured though it was, Romanov was enraged and it looked like the Gulag for the three of them. Insurrection – even as mild as this – was simply not tolerated. The rebels' days were indeed numbered and the trio, who became known as the Riccarton Three, would be shipped out one by one. Pressley and Hartley went to Celtic during the January transfer window before Gordon, the most valuable playing asset, was eventually sold to Sunderland for £9m.

Two years since Romanov had entered their consciousness, supporters were now coming to terms with reality: the team had reverted to their default setting well adrift of the Old Firm, the players were in revolt, they hardly knew who the manager was and the debt was mounting. It was not how it had looked in Romanov's brochure. Fans demonstrated their support for the Riccarton Three and for the first time "Romanov Out" signs appeared. The first full-scale revolt against him came after a home defeat by Rangers in November, 2006, when some 200 fans gathered outside the main stand chanting: "Can you hear us, Romanov?" He couldn't because he hadn't shown up. Not long before they'd been belting out his 'anthem', *La donna e mobile*.

The finances are not supposed to be a source of concern once a sugar daddy is in place, but, by the end of the season, the debt had risen to £36m and wages were paid late on several occasions. The wage bill had more than doubled with the foreign influx, but the club insisted: "The loss is in line with the board's expectation and is part of an approved long-term business plan for the club where investment and increase of costs are required to improve the performance." The 'long-term funding' was to be provided by a new main stand that would increase capacity to 23,000 and which, along with a hotel, offices and corporate entertainment, would offer other revenue-boosting streams. Even the most devout of the Romanov faithful could see this was a plan that made Peter Ridsdale look like Gordon Brown.

Romanov's state visits were becoming less frequent and one fan group described the situation at the club as "a circus freak show". But once again, the owner's silence would prove the lull before the eruption. In February 2007, Russian magazine *Futbol* reported an interview in which he said: "Celtic and Rangers? Even Kaunas are a match for them on the pitch. They have turned football into a type of showbusiness with their underhand games. They buy off players and referees. When it comes to weaker teams then nobody can help." Both Glasgow clubs threatened to sue him, but Romanov took refuge in the time-honored escape route of having been "misquoted".

The diversionary nature and timing of some of his rants were almost Mourinhoesque – although the Special One was never this deranged. Often they occurred after defeats or games against Rangers or Celtic.

Asked if he thought Romanov really believed Celtic and Rangers bribed officials or whether it was just sour grapes, Pilcher said: "I don't know – it's clearly not an alien concept where he comes from. I think he did believe that they got more than their share of favourable decisions. And I think everyone in Scotland who doesn't support either team has said that the Old Firm are treated differently." With Lithuanians reporting that Romanov "writes the plot for the championship" in that country, it was not a major leap for him to feel the Old Firm drafted the script for the SPL.

Meantime, the imports swelled almost to refugee proportions and their mediocrity made fans wonder if he'd given up on toppling the Old Firm and was now simply displaying his home-grown goods on a more fashionable high street. Defender Dylan McGowan was one of many Hearts veterans to lift the lid in 2013 and he told the *Daily Record*: "When I first signed, I was No. 74 and my clothes were kept behind the washing machine as there was no space for them." Back then the squad numbers were pushing 80.

In December, 2007, the owner's lengthy absence was explained – and fans found out that they'd not been the only ones being led a merry dance. Romanov had been preparing for – and winning – a Lithuanian version of *Strictly Come Dancing*. Nureyev he wasn't but despite his reported lack of finesse, he and dancing partner Sandra Kniazeviciute did enough to pick up a winners' cheque of £30,000. But with the Hearts owner involved, it was not as simple as that. Those who thought it must have been Kniazeviciute who stole the show had to think again – it was Romanov – by, allegedly, bribing the judges. At least he had the decency to give the winnings to his partner.

By now, changing managers was viewed much like the changing of the seasons with irregularities shrugged off as a meteorologist might blame global warming. Anatoly Korobcha was another who couldn't speak English but his appointment barely raised an eyebrow. Malofeyev had gone and, with one win in eight games, was officially the worst manager in Hearts history. Under Romanov, the competition was fierce.

What should have been Korobcha's honeymoon period might have been a sketch from Monty Python. Despite their inability to communicate, Stephen Frail was appointed as the Russian's assistant and during matches Frail would sit in the dugout with the translator while Korobcha watched from the director's box with another assistant, Angel Cerenkov. Every so often the translator's mobile would ring to convey the thoughts of the men above. Instant reactions were out, misunderstandings were in. After a 1-1 draw with Gretna in December, Frail was quoted as saying: "Sometimes it takes a while to get through with the translation and stuff – it's not ideal."

After Hearts plummeted to 10th in the league, it proved too farcical even for Romanov, who belatedly appointed Frail as the sole head coach in January 2008. Hearts eventually finished eighth – their lowest yet in the Premier League format. Losses in translation may have ceased at managerial level but the need for a strong presence in the dugout had never been greater. In the summer of 2008 Hearts simply couldn't find one. Not in this hemisphere anyway. In the end they settled on Csaba Laszlo, who was in Uganda, running the national side. 'About the only place they wouldn't have heard of him,' cynics sneered. The Romanian-Hungarian had been something of a wandering minstrel both as player and manager, but he got Hearts playing and up to second place in September. Late payments to players (and backroom staff) took their toll but Romanov denied the global financial crisis was having an effect.

Goals dried up, cuts were made and several high earners sold. The debt was reduced by £6m and Hearts somehow rallied to finish third. It was enough for Laszlo to be named Manager of the Year both by the Scottish Football Writers and the SPL. More remarkably, he survived until January 29 of the following season. In charge for 18 months, he was the longest-serving manager of Romanov's entire reign. By the owner's standards, it was gold watch territory.

Laszlo may have partly owed his longevity to Romanov becoming distracted – in March 2009 the Russo-Lithuanian announced that he wanted to become president of Lithuania. Call it egotism, call it megalomania, it did not surprise anyone who had followed his four years at Hearts with even a passing interest. Alas for him, this latest tilt at glory was doomed before it started – he was ineligible for that office because he was born in Russia. "I am disappointed," he said. "It made me wonder who I am."

Romanov may not have been entering politics but in January 2010 he made a populist move by replacing Laszlo with a club legend. Jim Jefferies, who had delivered the Scottish Cup in 1998, brought stability to the playing side to finish sixth and Romanov, whose interest appeared to wane again, remained eerily quiet.

He didn't stay silent for long however. After claiming to have almost bought Liverpool from Tom Hicks and George Gillett, he gravely mishandled the next crisis. In June 2011, promising right-back Craig Thomson was found guilty of 'lewd, libidinous and indecent behaviour' at Edinburgh Sheriff's Court after pleading guilty to pursuing two girls, then aged 12 and 14, over the internet. Thomson was fined £4,000 and placed on the sex offenders' register for five years. Romanov's scarcely believable response was to say: "There's no reason for Craig Thomson not to continue as a professional footballer and he will resume training with immediate effect."

Appearing more concerned with damage to the club than the victims, the Hearts boss once again blamed his old whipping boys, "the mafia" along with "crooks, criminals and thieves". It was worse than insensitive and provoked a universally irate response. Foulkes said: "Maybe people will realise why I resigned as chairman. I could not work with someone like Romanov. His statement is simply unbelievable. He has made some very strange statements in the past, attacking the media, the SFA, referees and agents. But this is the most bizarre of all. However, I don't think he will pay any attention to what I or anyone else in the UK says. He is immune to any criticism or outside reaction."

It took an outcry across Scotland and a potential boycott by Hearts fans and club sponsors before Thomson was suspended. The owner then said: "I have reviewed all the facts and understand he has done a wrong thing. This is a very bad example and he will not play for the club again." It was too late. Romanov had managed to lose credibility over an issue that never should have threatened it. Indeed, it made you wonder about his basic judgment as both owner of a public institution and human being; he was lucky it was before the world found out about Jimmy Savile.

Undaunted, he continued to steal the limelight. Having practised Mao Tze Tung's version of constant revolution he would now follow his lead as a swimmer. Where Mao had the Yangste, Romanov had Loch Ness. On July 10, 2011, encouraged by captain Oleg Adamov, a former commander of his old sub, he commemorated the 50th anniversary of its nuclear accident by swimming the width of the fabled loch in 26 minutes.

Some thought he missed an opportunity by not claiming to have spotted Nessie, but then he was not the type to play second fiddle to anything. It would not be long, however, before he reminded us that he could be a real monster with managers – two games into the new season he sacked Jefferies. And he had a suitably rabid statement ready. "Judging by the pre-planned squeals the media monkeys are making," he wrote, "Hearts has hit the point with the move. I believe that with only one competitive win in 15 games, only fools and idiots would not raise questions and suspicions. I now understand why Scotland is in 61st place in Fifa rankings behind such poor football countries like [sic] Lithuania, Albania and Gabon."

Craig Levein is neither a fool nor an idiot and, long before he returned to the club post-Romanov, noted: "I don't understand what boxes need to be ticked at Hearts to keep you in a job. You would need to be insane to do this job. At times it defies logic." Making the timing especially outlandish was that he had just sanctioned four new signings and Hearts were between legs in a Europa League qualifier, having gained a 1-1 draw at Hungary's Paks. But perhaps Jefferies should not have felt too aggrieved: Romanov once fired his basketball coach Darius Maskoliunas – in the middle of the Lithuanian finals series.

6

*"I made it clear to people there that Hearts is an institution and
if it goes to the wall it wouldn't just be supporters it would be the
Government in Edinburgh, the whole country that would feel it."*

Lord Foulkes, Lithuania 2014.

Next in the ejector seat was Paulo Sergio, a former Sporting Lisbon
boss. Another rolling stone, Sergio had played for 11 clubs and managed
six before he arrived at Hearts, but nothing had prepared him for the
turbulence of Tynecastle. The seatbelt sign came on in October when
salaries were not paid; in November the club was put up for sale. And
before that there was a 5-0 home annihilation by Tottenham in the
playoff for the Europa League group stage. Hearts earned respect with a
goalless draw at White Hart Lane but Romanov did not seem bothered.
He told Russian news agency RIA Novosti: "I want to leave football. I
have given the order to find buyers for all my clubs. I want to buy a
theatre and sell the clubs." The truth was that in business, unlike in Loch
Ness, he could barely keep his head above water. Even for Hearts, the
coming winter of discontent would be particularly severe.

Salaries were paid late for three months running in late 2011 and
a transfer ban was imposed. The oxygen masks were now dangling. In
January 2012, the club had to sell Eggert Jonsson for £200,000 to Wolves
just to stay alive. HMRC lodged a further winding-up order. Through it
all Sergio had Hearts playing some decent stuff and was providing his
own entertaining sideshow. With rants redolent of his boss's feistier
years, he found himself banished to the stands and summoned to the
SFA. Romanov saw a kindred spirit and withdrew his staff from all SFA
media events in sympathy.

With fringe players now told they could leave, Sergio did well to steer
Hearts to fifth in the table. But what secured him a place in Jambos'

folklore (and Hearts another Europa League spot) was thrashing Hibs 5-1 in the Scottish Cup final of 2012. It was typical of the bitter-sweet contrariness of the Romanov years that when the club's very future was being questioned they should enjoy one of their finest hours. The debt was actually reduced from £36m to £24m in accounts for the financial year of 2011/12 but the ship was sinking and the crew was jumping overboard: no fewer than 25 players departed. Sergio survived until the end of the season but quit when 'rewarded' with a new contract at a reduced salary.

After trying club legends, Lithuanians, Russians, a Romanian-Hungarian, a convicted sex offender and just about everybody but Pavlov's dogs – it was a surprise he hadn't tried himself – Romanov turned to a loyal servant. John McGlynn's appointment was further confirmation that funding was down to a trickle.

As Scottish Cup holders, Hearts took their place in the Europa League and for the second season in a row were drawn against illustrious English opponents. This time it was Liverpool and although Hearts made their customary August exit from Europe, they gave an altogether better account of themselves. Liverpool needed a late Luis Suarez goal at Anfield to edge through 2-1 on aggregate.

Hearts took pride in their performance but off the field the bad news kept on coming. In the autumn, Romanov revealed losses of £30m on his Lithuanian basketball team Zalgiris Kaunas. At his Birac factory in Zvornik, Bosnia, 1,000 employees hadn't been paid for months. Next came a winding up order – the sixth – from HMRC for an unpaid £449,692.04 tax bill whereupon Hearts issued a plea to their fans for "emergency backing". They got it and HMRC agreed to an extension of the payment deadline. Special mention must go to Scottish pub owner Salman Sarwar, who donated a day's takings of £7,500 to the club. By late January, Hearts could sign only under-21 players on a one in, one out basis. The catch for players of the future, however, was that Hearts couldn't guarantee having one.

In February, there were further signs that Romanov's empire was collapsing when his bank and businesses in Lithuania came under threat. On February 28, McGlynn was sacked with Hearts second to bottom in the table. Then Romanov gave a TV interview in Lithuania saying he was broke and might have to return to driving a cab to make a living. "On the day the bank went into administration," he said, "the authorities froze all my bank cards and accounts. All that I had left was the money I had in my pocket. I was forced to borrow money from friends and immediately sell my property to raise funds. As for what I will do next, I think I will become a taxi driver." When the *Daily Record* called Capital Cabs, Hearts fan John Stewart gave this response: "He'll have to learn English first and ken how to get to Niddrie and Drylaw. But he's a soor, moaning-faced git, so that works in his favour."

Fedotovus was quick to say that Hearts and the bank were separate companies. It did little to reassure but on the field the team had reached Hampden for their second final in 10 months. It was the 2013 League Cup final against St Mirren, but this time they could only rage against the dying of the light and went down 3-2. In the league they finished 10th – the lowest of the Romanov era. But they were still looking at a fate far worse than relegation. Following the collapse of his bank, Ukios Bankas, Romanov resigned from the board of Ubig, the company that held a majority stake in the club. He was then accused of embezzlement and fraud by the Lithuanian Financial Crime Investigation Service. He fled to Moscow where he was reported to be in hospital recovering from a stroke. As the Lithuanians waited in vain for him to return or at least explain why he hadn't, Hearts fans, as ever, reacted in wildly differing ways to the news.

A handful sent good will messages and sang his name at Tynecastle, but the vast majority nodded knowingly when a Lithuanian prosecutor said the medical certificate Romanov had sent "was missing some required particulars... it raises a certain amount of doubt." A Russian news reporter for RIA told a Lithuanian TV show that he was, "healthy and attending CSKA basketball games." The Lithuanians issued an arrest warrant but, as ever, there were conflicting stories – one had him being protected by bodyguards belonging to Chechen president and ex-war lord Ramzan Kadyrov; in another he was spotted by the swimming pool of a top Moscow hotel, talking on a mobile phone. Whichever version Jambos believed, they could safely assume he'd not started running his meter just yet.

On June 13 the club put all their players up for sale and, after they were hit by yet another embargo from the SPL and yet another winding up order from HMRC, Hearts finally admitted defeat. On June 19 they went into administration. The debt, which had peaked at £36m in 2007, stood at £25m – £15m to Ukios, which had been declared bankrupt, and £10m to parent company Ubig, which was claiming insolvency. Before the number crunchers had even set foot in Tynecastle, the immediate and sobering effect was a 15-point deduction with which to start the coming season.

There was, however, a glimmer. If anybody could save them, accountancy firm BDO could. After saving the basket case that was Portsmouth BDO's "Mr Fix-it", Trevor Birch walked into Tynecastle with Bryan Jackson, who had been the administrator at Dunfermline, Clyde, Clydebank, Motherwell and Dundee. "It's as desperate a situation as anything I have seen," said Jackson. "We've arrived here in June, with no income and 7,000 season tickets already sold. It couldn't be any worse, but the positive is the size of the fan base at the club. The estimate to carry on for the next three or four months is between £500,000 and £750,000. If we sell 3,000 season tickets within the next 14 days it relates to about £800,000 of income. Although that is a short timescale to arrange a CVA it gives us a chance to keep the door open and a squad together. If the season ticket money comes in there will be no need to have a fire sale of players and it will retain value for the new owner coming in."

It was desperate but it wasn't hopeless. Birch said: "It should be a no-brainer to run Hearts properly. It's such a shame it has come to this when it had the ability to be sustainable with 13,000 people coming through the turnstiles every week. You could run the business properly without having to go crazy. There is sufficient revenue to have a decent team and have some fun with it." Foundation of Hearts (FoH), who had quickly shot to pole position to become named as preferred bidder, were encouraged with Birch having delivered Portsmouth from dubious foreign clutches to the fans' very own Portsmouth Trust.

Hearts had not quite reached their target when the 14 days passed and Birch warned of a possible last resort scenario – the dreaded newco solution at Rangers. This was the new reality: one more thrashing on the balance sheet and there could be no more Hearts. But the fans weren't going to let that happen and rallied to the Foundation of Hearts started by Ian Murray, Edinburgh South MP and Hearts fan. He asked fans to make regular monthly contributions (between £10 and £500) to raise enough capital to eventually take over the club. And enough of them bought season tickets to allow Hearts to continue trading – and playing – until January. By then the administrators hoped to have come to an arrangement with the Lithuanians. It was vital breathing space and Birch thanked the fans for "a fantastic effort". But it would be a long and worrisome winter: a callow side under latest boss, Gary Locke, was stuck at the foot of the table and relegation looked inevitable.

On November 28 came both good news and bad. At a creditors meeting at Tynecastle, a majority (87%) of shareholders approved of FoH's offer of £2.5m toward the debt. But fans were told the club may not be able to exit administration until March or even April as Ubig were unable to sell their 50% stake. At least a CVA to take Hearts out of administration was approved on condition of the purchase of the club's majority shareholding. Both Murray and Jackson hailed the agreement as "a big step in the right direction" but March/April was a long way away and there might not be a club by then.

The need for reinforcements on the field was now critical. When Celtic came to Tynecastle and dished out a 7-0 humiliation, it was big Bhoys against little boys. Jackson wrote to the newly-branded Scottish Professional Football League (SPFL) for an easing of the embargo but was told rules are rules. Locke and his youngsters would have to battle gamely on. And not even the emergence of a potential saviour in multi-millionaire businesswoman, Ann Budge, could allay the sense of foreboding. Budge, 65, agreed to bridge the gap by taking over until FoH had sufficient funds, but to succeed, her intervention was still dependent on the creditors agreeing and Hearts surviving till they did so. A lifelong fan and season-ticket holder, Budge made her £40million fortune by selling her IT company in 2005. She was named as the sole director of Bidco, the company formed by FoH to take over the club when the transfer of its ownership from Lithuania was completed. It would contribute all of the £2.5m that made up the CVA pot of cash which was accepted by creditors.

Dubbed 'Queen of Hearts', Budge would take no salary and the only 'profit' she would make on the £2.5m would be the same interest she'd have if it had been in the bank. She was set to run Hearts for at least three years but didn't expect to be at Tynecastle for longer than five. By that time, Hearts hoped to be completely in the hands of fans and in a financially stable position.

In February, majority shareholder Ubig agreed to transfer its 78.97% stake in the club to the fans. Jackson reached a draft deal with lawyers in Lithuania but the proposal still needed to be ratified at a Ubig creditors' meeting, scheduled to take place in late March. Jackson told BBC Scotland: "From day one, I always thought procuring the shares was going to be the biggest obstacle. So, to me, it's a really big step."

But just when Hearts were thinking the finish line was in sight, the meeting was put back to April 7. By now the Lithuanians would be feeling what is known in their beloved basketball as 'a full-court press'. Foulkes arranged for Jackson to meet with Lithuania's ambassador to London, Her Excellency Asta Skaisgyrite Liauskiene, and then her UK counterpart in Vilnius, David Hunt. Foulkes said: "I made it clear to people there that Hearts is an institution and if it goes to the wall it wouldn't just be supporters it would be the Government in Edinburgh, the whole country that would feel it." Scotland's then First Minister Alex Salmond, a Hearts fan, spoke to the Lithuanian Prime Minister. BDO only had enough money to keep the club going until the end of April. Jackson, who, according to the *Daily Record*, had been "dismayed and perplexed" by the delay, was already preparing for a worst-case scenario.

The Saturday before the decisive Monday, Hearts were relegated. It ended a 31-year stay in Scotland's top flight but it was almost a sideshow compared to the momentous event to come. April 7 was 'D-Day' alright. Never in the 140-years had the club's very existence been in such jeopardy. A senior source inside Tynecastle put it at even money: "It is now 50-50 as to whether this deal happens or not – whites of the eyes time. The ball is in the court of the Lithuanians and this is going right down to the wire."

HEART OF MIDLOTHIAN

7

"It was the best bit of news anyone ever gave me in my entire life with the exception of the days my kids were born."

Hearts manager, Gary Locke, on hearing the club
had been saved.

Something told you it was not going to be that simple. This saga, already epic in duration, would have tested the patience of Job, the wisdom of Solomon and the negotiating nous of Henry Kissinger. It just had to have one more agonising twist. As Stuart Bathgate wrote in *The Scotsman,* "Ever been to a football match which, you are told, has to have an outcome on the day, only to find there will, after all, be a replay?" That was how it felt on April 7, 2014, D-Day for this famous old club. Replay? More like never-ending extra time.

The venue was Vilnius, the baroque beauty of the Baltic. Capital of Lithuania and home to half a million, the city reeks of civility and continental cool. The architecture of many centuries combines solidity and elegance, while the skyline is pierced more by Catholic and Orthodox steeples than high-rises. They don't hide the dark side, though, with the tourist trail including reminders of Nazi genocide and Soviet torture cells. Mercifully, the kind of calamity confronting thousands of their citizens in the spring of 2014 was only of the monetary kind – but livelihoods had been lost and lives ruined. Now, as they picked the bones of Ukios Bankas, a victim of a very capitalist crisis, and tried to salvage a pittance of their savings, the future of Heart of Midlothian FC would not have been uppermost in their minds.

It was perhaps this realisation that made the mood among the Hearts hopefuls as sombre as the cold, grey Baltic morning. The Lithuanians knew that Hearts' fairy-godmother, Ann Budge, had just sold her IT company for £40m and that Tynecastle High School, on a smaller slice of land adjacent to the stadium, had gone for £600,000. It was not beyond the realms that they might hold out for more money than the £2.5m CVA agreed in November. On the other hand, Hearts'administrators BDO had only enough cash to keep the club afloat till the end of the month. If Ukios wouldn't do a deal, BDO would have no alternative but to wind up Hearts and Ukios' creditors would get nowt. It was really a question of who would blink first.

More than 1,000 miles to the west, Jambos could hardly bear the tension. As with expectant fathers awaiting news of a difficult first birth, the hours were clocked off as if by sundial. They'd hoped for something on the news, on their phones, in the afternoon paper, from the club, and had been encouraged that Ubig had agreed in the morning. But since then there had been silence.

By evening Hearts were still not over the line. Their supporters had endured more shenanigans off the field in a year than most do in a lifetime as spectators. After Ubig had said 'yes' in the morning, Ukios' shareholders were expected to follow suit in the afternoon. Twice and for all, you might say. But Ukios' shareholders did not convene for a vote – they met Jackson instead and even then, after several hours, did not reach a conclusion. And thus D-Day ended like any other – in manic frustration.

As always, the half-glass full Murray tried to sound upbeat. "The agreement with Ubig should not be underestimated," he said in a FoH statement while the talks with Ukios were "lengthy and positive". But they could not dispel the sense of disappointment – even despair – with which many Jambos, finally daring to hope against hope, greeted the news. Besides confusion over the failure to get the deal done, there were genuine fears that the unwanted nuisance of two other late 'bidders' might cause a delay. Businessmen Bob Jamieson and Pat Munro came forward with rival offers on Sunday night and, even though FoH felt neither had credibility, such 11th hour interventions were the last thing needed at this delicate juncture. Still, in the cold light of day, the fact that Ubig had agreed to the FoH proposal and Tynecastle was signed over to them was really more than a halfway step. Neither Jamieson nor Munro had convinced Ubig they were worth a closer look and Jackson was sticking around.

But he would come home without clinching a deal, and there followed a long and an increasingly ominous silence. After a few days, Jackson, along with Birch, then returned to Lithuania but the wait went on. It was not until April 16, more than a week later, before white smoke was seen over Vilnius. Finally, finally, finally, there was agreement and at very long last Hearts could say they were home and hosed. A few details remained to be ironed out but the Foundation wrote on its Twitter account: "Four historic words for all Hearts supporters 'deal done, thank you'. More info to follow." Murray then said: "Ukios Bankas creditors met this morning and approved deal. Sale and Purchase agreement needs completed but we can say deal done."

Gary Locke called it: "The best feeling I've ever had from all my time in football... It meant that Hearts will still be here. It was the best bit of news anyone ever gave me in my entire life with the exception of the days my kids were born." It did feel like a rebirth. Jackson said: "I am delighted that the creditors' committee has today agreed the transfer of shares to Bidco. This is one of the final hurdles in the transfer of ownership of the club. I would like to thank the creditors of both Ubig and Ukios Bankas for agreeing to this deal and also the patience and forbearing of Ann Budge and the Foundation of Hearts. I appreciate that many fans will have wondered whether this day would ever come but we have been working tirelessly on behalf of the club to make this deal work. There is still some work to be done to conclude proceedings but we are now very close to a successful conclusion of the CVA."

There were to be no more injury-time hitches and, looking back, Foulkes reckons: "They ended up with a very good deal. I think Bryan Jackson surprised himself with the deal he got. I thought we were going to have to offer £6m or £7m which of course we hadn't got." On May 12, Budge duly took control with her Bidco 1874 company and the FoH stumped up £1m for the running of the club until the final exit from administration which was achieved on June 11. And so ended the tumultuous reign of Vladimir Romanov.

So, how do we look back on this period, one of the most tempestuous in the history of any Scottish football club? What lessons are there to be learned? Was Romanov simply a rogue, an unlucky rogue or simply unlucky? Was he a megalomaniac? An egotist? A narcissist? A nepotist?

Or a mere opportunist? Did he want to be Caesar? Or, in his case, Czar? There is not a simple answer: all are bona fide candidates.

We have heard from those who knew him that Romanov was influenced by the discipline and hierarchy of the Cold War society in which he grew up, and had been fond of talking about his military past. But, in classic oligarch fashion, he had been unable to resist the plunder that became available when it all fell apart. As a businessman, he liked to make a buck and had some affection for football, too, although, like many Russians, he did not quite have the knowledge, appreciation and quasi-religious fervour of fans in the West, and soon lost interest.

Among Scots, Mann probably knew him best. He says: "You have to understand where he came from. He was alive and in business at the height of the Cold War. It was when the KGB used to run and manage the Soviet Union. He did have a very successful business taken away from him by the KGB just because they could. So in that era of the early sixties he always had to know who his friends were. And because of that he often saw conspiracies where they weren't any. I think that was the biggest issue in terms of where it went wrong because he continued to see conspiracies in the football authorities, he saw them in the referees, in the players, amongst the agents, and it just wasn't the case. So it was a major clash of cultures that caused the wider problem."

Rollercoaster is a much over-used word to describe his reign and no mere fairground jolly could do such a tale justice no matter how white the knuckles. The last decade would have tested the resilience of a stuntman with its alternate tilts at the stars and bungee jumps into the abyss.

But what of Scottish football in general? And football in general? And what of foreign owners? In the first instance, Romanov's money saved one of Scotland's most famous clubs from ignominy, if not extinction, and for that it should be grateful. That he would plunge it back into an equally perilous plight erases most, but not all, of any credit balance. Gratitude has to go to several hard-pressed managers and players, Lord Foulkes for his steadfastness throughout, the administrators who also played a blinder, and in the end, the Lithuanian creditors for seeing reason, Ann Budge for coming in and, most of all, the fans led by Ian Murray.

In the eyes of the wider world, he has to go down as one of the game's barmier owners. *FHM* had made him runner-up to Real Madrid's Florentino Perez in a feature on '23 Men Who Killed Football'. Romanov was probably disappointed not to be No.1. He certainly would have been first on many people's list. Some of his rants were off the wall and downright slanderous. He dragged the game through the mud and didn't know when to stop. You have to ask (and many did): 'If football was so bad why did he keep pouring money into it?'

His initial idea of importing Lithuanian players might have worked had there been more than three or four that were any good. Just as his opening of a branch of his bank might have gained him a foothold in the second largest financial centre in the UK – if he'd followed it up. Developing Tynecastle was another idea that didn't materialise – that his plans were stymied by local planning regulations was something he just couldn't get his "soor, moanin'-faced" head around.

The initial fantasy did not last long. His reign was to somehow endure for nine and a half years yet the bubble was pricked in the second. And he did it himself. He never did accept that sacking George Burley was when he lost the plot and never apologised for it. It doesn't matter to whom you speak – almost all say that was when the dream died. So irrational, so outrageous, so loony was it that he never recovered. But according to Mcleod, "It was one of many turning points."

Winning the Champions League? That statement would be revisited and regarded as no more than bombast. In 10 fateful days in late October 2005, he lost not only his manager but his chairman and chief executive. And then he went and compounded the mess he'd created by hiring Graham Rix. Mcleod said: "We asked: 'What's this guy doing?' As soon as he had 90% of the shares, he started behaving strangely." He was a riddle, alright.

With hindsight – and something of a stretch – we can say that what became known as "the George Burley season" of 2005/06 was his own personal version of the Prague Spring. So much hope, so many possibilities – even a change in the balance of power – but in the end so many dreams were dashed it felt more like the Arab Spring. Romanov was not before his time – this *was* his time and he still blew it. It could have even worked. As both Foulkes and Mann noted, Romanov soon realised he'd struck a resonant chord with fans and a wider public over the Old Firm dominance and proceeded to hammer it whenever he could. But he overplayed it. "Mafia, thieves and criminals" was a bit much even for the most one-eyed Jambos to digest and to the rest of football – indeed the rest of the country – it reaffirmed his status as a basket case.

Having been able to bulldoze his way through the rubble of the collapsing Soviet empire, he was not accustomed to hurdles that are accepted protective mechanisms of Western society. In some ways he was smart but also dunderheaded. He hired Mann as his spokesman when an advisor was desperately needed – if he had been prepared to listen.

Nothing highlights his contrariness more than his claim to be a poet. A less likely purveyor of verse is as hard to imagine as the bowels of a Soviet submarine being its improbable hatchery. In 2013, this Bard of the Deep told Lithuanian TV: "If they put me into prison to sup porridge I will write a book just like *Mein Kampf*. I will show it to those perverts, I shall write them some poems." You'd bet he was more Adolf Hitler than Rabbie Burns.

His Hearts misadventure certainly cost him – he claims he put £50 million into the club – so what, we have to ask, did he get out of it? A harsh assessment would be two Scottish Cups, a bit of second tier European football and an awful lot of hassle. According to the *Daily Record*'s 'Insider' at the time: "He gets trusted English journalists in Moscow to translate his statements into English. Then they get pinged to Edinburgh to be issued. There would undoubtedly have been an attempt to tone things down but very often he will not listen to a word of criticism and demand it goes out verbatim. He is not an easy man to talk down. Another problem for him is that Russian is a difficult language to translate into English with accuracy in terms of nuance and meaning."

Romanov went through 11 managers during his time in power at Tynecastle and surprised no one when, asked his favourite, replied: "Me." Mann believes there was a missed opportunity because he could not find a balance with officials in general. The former spokesman said: "There was a car crash in terms of the way Vladimir Romanov runs his businesses and the way we operate in the UK and particularly in

Scotland. He expected people to do things his way. He could have come a lot more towards us. We could certainly have gone a bit more towards him." That's the considered view of a man who, after the Craig Thomson rant, said: "The volcano has erupted."

As for the volcano himself, he was spewing lava to the last. In a *Daily Mail* interview in December 2012, he told Graeme Croser: "I believe I have achieved much more than taking the first place in Scottish football. We've created more competition in football, a better atmosphere. I was able to point out that mafia exists in sport. And I believe, because of that criticism, refereeing became different – the referees were able to breathe freely. You are also well aware that, in 2004, there were [only] a few thousand people coming to watch Hearts and the club was on the brink. Overall, attendances in Scottish football were not peaking. With us coming and creating a change, I believe the whole game in Scotland picked up."

Good for the Scottish game? He spent most of his time lambasting it and was perhaps fortunate that his rants were so over-the-top that many were not taken seriously. Fines were dished out but punishment was often withheld as, in the opinion of many, he was only one rant away from being sectioned. What is down to him though – and him alone – is the prolonged tenure at Tynecastle. He also created a buzz about the place that had never been felt before.

But the successes weren't that many and the harsh truth is that Hearts were more consistent before his arrival – even against a backdrop of impending doom. Pre Romanov there were three top five finishes in six years and they were never lower than fifth whereas in the six that followed his arrival they also managed the top three on three occasions, but yo-yo'd to sixth and eighth as well. Only in the first – 'the Burley season' – did they come second and that remained the highwatermark. And Mann strikes a sobering note when he says: "George Burley said to me that he didn't think he quite had the squad to win it that season. He thought he'd go close but some of the players didn't have that level of experience to win a title against Rangers and Celtic."

Pilcher sums up the dilemma many Jambos have when he says: "I think there's a certain fondness for him given the success he enabled, whilst at the same time acknowledging he's an absolute zoomer who nearly put the club out of business." That contrasts with the hard line view of Dundee chief, John Brown, who described Romanov as the Tynecastle version of disgraced former Rangers chairman, Craig Whyte. Brown told *The Sun*: "Romanov's a rogue. From day one at Hearts you could see what he was going to do and there is not a great deal of difference between him and the Craig Whytes of this world."

Comparison with the Rangers shambles was inevitable but one huge difference was that the Ibrox saga involved a burgeoning cast whereas Hearts was all about one man; and Rangers went under and were regurgitated while Hearts survived. But the unseemly squabbling in Glasgow provided Hearts with a graphic and concurrent example of how not to go about things. The way the Foundation of Hearts led by Murray, the fans and latterly Budge, went about the rescue of the club could not have contrasted more starkly with the vultures picking at the carcass on the Clyde. Murray was the only Labour MP in Scotland to survive the 2015 General Election but played down his support for Hearts as a factor. "If it had any effect whatsoever it was very marginal indeed," he replied to my query. "I would suspect it would have been in the tens or hundreds maximum."

If 1914 was a landmark year in Hearts' history with the fabled team topping the table before joining the McCrae battalion that fought and died in WW1, 2014 will be remembered as when the club itself fought and nearly died. Of course, no one can compare it with the supreme sacrifice that those seven Maroons made, but in a modern context of football survival, to call it 'heroic' is not out of place. Mercifully, the later sacrifice was only financial and the effort emotional, but each took a considerable toll. The rallying to the cause, the leadership shown and the sheer bloody-minded determination not to be beaten was such that everyone concerned should take a bow. At a time of austerity and with the on-going Rangers reminder that it could all go unimaginably wrong, the commitment deserves a special place in the annals of the game's great survival stories.

Mcleod sums up the tenure like this. "He bankrupted this club and people lost their jobs because of it. But on the Romanov period, it's difficult not to look back on him as a lovable rogue. I don't think he was trying to do us deliberate harm. Events overtook him and he ended up in dire straits." And to think all this could have been avoided had the Lithuanian ambassador to London been consulted. When Foulkes spoke to Her Excellency Asta Skaisgiryte Liauskiene about the Ukios and Ubig creditors, she told him: "If you'd asked my advice [in the first place], I would have told you to have nothing to do with it."

The irony is that without Romanov having grabbed Hearts, shaken it and taken it to the brink of extinction, it is hard to see it being the vibrant Premier League force it is now; hard to see the finances in such robust shape, the main stand being redeveloped and claiming a place in Europe.

But judgment on his reign is inevitably coloured by the resurrection of the 2014/15 season and even if some Jambos are saying the recovery wouldn't have happened without Romanov's interregnum, he ought not to benefit from such maroon-tinted hindsight. It's akin to thanking a negligent stable boy for the new alarm system after your prized thoroughbred has made his excuses.

Manchester City

MANCHESTER CITY

1

"We're not really here, we're the fans of the invisible man, we're not really here."

Manchester City fans.

Of all the witty riffs in football fans' eclectic repertoire, none can surely be more apt than Manchester City's 'We're not really here...' No matter that it isn't the official anthem, its origin is disputed and its lyrics are hardly John Lennon: it sums up the sense of disbelief that many Blues feel about their rarified perch in the game's global stratosphere. Even now.

They are the richest club in the world, owned by one of the richest men, Sheikh Mansour bin Zayed Al Nahyan, a member of the royal family of one of the richest per-capita nations. To borrow a pertinent title, they are *Richer than God*. With the Abu Dhabi Investment Authority's $900 billion reserves under their desert mattress, their Manchester derby will never again be against Macclesfield. Nor will they hesitate to blow £35,000 on a new centre-back: today they blow £35 million.

But back in the nineties, the club haggled over loose change. Those were the days when an irate fan interrupted an AGM to say he was "sick of 20 years of shit," and when Franny Lee said: "If they awarded cups for cock-ups you wouldn't be able to get into our boardroom for silverware."

Many are well-documented but to fully appreciate the scale of the morph from mangy caterpillar to gaudy butterfly, we must revisit the time the script might have been written for a *Carry On* film. It was when the audience yelled its 'till I die' appreciation and could explain today's occasionally diffident reaction to the tampering with the club's DNA.

You could always tell City fans back then – they'd start chewing their fingernails and end up at A&E. Their blood pressure could be mistaken for the cricket scores and they wanted time added on in writing – even when 3-0 up. City did not just snatch defeat from victory's jaws, they were into purging.

To help cope with this black comedy, their fans indulged in their very own vaudeville. Famous for their humour, they brought it back to the terraces at a time of post-Bradford, Heysel and Hillsboro gloom. They started the inflatables craze, had the best cross-dressers and top celebrity fans as well as the best – and worst – jokes: anything to distract from what was happening on the field. 'Typical City' and 'It could only happen to City' became time-dishonored prefixes. You half expected James Alexander Gordon to read them out as he announced the inevitable at 5 o'clock on a Saturday.

For more than two decades, City performances plumbed the depths with a frequency that would have made Jacques Cousteau jealous. Just when they thought they'd reached the bottom, they'd discover a new low. Halifax away in the Cup; York, Lincoln and, yes, Macclesfield, were notable pit stops en route to a dark and murky doom. And it wasn't just that they lost – it was the ways they found to lose. And sometimes even when they avoided defeat, they would 'lose'. Like against Liverpool when Steve Lomas was told they were safe from relegation at 2-2 and dragged the ball into the corner to waste time. They weren't and went down. It wasn't the first or last time City would get their maths wrong. It was almost as if there was a special City Law – Sod wouldn't have been as cruel. They once won 5-2 at Stoke and still got relegated on goal difference. And five days after United had won their second European Cup, the lowest of the low, deep in the enveloping blackness of League One – Gillingham in the playoff final and 2-0 down with hardly any time left.

There is nothing like an escape when your fate looks sealed. Ask a condemned man who has had a reprieve on Death Row; ask a City fan who was at Wembley that fateful May afternoon in 1999. They were so far gone that even when Kevin Horlock pulled a goal back, no one got too excited. Many had already left. The appeal had fallen on deaf ears, the electrodes were in place and the governor's phone was on silent. But when five minutes of added time was signalled, there was a glimmer – and possibly a god. And when Paul Dickov levelled in the last move of the game, there was... delirium. Never had such a joyous collective madness been seen in a City crowd. Neither team could score in extra-time and many couldn't bear to watch the penalties. In 'typical City' fashion, Dickov missed his. But somehow, thanks to the heroics of keeper Nicky Weaver, City prevailed.

League One was their Jules Verne season – two 'leagues' under the top flight but it felt like 20,000. The lowest depth City reached was when defeat at York – their sixth of the season – sent them down to 12th place and 56th in the overall scheme of things. It was December 1998 and the game had all the 'typical City' trappings. One-all at half-time, City dominated the second half only to miss a golden chance to win it at the death. There was, of course, still time for York to nick it – which they did with the first touch in league football of a 19-year-old debutant.

City had ventured to Bootham Crescent on a five-game winless run that included losing 2-1 to Mansfield Town in the Auto Windscreens Shield before 3,007 at Maine Road. It was the lowest home gate in City's history. Typically, just 24 hours later, Manchester United played Bayern Munich at a packed Old Trafford. It was not the only time that City felt the Devil himself was arranging the fixtures.

At Wembley, oblivion had been sold a massive dummy and, carried by their momentum and still-euphoric support, they won a second successive promotion to find themselves in the top flight. But they soon reverted to old habits – and went straight back down. The club hadn't recovered from the traumatic nineties when they had had all those not-really-here managers and were fighting on two fronts – to stave off both the bailiffs and relegation. Even Lee couldn't save them. Indeed, 'Forward with Franny' only took them backwards. That was when the jokes really hit home.

City had not won a trophy since 1976 and – briefly in late 1998 – were Greater Manchester's fifth-ranked club. They were behind United, Bolton, Stockport and Bury, defeat to whom led to one of the most storied anecdotes even in City's bulging lexicon. The moment the Shakers took the lead, a City fan ran onto the pitch and ripped his season ticket up in front of the directors' box. Three days later he got it back in the post, pieced together, with a note that read: "Why shouldn't you have to suffer like the rest of us?"

It sounds apocryphal but the best tales do. A real-life fan, Chris Morris, then 36, related it to the *Manchester Evening News*: "Another fan had ripped his ticket up on the pitch and I couldn't stand it anymore," he explained. "So I ripped my ticket up without thinking. People congratulated me. I had an immense feeling of relief, no more garbage, no more working around City matches, and no more overtime. But on Tuesday it arrived back in the post with that note. It seems you can't get away from the club no matter how hard you try. So I'm going back to Maine Road for the West Brom game on Saturday and looking forward to it."

Fact often outstripped fiction where City were concerned. Way back in 1904, triallist Harry Kay scored four times for City reserves. Was this a new hot-shot goal poacher they'd discovered? Was it hell! Due to the fuss made, Kay got arrested – he was an army deserter. The same year, City narrowly missed out on the double, winning the FA Cup and coming second in the league. But two years later, they became embroiled in a match-fixing scandal in which 17 players were suspended and their star, Billy Meredith, somehow ended up at United.

In 1927, going head-to-head with Portsmouth for promotion, City won their last game 8-0 – only to miss out with an inferior goal average of 0.02. It could only happen to City. Just as in 1938 when they became the only club ever to go down the year after winning the title. Further 'only happen to' embellishments were dropping five places on the final day and being the division's top scorers. Despite all that, up until the Second World War there was not a lot to choose between City and United. United had won the League twice to City's once; City had won two FA Cups to United's one. And the Cup meant an awful lot more then of course. City would also claim the largest attendance (84,569) ever on an English league ground in 1934. They were very different clubs in those days – pre-Munich, pre-Fergie, pre-Abu Dhabi and pre just about everything we associate them with today.

After the war, City were typically forgiving. They allowed United to play at Maine Road after a Luftwaffe bomb caused a crater in the middle of the Old Trafford pitch and then hired a former German POW to keep goal. Bert Trautmann's defiance – broken neck and all – helped win the 1956 FA Cup final. And in 1961, there was a classic 'it could only happen to City' scenario when Denis Law scored all six goals to lead Luton Town 6-2 deep into the second half of an FA Cup tie – only for the game to be abandoned when the pitch became waterlogged. Law scored again when it was replayed but City, of course, lost 3-1.

Law would be best remembered at United when the two Manchester clubs went toe-to-toe in the gilded late sixties. For United it was Law, Best and Charlton; for City, Lee, Bell and Summerbee. Both trios were dubbed 'the Holy Trinity' by their adulatory fans. If United had a slight points lead in stardust, City made up with Big Mal. United boasted a revered national institution in Matt Busby but for charisma – and tabloid tittle-tattle – Malcolm Allison was the *non-pareil* of his day, a sixties Mourinho with a dash of Errol Flynn. There was a fedora, a craggily handsome face and jaunty London vowels, his tongue as loose as his trench coat. Busby had his Babes but so did Big Mal. And Busby never got into the team bath with a *Playboy* model as Allison did. That was at Crystal Palace but under the wise-owl gaze of Joe Mercer at City, Big Mal's flamboyant excesses were reined in and as a coach he was able to flourish at his inventive best.

For a tantalisingly brief golden age City were superior. United achieved the Holy Grail with the European Cup triumph at Wembley in 1968, but couldn't follow it. City had pipped them to win the League two weeks earlier. And while United, sated by the magnitude of their feat, slumped, City remained hungry. They added the FA Cup a year later and then the European Cup-Winners' Cup and League Cup double in 1970. United fell apart and with Busby upstairs and their Holy Trinity in unrighteous disarray, were relegated in 1974 thanks to a famous back heel from the Lawman – now back at City.

The backbone of that great City side was centre-half Tommy Booth, who played 382 games between 1969 and 1981 and won four trophies. He told me: "For six or seven years we were definitely top dog. We outplayed 'em time and time again, and I think United were scared of us in them [sic] days. You never thought of them as a superior side to us. The first City team I played in with Summerbee, Lee, Bell and Doyle was a helluva side and we didn't fear anyone."

In 1972, City almost won the league again and probably would have if Big Mal – now on his own after Mercer quit in an acrimonious split

– had not added Rodney Marsh to the mix. They missed by a point but still held the local bragging rights. However, like a beautiful dream, the superiority couldn't last. Enter Peter Swales.

A fishmonger's son who had owned non-league Altrincham, Swales had made his fortune in TV sales and rentals. With City riven by boardroom disputes, he talked his way in by promising to make their ascendancy over United permanent. He would later admit: "I had no bloody idea, none whatsoever". Twenty years later he still hadn't.

With ever-willing caretaker, Tony Book, again in charge, they won the League Cup in 1976 and chased Liverpool to within a point of the league title the following season. But it was not enough for Swales. United, now under Tommy Docherty, had bounced straight back in 1975 and come third the following season as well as being FA Cup runners-up. Feeling their hot breath, Swales sacked Book and brought Allison back for what he called "the final push". Big Mal quipped: "It was the final, fucking push alright." Of his first meeting with Swales, he said: "I looked at him, saw the comb-over, the England blazer and the suede shoes and thought 'this isn't going to work.'"

It didn't but Allison must carry much of the blame. When a touch-up might have done, Big Mal dug up the foundations. Much-prized homegrown stars Peter Barnes and Gary Owen were sold off cheaply while he over-spent hugely on inferior replacements. Barnes remembers it bitterly: "He came back and wrecked the club, tearing the heart out of the team. Six or seven internationals were let go in a few months." It wasn't sour grapes.

King of the Kippax editor, Dave Wallace, has seen it all and, when asked the 'where did it all go wrong?' question, he said: "Without a doubt it was when Big Mal got rid of those seasoned professionals and spent a lot of money we didn't have. We went down in '83 and the financial situation and repercussions took us 15 years to get back on our feet. United didn't really hit the top until the Premier League started and they got all the money from that and the Champions League. And Ferguson, of course, and it all changed." Big Mal was put out of his misery after 15 catastrophic months. Mercer had given him just enough rope; on his own, he hanged himself.

Swales clung on till January, 1994 when he was outflanked by popular support for Lee. Swales, who maintained his love for City until the saddest of ends, died three years later. He was 63 and, in the words of *The Guardian's* David Conn, "a broken man shattered by his ousting". Allison almost broke City, wheeling and dealing in expensive duds – £1.4m for the journeyman Steve Daley being the most mind-numbing. When he was driven away from Maine Road for the last time, we had only a fleeting, shadowy glimpse through a closed window, but what a poignant peek at harsh reality. The Fedora had gone and so had the sparkle, but it was him alright. Was it a tear in his eye or rain on the window? It hardly mattered as it was no longer larger-than-life Big Mal – just a crumpled and diminished version. Like Swales, he would never be the same again.

MANCHESTER CITY

2

"If City were the only thing in your life, you'd probably top yourself."
King of the Kippax editor Dave Wallace in the bad old days.

For all the off-field shenanigans, on-field triumphs and one real and terrible tragedy, City and United ended their first 100 years of co-existence pretty much as equals. They had jostled stride for niggling-neighbour stride throughout, and whenever one assumed the bragging rights, the other would redouble his efforts to reclaim them. Even their 'Holy Trinities' crossed celestial swords.

But toward the end of the 20th century, a significant gap had appeared. Like the distance runner kicking for home at the bell, United left City for dead. Once they started winning trophies, Fergie's side couldn't stop and their league title drought was followed by a period that would have had Noah calling for the shipbuilders. By the mid-nineties, City were left wondering which way the bad guys had gone.

As a team and a business, United disappeared into the red yonder. Having launched on the stock market in 1991, they soon found themselves in another financial league. Whether mining sponsorship gold or milking 'followers' with their tat, they were building a global empire. City, as usual, were in survival mode and pretty ham-fisted about that.

Lee saw himself as a saviour and was duly annointed chairman in 1994. Worshipped as a player, he was as shrewd and direct in business as he had been on the field, and made a fortune out of recycled paper. Affectionately known as 'the bog roll millionaire', Lee had no trouble mobilising an army of supporters. 'Flush with cash' was the irresistible quip and the intention was to make some for City and catch United. But when he took over he struggled to find a manager and ended up appointing old England mate Alan Ball – his fourth choice. Bally started badly and it went downhill from there.

Phil Neal (as caretaker), Steve Coppell (twice) and Asa Hartford (caretaker) came and went with alarming speed. Others turned down the job and gloom descended on Maine Road. But it didn't stop the jokes. One of them had Lee encountering an old lady who was struggling with her shopping bags. "Can you manage, love?" asks Lee gallantly. The old lady fixes him with her gaze and replies: "You're not catching me out that easily."

Lee's idea was to copy United with a flotation, but City, being City, were not flush enough to pull it off. Within two years of him becoming chairman, the club was in debt and going down. Where United had exploded with a Big Bang, City had merely farted in their general direction.

Lee found himself between a tip of a ground and a joke of a team. Saddled with the burden of modernising the Kippax, he became aware of Manchester's ambitious bids for the Olympics and Commonwealth Games. If there was going to be a new stadium, he wanted City to be playing in it, but a neglected Maine Road still needed fixing in the meantime. What is best remembered is a roofless temporary structure which, with typical City wit, was dubbed the Gene Kelly stand – by occupants accustomed to "singing in the rain".

While Lee and fellow investors took a bath, visiting teams complained of having to do so in cold water. A boiler hadn't worked for three years and when Lee looked at it, he found it held together by sticking plaster. He quipped: "It looked like the African Queen." He could have said the same about the team. Vice-chairman David Bernstein, who would eventually become chairman of the FA, said City had been "under-capitalised and over-borrowed for years." Division One would prove no more than a protruding outcrop that broke their fall, but on which they could not gain a foothold. They slipped again – this time to uncharted depths.

After just over four years of frustration and acrimony, Lee's tenure was an undoubted failure. "It was a bigger mess than he ever thought," says Wallace, "and I think he regretted coming back." Joe Royle became Lee's seventh manager in four years – a turnover that was outdoing even Swales (11 in 20). The sixth, Frank Clark, noted: "It will take a very, very long time to sort things out – it's a rat-infested place."

Lee's reputation inevitably suffered and there was a campaign to get rid of him which City humourists called 'Free the 30,000'. And the club could not complain when Docherty cracked his Oxo cube joke – light blue was indeed for laughing stock. In the late nineties, as United couldn't lose and City couldn't win, *The Guardian's* Simon Hattenstone wondered if a club could have a breakdown. He felt City's may have occurred in 1996 when the manager's door nearly came off its hinges. Other City fans still saw the funny side. To Old Trafford's theatre of dreams, now-disgraced broadcaster, Stuart Hall, dubbed Maine Road "the theatre of base comedy". Comedian Eric Large once gave the halftime team talk. It was at Bournemouth in 1989 and City were 3-0 up but needed a win as they were chasing promotion. They drew 3-3.

Catching United certainly seemed a despairing chase to former world champion boxer and lifelong City fan, Ricky Hatton. "All my life, it's been United, United, in your face," he told *The Observer* in 2012. "Every time you go to a pub or switch on the radio, you've had to duck it. You've had to have a sense of humour, the crap we've put up with over the years... But we've stayed a people's club, getting crowds of 30,000 even when we were in the third division, and we've been through thick and thin."

Manchester was now a city of two tales. In February 1998, *The Times* printed two lists about each club since Fergie had taken over United. The red half had four league titles and one runners-up slot; three FA Cups and one as losing finalists, and one League Cup and one as losing finalists. They'd also won the European Cup-Winners' Cup. City's list was just about as long – it was of the 11 managers they'd had. Honours? None.

By now, there was a bitterness about the rivalry with United fans easing from mere disdain to blatant mockery. They unfurled the banner at the Stretford End reminding City that they hadn't won a trophy since 1976. City fans bridled at the onslaught. They saw themselves as the native sons of Manchester upholding the football faith as opposed to bandwagon types from the four corners who would not find the place on the map. United, they felt, had sold their soul as well as their Manchester roots to become a global brand.

But United's appeal to outsiders began long before the commercial aspect kicked in, according to Wallace. He says: "United have had a new type of fan since the Munich air crash. That made them appeal to a lot of ladies. The number of different accents we heard when we went petitioning at Old Trafford in the 80s was phenomenal." Hattenstone agrees, even explaining what City fans mean when they scream "fucking Munichs". Although it sounds like the ultimate profanity, he argues that it is not about abusing the dead but about United loosening their ties with Manchester. "There is a broader meaning to the phrase," he writes. "After the air disaster Manchester United became the world's favourite football team. Today you're as likely to find United fans from Belfast and Japan and China."

For more than half a century the name Manchester United has resonated around the world like no other. It has just one more syllable than City's but for 20 years had so many more selling points. And when United began their hard sell, those they now call "customers" bought in. You get the feeling they could flog bog roll to Franny Lee.

City fans took refuge in humour – gallows humour. "We always lose at home, and we always lose away, we lost last week and we lost today, we don't give a fuck cos we're all pissed up, MCFC OK." Who says they didn't wallow? While this has slipped off the menu, other ditties from the cock-up days have soared up the charts. 'I'm not really here' is one but doubt surrounds its birthplace. Millwall, Luton and Macclesfield are in the mix – all places where City fans wished they had been invisible. Another claim is that it started in the Swales era of dubious attendance figures. Whatever the truth, it resonated: Paul Lake, a gem of a player from the youth set-up whose career was cruelly cut short by injury, even used it as the poignant title of his biography.

Even in the darkest days, City packed them in. Once in the third tier they got the fifth highest gate in the country... against Wrexham. They were portrayed as masochists – a term which Wallace doesn't exactly rail against. Asked what it was like being a City fan at the end of the 1998 season, he told *The Sunday Times*: "A way of life, a very frustrating way of life. You wonder why you keep going back for more. If City were the only thing in your life, you'd probably top yourself." The Samaritans missed out when they didn't open a branch at Maine Road.

When I ask Booth if he thinks City fans wallowed, he says: "I think, because there was such a gulf in class [with United], City fans got used to it. And they thought of a way to deal with it. It was about thinking up jokes about ourselves so we could basically laugh at ourselves and the club. What took it totally out of hand was what United were doing. They were winning everything and City fans took so much stick it was really, really hard to come to terms with it. We'd win the odd game but they were superior to us and annihilated us home and away most seasons. I don't think we were wallowing in self pity – it was like a protective shield. And some, especially the older fans, are still like that."

Hattenstone refutes any suggestion of masochism, though: "Bollocks. We hate failure. We have always wanted to be the best," he wrote in *The Guardian* in May 2000 as he celebrated back-to-back promotions. He savoured "fluked" victories and claimed "winning games in the last-minute after being outplayed is as good as it gets..." Such reversals of fortune were pure nectar to a City fan and no win was ever sweeter than Gillingham. But it needed to be. Five days before City scraped past their Third Division opponents, United came from behind to beat Bayern Munich in the Champions League final and complete an unprecedented treble. The chronology was 'typical City'.

The drama of Gillingham – the name resonates like Dunkirk did with survivors – obscured the quiet work behind the scenes that would be just as crucial in keeping the club afloat as Dickov's equaliser. A year earlier, Bernstein had replaced Lee as chairman. A chartered accountant, he was the safe pair of hands the City board had long needed and came with a reputation for saving companies: he now had his ultimate test.

When Manchester City Council bid to host the Olympics, it felt like Ena Sharples entering Miss World. But despite the mockery and the knockbacks, they persisted. And in 1995, Manchester won the right to stage the 2002 Commonwealth Games. Bid leader Bob Scott admitted it was "a consolation prize," but still vindication for all those re-jigged drawing boards: the 'Rainy City' was to get a facelift – and a new stadium.

With first Lee and then Bernstein pushing for City to play in it and the council anxious to avoid it becoming a white elephant after the Games, the club got the stadium. Moving in 2003 proved a massive boost and fans, who had sung in the rain, were won over by its spanking appearance and bargain price: City were getting it for free apart from £45m reconfiguration costs. By any standards, it was a snip. And it was the fulcrum of a sports-led regeneration of a sizable slice of the urban area – a promised land duly delivered. This was not typical and no one could imagine how much promise it would have.

City had returned to the top flight in 2001-02 while still at Maine Road under Kevin Keegan, and broke both the club scoring and points records in doing so. It was the fifth season in a row they had changed division. They were no longer a yo-yo club, they were on a trampoline. But they were still City, struggling in United's shadow and enduring off-the-field squabbles.

Chairman and manager fell out over the transfer of Robbie Fowler from Leeds and Bernstein resigned. Keegan, disillusioned with the game in general, followed in March of the 2005 season. After a bright start, Stuart Pearce found that even in the new surroundings, old habits refused to die. With City on the cusp of European qualification, all they had to do was beat Middlesbrough in the final game of the season. But Fowler's injury time penalty was saved by Mark Schwarzer and it ended 1-1. The extra funding from a UEFA Cup campaign went begging.

The importance of that miss became apparent two months later when Pearce was ordered to sell Shaun Wright-Phillips. "The club had sold the club shop, sold the ground to the council, we were paying on the never-never for the Anelkas of this world," Pearce told *The Mirror*. "It really was a case that the owners said, 'Unless Wright-Phillips goes, we go.' On the Monday morning they pressed the button and Chelsea put £21million in the bank which bails the club out." Chairman John Wardle and director David Makin had been paying the wages and could not carry on. Chelsea's offer was one they were not going to haggle over. It was 'a Gillingham' of the balance sheet.

But this time there would be no bounce and two seasons of steady decline saw City go from goal glut to goal drought. They managed 10 at home all season and none at all after New Year's Day. Relegation was avoided but Pearce paid the inevitable price.

MANCHESTER CITY

3

"I know it was a bit dodgy, like, with this politician wiping out the drug dealers, but some of us joked that, 'Hey – some of them were probably United fans!'"

King of the Kippax editor Dave Wallace on the arrival of
Thaksin Shinawatra.

By the mid-noughties there were unmistakable signs that City's decline from 'massive club' to figure-of-fun mediocrity had become terminal. And they weren't as funny anymore. They had somehow remained in the top flight for five years but even for a following as defiantly loyal as City's, aspirations of greatness were becoming delusions. It was nigh on three decades since they'd won a trophy and they'd tried everything. They'd moved to a brand new stadium and been promoted in time to share in the TV rights windfall. Their previous two chairmen were respectively an iconic former player and a chartered accountant renowned for saving companies. The current chairman was paying the wages out of his own pocket. The previous two managers had been among England's most inspirational players. They had promoted kids from the best youth squad in the country and mixed and matched them with big-name ex-internationals. And they were still in a mess. And all the time that banner at Old Trafford was racking up the years. Ticking. Taunting.

About the only thing City hadn't tried was selling to a former prime minister of a faraway land of which they knew little. A leader who had been deposed in a bloodless coup, kicked out on corruption charges and accused of 'human rights abuses of the worst kind'. Oh, and had suppressed the media while ordering his military to take care of an uprising and a drugs problem. An estimated 2,500 'dealers' had been killed. Not many boxes ticked, then, but Thaksin Shinawatra had the cash. Well, they thought he had. Amid the negotiations there was an 'it could only happen to City' hiccup when the junta froze his assets. Still, it didn't deter the club or the authorities: welcome to the Premier League, the 'fit and proper' ex-prime minister of Thailand.

After being ousted in 2006, Thaksin had taken refuge in London. He denied all the charges against him but, with his image in urgent need of a brush-up, he hired Edelman, the world's third-largest PR company. Intent on returning to his native land and his old job if possible, his priority was to remain visible to his people. Edelman lobbied politicians in Europe and America but Thaksin was getting advice from other sources, too: the sure-fire way of staying in the limelight, one told him, was to buy a Premier League football club.

The former Thailand leader's name figured prominently not just on the 'Wanted' lists of Amnesty International and Human Rights Watch (HRW), but on the speed dials of football agents – the high-end ones who don't just find superstars for big clubs but billionaires who want to buy those clubs. And it was one such operator, Swiss media entrepreneur Philip Huber of the Kentaro agency, who proposed Manchester City. "It is a huge brand with a lot of potential, and we felt it was a great opportunity," Huber explained. In tandem with Jerome Anderson, who had his own SEM agency, he convinced Thaksin that City were a better deal than Everton, Spurs or Liverpool, who were all mulling moves or expansion plans. City had a new stadium and the blind faith of the 30,000 dying to be freed. And at less than £60m all in, including the loans to former shareholders, they were going for a relative song.

At this point, City were still without a manager and they'd tried just about everything in that catalogue too. Old hands, new thinkers, disciplinarians, tracksuit types, loved ones, neglected ones. Mel Machin was sacked because he "lacked charisma" while Big Mal had too much. No less than 28 had supped from the poisoned chalice in the 31 years since Tony Book had held the League Cup to his lips. But what City hadn't tried was a foreign manager. A continental *bon viveur* who had won trophies in Sweden, Portugal and Italy, but one who, in England, had more success with the fairer sex than the 'golden generation'. Anderson proposed Sven-Goran Eriksson.

"I had never heard of Thaksin Shinawatra," Sven told me, "but I said 'yes' immediately." On July 6, he was appointed. He also said it never occurred to him to check up on his new boss. Indeed, the only war chest Sven was worried about was the one to buy players. "I signed a two-year contract; the job was exactly what I had hoped for. There was money for new players and I had five weeks to build a team."

City fans didn't quite know what to make of it all but even before the owner's name had morphed into 'Sinatra' or 'Frank', they knew how to pronounce 'billionaire'. A few bristled on humanitarian grounds but the majority applied the football fan's time-honoured deaf ear/blind eye principle: Thaksin might be as bent as a nine-baht note, but most Blues didn't give a toss if he were bankrolling an exciting new side.

Sven, who knew the continental scene and now had the similarly well-connected Anderson and Kia Joorabchian in tow, went to work with impressive haste. No fewer than nine players came in before the end of the transfer window. There were some that fans had never heard of but that didn't matter. Roland Bianchi, Martin Petrov, Gelson Fernandes, Elano, Javier Garrido, Geovanni and Vedrun Corluka were the most notable and after a bewilderingly comfortable opening win over West Ham, City fans chorused: 'What the fuck is going on?"

There were quibbles about the fees, whether the new men would gel and the preponderance of foreigners at a club that prided itself on developing English youth. But all agreed it was vital to make an instant impact. As for the reaction of existing players, Didi Hamman told me: "We won the first three games and beat United. We were top of the league and everyone was delighted." No qualms about Thaksin then? "It was none of our business. There's a 'fit and proper' test and if he passes that he's free to do whatever he wants. The club needed investment. We weren't bothered – we just got on with the job. Most of the stuff came out later anyway – we were paid to play football and not to give our opinion on political issues."

The fans were not aware but Thaksin was not putting as much money into the club as first thought. Missing was investment in the culture and infrastructure. According to Garry Cook, who would soon come on board, it was nothing like the subsequent Sheikh Mansour takeover. "I'd take that a stage further," he said. "In the financial model that is very common in Asia, it was an operation of leveraging the existing assets.

So it could be anything from season ticket sale revenues, which could be brought forward, to making only a downpayment on a player and stringing the [rest of the] payments out."

But Cook also felt there was more to it. "There was an emotional play as well. I think he [Thaksin] wanted to own a football club, there's always that in professional sport. And it was also about his profile." Whatever the reason – and few doubt that politics was the primary one – City ended up acquiring almost a new team without Thaksin having to break his off-shore bank. For the new owner, who said he "had dreamed of owning a club for many years," it was beyond even that.

Thaksin's claim that he was a democratically elected and popular prime minister removed illegally by the military may not have convinced many. But a beatific smile at a club riding high in the Premier League in front of a worldwide audience, blue and white scarf around his neck, was something a PR company simply couldn't provide. And he'd done it on the cheap. A derby win over United and he'd cracked it already.

He needed to. On August 14, Thailand's Supreme Court had issued an arrest warrant against Thaksin and his wife, Pojaman, after they failed to answer more charges of criminal corruption in Bangkok. They stemmed from Pojaman's 772 million baht ($22.3 million) purchase of land in central Bangkok (while her husband was prime minister). It was in a 2003 auction at which other bidders dropped out. The couple maintained their innocence and said they would not return to Thailand until democracy was restored. But there would be more trouble to come as investigators warmed to the task of untangling the City owner's empire.

There were questions in Britain too – from the City supporters trust, HRW and the British Government about Thaksin's right to own Manchester City. "Under any definition, I don't see how Thaksin can be fit and proper," HRW's Brad Adams told *BBC Sport*. "I've written a letter to the Premier League asking what this test means." Thaksin's lawyer, Noppadol Pattama, told *BBC Sport* that the allegations were completely unfounded. "The civil and human rights charges against him have never been proven." Still, it was enough for Tommy Booth to wonder: "When there was talk of his wife going to jail for him, I thought: 'Hang on a minute, what have we got here?'" The supporters trust warned: "Our club should not be the meat in the sandwich between rival political factions in Thailand." Even Sven began to wonder. He wrote in his autobiography: "It was not our business to investigate Thaksin's affairs. I focused on the football. The plan was to finish in the top 10 in that first year. At the same time, we wondered why Thaksin had bought the club. Did he want to make money? Was it to enhance his standing in Thailand? Was the footballing business a cover for his other affairs? We never got an answer to that."

On the field, for once things were less complicated. The win over United in the third game of the season sent City to the top of the table and their fans into that long-forgotten state of euphoria. It was enough for Sven to earn their undying affection and the Manager of the Month award for August 2007. "Everything was almost too good to be true," he said. Except that Sven thought Thaksin was clueless about football. After a loss to Arsenal, when Arsene Wenger had praised City's performance, he called the manager. 'Schwen,' he said, – 'Thaksin had difficulty in pronouncing the 'sv' in Sven – 'Last week, you were very good. This week, you're very bad'." 'Schwen' got the message.

On owners of Thaksin's ilk, the Swede had this to say: "They think it's a business. If they put £50m in they think they should win. They think it's as simple as that and of course it isn't." Was he an interfering owner? I asked. Sven smiled: "He asked me to play Kasper Schmeichel in goal as the girls in Thailand loved his blond hair and blue eyes, but aside from that, no."

The 'Thai spring' of early season couldn't last and City's form dipped with the temperature. The only highlight of the second half of the season was the 2-1 victory over Manchester United at Old Trafford on the 50th anniversary of the Munich air disaster. It completed a League double over United for the first time in 38 years and prompted chants of "There's only one Frank Sinatra". They stopped when Thaksin showed he would do things "my way" by firing the Sven even though it was the club's best season in years. The trigger was a reoccurrence of 'Cityitis' against Fulham, one of the few matches the owner attended and which they contrived to lose 3-2 after leading 2-0.

Hamman recalled: "The players were very unhappy. We couldn't understand it as he was a very good and well-liked and manager, and performances dropped." They culminated in an 8-1 humiliation in the last game of the season at Middlesbrough. On the same day, United were crowned League champions for the 17th time. For City, the cruel symmetry suggested normal service was being resumed. But the fans still launched a Save Our Sven (SOS) campaign. After initial hesitation, they had taken to the Swedish Lothario and while still in the cups, had sung in tribute: "Sven, Sven, you can shag our wives on our settees as long as you get us to Wemberlee."

The fans turned against Thaksin for the first time and gathered over 14,000 signatures for SOS. But it was to no avail. For Eriksson, it meant he would not be around to wield the gold-embossed cheque book of Sheikh Mansour. "I was a bit too early for that," he said matter-of-factly. "I am convinced that the new owners would not have got rid of me. But I never lost any sleep over it. You had to accept that it was all part of football. A lot of football was controlled by men who knew nothing about the game."

MANCHESTER CITY

4

"At the time I signed, I was supposed to meet the owner, but then he had to cancel it to go into hiding somewhere. It was a bit of a funny situation."

Vincent Kompany.

No one knows the inside story of Manchester City under foreign ownership better than Garry Cook, a Birmingham-born, American-made marketing wizard who had been president of the Jordan brand at Nike. Head-hunted back to Britain as CEO on a salary of £1.5m a year, his own tenure at the club would be almost as tumultuous – albeit in a sporting sense – as Thaksin's had been in Thailand. Cook arrived in the twilight of the Thai's reign and departed when the Sheikh's had never glowed more brightly: the league title had been won three months earlier and a golden future beckoned. In straddling City's two foreign dynasties and the huge disparities between them in just about everything, he has a unique perspective. As for 'the project', he wrote it.

I caught up with him via Skype the day before he flew to Las Vegas to take up a presidential role at Ultimate Fighting Championships (UFC). He was approaching the new sport with the same missionary zeal that he'd tackled the Blue Moon and the Swoosh, and it was impossible not to warm to his frankness and marvel at his enthusiasm. Yes, there were lots of 'globals', 'brands' and 'leverages' in his oft-derided corporate-speak but only a couple of 'projects' and just one 'trajectory'. Underneath it all there was the former Birmingham City ball boy but now Manchester City convert recalling his time as front man for two foreign regimes at the world's richest football club. "Yes, I grew up as a Birmingham fan but you can get divorced," he reasoned. It may sound taboo, but no one has sweated, sacrificed and achieved more for the Blue Moon than he did.

Despite the parlous state that both Thaksin and the club were in, the head-hunting of Cook meant the Thai still had major ambitions for

Manchester City. Cook recalled: "It was a club in survival mode when I walked in – not quite the dream it seemed. But the move to the new stadium had been a massive boost and Man City was an appealing proposition because of that. But infrastructure also means people and processes, and theirs was not fit for purpose. I was surprised. There was no human resources department, no legal team. People looked at them [City] and thought 'they put on matches so it must work'."

I asked what his brief from Thaksin had been at what was then called Eastlands. "To turn the football club into a global brand," he said. "Thaksin was ambitious and I put a plan together. That's what I've done for 20 years – it's my job just as a bricklayer lays bricks – and what I do whoever the owner is. I know nothing else. For me it was about where the opportunities were in football, what was happening with the global media and beyond that the attraction of global sponsors and global partners. All that had been going through an explosion in the last 15 years. But things obviously took a swift turn when Shinawatra's assets were frozen."

I asked if the Thaksin experience had been like a trial run for the Sheikh? He answered: "The plan that's in existence today is not that much different to the one I presented to Shinawatra. Which was 'City is the brand, blue is the colour and European success will determine your global success on the field'. Off it, it's about becoming consumer-centric or fan-centric – don't worry about the 37,000 who come through the turnstiles every week – there's 6.4 billion fans out there who may never visit the stadium. I don't think any of those things really changed – it was the ownership that changed."

Given what we know now, I asked if the season under Sven had seemed like a false dawn? "Did we make Man U quake in their boots? Absolutely not. But it ultimately led to the Abu Dhabis. For the first time, City had taken on board the thinking of a foreign coach. Shinawatra definitely moved them forward by virtue of changing the thinking."

As for the premature sacking of Sven, according to Cook, the manager's failure to make a long-term commitment such as buying a house in the area – the Swede preferring a suite at the Radisson – "was one of the things that didn't endear him to the owner." But Thaksin still couldn't understand why the team were not doing better after he'd pumped money into it – and brought in a *feng shui* master. Magic crystals and porcelain elephants were buried at strategic points beneath the pitch to 'energise' the players and 'create harmony' at the stadium.

As to what sort of bloke the owner was, Cook said: "He was a very emotional man, a passionate man and he loved his football. He, Mark Hughes and I used to have conversations about football and he was passionate about it." I ventured that Sven disagreed but Cook insisted: "He could hold his own in a conversation about it." He got to know Thaksin on the golf course which triggered the most infamous of his gaffes early in their relationship. Once, while being grilled about the Thai's reputation, Cook had responded: "Is he a nice guy? Yes. Is he a great guy to play golf with? Yes. Has he got the finances to run a club? Yes."

Cook deeply regrets these comments, saying: "I was unaware of what he was accused of and it wasn't deeply known at the time. What developed and came out later on clearly showed an error in my judgment. However, at the time, I felt I was not in a position to pass judgment. I was there to run a football club that he owned and he was considered a fit and proper person."

In trying to maintain a positive profile in Thailand, Thaksin entertained Thai dignitaries at home games, hosted the Thailand national team in Manchester and even wished the king 'happy birthday' on the Eastlands scoreboard. He had City undertake a goodwill visit to his homeland but none of this impressed the generals sufficiently to prevent prosecution or allow him access to his nest egg. As for the team, Thaksin had shown his ambition by bringing in an up and coming manager in Hughes and soon afterwards Brazilian striker Jo for an out-of-the-ordinary £19m from CSKA Moscow. Well, 19m was the total fee...

The summer of 2008 would be the most momentous in City's history – and hair-raising even for Thaksin. The club did not have two Thai baht to rub together. Incoming players were being signed practically on tick while staff were going home at night not knowing if they would have a job to return to in the morning. "The fabric of the football club had been taken away," Cook told me, "and it was at this point that I had to inform Shinawatra that he had no option but to find a buyer. If he hadn't taken my advice, the consequences for City would have been absolutely disastrous. I have to be honest: we were standing on the edge of the precipice. The business model was not sustainable. We were leveraging money against future television revenues to put deposits down for new players. City had been, quite literally, just moments away from it all going horribly wrong." In July, they borrowed £25m from Standard Bank secured by the club's projected TV revenues over the next two seasons. They were 'living the dream' a la Leeds under Peter Ridsdale. All that was missing was a tank of light blue goldfish.

On July 31, Thaksin's wife Potjaman was found guilty of tax evasion in Thailand and sentenced to three years jail in her absence. But that did not stop the couple flying to Beijing for the Opening Ceremony of the Olympic Games just over a week later – and thus violating their bail terms. Nothing sums up the fluid situation more than the arrival of Vincent Kompany from Hamburg on August 21. The stalwart skipper has since reflected: "At the time I signed, I was supposed to meet the owner, but then he had to cancel it to go into hiding somewhere. It was a bit of funny situation." It was 'funnier' than Kompany imagined but no one was laughing. The eventual fee would be £6m but only a £2m loan from John Wardle kept the club going. Although the former chairman had severed his official ties with the club and was still seething about the sacking of Eriksson, he agreed to help. He is an unsung City hero if ever there was one. Thanks to him, the club had survived a financial 'Gillingham'. Another one.

In retrospect, Cook's pronouncements in the last days of the Thaksin regime carried echoes of the Iraqi Information Minister's when American tanks rolled into Baghdad. "Before the new owners had taken over," he stated, "we were having conversations with Ronaldinho, with the Brazilian Ronaldo, and we had investigated Kaka at the time. Unlike the unfortunate Mohammed Saeed al-Sahhaf, however, Cook knew that rescue was on the horizon – it was he who had brought in the cavalry. And thanks to him City managed to snatch an atypical victory from the jaws of impending doom.

"It was very quick – three to four weeks was all it took," he said. "Negotiations started at the end of July/beginning of August. Then I met Amanda Staveley [the Gulf's British Ms Fix-it for selling to the

Sheikhs] at a Man City home game with West Ham in 2008/9 and I presented a plan of why City was a good investment. Her people went for it and Sulaiman Al Fahim led the Sheikh's acquisition. I still have the PowerPoint presentation that I made to executives of the Abu Dhabi United Group. I would never say I was the saviour of City but I do feel blessed to have had that experience."

Wardle was repaid in two days and his loan not only saved the club, it enabled Thaksin to make an unexpected killing. When the Abu Dhabi deal was signed the Thai leader made, by all accounts, a profit of close to £100m. City were even more fortunate.

Just a few days earlier, Cook had come out with another of his classics: "China and India are gagging for football content and we're going to tell them that City is their content. We need a superstar to get through that door. Richard Dunne doesn't roll off the tongue in Beijing." Dunne happened to be the club captain and Player of the Year for the previous four seasons. The media had a field day with it, but in a sign of how the sands of the game were shifting, the Abu Dhabi United Investment Group (ADUG) agreed with Cook. They smashed the British transfer record by buying Robinho from Real Madrid for £32.5m. It was a statement alright and would have been heard in Beijing.

"When we signed Robinho we needed to have a big-name player in the team," said Cook. "We'd contacted plenty of them – it was part of the agreement with Abu Dhabi that we'd acquire one big signing during that window – in order to make a statement. He was the chosen one and he played his part."

Al Fahim also talked big and City fans could scarcely believe what was happening. But even then, generations of half-glass empty wariness made some fans sceptical. The Thai interregnum had only fed that negativity even if, unusually for City, it had eventually turned out for the best. I asked Cook how much Thaksin had put in? He said: "At max £50m and that was accelerated when the club was close to being sold. As for buying players, he bought a few. But you're only ever in debt to about 20% of their value because of the model works on placing down payments."

Prominent among the sceptics was Arsene Wenger. In the October issue of the official Arsenal magazine, the Strasbourg University economics graduate wrote: "I don't know why these people are in there. It doesn't look like they are there to make any money. So if they are not there to make money out of it, then are they buying it out of love? Well, I am not sure these people are supporters of Manchester City from a young age. So then comes a further question: Why are they doing it? Why have they bought the club? I can't really find a rational answer. If it is just a toy for them then it is even more dangerous. You can have 20 billionaires in the Premier League, still only one can win it and one will come last. The problem is that when these people, who have bought into football, get tired of it, what will they leave behind? That is the real question you can ask. If their investment is purely strategic, based on the market interest, then they could easily decide one day that it is not strategic to be in that market any more, and then they will leave."

But it was apparent from the off that even among today's global big boys, City are a special case. The new ownership is a considerable step up from bog roll and telly millionaires like Lee and Swales. And no, the Al Nayhans had neither played for nor supported the club. But in Al Fahim's introductory remarks, Wenger would have had his answer to why they bought it: "It is for the greater glory of Abu Dhabi."

MANCHESTER CITY

5

"The market is worldwide. There's something not right about sitting in a bar in Bangkok, Beijing or Tokyo and seeing 'Fred Smith's Plumbing. Call 0161...'"

Garry Cook.

'The project' may have been the same but Cook now had backers who could make it happen. Where Thaksin had to beg, borrow and employ high-roller survival instincts to ensure the tea ladies were paid, Sheikh Mansour could buy a World XI without having to check the oil price. And the man to deliver it was already in place. Cook sees the curvature of the earth when many in the north of England do not look beyond the Pennines. He targetted fans not from Chorlton-cum-Hardy and Whalley Bridge but from where they were "gagging" for it. "The market is worldwide," he explained. "There's something not right about sitting in a bar in Bangkok, Beijing or Tokyo and seeing 'Fred Smith's Plumbing. Call 0161...'

The sheikh was more than a fantasy Father Christmas to Cook – and it wasn't just the stuff on the sleigh. Cook found the sheikh's team was not just on the same corporate wavelength but spoke his dialect. I asked if this lottery-like win was a dream realised?

"This may sound a little strange but the money wasn't the important part for me," he answered. "The important part was that we'd found the right partner for this football club that, I truly believed, had an opportunity to become a global brand. The purpose for them was they were looking for proxy brands to develop their nation. Etihad Airways would be part of that – part of developing a world outside of Abu Dhabi so that people can become more aware of Abu Dhabi and its intentions. They are investors and look at the long term. Man City was a vehicle by which Abu Dhabi would communicate to the world that they invest in sport. When the owners agreed to come in, I knew they had lots of money, absolutely, but for me it was not so much the scale, more important was their commitment and what it meant to Abu Dhabi."

I asked if Manchester United, from the same city, with almost the same name and 600 million 'followers', were not an impediment? "No, it's called competition. In any business, when you're a new entry into a market, there's always a competitor ahead of you unless you're the first. If you were selling a shirt with Cantona on it, there's a pretty good chance you'd sell more globally than if you had Elano or Dickov on it for a team that nobody was supporting. Every time you mentioned Manchester people thought it was United. Every time you went to an airport, you'd see Chelsea, Arsenal, Liverpool and Man United paraphernalia on sale. That was the competition. You beat them by opening up new markets, by developing on-field presence, and a better football club than the one that already exists. And, lo and behold, wherever you go in the world today, you'll see a City shirt. Wherever you go, you'll see Etihad Airways or Abu Dhabi mentioned. The only way to beat competition is through time and perseverance. I didn't look at it any other way.

"The message to team members was that we've got to stop becoming Manchester United myopic; that we must rise above it and take on a grander scheme. We were going to become noisier because we were trying harder and trying something a little different. The two most common mantras at the football club were 'typical City' and 'City till I die'. If you're 8-10 years of age, I'm not sure death is on the horizon. 'Typical City' is an admission of mediocrity so we were all trying to build out of that. Any time we did anything it was felt as if it was above our station which I found most offensive."

What about surpassing United? "You have to be very careful in making those statements. I've made mistakes in the past. But I definitely feel that City are surpassing not only Man United but many around the world in organisational capability. The football achievements? There's a long way to go, of course, but we've set off on a very good path. And this ability to regenerate an economy by virtue of its investment in a city is unparalleled anywhere in the world. I think we've already surpassed Man United in that."

But weren't you in the shadow of MU? "Not if you look at through the eyes of the Abu Dhabi investment people. Opportunities were available that were not available anywhere else. Being a London club was not important to them. The biggest brand in football at the time had the same name. Manchester was one of the forerunners of economic development in Great Britain under the guidance of Howard Bernstein and Richard Lees. All of which made sense to Abu Dhabi. That's why we entered into a joint-venture with the City of Manchester. This was not a back-of-the-napkin plan and certainly not without vision."

Playing Devil's Advocate, I press him over City not being the most obvious club to buy. "There were three other clubs who Abu Dhabi were looking at," he said, "but we ticked all the boxes. We could deliver the name Manchester – and I'm not ashamed to admit I used our rivals Manchester United to push our cause; we could deliver the name City – something that could become a powerful brand – and we could also deliver a fantastic stadium surrounded by 230 acres of land that was ripe for development. I addressed men of real intelligence and insight who recognised the potential of Manchester City. They knew the dream I had was realistic. Ironically, I had a much harder task convincing people at the club and many of City's supporters. When I went to the Burnage branch of our supporters' club to tell them that we would beat United and that one day we would win the Premier League and the Champions League, they looked at me as if I was mad. They'd been used to thinking no further than the 40 points needed to stay in the Premier League. So there was 35 years of failure to address. We had to change the culture of the club. It had to be revolution rather than evolution. There could be no looking back – it had to be year zero.

"I came from an American culture. I came from a great company like Nike, where we never once worried about what Adidas were doing: we looked at what Disney were doing. So when I came to Manchester City and I was told that Manchester United were *the* team we had to challenge, I didn't stop for a second to think about how we could emulate what they were doing at Old Trafford – the clubs I set my sights on were Barcelona and Real Madrid."

This was vintage, carafe-overflowing Cook-speak, the kind that a cynical media might ridicule, but Cook knew his audience when he made that presentation. The buyers were never likely to be impressed by Mr Micawber. Or Fred Smith. Like Cook, happiness for them was conquering the football world.

As for the 230 acres, he said: "That campus didn't take three years to build, it took six years to develop. I took the football team to Portland, Oregon and I took Khaldoon [Al Mubarak, the City chairman] to the Nike campus. I wanted it to be the best in the world and to put Manchester City on a par with the greatest institutions of the sporting world. The like of Man City in the sporting world has never been seen and may never be seen again. These were all the plans we put in place and sold to Abu Dhabi. I really feel it when people ask if you were anything to do with it – of course I was something to do with it – I was driving it."

MANCHESTER CITY

6

"We felt this was an opportunity to show our ambition with a tongue-in-cheek approach that had the audacity to say Man City and Man United can live on a par."

Garry Cook on the 'Welcome to Manchester' sign.

When Robinho appeared, Hughes wore the look of a man who had desperately wanted a Mercedes but had been given a Ferrari. Besides there being no room for the kids, he knew it would be high maintenance and would it start on a wintry night in Stoke? But he appreciated the logic and now had to fit the Brazilian in along with five other more roadworthy additions.

City were undoubtedly stronger on paper than last season and although the big hopes were for the longer term rather than the immediate future, a middlin' start was a bit of a letdown. And in January, although Hughes brought in Wayne Bridge, Craig Bellamy, Shay Given and Nigel de Jong – all internationals – there was no new name to "roll off the tongue in Beijing". And the only one that did, Robinho, was not living up to the hype. No one was more aware of this – and that another 'statement' was needed – than Cook who came within a prime ministerial intervention of one of the most sensational transfer coups in football history.

They did not come bigger than Brazil's 2007 *Ballon d'Or* winner, Kaka. City were prepared to pay €100m for him as well as a salary of £500,000 a week, and entered prolonged negotiations with the player, his father and AC Milan. It seemed that Cook had got his man until Milan president and Italian Prime Minister, Silvio Berlusconi, suddenly realised that selling the team's talisman could cost him votes in the forthcoming election and blocked the sale. Cook famously accused Milan of "bottling it," but had to cop a lot of stick for the way it unravelled. He remains defiant: "I still have the documentation and picture of Kaka in a City shirt," he told me.

You can scarcely begin to imagine his frustration as City, bank balance bulging but still lacking the X-factor, continued to be maddeningly inconsistent. At home they had the best record in the division but away they were among the worst. They reached the last eight of the UEFA Cup, lost both derbies and ended up 10th in the league. The previous season, even with Eriksson's impending dismissal causing a dip, they had been ninth.

The owners and the fans had so far been patient but Hughes suffered from comparison with Eriksson's single energising season. He finished only one place above but Sven's men were intriguingly foreign compared to Hughes's mostly familiar faces and they had done the double over United. The Welshman had 'won the lottery' but it was as if he were still living in the same semi-D, still shopping at Asda and still driving a Ford Fiesta. It may have been the feet-on-the-ground way to react in real life but this was the rarified realm of mega-rich owners with commensurate ambitions. And he was not the owners' man. He knew he had to make that summer's transfer window count.

In came Gareth Barry, Roque Santa Cruz, Emmanuel Adebayor, Kolo Toure, Joleon Lescott, Sylvinho and, lastly, Carlos Tevez from United. Serious money was spent but the only real tongue-roller was Tevez who would create more noise off the field thanks to that infamous banner. The Argentine did make a difference, though, and helped City come flying out of the blocks to win their first three games. The fourth was at Old Trafford in which Tevez scored twice but City ended up losing 4-3 in a thriller that was voted the Greatest Premier League Game. If there was any consolation, they were getting under Fergie's skin.

He called City "noisy neighbours" because of the infamous 'Welcome to Manchester' billboard featuring Tevez who City had just acquired from United. "We felt this was an opportunity to show our ambition with a tongue-in-cheek approach that had the audacity to say Man City and Man United can live on a par," said Cook. "That's essentially what it was saying. I didn't realise that it was going to go around the world and have the impact it did. The biggest challenge for Man City at the time was attracting footballers to come and play for the team. If you remain quiet as a mediocre football club, trying to get great players to come to it is a bit of a challenge. You have to lead from the front at some point."

City's season never kicked on and Robinho, who had finished the previous campaign as fourth top scorer in the league with 14 goals, never got going. Injury and indifference saw him play just 12 games, scoring only once, and in January he left for Santos on loan. By then City had a new manager in Roberto Mancini, patience having finally run out with Hughes. "The trajectory of recent results was below the requirement and the board felt there was no evidence the situation would fundamentally change," explained Cook.

Some felt the Welshman had been a dead man walking from the moment the 'Abu Dhabis' took over, but no one gives a corpse £200 million to spend and 15 months in which to do it. That's how much and how long Hughes had since the takeover although not all signings were his idea. The owners had always promised "to do things differently", but the manner and timing of Hughes' dismissal was straight from the Doug Ellis school – just before Christmas, well-advertised and messy. Everyone – including Hughes – knew it was coming. It happened after City had beaten Sunderland 4-3 and there were poignant scenes as the Welshman waved goodbye to the fans before he'd officially been fired. Unbeknown to him, his successor was at the Lowry Hotel in Manchester and had already dispatched scouts to watch City's next opponents, Stoke, at Aston Villa.

Cook maintained that Roberto Mancini "didn't want to come and manage Man City". It had taken the personal intervention of Sheikh Mansour and nearly three weeks to swing it which goes some way to explaining the delay. Mancini, for his part, tried to make light of it, saying: "It's normal. I am sorry for Mark. But when you start these jobs, this kind of situation is always possible. I was at Inter for four seasons and won seven trophies and then they sacked me. It's football."

The matter could have been handled better and Al Mubarak has since said it is one of his principal regrets. In *Richer than God*, David Conn wrote this of the chairman: "He was adamant, looking back, about his two most difficult challenges at City: the sacking of Mark Hughes...

and the stand-off with Tevez. He said: 'We were criticised for talking to Roberto first – of course: I'm not going to fire the guy running the ship without having a replacement in place. People looking at it say we were cold-blooded and harsh, but for me it is business.'" He also said they were right to take a stand over Tevez. Fergie said they were hypocrites to call it off – but they won the league. They tried to be principled but were also pragmatists.

Besides the sluggish progress on the pitch, another surprise for the new owners was just how amateurish it was off it. Like Cook, Al Mubarak had also noted the absence of human resources and legal teams, while one player described the gym at the Carrington training ground as "like the treatment room in M*A*S*H". "I found it shocking in the famous Premier League, to be without such basic functions," Al-Mubarak told Conn. And like Cook, another thing the marketing whiz-kids of ADUG couldn't get their heads around was the morbid expression of loyalty in the song, *City till I die*. Nor would they have been impressed by the self-deprecation of the 'Can you manage, love?' era. Cook said such sentiments were beyond the new owners' comprehension.

Al Mubarak already knew Mancini who appeared just what he was looking for – a winner and someone who could stand up to Fergie. Mancini's *Serie A* record was inflated by the *Calciopoli* match-fixing scandal of 2006 that took the title from Juventus. But he had brought success to the blue half of Milan after a lean couple of decades when the *Rossoneri* had lorded it over Italy and beyond. Europe was the only box he didn't tick. Taking over in December, it was cold enough for him to wear a scarf. Folding it as Giorgio Armani would have, he prowled the technical area like Don Corleone waiting to hear if the drop had been made.

Like Eriksson, his mentor at Sampdoria, he enjoyed an early victory over United. It came after four successive wins in the league and was the first leg of the League Cup semi-final. Although United overhauled it in the second leg, it goes down as a derby win and no one could take it away from him. The fans were already onside. In the January window he brought in only Patrick Vieira – a trusted old hand – taking the view that it made little sense to spend big before he had got to know his squad. And his prudence was all but rewarded. City reached the top four by the end of April only to lose 1-0 at home to Spurs in the final match and miss out on a place in the Champions League. It was 'typical City' but the Abu Dhabis stuck with Mancini.

The manager made up for an abstemious winter with a summer splurge. No less than six internationals arrived, only this time there was a serious upgrade in price and standing. In came Jerome Boateng, Yaya Toure, David Silva, Aleksandar Kolarov, Mario Balotelli and James Milner, with Edin Dzeko added in January. Mancini and Brian Marwood were identifying the players on whom they had 50-page dossiers, but Cook was securing the deals. "It wasn't easy to get people to sign for Man City," the CEO admitted. "We were selling the club and an idea. And Yaya Toure was the one we wanted." City had to prise him from Barcelona and offered him an extraordinary £220k a week. Cook said: "Yaya was different. He came and said, 'I'm going to make this club great'. He was THE ONE. After we signed him, every top player began to see the possibilities at City. Take David Silva, for example. If we hadn't signed Yaya, I don't think David would have come. He was like a Pied Piper. The story we'd always tell would be 'you can go to a big club and be part of the system or you can come to Man City and change the future of the football cub forever. And when I look at those players now – Dzeko, Aguero, Silva, Yaya Toure, Tevez... these were the players that did it."

There were big expectations for Mancini's first full season. He had his own side and he did not disappoint: once City had established themselves in the top four, they stayed there. There were frustrations in the League Cup and Europa League, but City's overseas stars embraced the FA Cup with surprising enthusiasm. After edging a tight Manchester derby semi-final 1-0, there came the chance to end the trophy drought – now 35 years – and force that banner to be taken down. Toure's second half goal saw off Stoke and sent the Blue Moon into a whole new orbit. City had won a trophy, were in the Champions League and, although United had won and drawn the league derbies, a new respect was discernible. That pennant to purgatory at the Stretford End was finally rolled up.

How crucial was the first trophy? I asked Cook. "Absolutely crucial – to me that was the game changer," he says. "It was a game changer on many levels. First, the fans could actually see the manifestation of all this investment and ambition. One of the quotes I used when I first joined the football club was 'build a trophy cupboard' because we didn't have one. We had nothing to put in it. It [the FA Cup] represented so many different things and changed a lot of people's lives. Many grown men and women were crying that day. It meant an awful lot to an awful lot of people. And to the team, to the organisation, the staff that had worked so hard because they knew we had a dream, a vision – and it was partly the manifestation of that dream. Football was ready to sit up and pay attention and the owners were given their just rewards."

MANCHESTER CITY

7

"Before kickoff I remember turning to my brother and saying: 'How can we mess this up? I used stronger language than that."

Garry Cook.

In the summer window of 2011, Manchester City could hardly have made a bigger statement of intent than breaking their transfer record. The standout among another raft of signings was Sergio Aguero, the brilliant Argentine striker from Atletico Madrid, for whom City lavished £38m. Just 23, the lethal target man provided Mancini's side with the firepower to make a serious charge for the title. With eight goals in his first five league games, he hit the ground at a sprint and only injuries have slowed him since. But not enough to prevent him becoming a City legend and one of the world's leading strikers.

Early in the 2011/12 season, City were swatting aside all comers and looking unstoppable in the league. But then came a rude reminder of the pitfalls of a multi-pronged campaign with their first venture into Europe's premier tournament. Not only did they find opponents cussed – defensive-minded Napoli held them to a draw at the Etihad – their own players could be too.

It was deep into their second Champions League group game. City were trailing Bayern Munich 2-0 in the Allianz Arena when Mancini ordered Tevez to warm up. The Argentine did not budge. Amid confusion on the bench, he refused to take the field and City failed to claw back the deficit. They would not recover from their poor start to the campaign and did not qualify for the knockout stage. It set a Eurosceptic trend which they have struggled to shake off. What it showed the City strategists was that even with the most meticulous planning, there's no filter for stroppiness. Barely controlling his rage, Mancini said of Tevez: "If I have my way he will be out. He's finished with me." City backed the manager, suspending and fining Tevez the maximum allowed. The Argentine spent the next four months on gardening-cum-golfing leave at home while efforts were made to find him a new club.

Tevez was not the only player who many thought would not survive a second glance let alone 50 pages of scrutiny. Indeed, one look at the new recruits and you knew the manager was getting his way. There were no shrinking violets in a squad that could look after itself. However, Mario Balotelli couldn't always do that off the field.

Dismissed by Jose Mourinho as having "two brain cells", he was to prove a slap-stick disaster zone but his many 'moments' were more stupid than sinister. And it was Mancini's reputation that suffered more – in the way he handled his *enfant terrible*. While the rest of football laughed, Mancini lost his rag. But he also appeared to indulge his fellow Italian and the mutinous feelings among the squad built up from there. Nor did it impress the former players. And the manager, for all his dress sense, did not always cut a dignified figure on the bench nor act as a gracious loser. Peter Barnes said: "I didn't like his body language at the side of the pitch. He never shook players' hands when they came off. I found him arrogant." But none of that mattered to the fans who loved him – or the owners while he was getting City to win.

At least Balotelli could laugh at himself as he did by unveiling his 'Why always me?' t-shirt after scoring in the 6-1 thrashing of United in October 2011. It was the worst humiliation of Fergie's career and City's superiority was such they looked certs for the title. But their form tailed off and they trailed United by eight points with six games left. The January transfer window had long passed with no suitors for Tevez so the Argentine returned to Manchester and an uneasy truce was brokered. Tevez needed to play and City needed Tevez – he had a knack of scoring vital goals and his energy was just what a flagging squad was crying out for. Just when the title seemed to be slipping from their grasp, he was no longer "finished" with Mancini: he was back in the side.

City then went on a storming, unbeaten run to overhaul United and Ferguson was not amused. "Taking him back showed desperation. In terms of his prestige as a manager, he let himself down," he would write of Mancini. Perhaps, but this was football and there was a title at stake:

City wouldn't be the first to put points before principle. And so it came down to the final day of the season. All City had to do was beat Queens Park Rangers at home to clinch their first title for 44 years. City had dropped only two points at home all season while QPR had won just 11 points on the road. And if City won, it wouldn't matter what United did at Sunderland. City couldn't, could they? On that fateful Sunday morning, Mancini visited the chapel at nearby St Bede's college – and prayed.

It shouldn't have been necessary but City never had done shoo-ins. With so much at stake – the visitors were fighting to avoid the drop – it was a scrappy, error-strewn affair. The crowd was on edge, nails were gnawed, faces drawn. And City, hamstrung by the enormity of the occasion, couldn't get going. Even when they took the lead six minutes before the break, the tension barely eased. And when, soon after half-time, Rangers levelled, you could almost hear the nerves jangling. Then Joey Barton was sent off after a clash with Tevez. But still City couldn't find a way through. Then on 66 minutes Rangers took the lead. United had done likewise at Sunderland and 48,000 ashen faces told you that Cityitis was making the mother of all comebacks.

Hughes, who by a strange twist was now managing Rangers, had said there is something in City's DNA that makes them believe that 'if it can go wrong, it will go wrong'. It was looking that way – with all the looming consequences. Fergie had said if City don't win, it could take them years to recover. Cook, who was in the stands eight months after resigning, told me: "Before kickoff I remember turning to my brother and saying: 'How can we mess this up? I used stronger language than that." Not strong enough though for City going behind after taking the lead against 10 men. Older City fans, who still bore the pockmarks of previous traumas, couldn't recall anything on this scale. The mockery would be unthinkable, Fergie insufferable. Years to recover? City may never.

As the QPR defence continued to hold firm, on the touchline Mancini was coming apart at the Armani seams. Dishevelled didn't do it and you feared his precious scarf might become a noose. But frazzled though he looked his football synapses were still functioning – on 69 minutes he sent on Dzeko. Seven minutes later he played his last card – none other than Balotelli. Up in Sunderland, red ribbons were being tied to the Premier League trophy.

At this point you had to wonder just what were they making of it in Abu Dhabi. All the planning, all the money, all the dossiers, all the research... and still United end up winning! Was that what they were thinking? Could they even pull out?

Ninety minutes were up. There would be five minutes of stoppage time – the same as for the Gillingham game. And as in '99, two goals are needed. No one dares mention fate. But one minute, 15 seconds in Silva's pin-point corner is headed home by Dzeko. City are still alive but the roar is well-short of full throttle – as it was when Horlock had scored against Gillingham. City lay siege. Last two minutes. On the edge of the QPR box. Balotelli. He falls over but manages to find Aguero. A shimmy past a defender into the box and then... the net bursts and so does the blue half of Manchester!

The winner to beat all winners. Cue bedlam, cue delirium, cue pandemonium. This was the finish of all finishes. The most dramatic climax in Premier League history. 'Who is writing this?' asked commentator Ian Darke. No one. No one could write this. If they did, it would be rejected. Three minutes, 20 seconds into injury time. Thirteen seconds after United's final whistle at the Stadium of Light. The Michael Thomas moment had nothing on this. For City, nor did Gillingham.

Just how crucial was winning the league? I asked Cook. "It was a game changer on many more levels [than the FA Cup]. The definition of success in football is the League championship and so it was the representation of that and also how near to failure you can be." Mancini, whose substitutions had been crucial, gave the credit to a higher authority: "God was looking down on us," he said. Cook added: "What it meant was that the dreams we all live and die for in live sport came upon us in a three-to-five minute period. Up in Sunderland, the chairman of the Premier League held a trophy festooned with the colours of the wrong club – and it was quickly shovelled into a cupboard. It meant an awful lot to Man City and to Manchester. Now there are two teams here and it could say if Wembley was the home of football, Manchester is the heart of football."

I had to ask: if you'd not won it, would it have been back to 'typical City' with bells on? "It certainly would have been. People say that even now. And I was so adamant we had to lose that moniker as it smelled of mediocrity. Edin Dzeko and Kun Aguero, both of whom I'd signed, will go down in folklore as the two who changed the club from being 'typical City' to global player. It [failure] would have been talked about in much the same way as Greg Norman failing to win the Masters or Bayern Munich failing to win against Man United in Europe or Milan v Liverpool. It would have had an impact."

City did not go back but did not push on quite as quickly as Cook or anyone else expected. The trajectory took a dip as did the careers of both the CEO and the manager. Cook had already resigned over an errant email. Both men are still fondly remembered at City. The summer signings were nowhere near the standard of previous windows and haven't been since he quit. And although City were solidly in the top four, they once again bombed in Europe. It was a genuine group of death – Real, Borussia Dortmund and Ajax – but City should have been getting the hang of this by now. Meanwhile, relations between Mancini and Balotelli spilled over into a training ground spat that got physical. The photos were awful but diverted attention from Mancini's rows with the rest of the team. City managed to reach the final of the FA Cup where they were heavy odds on to take a consolation prize for a dismal season at the expense of Wigan. But such was the discontent in the dressing room they did not turn up in any recognisable competitive shape – and the underdogs stole a famous victory. Mancini was sacked two days later for "poor communication and relationships with players, executives and board." City tried to dress it up saying the decision was a result of senior figures having "identified the need to develop a holistic approach to all aspects of football at the club". It didn't wash with those in the know – he was a victim of player power.

But Wallace insists: "Most City fans recognised the leap he gave us – beating United in the semi, winning our first trophy for 35 years, winning 6-1 at Old Trafford, winning our first title since 1968, taking on Fergie and beating him at his own game. That was the bottom line which fans focus on. All the infighting and non holistic stuff mainly passed fans by – most thinking that the players should be treated and accept being treated as adults earning a lot of money."

It didn't go unnoticed that City opted for the temperamental opposite of Mancio as his successor – the urbane, dignified and long-fuse, Manuel Pellegrini. With the title regained and the League Cup won in his first season, it seemed a wise choice. But once again, City couldn't build on that the following season when they failed to win a trophy and still seemed in awe of Barcelona in Europe. The campus opened in the autumn of 2014 to universal acclaim and wonderment, but results didn't quite match. The club had arrived as a major force in England, but with as much enthusiasm for Europe as a Brexiteer, they were not yet where Cook had wanted them to be. For one reason or another – meeting Barca in successive years in the Round of 16 being one – the players did not bring their 'A' game to the competition while the fans felt on the wrong end of some arbitrary UEFA rulings. It led to a widespread antipathy to the Champions League, with booing of the anthem and a failure to fill the stadium. With all the planning and all the dossiers and all the money in the world, becoming bigger than Barcelona was still the tallest of orders. It had eluded even Fergie.

MANCHESTER CITY

8

"I resent the fact that the club I have supported since I was five years old is now simply the vehicle for the geo-political ambitions of an oil-rich emirate in the Middle East."

Colin Shindler.

There is luck, there is winning the jackpot and there's Manchester City's second foreign takeover. Back in the summer of 2008, they were for once ahead of the curve – about to fold before Lehman Brothers. After the global meltdown, there would have been little hope of a buyer with Financial Fair Play looming. City had a mediocre team, resided on the wrong side of the tracks and their owner was a wanted man. Even now we know the rest there is an unmistakable "of all the gin joints, in all the towns, in all the world" feel to one of the world's richest and savviest investors "walking into" East Manchester back then.

A clutch of trophies, a £200m training campus, an enlarged stadium and Pep Guardiola later, it is easy to say this is what one and a half billion quid can buy. But what makes it seem like City have won the jackpot twice is that Sheikh Mansour's regime has delivered all this while largely respecting the traditions of the club and sensitivities of the fans. There have been stumbles over managerial dismissals, Carlos Tevez, seating and ticket prices for the Champions League, but nothing like the cardinal stuff committed by other owners we could mention. And Cityitis, if not eradicated, has been pretty well contained.

All this has been achieved while 'the project' is as much about demystifying the kingdom as glorifying City. Abu Dhabi is never going to challenge Sweden when it comes to human rights; nor ancient Athens as a founder of democracy. And it certainly can't claim blood brotherhood with the Kippax in terms of 'till I die' support. But through its reboot of City, it projects a more positive image to the world. The Sheikh has attended only one game yet no owners have invested more in the fans than 'the Abu Dhabis'. They may not be everyone's cup of *karak chai* but in changing the fortunes of this football club they've managed to keep the majority of the faithful on board while making a giant leap into the future. The main quibble is with the soul – more of which later.

Their arrival showed that boxes can be ticked even when a club is down and almost out. But when it came to the hard sell, potential counted for more than history – in City's case, support, stadium and surrounds mattered more than Trautmann or the Holy Trinity. Where other foreign owners have been lured by the glamour of London, these well-heeled go-getters were not deterred by the grotty remains of a bygone industrial age in the grim north – they had so much money they would transform the place as they would the fortunes of a bygone team.

From the moment they snaffled Robinho from the pocket of Roman Abramovich's jeans and reduced Dimitar Berbatov to hiding under a blanket in the back of Fergie's car, they have demonstrated their reach and intent – and shown the Chelsea owner that he's no longer the biggest cheese on football's billionaire's row. But where the Russian has never pretended the London club is anything but an expensive indulgence, Sheikh Mansour is strictly about business. The spending has been similarly huge but incremental and more focused, and it took longer for silverware to arrive. But where the oligarch was scattergun with signings and trigger-happy with managers, the Sheikh showed patience and had a plan. And where Abramovich wasted a decade looking for an alternative ground in London's urban jungle, Mansour simply enlarged the existing stadium while creating the world's best training centre-cum-campus right next door.

He also sought a global reach and City became the hub of an empire which acquired fledgling clubs in Melbourne, New York and Yokohama under an umbrella called City Football Group (CFG). All that has left the fans a little nonplussed but they are far from neglected – City have consistently had the cheapest season tickets in the top flight. Besides buying superstars, they consult with fans over seating, a change to the badge and, unlike their neighbours, do not demand season ticket holders pay in advance for cup matches they prefer not to watch. As Henry Winter put it in *The Times*, "They are organised, professional and slick, but have not lost the soul and community feel that has always characterised City. They have the balance right. Other clubs should look and learn. Especially the Glazers at United."

The more they are compared with those Devils incarnate, the more saintly 'the Abu Dhabis' become. But some question whether City still have a soul. The changes have been root and branch with nary a twig surviving. It is no longer a people's club where self-deprecation was a founding principle. And there's not much of the old humour or spirit left when the UEFA anthem is booed, seats are left empty and the players can't be arsed. When they arrived, City were a well-documented nowhere while United were kings of Europe. Initially, United maintained their domestic dominance with three more title wins, but took Spanish gold for Ronaldo and then could not have cocked up the Ferguson succession any more if they'd used Louis XVI as a template.

Since Fergie first heard the racket from the "noisy neighbours", City have been on the rise as a team and an organisation. Once, when asked if City would ever start favourites in a Manchester derby, the United boss sneered: "Not in my lifetime." City didn't even wait for him to retire. Dominant in the derby, they are now making a profit off the field. And whatever City have lavished on players, it is not as much as United have spent in interest on their massive debt. On December 1, 2015, City announced a £265m investment from the Chinese government and two months later secured Guardiola, the most coveted manager in the game, who joined on July 1, 2016. The City owners had once again showed their pragmatic side in sweetening the China deal: but by inducting Chinese journeyman, Sun Ji-Hai, they forever devalued their Hall of Fame.

As United continued to flounder under Louis van Gaal and their share price tumbled, City stood poised to eclipse their rivals off the field as well as on it. The China deal valued City at £2 billion just a few bob behind United at £2.05b. Indeed, it is widely believed that a reluctant United were jolted into sacking the Dutchman and hiring Jose Mourinho by Pep's impending arrival on the other side of town.

But not everyone buys into this metamorphosis. Colin Shindler, whose *Manchester United Ruined My Life* chronicled his City devotion during United's dominance and became a best seller, is prominent among the disillusioned. In a story of "sorrowful disenchantment," he pens a sequel entitled *Manchester City Ruined My Life*. It is a lament of how his home town club, on the instruction of its new foreign owners, turns itself remorselessly into a global brand. Even after Aguero's winner against QPR – a moment of unfettered ecstasy for most Blues – he writes: "I wished I could share their unrestrained happiness but still the thought nagged away at me that this triumph had obviously been bought with a cheque cashed on the bank of Abu Dhabi and its integrity had therefore been significantly devalued."

When asked if his disenchantment was more with the way football in general has changed rather than with the City owners in particular, he told me: "I loathe the Abu Dhabi lot because they've ruined my home town club but I suspect there are supporters of all Premier League teams (particularly of my age) who feel similarly so the disillusion of the club and the game in general bleed seamlessly into each other." A day later he wrote: "Actually the phrase that best sums up my frustration however wonderful everyone else thinks these people are is as follows: I resent the fact that the club I have supported since I was five years old is now simply the vehicle for the geo-political ambitions of an oil-rich emirate in the Middle East."

David Conn is another childhood Blue who admits to feeling a certain detachment as early as the Gillingham game. In *Richer than God*, he writes of the Dickov equaliser: "And yet even in that moment I had to realise that something was missing; I was not quite feeling it. I was not beside myself; I was not the boy who kissed Franny Lee on the telly, nor the young man who had struggled for breath when I heard that our young City had beaten United 5-1." When I asked him recently, he said he hadn't changed his opinion.

Wallace takes a different view: "I don't think you'd find many who would concur with Colin Shindler's views," he told me. "We had to catch up with Arsenal, Liverpool and United who had all been in the Champions League all those years and got all that revenue. The only way was to get an owner with big investment. It's been remarkable since they've taken over. We've become one of the top teams despite our worries about being the daftest team in the world – and whether that would continue. We still have our moments, of course, but we've won the League a couple of times, the League Cup a couple, the Cup. They've developed the academy which is fantastic. They've put on a new stand at one end of the ground that is absolutely immense and are hoping to do that at the other end taking the capacity up to over 60,000. At the moment we've got a capacity of 54,000 that's pretty well full for every Premier League game.

"They still don't do all things quite right but, compared to the fiascos elsewhere, the things they get wrong are very minor. They've done a fantastic job and I don't think they get the credit they deserve. They've done a lot for the city of Manchester with the academy, the facilities that are open to the community. We had all the jibes when they came in about it being a plaything and it was just going to be a couple of years and they'd get fed up, but they really are in it for the long term and with snapping up Pep you cannot see us doing anything but moving on and getting amid the Real Madrids and Barcelonas even."

Hattenstone, who has criticised Roman Abramovich in the past, was accused of hypocrisy by some *Guardian* readers for continuing to support City after the cash poured in. He summed up the conscience debate best on the eve of the 2011 FA Cup final: "Blood is thicker than principle when it comes to football. Could I walk away from my team after all these years? No way. Your team is your team is your team, however much it embarrasses or shames you. Anyway, it's not as if United haven't bought success. Was I desperate to win a trophy whatever the price? Of course. Was there a grotesque chasm between what I preached and what I practised? You bet. That's football."

When I asked another lifelong City sufferer and late friend, Geoff Bennett, about the morality issue, he was unequivocal: "Do you think I've got any qualms about that after 30 years of pain, misery and ridicule?" Judging by the support, it appears the vast majority agree it was time for martyrdom to end. Nothing summed up the change in outlook more than City's capture of Guardiola. It was a stunning coup by any standards, but for a club that, it was joked, once chose John Benson to replace John Bond because his initials saved buying a new tracksuit...

City took a calculated risk in revealing the Guardiola deal in mid-season and inadvertently condemning Pellegrini to lame duck status.

Parallels with United's premature announcement of Fergie's first 'retirement' and the subsequent effect on motivation were made. But with speculation mounting, City gambled on the players wanting to prove themselves to the incoming boss. Instead, many played as if resigned to being shipped out by him. Still, the owners are banking on Guardiola attracting players and taking City to the next level – especially in Europe where, until the 2015-16 season, they had been disappointing.

The jewel in City's crown is the Etihad campus, the £200m training centre-cum-academy which is designed to attract the best youngsters in the world, not only providing for their football futures but giving them an education as well. Even some former United stars enrolled their sons there and Lionel Messi's jaw dropped when Barca paid a visit. No expense is spared and nothing is left to chance – City players' sleeping positions are incorporated into customised ergonomic mattresses. Zonal sleeping? Whatever, it's a long way from 'the African Queen'.

City visited over 30 sporting institutions worldwide before Garry Cook's masterpiece came into being. It's built in an old, forgotten area of Manchester where an India ink factory once turned the ground purple. But the soil has been washed and the contaminants filtered out. Recruitment of staff and procurement of materials were 90% local: the paint is from Beswick, the tiles from Stalybridge. It symbolises both the fixing of an organisation from top to bottom and commitment to the community. No visitor goes away thinking City ruined anything – certainly not football.

Their winner's luck is no more apparent than in the timing. Two years later and Michel Platini's FFP googly would have had them plumb in front. That well-disguised attempt to protect old money by blocking new could have put the handbrake on further progress. City didn't escape altogether, incurring a €50m fine and player restrictions in 2014, but they were more than able to weather the storm by then.

The bottom of the curve was 2010 with a world record loss of £197m, but since then they've halved it progressively. The next year the loss was down to £98m and in 2012 to just £45m. In 2013 they broke even and since then have made a profit. Far from a rich man's plaything, this is business – even the campus is intended to be self-sustaining in a few years – and the sheikh and his henchmen are not in it just to watch City play. They do – the highly respected Al Mubarak attends two-thirds of games despite his portfolio extending way beyond City. "He's an incredible guy and a global big-hitter," said an insider. As for the Sheikh, he never misses the telecast. When I asked why he hadn't been to more than one game, I was told: "It's like trying to get the queen."

For a "daft" club with a history of cold showers, roofless stands and sticking plaster managers, there is a "they think of everything" feel to it now. Even the bridge linking the campus with the stadium is seen as symbolic in that it connects the community and youth to the heart of the club. I asked Wallace: 'Would you say it was like winning the lottery twice?' "Oh, without a doubt – especially when you look at Leeds and one or two others," he laughed. "But there are City fans who say to me: 'It's not like the old days because now we have to win every game and we're disappointed if we don't whereas back then, if we win that's great, if we didn't win, we'd have a good booze-up or a good day out.' We've been so, so lucky – we have the best [owners] in the business as far as we can see."

But are City where they're supposed to be? Are they really here? Even now, eight years on, with many promises fulfilled, five trophies won and Pep delivered, they are still not bigger than Barcelona or Real Madrid, still not the Harlem Globetrotters of football. Will the academy produce the goods? And could the pampering backfire? The first team has looked soft and uninterested at times – even a Champions League semi-final at the Bernabeu couldn't rouse them. And could they be banking too much on Pep? He's very good but it seems he's expected to lift not just the team but the whole club.

You can't help feeling that some City fans are like the jackpot winners who have everything – new house, new car, holiday home – but at times pine for the old days in the two-up, two-down, driving a beat-up Vauxhall Corsa when they were... happier. Back then they knew their modest place and were comfortable in it whereas today's undeniably spanking upgrade can leave them confused as to how to behave. There is also a sense of distance from the essentially foreign hierarchy as well as a feeling of excess. Compared to the warm, fan-friendly Cook, CEO Ferran Sorriano is an aloof figure while the fees and wages paid stick in the craw when the lack of effort is observed. And the feeling of over-indulgence was fuelled by staff filling a sizable plane to the US to sell the club while Mancini 's entourage included a fellah whose principal function appeared to be to wash the manager's bike.

This may explain why Colin Shindler is not alone and why there have been enough spaces in the stands for the stadium to be dubbed "Emptihad" although mainly for Champions League games. Like an arranged spouse, it's a tournament that City fans have taken a long time to love. But City are already one of the mega clubs and Abu Dhabi is very much on the map. City's owners have been the most generous of benefactors and so far the cash flow has been all one way. Far from threatening the club's stability they have strengthened its foundations to support the lofty heights they intend it to scale. They are playing a long game.

Getting this far already challenges David Gill's view that City will never be as big as United. The former Old Trafford chief executive was speaking at an event to mark the 500th anniversary of Manchester Grammar School in 2015 and the audience lapped up his rhetoric. "I'm not being arrogant, but Manchester City will never be as big as Manchester United in Asia and certain markets," he said. "Look at Liverpool, the club haven't won the league for so many years but they are very popular in Asia. The big teams with history and heritage – Barcelona, Bayern Munich, Juventus and Real Madrid – have that." Across the city at the Etihad Stadium, one senior club executive opined: "Mr Gill had better be careful – 'never' is an awfully long time."

Nottingham Forest

NOTTINGHAM FOREST

1

"You can't fart around here without Cloughie's name being mentioned."

Joe Kinnear.

The European Cup is made of something called Silver 925, stands 71cm tall and weighs 24lb. It is one of the heaviest trophies in sport and Nottingham Forest know this better than most - they've lifted it twice in succession and had it hanging around their neck for 36 years.

Hailing from the smallest city ever to lay hands on 'Old Big Ears', Forest have found their back-to-back triumphs in 1979 and 1980 a mixed blessing: they were undreamed of twin peaks for a provincial club but set the bar unrealistically high. Although they did enjoy success, even winning silverware, in the subsequent decade, they could no longer sustain living at such a lofty altitude. It is now 17 years since they graced England's top flight and their recent efforts to return betray a mounting desperation.

Forest's story is that of the unlikely mountaineer who conquered Everest back to back and then fell into an abyss. Rescue came but since then he has been unable to reach even base camp despite resourceful backers. Forest's ascent is well documented but for the purposes of this book, I have gone back to when they first lost their footing. After that, the focus is on the two main rescuers whose *modi operandi* contrast as starkly as their characters and backgrounds. One was a publicity-shy local who may have erred on the side of caution; the other an extrovert foreigner who has been tripped up by his own impatience. One followed the other so their polar opposite tenures make comparison inevitable. I have therefore looked at both in some detail as each offers a convenient case study in their differing approaches to football club ownership in general and turning around the same fallen champion in particular.

For the actual kickoff of this tale there are several candidates: some obvious, some obscure. Death, relegation and resignations jostle with less-definitive watersheds, all having dropped unmistakable calling cards that things would never be the same again. The most tragic, and perhaps the most logical for this book's purpose, would be the Saturday lunchtime in February, 2012 when, in the Lincolnshire village of Skillington, Nigel Doughty, apparently fit and just 54, was found dead in his gym after going for a work-out. Four children lost their father, a young wife her husband, the Labour party a generous donor, British industry an enlightened captain and Nottingham Forest their saviour.

For all the chilling finality of that moment, however, it can also be claimed that Forest had entered the abyss four months earlier. It was October 2, 2011 and followed a woeful capitulation at home to Birmingham City. Five days before they had been thrashed 5-1 at Burnley. As the majority of fans straggled disconsolately away from the City Ground that Sunday evening, an angry mob – no more than 200 strong – mustered in the car park behind the main stand. It was hardly the Storming of the Bastille and their anger was directed as much at the deeply unpopular chief executive, Mark Arthur, and manager, Steve McClaren, as Doughty. What they forgot to recognise was that the club's head honchos were even more gutted than they were.

Frustration at the sudden belt-tightening in anticipation of Financial Fair Play (FFP) was felt by all, not least McClaren whose transfer budget had been slashed. He resigned minutes after the final whistle, biting his lip to say he was "on a completely different page to the chairman and the board". The manager, who had not been a popular choice, had become even more of a 'Wally' in the eyes of most Forest fans during his 112-day tenure. He was in such a hurry to leave he did not hang about for compensation. It was enough for Doughty to do the honorable thing. He said: "It was my personal decision to appoint Steve McClaren and that's why I'm going. I don't want to compound the error, basically." Since hiring McClaren in midsummer, impending FFP constraints had seen him turn to that 'different page'.

Unaware two coconuts had removed themselves from the shy, the demonstrators, in an act of epic ingratitude, unfurled 'Doughty Out' banners along with mouthfuls of vitriol. The owner, a genial giant of a man but blessed with neither the deaf ears nor the rhinocerous hide required for even minor insurrections, was the most wounded of the three. "As far as Forest were concerned, he was never the same man after that," said one associate. Nor was the level of his funding. After more than a decade in which he had poured nigh on £100m into his precious club, the question he must have asked himself as he drove back to the lush folds of the Vale of Belvoir was: is that all the thanks you get? Football can be a cruel and ungrateful business, and it seemed that way that late autumn evening. The leaves were in free fall and so was Doughty's interest: he would never see his beloved Reds again.

Alternatively, the story could be said to have begun a quarter of a century earlier in a place far removed from Doughty's sequestered vale - the sweltering harshness of Kuwait City. It was when the man who would succeed Doughty as Forest's owner, then an impressionable teenager, first clapped eyes on the genius who transformed the club from provincial nobodies to kings of Europe. When it comes to Nottingham Forest, all roads lead to Old Big 'Ead.

As *The Times* put it in 2013, "From his mansion, a young Kuwaiti boy saw Forest dominating Europe, the larger-than-life Clough on the touchline, and that was it." Fawaz Al Hasawi would get a closer look when Forest actually visited Kuwait as European champions. He says: "I remember standing in the pouring rain to watch Forest play against Qadsia [one of Kuwait's leading teams which he would come to own]. I remember the excitement – the best team in the world had travelled to my country and their manager was Brian Clough! My hero when I was a young boy. Despite the rain, I remember the excitement. When they had won the European Cup, everyone all over the Gulf and Asia was talking about them. They were the greatest of sides – a bit like Manchester United today."

Back in Nottingham, it was why fans would refer to events that were pre-1975 as 'BC' – Before Clough. It is also why there's a bust of the great man in the entrance to the City Ground and when the players emerge from the tunnel the imposing double-decker stand facing them is adorned with his name. It is why there's a statue in the centre of Nottingham and why, as one of 19 failed successors in 24 years, Joe Kinnear quipped: "You can't fart around here without Cloughie's name being mentioned."

Fawaz's fascination may have begun during Cloughie's pomp but as a starting point for this story, I have opted for the very public occasion that Forest supporters first sensed the glory days might be coming to an end. It was more than a moment – just under 15 minutes of lingering excruciation - when we saw with disbelieving eyes that the Midas touch had deserted him. This was when the club would start its tortuous descent from all-conquering royalty back to hard-up East Midlands hoi polloi.

The 1991 FA Cup final is best remembered for Gazza getting carried off and Des Walker's own goal. But it was also when Forest's greatest manager showed he had lost the plot. It was the end of full time. The teams were locked at 1-1 and Clough still had not got his hands on the only major domestic trophy to elude him. Throughout his managerial career, he had preached that the league was paramount and had won it twice, once with Derby and again with Forest. He had surpassed that, though, and achieved true legend status with two European Cups. There were also four League Cups for good measure and several minor baubles. But the one that he'd never quite nailed was the oldest and most romantic of all, the FA Cup. And he had lately admitted he wanted it "badly". Here he was, a tantalising half hour of extra time away from what tennis players call a grand slam of titles. And sticking it on top of his telly that night as was his wont with previous trophies. Just a few words of inspiration, a pat on his young side's back, a kick up a couple of backsides and a wag of that famous finger... that was all it needed. And no one was better equipped to deliver: Terry Venables could talk but he was no Cloughie. The moment was crying out for the master motivator to show how he could reboot a football team.

The stage was set and the world was watching. But he did nothing. While El Tel exhorted his troops in the time-honored manner, Forest's young players – average age 23 - expected similar. It was not long since he'd been asked about injuries and replied: "I'm more worried about acne with this lot." But Clough remained in his seat, face indefatigable, arms defiantly folded. Inevitably, the cameras zoomed in and many thought it was another master stroke of his quirky psychology - reverse psychology. The players would know what to do, they argued, they would gain strength from being trusted while El Tel wasted his breath. You could just see it being written up that way if Forest prevailed. And their manager hailed as an even greater genius.

But not all Forest fans were subscribing to that view. Many were uneasy as the team's callow youngsters had allowed Spurs back into the game. From every drooping forelock, they looked as if they needed a boost. Right-back Brian Laws, one of the older hands, said: "It was crying out for more support on the pitch." But as then *Nottingham Evening Post* reporter Duncan Hamilton would later reveal in his award-winning *Provided You Don't Kiss Me*, Clough had a bad feeling about it. He feared that Forest's brilliant spring form was petering out and that he was destined never to land the coveted trophy.

If that didn't sound like the Brian Clough the world knew, his 'premonition' was spot-on. Des Walker - "You'll never beat Des Walker", the Forest faithful sang – beat himself, heading into his own net and Spurs were victorious. Clearly, the man we saw in the dugout was no longer the all-conquering maestro who could live up to his boasts: indeed, he was so far removed from him as to bear no resemblance. Those in the know put it down to his drinking. They were already aware of spots and puffiness in his face which, to a wider audience who still remembered the telegenic features of his punditry pomp, would have come as a shock. But the bigger surprise was that the inimitable voice remained mute.

However you look at it, Clough's non-intervention was a miscalculation that may have cost him a career-capping moment. Forest would be back at Wembley the following year in the League Cup final, but a strangely subdued performance saw them bow 1-0 to Manchester United. They won the Full Members for the second time in four years and two more appearances under the twin towers in May had led to Clough quipping: "Wembley's our second home." But insiders were not fooled. It put a bit of false gloss on a crumbling dynasty. To make ends meet, Walker was sold to Sampdoria, Teddy Sheringham to Spurs. They weren't replaced. Roy Keane was arrested, Charles fined, Stuart Pearce and Neil Webb crocked for the season. There were whispers about more erratic behaviour by the manager. His already rare training ground visits all but ceased. He no longer walked on water and the riverside nettles, through which he made generations of players run bare-legged after a poor performance, grew tall.

The worst stories would only come out later in the terrible denouement. Forest would go down in 1993 just weeks after tabloid revelations about his drinking. All this came around the time Clough was given the Freedom of Nottingham for his services to the city. It made his demise seem even more poignant. Forest director Chris Wootton had a tape recording of the once razor-sharp pundit slurring his words while attempting to do a TV commercial for *Shredded Wheat*. There were even claims he had buried vodka bottles in his garden and once been found drunk in a ditch at the side of the road. With Forest looking doomed, the club's handling of it was just as crass. It was finally agreed with Clough that he would retire at the end of the season. The only trouble with that was, the manager claimed, it wasn't supposed to be announced until the season had ended: Forest blurted it out straightaway. There was an inevitable feeling that they couldn't get rid of the greatest manager they ever had fast enough.

Forest had done exceedingly well to hang on to him for 18 years and were always paralysed by fear at the merest hint of his leaving. For both the club and their iconic, irreplaceable manager, the 1991 FA Cup final was the occasion to have ended it. There was no disgrace in losing to Spurs after extra time: downbeat would have been better than deadbeat. But that is easy to say with hindsight. Alas, no one could imagine the depth of the coming crisis even though Clough's Wembley silence was its deafening siren.

NOTTINGHAM FOREST

2

"An owner only has to make one good decision – and that's getting the manager right. If you do, your Saturday nights in front of the telly are fabulous; get it wrong and they are totally miserable."

Brian Clough

As gut-wrenching as the double blow of losing Clough and Premier League status was, Forest defied the doom-mongers by bouncing back at the first time of asking. The appointment of Frank Clark, the ex-player whom Clough had endorsed as his successor, meant they were in safe, Forest-friendly hands. Armed with a war chest from the sales of Roy Keane, for a British record £3.8m to Manchester United, and Nigel Clough, to Liverpool for £2m, they were able to rebuild. In came Stan Collymore from Southend and Colin Cooper from Millwall, who belatedly filled the gaps left by Sheringham and Walker. Collymore's 25 goals carried Forest to automatic promotion behind champions Crystal Palace while Cooper sealed the defence as well as popping in nine goals. In their first season back in the top flight, bolstered by Dutch winger Bryan Roy, Forest came third. It remains the highest finish by a newly promoted side and earned a place in the UEFA Cup. Perhaps they weren't missing Clough that much after all.

But those in the know were not getting carried away. Finances were a constant problem and Forest could no longer hang on to their latest prized asset. For the second time in three seasons, they picked up a British record fee – this time for Collymore who had bagged 22 goals and went to Liverpool for £8.4m. Forest slumped to ninth in 1996 but reached the UEFA Cup quarter-finals before a 5-1 thrashing by Bayern Munich at the City Ground dashed any delusions of another continental triumph.

Even getting that far was a welcome diversion from the reality of debts that had grown to £8 million by February, 1997. Despite the big bucks sloshing around the game, Forest, third-oldest league club in the world and Byzantine in constitution, simply could not compete with the big boys. With their iconic manager gone, they were falling over just trying to hang on to fast-disappearing coat-tails. But in certain predatory eyes, that made them ripe for the plucking.

Margaret Thatcher had left the building but Thatcherism was still the rage in football's corridors of power, flotation the buzz word. Irving Scholar was its poster boy and he pioneered the Spurs' flotation in 1983. Millwall followed in 1989 and a slowly-awakening Manchester United in 1991. No less than 16 more clubs would float between 1995 and 1997. Forest were owned by 209 shareholders, who had one share apiece, and this could not be changed - and Forest could not be floated - unless 75 per cent of them agreed.

On Trentside, there was an unseemly scrum to get snouts in the trough and fans were rightly sceptical. Scholar, now Monaco-based and persona non grata at White Hart Lane, fronted the most determined group that was dubbed the Gang of Four, his cohorts being Nigel Wray, Phil Soar and Julian Markham. The joke was that 97 percent of fans were against them but the three percent in favour were the shareholders. Wooed by a slick media and flesh-pressing campaign, they voted 189-7 in favour of Scholar's Bridgford Consortium.

Wray became chairman and the plan was to float on the Alternative Investment Market with a figure of £20m targeted. Forest were bottom of the table and being managed by skipper-cum-caretaker Stuart Pearce at the time. Scholar's group swiftly appointed Dave Bassett to take over from the England full-back and signed Pierre van Hooijdonk for £4.5m from Celtic. But for the second time in five years they went down and the float raised a derisory £2m. Scholar, Wray & Co had been denied their quick killing and lost interest. Disaster loomed both on and off the field.

Against a backdrop of boardroom turmoil, Forest began the 1997-98 season in defiantly positive fashion – as they had after their previous relegation. This time they romped to the title with Van Hooijdonk bagging 34 goals and Kevin Campbell 23. Having switched divisions four times in six years, Forest were now fully paid-up members of the yo-yo brigade, a label that seemed certain to endure when the owners told Bassett there was no money for new players in the coming season. Worse still, they sold Campbell behind the manager's back before a ball was kicked. Losing his partner prompted Van Hooijdonk to go on his infamous 'strike' which meant Bassett lost his two main men. The Dutchman would eventually return but his motivation and all respect for him was gone. Ditto the owners. It would be a long, hard winter and Bassett survived only until January. He and Forest had been doomed before the season began.

If the takeover battle had elements of the Hicks-Gillett saga at Liverpool, the way the club was being mismanaged was a precursor to the Mike Ashley regime at Newcastle. No one actually called them 'the Cockney mafia' but the perception in Nottingham was that the club was being shafted by "shysters from London". Soar was a fan and in situ but Scholar was acting as director of football from the *Cote d'Azur*. Bassett had certainly been shafted before being replaced by Ron Atkinson. Big Ron was promised a £1m bonus if he could keep them up. He never came close and Forest finished bottom again. Maybe it was the mist rolling in from the Mediterranean.

Relegation finally convinced the Gang of Four that Forest were not going to be their cash cow. At least Wray, who had dubbed the Nottingham public 'hypocrites' for their reluctance to back the float, had the decency to suggest the club would be better off if it were run locally. He handed over to local businessman Eric Barnes who duly said he intended to put "the Nottingham back into the club." Well, Newark was near enough.

Barnes brought in Nigel Doughty who had been a Forest fan since he was in short trousers and had bid against the Bridgford Consortium. Born on a council estate in Newark, Doughty had been a season ticket holder even before Forest's European heyday and enjoyed a rise as unlikely and spectacular as his team's. A venture capitalist, with partner Dick Hanson he bought and sold billion-pound companies and made a fortune. Doughty appeared on the *Sunday Times* Rich List, donated to the Labour party and dined with prime ministers. Forest-daft, he would interrupt business meetings in European capitals to follow the Reds on line. But it was not a venture he committed to without guarantees and he drove a hard bargain. He agreed to invest £12 million in return for a controlling interest in the club and a say in the selection of a new manager. Asked why he came in, he said: "I did not want to see Forest decline any further, both in terms of its competitiveness and its links with the community it represents."

Doughty became the major shareholder of Nottingham Forest on May 17, 1999, the day after they had gone down. There was immense relief that an even worse fate had been avoided, but no sense that a mega-rich owner was about to magically transform its fortunes. It was before the gold rush of the next millennium and Doughty was little known and merely rich, not mega-rich. His money would come in incrementally, in carefully calibrated tranches, and he insisted he would not make signings "for PR reasons". Although he wasn't a recluse, his firm Doughty Hanson was described as "Britain's most secretive private equity firm". When he took over Forest, he said: "I don't do pictures and I try to keep a low profile." He was certainly no Caesar and the very antithesis of Fawaz Al Hasawi. And he'd also put some important noses seriously out of joint: Scholar and Markham in particular cried foul.

For all the ill-feeling generated by the previous regime, Forest were in better shape off the field than on it. When the players returned to pre-season training, Atkinson had long since returned to the sun lounger, Van Hooijdonk had been sold and Scholar had resigned. Veteran keeper Mark Crossley warned: "We could do a Man City." City had just dropped from first division to third in two seasons.

Doughty's biggest mistake was his first and it was to blight his entire reign. Cloughie once said: "An owner only has to make one good decision – and that's getting the manager right. If you do your Saturday nights in front of the telly are fabulous, get it wrong and they are totally miserable." Doughty's reign would be one of almost total misery.

Of all the managers' names bandied about – Glenn Hoddle, Roy Evans, Martin O'Neill and Brian Little among them - he opted for David Platt. A curious choice, Platt's only stint in charge had been to relegate Sampdoria without his coaching badge. Still, it was felt his Italian contacts could be to Forest's benefit. They didn't expect Baggio but for £6m they were hoping for better than Moreno Mannini, Salvatore

Matrecano and Gianluca Petrachi. Aging and injury-prone, they were nobodies in their local trattoria. Gone in three months, they would have a lasting effect on Doughty's tenure. The owner's pockets were burnt so badly he came up with a Transfer Acquisitions Committee (TAC) so such profligacy could not be repeated. It would be an albatross around the neck of every subsequent manager.

Somehow Platt survived, but with a 14th place finish and no money for new players in the summer, the City Ground was a hotbed of discontent. In August 2000, Doughty tried to explain why he was being frugal. Citing Crossley's 'Man City' Doomsday scenario, he feared Forest might do the same: "It was a probability rather than possibility," he said. "It's difficult to catch a falling stone." He had to loan the club another £6m to get by but there was no discernible improvement on or off the field. As fans demonstrated against Platt, Scholar and Markham began legal proceedings in January 2001 that, if successful, would effectively have brought bankruptcy.

But acknowledging the damage it would do, the pair withdrew their demands for repayment of Doughty's investment and sought compensation by forcing the individual directors to buy their shares instead. The case was dismissed. The judgment in favour of upholding the Doughty investment and dismissing all the litigants' claims (as well as awarding costs of up to £3 million to the club) was not just a lifesaver for Forest but a significant victory for football.

Mr Justice Hart, who passed the judgment, is not listed among Forest's heroes but without him there may be no club today. His ruling is regarded as a landmark in the history of the game and makes it into David Conn's *The Beautiful Game: Searching for the Soul of Football*. Justice Hart remarked: "The board were seen as a collection of out-of-town investors who had invested for narrow financial motives... Mr Scholar was known to be a passionate supporter of Tottenham Hotspur. Mr Markham is also a Spurs fan. Neither Mr Wray nor Mr Leslau [Nick Leslau, a former non-executive director of the club] were natural fans of the game of football. None had local Nottingham connections."

Relief at the verdict was tempered by disappointment on the field where Forest slid even further from Europe's elite – they were now embedded in mid-table. It is for delivering this new, unwanted status and for showing no affinity with the club that Platt is still vilified in Nottingham today. Mercifully after two tortuous years, his former mentor in Italy, Sven-Goran Eriksson, extracted him to be England Under 21 manager. In two years, Forest's debt had spiralled to £15m.

Desperate to rein it in, Doughty made youth team coach and former central defender Paul Hart his next manager with the brief to promote academy prospects. With losses of £100k a week, Forest put the entire squad up for sale and Hart was told to cut the wage bill a week before the start of the 2001-02 season. In December, Doughty bought another 45 percent of the club – by then he was the only show in town.

NOTTINGHAM FOREST

3

"Given football's self-destructive economics it is – to my friends, family and business colleagues – the closest unqualified declaration of insanity they will ever see."

Nigel Doughty

Einstein had his theory of insanity and now Nigel Doughty had his. On Tuesday, April 30, 2002, it was with these words that the new chairman of Nottingham Forest announced his position as official top dog instead of mere saviour, man in the shadows, bitter-sweet sugar daddy or whatever else he happened to be called. At this point, he had put in around £20m without much hope of getting any of it back. Even so he came in for a lot of stick. It appeared to confirm that here was another otherwise astute, hard-headed businessman going soft at the roar of the crowd; another member of the millionaires' club who left his business acumen in the car park when it came to football. Well, he was admitting as much himself.

For Doughty it wasn't as if he was getting any glory and there were absolutely no thanks. The club he cherished was on the downward spiral from the unprecedented highs it had so recently known. He had merely tried to stem that slide which, despite his best efforts, was in danger of careering out of control. The way the game's finances were changing he knew that he could be putting good money after bad. The previous stratosphere at which Forest had flourished was fast becoming unattainable for a club of its size. The chilling reality was that Forest, for all their European pedigree, were an awful lot closer to doing an Accrington Stanley than a Real Madrid ever again. Just three months earlier, Eric Barnes had revealed that they were £11m overdrawn with NatWest and that the club would have been insolvent if the bank had called in the guarantee. And then there was the hassle and the aggro from ungrateful fans who, for one millionth of Doughty's commitment every other week, thought *they* owned the club. And all this after the legal challenge from fellow millionaires who thought *they* did.

Looking back now, few Forest fans can bring themselves to criticise Doughty although many did during his tenure. Death can draw the sting of the fiercest of foes, quieten the loudest critics and alter the most jaundiced of perceptions. The shock at Doughty's sudden demise also led to sober reflection, not to mention sheer blind terror at what may follow. It made everyone appreciate the man rather more than they had during the most exasperating periods of his reign. Even players had sounded off at his tight grip on the purse strings. Twenty million down the Trent and a tight grip? That's football ownership for you.

Hart's first season had been a constant struggle with an even lower (16th place) finish and jewel of the academy, Jermaine Jenas, sold to Newcastle for £5m. But the new (2002-03) season saw a notable upturn with a young side grabbing the last playoff place. Only a dramatic second leg collapse at Sheffield United denied them a Wembley final and a shot at the Premier League. It was the closest they have come.

Another telltale sign of Forest's new downstairs status came when, after scrapping plans to build a new main stand "to concentrate on promotion", they flirted with an unthinkable second relegation. Hart was replaced by Joe Kinnear as Doughty worked his way through the menu with managers.

The portents were not good when on June 29 Forest announced that they couldn't pay the £4,516,584 sum owed to the City Council on the Trent End Bond. In his letter to the Nottingham City Council explaining why, Doughty referred to Forest as "this slot machine of a club". Before the 2004-05 season had kicked off, Andy Reid claimed that "playing for Forest is like playing for a club in administration".

With peanuts to spend and a capricious approach to training, Kinnear alienated fans and hierarchy alike, and once he'd committed the cardinal sin of describing a loss to Derby as "just another game", he was on his way. Gary Megson, who Clough had famously claimed "couldn't trap a bag of cement", came next and was introduced as 'the man who knew how to get out of this division'. Within four months he had delivered – taking Forest down to the third. They were the first European champions to descend to such depths. There were some bitter cup moments too. What might be called an imperfect hat-trick of knock-outs: in the League Cup, which Forest had won four times, they went down to Macclesfield; the LD Vans Trophy (!) saw a 3-2 loss to Woking and they bowed out of the FA Cup to Chester. From kings of Europe to a falling stone.

The following season promised even worse and when the Reds hovered just above the relegation zone, Megson left by mutual consent after a year in charge. Doughty just couldn't get the right man and swung like a pendulum in his choices. He went from "the future" in rookie Platt to the past in old hand Hart; from the cavalier Kinnear to the roundhead in Megson. It was a pattern that would be repeated by his successor albeit with the fast forward button pressed.

Having almost snatched an unlikely playoff spot with a late run under joint caretakers Frank Barlow and Ian McParland, Forest appointed Colin Calderwood who duly reached the top six in his first season (2006-07). But not before a few more hang-yer-head-in-shame moments along the way: there was a 2-1 win at Gillingham before just 1,817 souls. From retaining Old Big Ears, Forest were dukin' it out for the Johnstone's Paint Trophy.

After beating Yeovil 2-0 in the first leg of the playoff semifinal, Forest contrived the greatest humiliation in their history when they went down 5-2 at home in the return. Everyone at the club was stunned. But they did manage to buy their chief tormentors, Arron Davies and Chris Cohen, at the start of the following season. And they went up automatically at the third time of asking.

But with the debt now above £30 million, Doughty refused to be "held to ransom over potential signings". Having given up on developing the City Ground, Forest raised more than eyebrows in June 2007 when they announced they were considering relocating to a new stadium in Clifton, to the south of the city. Stadium plans seemed an odd priority, especially one holding 50,000. Two years on it was switched to Gamston as part of England's World Cup 2018 bid. They were clearly hoping someone else would be footing the bill.

Delighted to be away from the dead men, Doughty sanctioned something of a pre-season splurge in the hope of making Forest competitive in the higher strata. Most notable of six signings was Robert Earnshaw, a renowned goalscorer at this level, who cost £2.65m. It represented a significant departure from previous cost-cutting ways. But still Forest failed to kick on and with the prospect of becoming a yo-yo club all over again, they sacked Calderwood in December 2008. Enter Billy Davies.

The Scot was considered another expert at getting clubs out of the Championship and at least his had gone in the right direction. He'd taken Derby up and Preston to the playoffs twice, but his first task was to keep Forest in it – which he would consider his finest achievement in football. It was close but the team had played with purpose over the second half of the campaign which gave rise to discernible green shoots for the next one. In Davies's second season, bolstered by £5m's worth of new additions, Forest appeared genuine contenders for promotion. Second in the table in January, Davies asked, not unreasonably, for two more players to maintain the push – his squad was thin and injuries were taking their toll. The request fell on deaf ears.

Forest limped into third place and it would prove a costly misjudgment. The fans once again didn't quite know what to make of the owner – occasionally generous in the summer, mostly niggardly in the winter – and Forest ended up being beaten by sixth-place Blackpool in the playoff semifinal. After the defeat, Doughty was quoted as saying: "I guess we saw £90m go astray in 90 minutes." For Davies and many fans, it went astray in January.

The tall, urbane chairman and fiery pocket battleship of a manager were not natural bedfellows: more like cautiously benevolent owner and not entirely appreciative shop steward. Davies, in true Glasgow tradition, does not suffer fools and although he did not think Doughty was one, he certainly believed the TAC was an especially brainless idea. Having to consult with Doughty, Arthur, chief scout Keith Burt, finance director John Pelling and football consultant David Pleat before a move could be made drove him to well-documented distraction. Davies was relieved he didn't have to run it by the groundsman. This was, after all, a man who, to quote a former colleague, "wants to manage the world

XI, and yesterday." Clear the air talks were held so often Forest could have used a fumigator. Forest fan and *Guardian* football correspondent Daniel Taylor wrote: "They all need their heads knocking together."

Despite the narrow miss Doughty kept his wallet firmly shut in the summer of 2009. And a sixth-place finish saw them back in the playoffs where they met Brendan Rodgers' Swansea. With just Cardiff or Reading to beat from the other semi-final, there was a feeling this really could be the Reds' year. But the playoff jinx struck again and, for the fourth time, Forest were denied a place in the final.

Many fans felt that the Scot had not had the backing he deserved since that initial summer window. He had turned Forest around from sinking shop to vibrant force but the truth was that long before the denouement, he was a dead man walking. Davies, whom Doughty had described as "probably the best manager at this level in the game," had not helped himself with his unrealistic demands for "stellar signings" and it is known on good authority that he would have been sacked even if Forest had been promoted.

In another pendulum swing, Doughty replaced Davies with Steve McClaren – for whom it would be another hospital pass. No sooner had he settled in than "the parameters changed," as he would euphemistically put it – Doughty suddenly realising that the impending FFP rules would have teeth. Like Platt, Kinnear and Megson, McClaren seemed the wrong fit for Forest in the first place. His signings – Andy Reid's return excepted – were uninspiring, results were poor and then came the debacles against Burnley and Birmingham. It is a widely held belief that he would have resigned after the second game even if they'd won. That really was where Doughty's interest effectively ended. It was a sad business even before the tragedy that followed, but illustrated just how difficult it can be to own a football club that you love.

On the face of it, he was the ideal benefactor: rich, knowledgeable, a genuine fan of long-standing, with the club's best interests at heart and a local to boot. He did not just tick all the boxes he attached impressive appendices. But over 12 tumultuous and, let's face it, mainly frustrating years and failed managers, it hadn't worked. He had saved the club, undoubtedly, but that long out of the limelight could only be deemed a failure. He had tried hard, switched managers and gone for youth, but had to sell the latter before the crop matured. As he had once said: "We are trying to push the boat out, but in a gentle fashion."

It was neither one thing nor the other. He pushed at the wrong times and too gently when a shove was needed. And he didn't have much luck. It was, as he had said, insanity. After resigning, his continued patronage could no longer be taken for granted. Mark Arthur warned: "When you are putting in that sort of money and getting the abuse he has received, it must make you think about it [quitting]." It did.

Next in charge was Steve Cotterill who had impressed on the other side of the river when taking Notts County to the League Two title in 2010. Since then he'd been at Portsmouth where he was to write a whole new syllabus in crisis management. After that, Forest must have seemed like a breeze – he had merely a relegation battle, no money and a disillusioned owner, but at least he knew who the owner was. Just over three months later, however, he couldn't be sure about that: events were to take a tragic turn.

With Doughty's death on February 4, 2012, the future of the club was once again in jeopardy. But in a remarkably heart-warming gesture less than three weeks later, Doughty's family decided they would not leave the club in the lurch. Arthur stated: "We are very pleased to announce that the club will have the financial support of Nigel Doughty's estate through to next season while we are seeking a new owner. This will enable management and players to focus completely on the task of retaining our place in the Championship for the 2012-13 season." Cotterill still had to wheel and deal, and his football was not always appreciated, but in extremely fraught circumstances he did well to steer Forest to safety. No one knew at the time just how crucial staying up would turn out to be.

NOTTINGHAM FOREST

4

"Owning Forest is like having a classic sports car sitting on bricks, rather than a sensible saloon with a full service history (say, Stoke). A romantic choice."

Alison Kervin, The Times.

New seasons come more quickly for the unprepared. Delays in funding can leave a club with barely 11 players for the kick-off. Contracts cannot be signed, shirts cannot be printed, season tickets cannot be sold. Three weeks into the summer of 2012, it looked as if no one at Forest had ever joined the Boy Scouts. There had been rumours of a possible buyer for the club but nothing to rustle those nettles on the banks of the Trent. They were still relying on the support of Nigel Doughty's estate but the start of the coming campaign was edging closer. "I don't think Michael and Helena would have let Forest go to the wall," said one insider of Doughty's adult son and daughter. "They're big fans." If that was reassuring, it needed to be. As Paul Taylor wrote in the *Nottingham Evening Post* on May 24, 2012, "With every day that ticks by now, the chances of staying clear of League One again in the future become slimmer and slimmer. With only one senior defender currently under contract it could, in fact, quickly become an impossible task. Particularly being as that player, Chris Gunter, is arguably their most saleable asset."

Forest were still without a new owner, a shirt sponsor and much hope. The harsh truth was that apart from their history, there was not a lot to sell. They didn't even own the ground, half of which was in need of an upgrade anyway. A fire sale of players looked inevitable. Then in mid-June a press conference was called... to announce a shirt sponsor. Local auctioneers, John Pye & Sons, had stepped in but that could have been taken the wrong way: "Give me a pound, two pounds, the gentleman on my right..." Forest would not be flogged off in such a manner but it was the firm's CEO, Adam Pye, who let the moggie out of the rucksack: the club, he claimed, might be in for "an exciting future". It was enough to spark a social media frenzy which was ratcheted up further by news from Kuwait, of all places. A teenage girl there had been spotted wearing a Forest shirt. The girl's father happened to be one of the richest men in the country and had just resigned from the Kuwait champions. Then came the announcement on July 10: the Al Hasawis, one of Kuwait's richest families, were buying Forest.

They introduced themselves at a City Ground press conference on July 14, 2012. With Abdulaziz Al Hasawi in the chair, it was handled smoothly in both English, in which he was almost flawless, and Arabic. He came over well: ambitious, but realistic. Asked if they were going to do 'a Manchester City', he answered: "We'd like to be but we're in a different league. We do have ambitions, we do have hopes, but we will start and some day, yes, we will probably play with Manchester City or Manchester United."

The question 'why Forest?' was inevitably put. The answer was: "We are here because we felt that the club, with its rich history in this wonderful city, was an ideal place for us to use our years of footballing experience and passion for the English game. This club is one of the best in the world, and we intend on working hard to improve its global standing. We know that for most football clubs, success does not happen overnight. That's why we are here for the long haul. It is important to remember that running a football club is a marathon, not a sprint." Again he stressed patience although none was shown to Cotterill who was removed with immediate effect.

On the question of money, Abdulaziz said: "It's not all about money, it's more about passion isn't it? Football is really in our blood, we've been following football since we've been very young. My brother Fawaz has been involved in football for almost 15 years so he has a big input in this. Certainly this isn't easy, we fully understand what's up ahead and we accept the challenges."

Few outside of Kuwait had heard of them. They were not in oil but refrigeration, air-conditioning, hotels and real estate – and they were well-connected – to the Kuwaiti royal family no less. A story emerged that this diverse empire had blossomed from a humble fridge repair shop opened in 1962 but that's denied by Mohamad Said, deputy sports editor of Kuwait's *Al Qabas* newspaper. What he told me was far more romantic if you don't mind going back a bit.

Back to 1866, in fact, when Forest, founded the previous year, played their first ever game – against Notts County. It was also when the ancestors of the club's current owners embarked upon an adventure of their own. They began the trek from the oasis region in the east of Saudi Arabia, to the northern shores of the Persian Gulf and what we now know as Kuwait. "They were Bedouins," according to Said, "and several generations moved between 1866 and 1892. They were called Al Hasawi as they had come from Al Hasa. The family fortune was made by the father of Fawaz and Abdulaziz, Mubarak Abdulaziz Al Hasawi, who was born in Kuwait in 1925. He started work at the port as a welfare officer for seamen but in 1956, went to Alexandria in Egypt where he bought and sold real estate. He became a member of the Kuwait parliament and died in 2005."

What of Fawaz himself? I ask. "He was not a great student as his mind was always occupied with football, especially local champions Al Qadsia. His mother wouldn't let him play football unless he had a university education so he was sent to the American University in London to study business and marketing. When he finished his studies he returned to Kuwait to work in insurance and shipping. He soon established his own company and got into real estate and hotels as well as the other family business of air-conditioning and heating. Besides their manufacturing empire, they are involved in retail and own real estate across the Middle East. His wife Sheikha Asmaa Al Saba is a member of the royal family." Fridge magnates indeed!

"They are not fly-by nights," assured David Lloyd, a senior consultant at London-based trade body the Middle East Association. He was not alluding to the Al Hasawis' nomadic heritage. "I would have thought they would come with considerable funding," he added. But why Forest? According to Simon Chadwick, professor of sport business strategy and marketing at Coventry University: "It makes a great deal of sense for an investor to buy into a club of Forest's stature. There is some equity in the brand amongst fans and potential fans that dates back to their successes in the late '70s and early '80s. This brand equity can offer things to customers and investors that other organisations can't."

Given the club's plight, it seemed that Old Big 'Ead was still working his magic. Without the success he had forged, Forest's "brand" would hardly have merited a second glance. But because of it, an otherwise unattractive asset was eagerly snapped up by wealthy foreigners. Thanks to Cloughie, 33 years after they first won the European Cup and almost eight since his death, Forest still had 'stature'.

Said told me: "Fawaz first got into sport through his beloved Al Qadsia, one of the famous clubs in the Gulf. He became president and under him, they dominated, winning five trophies. He was the main financial provider for football and other sports, buying players out of his own pocket. But other members of the club treated him like a [cash] cow. They just expected him to pay, pay, pay and didn't thank him for or appreciate his efforts. That's why he left. He was very angry and there was a lot of in-fighting, so eventually he resigned and said he wanted to buy a club in Europe."

According to Said, Forest were not his first choice. He said: "He looked at many clubs and Leeds, another big one, was who he first wanted, but because of the big debts he turned away from them and went for Forest instead. Forest didn't have much debt." I ask how rich are the Hasawis and if he expected them to spend big? "Fawaz is a very big [sic] millionaire but not a billionaire. The family are billionaires. His dream is to get into the Premier League. I advise supporters to be patient. An interview I did with him in November 2013 and published in *Al Qabbas* was entitled, 'You cannot return Nottingham Forest to their original position in one night.' "

Are Forest lucky to have him? I ask. "Yes, of course. There are not many big millionaires interested in buying a second division club." But Said warned that the Al Qadsia experience was not an ideal apprenticeship for English football. "At the beginning, I thought they would not do well because they are like amateurs compared to the professionals of the English league. And some of the people advising him know as much about football as you and I do of the Chinese language."

But on that midsummer Saturday, the first impression was overwhelmingly favourable. They said all the right things, used most of the right cliches and had even decided to retain Frank Clark as an ambassador as well as Mark Arthur as CEO. The only quibble was over the manager. All but Cotterill's harshest critics thought his treatment unfair, but few worried if this might be the shape of things to come. They promised an "iconic" manager but hot favourite Mick McCarthy would not have been on many lists either. Still, it was not enough to spoil their weekend. When McCarthy turned the job down, fans did wonder why – even those who were relieved. But no one knew it would set a trend. Expectation mounted as to who would be the eventual choice. Glen Hoddle was the new favourite with Harry Redknapp and Duncan Ferguson also mentioned. Then they appointed... Sean O'Driscoll of Crawley Town.

They couldn't have done more to bring us back to earth if they'd arrived in an aging Vauxhall Corsa, dined in the local chippie and put up at a B&B. But then it was revealed the players had lobbied for him. O'Driscoll had been at Forest at the back end of the previous season under Cotterill and had impressed hugely with his coaching. He was a disciple of the passing game – his Doncaster sides were pleasing on the eye – and he knew all about this division. Well, at least the owners were listening. Signings were made, 11 in all. A skeletal squad needed bodies and these players, although their names "didn't roll off the tongue" in Kuwait City, to borrow a notable phrase, they were generally sensible additions. Most notable were Henri Lansbury for a giveaway £1m from Arsenal and Adlene Guedioura, an Algerian midfielder who had become a fan favourite during his loan spell from Wolves.

The season started slowly but encouragement came with a fine win over title favourites Cardiff. But then Forest drew too many games they might have won. As for the promised Kuwaiti influx, goalkeeper Khaled Al Rashidi arrived but was made to wait for his work permit. As autumn turned into winter, Forest weren't yet promotion contenders but then the owners had talked about a "three-to-five-year plan" and "a marathon not a sprint". At that point, no one was too concerned.

In December, however, the first alarm bells rang. The last thing expected at a newly enriched club was for the players' wages to be late. A glitch with the BACS system, apparently. Then it was agents and suppliers who had not been paid. This news emerged after Forest's credit card had "bounced" during the trip to Brighton. The number had been read out wrongly over the phone. Apparently. It all added up to some red faces at the City Ground and the first furrowed brows among fans. Chairman Omar was removed "for personal reasons" and Fawaz was to be more hands on. Omar, who had been running the club at the time, was paying way over the odds to get players in quickly. They couldn't wait to sign on the dotted line. The Hasawis looked at the deals again and realised what they'd done. Then they decided they couldn't wait three years – but had to get promoted that season.

O'Driscoll was informed of the change of gear the day before the Watford match on the 22nd which Forest lost 2-0. Four days later, in the big Boxing Day clash with Leeds, the manager appeared to have got the message. Forest turned on the style in front of the cameras, winning 4-2 and closing to within a point of the play-off places. Adding to fans' bewilderment over the finances, two giant screens costing £1m were unveiled. But that was nothing to the news they woke up to the next morning.

So much for patience, so much for the marathon, so much for O'Driscoll deserving a chance: within hours of overseeing the team's best performance of the season, the Forest manager was sacked. The news was greeted with disbelief in Nottingham and the wider football world. A quick poll in the *Daily Telegraph* revealed 81 per cent of respondents were against it. The decision had been taken on Christmas Day and the owners had to be persuaded not to announce it then. Fawaz told the club's official website: "The timing of our decision may look a little odd after the win over Leeds but sometimes you need to make changes with the long term future in mind. Sometimes those changes need to be made from a position of strength rather than weakness and that is what we are trying to do. We are looking to bring in an ambitious manager with Premier League experience." It did nothing to stem the tidal wave in the tabloids and social media. "Madness", "crazy", "crackpot" and comparison with the Venky's were common reactions. And it would get worse.

NOTTINGHAM FOREST

5

"Billy will be with us like Ferguson is with Manchester United."
Forest chairman Fawaz Al Hasawi, March 2013.

By now, we had seen a sea change in ownership style from Doughty. Alex McLeish was swiftly installed to become Forest's third manager of the season – Doughty had given even the duds a year in the job – but none were 'iconic' and neither Cotterill nor O'Driscoll deserved to go. Yes, McLeish 'knew' the Premier League but one fortuitous League Cup win apart, he knew its downside. Forest fans were well aware of the Scot's inglorious failures at Birmingham and Aston Villa, where neither was ever mistaken for Barcelona. However you looked at the decision, it made little sense – there was more compensation to pay and Forest had become one of the prime exhibits in the xenophobia-laced debate about foreign owners not knowing their well-upholstered arses from their predatory elbows. Fawaz claimed: "With the January transfer window approaching, we feel it's the right time to make a change."

When the window opened, Fawaz would barely tap on the pane yet still managed to trap his fingers. There were hopes that he had lined up some big names but only Stephen McLaughlin from Derry City (for a small fee) and Darius Henderson (on a free from Millwall) came in. But if it was eerily quiet in terms of player recruitment, the opposite was true off the field: on January 17 a veritable Night of The Long Knives saw the axing of three senior executives including the esteemed European Cup winner, former manager and chairman, Frank Clark. Long serving CEO Mark Arthur and scouting director Keith Burt were also out.

'Marthur', as fans dubbed the CEO, was little lamented but sacking the head of recruitment halfway through the transfer window? As for Clark... No reason has ever been given for any of them. After a dismal month with one win in six games that included a dire FA Cup defeat at home to Oldham, Forest attempted to sign George Boyd, who had been on loan two seasons earlier, from Peterboro. But on the last day of the window, in a now-infamous incident that really did take Fawaz to the verge of Venky territory, it was announced that Boyd had failed an eyesight test and the club had pulled out of the deal. Peterboro chairman Darragh McAnthony was predictably incandescent: "Total disgrace, the whole thing," he tweeted. "I'm devastated for George. I got a phone call off him in bits." He added: "George agreed terms with Forest and went there for a medical. He said that he passed the medical then they made him do an eye test. He's played 300 games and scored from the halfway line the other month, but Forest say he has an eyesight problem. The whole thing stinks."

The problem, it was widely assumed, was not Boyd's eyesight but Fawaz's cold feet about McLeish as manager - and how to ease him out. Judging by how quickly a replacement came in, the owner had developed frostbite prior to Boyd's alleged visual impairment. The Scot held his fire. Up next were Birmingham and, showing admirable bottle, he was not going to shirk a return to St Andrews. He duly copped plenty of Black Country stick and yet another defeat. A few days later he came to an agreement with Fawaz and left – after 41 days. McLeish cited "a difference of understanding of the development strategy" as the reason for his premature departure from the City Ground. Big Eck, whom the *Post* called "a top bloke", was simply the wrong choice and deserved more respect from the owner. As did his two predecessors. According to the *BBC*'s Pat Murphy, Forest were now "a shambles". It had taken only six months.

The papers were never going to overlook this particular gift horse. "Venky's 2.0: With McLeish gone, Forest's farcical owners are rivalling Rovers for managerial madness," was the *Daily Mail* headline, while *The Guardian*'s Barry Glendenning wrote: "... Al Hasawi and his co-owners have pulled off the spectacular feat of making Venky's at Blackeye Rovers look better organised than an OCD-sufferer's desk tidy."

Such things had never happened under Doughty. The Newark man had often got it badly wrong when it came to managers, but would never have considered "anyone from Richard III's skeleton to Cookie Monster from Sesame Street," as Glendenning suggested Fawaz might. Forest were never made fun of, never compared to the game's basket cases. But in the winter of 2013, they were. Another defeat – this time in true karmic fashion to Bristol City managed by Sean O'Driscoll – and we wondered how Fawaz was going to get out of this. Just who would want to come and manage the club now? We should not have underestimated him – he had perhaps the only man outside of Fergie, Mourinho and Pep Guardiola who could have quieted the unrest. He brought back Billy Davies.

The Scot had not had a job since his brusque dismissal in 2011. He'd held talks with Blackpool two days earlier but Fawaz moved swiftly and Davies could not resist the chance to return to Nottingham. Fawaz, delighted and relieved to get his man, was glowing in his appraisal of Davies's managerial abilities. He told the club's website: "Billy has unfinished business with the Reds and we know how hungry he is for success. In returning to the City Ground we believe his leadership will help us fulfil our ambition of making it to the Premier League."

Fawaz used the phrase first but Davies would claim copyright. He said: "As my new friend Fawaz says, I have 'unfinished business' here at Forest and I am relishing this great opportunity to return Forest to its former glory. My tenure at the City Ground was cut short last time and I can't wait to get my boots back on and training the lads. We have a great squad and I know I can get the best from them. Coming home to the Reds is a dream-come-true."

It was a move Doughty would never have made but it was populist and won over most fans at a stroke. And even the doubters would soon be convinced – Davies had not lost his touch and inspired a winning run that took Forest back into the promotion race. The Scot had made his customary instant impact and, for a few weeks, Fawaz must have thought he'd pulled off a masterstroke.

But then came an international break and Fawaz, perhaps now feeling he could finally flaunt his wealth, took Davies and his No.2 Ned Kelly to Kuwait along with a *BBC East Midlands Today* team to record the trip. What we saw took the breath away. An Arabian palace with all the trimmings as well as life-sized murals of England winning the World Cup in 1966 – two years before Fawaz was born! A fleet of fabulous cars!

A family fluent in English and Forest lore. Fawaz's wife and mother of three, Asmah, even told presenter Natalie Jackson: "Forest are like our fourth child."

After the financial glitches, many thought this blatant display of opulence would put paid to worries about the size of the family piggy bank. But there were plenty who thought it over-the-top. Had a PR company written the script? Had the painters been in to daub Bobby Moore and Geoff Hurst on the living room walls? If you're that rich, you don't need to flaunt it, do you? From the footage we saw, Davies didn't look entirely sure what to make of it himself. He should have been delighted. Fawaz said: "Billy will be with us like Ferguson is with Manchester United. I mean that. I would like him to stay with us. When I bought Nottingham Forest it wasn't like this. But now I am a really big, big fan of Nottingham Forest. I want to stay for a long time, not for one or two years. For me it is a hobby more than a business. I like the challenge and I want to put Nottingham Forest in the Premier League. I don't care about the business in football because I have other businesses. If I am a dictator I would not bring Billy Davies into my club because he doesn't like people to interfere in his job; he is a strong manager. I have known Billy Davies for two months, maybe less, but it feels like I have known him longer. The relationship is very good."

It was an unlikely double act: one was from the mean streets of Glasgow, the other from a rich family in the Gulf, but they did share an ambition. And Fawaz's was not confined to securing domestic glory. Asked if he wanted the side to be crowned European champions for a third time, he said: "Why not? We were there before and we can do it again. Maybe one day I will put a third star on the shirt for Nottingham Forest." Even that didn't seem impossible as viewers were whisked through the visual splendour of Fawaz's gaff. Little did we know that reality would make such a swift and devastating comeback.

The break had come at the wrong time for Forest whose runaway form was suddenly reined in. Momentum was lost and the next three games were drawn. Then the following two were lost, including a 3-0 hammering by Cardiff. Key players were getting crocked. They would have to beat Leicester at home in the last match and hope for favours elsewhere. A pulsating game ended agonisingly with an injury time goal seeing the Foxes through 3-2. Forest had missed out on sixth place by a single point. It made you wonder what difference it would have made had the international break not occurred when it did.

Frustration was palpable – especially when it was their local rivals who had nicked the last ticket to paradise – but by the summer there was optimism anew as several judicious, albeit not 'stellar', signings strengthened the squad. The exception was the most expensive - Algerian Djamel Abdoun for £2.5m and £30k a week from Olympiakos. A flashy winger who had played in the Champions League, he was assumed to be 'the chairman's signing' as he was way over budget and bypassed all of Davies's traditional boxes. It was also a sign that despite Fawaz's claims to the contrary, he *was* interfering and would do so again. And not even a "strong" manager like Davies could stop him. By then Davies, who had brought in his cousin, Jim Price, to oversee affairs off the field, knew he was on to a good thing.

Yet again among the favourites for promotion, Forest began the new season well and in October sat fourth in the table, having won six of their first 11 league games. Optimism abounded and Price tweeted: "I think Fawaz will be known as the man who saved the club. Billy will be the man who took nffc back into Europe." It was enough for Fawaz to offer Davies a new four-year contract. He told the club's official website: "This is a fantastic day for Nottingham Forest. Billy and I have the same long-term vision for the club and I am absolutely delighted that he has agreed to sign an extension to his contract."

For the second time he had wrought a remarkable transformation to Forest's playing fortunes and, as long as they were winning, fans and chairman would stay with him. And Davies did know how to fix a team. Andy Reid was in no doubt: "Billy Davies is absolutely fantastic. His tactics are second to none. We go into matches knowing exactly what we're up against and how we're going to beat it."

But Davies and Price were giving Forest, once many fans' second favourite club, a bad name. Barred from practising as a lawyer in Glasgow, Price could not be appointed CEO as he belonged to that rare species that might actually fail the 'fit & proper' persons test. He saw his primary role to protect Davies and did so with a vigilance not seen since

Rosa Kleb took care of Blofeld. Davies did need protecting as he could, to bend Fergie's phrase, beat Dennis Wise to the punch in an empty room. Except that no room was ever empty – Davies carried so much baggage. He was not above challenging photographers to show their credentials on the touchline or banning fully-accredited reporters from the press box. And when he did speak to the media, the best they could get from him was: "It is what it is." Referees also copped it and he was given two five-game bans that season. It all led to the CEO of a rival dubbing Forest: "The Midlands' answer to North Korea." As *The Guardian* put it: "Clough said he could walk on the Trent, Davies seems intent on polluting it."

NOTTINGHAM FOREST

6

"It's about pay back. Vengeance is best served cold. Trust me the innocent will not be harmed."

A tweet from Billy Davies.

Almost 13 months on from 'The Night of the Long Knives' came 'The Valentine's Day Massacre' – and this time 'the blood' was not on Fawaz's hands. The culling of four senior staff on February 14, 2014, was all down to Davies and Price who were in charge in the owner's absence. Fans were once again wondering just what was going on. Four more head honchos – with a combined service of almost 60 years and massive expertise in all aspects of the football club – were axed. They were financial director John Pelling, academy director Nick Marshall, press officer Fraser Nicholson and operations manager Brandon Furse. Even the most casual observer had to query what was behind such carnage. Few were aware that what Davies had meant by "unfinished business" was not just winning promotion, it was gaining revenge. More precisely, getting back at anyone associated with the Doughty regime who, in his view, had been party to his sacking. And if there were doubts, there was the celebrated tweet, purporting to be from Davies but possibly written by Price: "It's about pay back. Vengeance is best served cold. Trust me the innocent will not be harmed."

Although not a suspect in this matter, Fawaz had not impressed fans by his transfer dealings. He'd promised that on-loan defender Jack Hobbs would be at Forest for the season only to have him recalled by Hull in January. And then came what can only be described as another vanity purchase. Anxious to give Forest a wider appeal in the Arab world, he had brought in Rafik Djebbour, another Algerian from Olympiakos, initially on loan but eventually for a €1.5m permanent deal. A striker, known as "The Terrorist", with just one goal in seven games he turned out more of a pacifist. Davies was not happy about it, especially when denied his own "stellar signings", but was only three months into that new contract after all. Still, the Reds were in the playoff mix and thrashed a pre-pubescent West Ham 5-0 in the FA Cup. Then, wracked by injuries, they went on another run, as they tended to do under the Scot, only this time without winning.

An eight-game winless streak culminated in a 5-0 annihilation at Derby, of all places. Given that single-goal defeats in this fixture had ended the reigns of managers of both clubs, not even Davies could survive this. Coupled with the off-the-field shenanigans, he simply had to go and most Forest fans accepted the fact – some more than others, it has to be said. A failure to even acknowledge the Reds' faithful at Derby after they'd endured a wretched afternoon did not endear him to anyone. Nor did ducking the post-match press conference. As Ned Kelly fought valiantly to hold off a braying media pack, Davies and Price were already heading for East Midlands Airport for the flight to Glasgow. They wouldn't be coming back.

Fawaz did the inevitable on the Monday and so ended his latest attempt at a managerial dynasty. It was just over a year since the Kuwait trip, when Davies was anointed as the new Fergie, and only weeks since the *Daily Telegraph* had claimed Forest were "thriving under a siege mentality". Now the same newspaper had already switched to saying Davies "was destined for failure after a year of drama, fallouts and media blackouts". It had happened quickly, it always does. Davies looked a beaten man at the end. In mitigation, he had suffered an injury crisis rarely seen in peacetime. As February turned to March, as many as 14 players were crocked. But the surrender at Derby was abject and unforgivable.

Despite the false dawn of Davies's tenure, Fawaz had once again made the wrong choice – the Scot might have taken them up without the injuries but the damage to the club's reputation would take some repairing. Fawaz had been smitten: Davies was his fourth boss in seven months and this time the owner thought he'd found 'the one'. Only he got it wrong big-style. He had given Davies and Price the keys to his kingdom and they ran it as their own personal fiefdom. Another example had been Davies's press conference *before* the Leicester game at the end of the previous season, a game which could have seen Forest in the playoffs. Had they made it, there would have been no comments from the manager on the genuine prospect of a return to the top flight after 15 years. Not even an 'it is what it is' because he didn't know what it would be.

But 'innocents' *had* been harmed and after the two inexplicable culls of top dogs – the first was pre-Davies – kids were left doing senior management jobs. Another negative aspect of Davies's reign was how little time he spent in Nottingham. As he had in his previous stint, he'd been put up in a flat in nearby Riverside, convenient for both City Ground and training ground, but was a rare presence. He would not be seen on a Monday and would catch the 8am flight from Glasgow on Tuesday with Ned Kelly picking him up at East Midlands on his way from Birmingham. He would go to training but by 4pm he was on the flight back. Then he would fly back south on Thursday and stay till after the game. For someone whose attention to detail was forensic in other aspects, this hands-off approach may well have sown the first seeds of doubt in the players. He was there so little he made Joe Kinnear look like the Sheriff of Nottingham. At least with the ex-Crazy Gang member, there was humour; with Davies, he would crack a joke on the team bus and look around to see who laughed. If you didn't, you were in trouble.

After pulling the plug on Davies, Fawaz finally acknowledged that he needed a little local guidance and appointed Forest's two-time European Cup-winning captain John McGovern as ambassador. As a player, he had been one of those unsung heroes that did the simple things managers and teammates appreciate more than fans. I asked him what his role entailed and he replied: "My role has no definite description, so I literally go to support whoever needs help. Similar to my role as a player." It was a void that had been crying out to be filled since the Al Hasawis had taken over. Unfortunately, though, McGovern couldn't prevent the next managerial snafu.

As was his recent custom, the owner had a replacement in mind for Davies. Neil Warnock was "the chosen one" this time and although that didn't please all the fans, there was logic to it at least in the short term. Forest were still within a shout – although admittedly a distant one – of the playoffs and Warnock, who had a Marmite reputation but was a fine motivator, said he could get them there. And it was not idle bombast – he had got seven teams promoted in his time. But confusion over loan signing Lee Peltier, whom the Yorkshireman wanted, and a sixth sense about interference led to him declining the opportunity. Warnock wrote in his *Independent* column that "the situation with Lee's transfer showed Forest need a chief executive type who knows the English game to run the club day to day". He expressed similar sentiments on Nottingham local radio stating: "There was nobody at the club English-wise that knew about football." He insisted that he had no problem with Fawaz, adding: "This guy's put a lot of money into Forest and they (the fans) like him, they think he's a good chairman and I haven't got a problem with that." But he did suggest that some managerial decisions might be difficult under Forest's structure. Fans did not need the Enigma machine to figure out what he meant.

But then came the knockback that no one was expecting – from Stuart Pearce. Just as Fawaz had turned to Davies in times of trouble, he again went for the populist option. And this time it was a different kind of 'unfinished business' that got in the way. Pearce said he was not ready because of family matters and media commitments. It didn't sound like the 'Psycho' fans had once idolised. They'd expected him to jump at the chance with the same unbridled zeal he'd shown in the tackle during 12 unhesitating years as a player. But when Forest asked him a second time a week later, he changed his mind. Pearce said: "This club probably has more of a pull than any club in the country... By the time I've finished with management if ever I felt I had the opportunity to become manager here and turned it down, then I would not be fulfilled."

Relieved to get a 'yes', Fawaz put academy head Gary Brazil in charge of the first team and Forest limped to an 11th place finish. In fact, they practically ended the season on crutches. No less than 13 players were unavailable on the final day through injury, illness and suspension with three more – Djebbour, Abdoun and Kevin Gomis – out of contention because, according to Brazil, "they lacked the right attitude". Forest were so concerned about the crocks they launched an investigation but it really was down to dastardly luck.

Once again, fans wondered what might have been. Had they not suffered so many injuries; and had Psycho or Warnock taken over straightaway, they might just – with the new manager bounce – have made the playoffs. But there was an important lesson from this episode – Warnock had highlighted the fact that no one in the back office had a clue what was going on. Sixty years of experience and expertise had been lost in one night. Which was why, besides the perennial desire for a 20-goals-a-season striker, a left-back and a defensive midfielder, there was another position fans desperately wanted filling. Such had been the scale of ineptitude and embarrassment off the field that the fans were crying out for... a chief executive.

NOTTINGHAM FOREST

7

"No disrespect to Derby. But I have to say I could never work for that club in any capacity. And I mean never. People might say I'm being ridiculous but that's just the way it is. Even if I was desperate and they were the only club around, I couldn't do it. I'd rather go on the dole and take my chances."

Stuart Pearce in 2005.

The selective amnesia of football fans is never more evident than when a favourite son returns to the fold. Forgotten can be damning mediocrity elsewhere as nothing is allowed to sully the memory of his marauding pomp in home colours. A textbook example was the blind refusal of many among the Forest faithful to consider the post-playing career of Stuart Pearce. Those who did warned it could end in tears, but their voices were drowned by the din from the geed-up majority. Before his failures at Manchester City and the FA there had been a dozen refulgent years in the Garibaldi. He had played for Forest like no one else has played before or since. He wasn't just hard – he tackled as if he'd been quarried. And when he'd done defending, he would embark on a cavalry charge, thunder thighs pumping, elbows driving like demented pistons. Opposing defences would part like the Red Sea before he'd deposit an artillery shell into the top corner. Cavalry? Artillery? He was a one-man army, he was Psycho.

Not even the rarity of top players becoming top managers could quell the optimism surrounding his return to the City Ground. Pearce was an all-time Forest great through his own manic efforts to make the most of an ordinary talent. The assumption was therefore that once back in his spiritual home, he would be able to extract similar quantities of blood from subordinate stones. All Reds' fans could remember were the sheer guts and application that turned the former part-timer at Wealdstone, who had once advertised his day-job in the Forest programme, into a living legend. The ex-sparky, who had fixed Cloughie's kettle, had rewired the whole City Ground.

At 2.58 on August 9, 2014, that ground crackled once again. The sun shone, the teams were on the pitch, an almost full-house expectant. But there was more in the air than optimism about a new season: there was an unmistakable sense that this could be the dawn of a new era with a glance back to a previous one. Forgotten was the hesitancy of his acceptance three months earlier; forgotten also was the snafu over transfers five days earlier: all was now well with the Forest world as, clad in sharp blue suit and red and white club tie, he strode purposefully through the tunnel. The moment he emerged the roar could be heard for miles. This was welcoming back the club's favourite player of all time and the din did not subside until the referee's whistle signalled 3pm. Psycho was back. Or so everyone thought. With a wave to all corners of his old stomping ground, he acknowledged his faithful and took his seat in the dugout. The thought occurred that sacking him would be like beheading Bambi.

But ever since he'd taken up the official reins at Forest on July 1, he'd stressed that he wasn't Psycho any longer. He made the message clear to players, media and fans alike: the suit should have told us. But there were other non-sartorial signs that the old image had indeed been shed. Besides the hesitancy in taking the job would 'Psycho' have stood for the chairman flogging two of his best young players behind his back days before the season kicked off?

After doing quiet but astute business in the previous weeks, Forest had suddenly sold goalkeeper Karl Darlow and centre-back Jamaal Lascelles to Newcastle for a combined fee of £6.5m. The double blow was softened somewhat by having the pair loaned back for the season with their wages paid by the Premier League club. Still, the fee was not considered enough by most fans, while the willingness to sell did not stack up against the summer long strengthening of the squad. Was there a sudden shortage of cash? Or, more worryingly, did it suggest a lack of ambition? Fans were perplexed and angry. In terms of undermining a new manager, it couldn't get much worse. The *Daily Mail* said the club was "descending into chaos".

The manager said he was "disappointed" but added: "I don't know the financial constraints the club are working under. I plan to find that out, very soon. Then perhaps I can understand this decision." Fawaz put out a statement on the club's website making his position clear. "The manager and I openly discussed the proposed sale of Karl and Jamaal and he was aware of the negotiations throughout. The business side of football is changing and the requirement to increase revenue means, unfortunately, difficult decisions have to be made." We need not have worried how they were going to reconcile the irreconcilable as Pearce would soon explain: "I saw him (the chairman) before the game and we had a little kiss and a cuddle. So that was fine." No political spin doctor could have put it up better. But it didn't sound like Psycho.

What placated Pearce and the fans was that Forest spent the money the next day. In a move every bit as positive as the Darlow-Lascelles deal had seemed fire-sale negative, they bought Britt Assombalonga for £5.5m from Peterboro and Mikhail Antonio (£1m plus) from Sheffield Wednesday. Assombalonga, especially, was a big gamble for a Championship club but with the dual purchase, Forest had added hugely to their firepower. It was only made possible by accepting Mike Ashley's shilling.

The truth was that Pearce and Fawaz needed each other. A Psycho walkout before a ball was kicked would have been the kiss of death for the Al Hasawis as a credible regime. After O'Driscoll and McLeish, Boyd's eye test and unpaid bills, rejections from McCarthy and Warnock, it would have taken them deep into crackpot territory. According to the tabloids and certain Trickie trolls, they had already strayed into it several times. It would also have looked bad for Pearce even though he'd have had the sympathy vote. He would have gained kudos for principle, but for a manager trying to re-establish himself a false start would have been the last thing he needed. But still there was the feeling that it was perhaps only because it was Forest that he stayed.

Having skippered Cloughie's second best Forest side, he was familiar with the club's exalted status. But in 2014, 17 long and humbling years since he'd left, he was all too aware of how far they had fallen. Recalling his introductory speech after accepting the manager's job, he said: "I hate the 'sleeping giant' tag. I went and addressed all the players and staff in May and told them to forget that. Why do Forest have any more right to promotion than another club?"

It struck some as overdoing it. Players not born when Forest bestrode Europe surely needed a history lesson while to the fans Forest *were* a sleeping giant that desperately needed reawakening. It is the nature of supporters to believe the all-time peak is the default setting of their club no matter how fleeting the stay on the dizzy heights may have been. But Forest did scale the ultimate summit and stayed there for a while – it was why they had attracted the Kuwaiti cash after all: as we have heard, their "brand" still had value. To Generation Y players, however, for whom football was created by the Premier League, Forest may not have seemed a giant of any kind – sleeping or comatose – but merely a modest, second-tier provincial outfit. To them, even with the trophies, bust, statue and stand to remind them of who once stalked these corridors, calling Forest a giant was akin to looking at a 1950 atlas and thinking Britain should still be calling the shots because a quarter of the world was coloured in pink. Or was it? Fawaz had said: "My dream is for us to be back in the Champions League. It's important that everyone has a dream and that is mine." Billy Davies had talked of "returning to former glory" and even Steve McClaren had "sniffed the history". Could Pearce have lowered expectations too much?

That sunny first Saturday they were still pretty high. Forest won 2-0 with two of the new signings scoring. They would stay unbeaten for 11 games. It was a scarcely believable start to the campaign for Pearce with his big-money buys looking like bargains. They did not taste defeat until October but they had ridden their luck and were not totally convincing. Pearce was tinkering too much, players were played out of position and Assombalonga was feeding on scraps. Off the field, Fawaz had finally appointed a CEO – Paul Faulkner formerly of Aston Villa – while Pearce, as a diplomat, was being lauded for repairing the damage of the previous regime. What could possibly go wrong?

Injuries, of course. Two of their best players (Cohen and Reid) were crocked for the rest of the season and a third (Hobbs) for a big chunk of it. Form faltered and Forest were losing touch with the top places. Doubts grew and sights were readjusted from possible automatic promotion to a playoff place. But no one envisaged they would go nine games without a win. Or 19 games with just two victories.

By December there was a sense that the early season form had flattered *and* deceived. Leaks had emerged from within the club that the players were not happy with the manager; that he couldn't motivate them and was tactically clueless. But he was nurturing the academy, which had been almost forgotten under Davies, and even persuaded clubs to loan players again after Forest had been refused because of late payments. Despite the miserable run, the bulk of the fans were still very much with him but wished he would stop saying things like, "I'm still learning". He was 52 – nine months older than Jose Mourinho.

The manager was not helped when the long anticipated transfer embargo was imposed, ruling out January additions that were badly needed. There were dire defeats at home, and even an FA Cup KO at Rochdale. With each sickening loss, more fans were sadly admitting it was not working and it was a surprise in some quarters that an owner with Fawaz's track record did not act. Had Pearce not been who he was, the consensus was that he wouldn't have lasted this long. Then came high-flying Derby away. The spectre of that 5-0 defeat of the previous season loomed and it was hard to see how the injury-ravaged Reds could avoid another hiding. And if they didn't, Pearce, like Davies before him, would surely pay the price. Trickies had never travelled to the hated 'sheep' feeling more like lambs heading for the slaughter. But against all odds, Forest did the business and when the net burst for Ben Osborn's injury-time winner so did the manager and much of Nottingham. For Pearce it was Euro 96 all over again: the same contorted face and demented celebrations. They couldn't sack him now, could they? For a manic moment, Psycho was back.

NOTTINGHAM FOREST

8

"This is Fawaz's train set and he won't let anyone else play, which is the troubling thing."

Forest fan and journalist Nick Miller.

Fawaz couldn't and he didn't, but two miserable defeats later and he had no choice. In the end, it was almost merciful as it wasn't 'Bambi' any more: Stuart Pearce was definitely no longer Psycho. He'd been telling us all along but we wouldn't listen. The punk rocker had merely tinkled the ivories and couldn't find a tune. His fate was sealed by a dismal home loss to League One-bound Millwall, and it says everything that most fans felt he had to go. They still loved him as a player but reluctantly accepted that he wasn't much of a manager.

An exasperated Faulkner followed in protest – partly about Pearce but mainly about not being allowed to do his job. Failure to consult him on Pearce's sacking – which he opposed – was the final straw for a man who could never get past the two Gamorrean guards, Kuwaitis Lalou Tifrit and Hassan Saef, who looked after Fawaz's interests. The *Guardian's* Nick Miller, a lifelong Forest fan and then a freelance, noted: "I was saying to someone before the [recent] Fulham game that I'd be amazed if Paul Faulkner lasted the season. This is Fawaz's train set and he won't let anyone else play, which is the troubling thing."

Losing two leading lights inside 24 hours dragged Forest back to familiar territory under the Al Hasawis – and the sense of crisis was fanned by an inevitable Twitter outcry. Asked if he would ever step down as chairman, Fawaz appeared pretty fed up himself, responding: "I'll soon from everything." Whatever was missing from that sentence sparked another frenzy of speculation. Like Doughty, he was thin-skinned and did not take kindly to abuse from the twitterati. He even threatened to sue and his friend Emad Alqahtani, told the *Daily Express*:

"We now have all the accounts that did swear to [sic] him and abused him for a week all captured and ready to take legal action. It's hard to know what goes on his mind these days but trust me on this one. The guy is so damn upset from the abuse he got from many."

Fawaz's frustration was understandable even if many problems were of his own making – and he didn't have to be on twitter. His next manager would be his sixth in less than three years. The club was under embargo and he was being assailed by head honchos and hooligans alike. He had not kept up the transfer instalments to Peterboro for Assombalonga and his car was damaged at Derby. Peterboro chairman Darragh MacAnthony said a missing payment had prevented his club from signing players. In a series of tweets, he noted: "This same club did this to us in August & now again. Truthfully its [sic] a disgrace & their chairman is the same. It has put us last minute in a terrible predicament. Its also a shambles the Football League allow this nonsense to carry on & not for the first time. I'm also sure we are not only club who its happened to but the knock on effect is outrageous." Other clubs, agents and suppliers were also understood to have been made to wait for their money.

But Fawaz had another manager in place – and for such an impatient man, it was a surprisingly sensible, low-key appointment. Dougie Freedman had also played for Forest but not like Psycho. He was a decent striker at the end of the nineties but a safe distance short of a legend. As a manager, he'd worked quiet wonders at Palace and striven manfully in even worse circumstances at Bolton. For the mess Forest were in he looked the ideal fit. No fuss, no outrageous promises and he never used the word "stellar". Even so, hired initially until the end of the season, he got off to a Daviesesque start. An unbeaten run of six games silenced the critics, took Forest to ninth place and even raised fleeting hopes of a playoff push – until reality set in. Making it even more praiseworthy was that Freedman had been hit by the cruellest injury crisis yet and a full transfer embargo. In only the manager's second game in charge, Assombalonga caught his studs in the City Ground turf and let out a howl heard in the stands: a broken knee-cap meant he was out for 14 months. The knee-capping of the club would last even longer – for two more transfer windows.

Forest hobbled to a 14th place finish, taking only two points from their final eight games. With Matty Fryatt also missing, their lack of firepower was brutally exposed. They were heavily reliant on Michail Antonio and some wondered if Freedman was the right man after all. But under him Forest were a lot more organised and Fawaz rewarded him with a two-year contract.

The summer of 2015 was Forest's second window under embargo and when Freedman was at his wheeling and dealing best. Restricted to freebies and loanees to whom he could pay no more than £10k a week, he bolstered the squad and cut the wage bill. He even managed to offload Fawaz's own follies, Abdoun and Djebbour, while Matt Mills, Jamie Ward, Daniel Pinillos and Nelson Oliveira, the last loaned from Benfica, were value additions. But, with Fryatt, Assombalonga, Cohen and Reid still missing, the merest fantasy about promotion disappeared with the sale of Antonio to West Ham for £7m on the last day of the window. Still in a financial headlock, Forest had little choice.

There was still enough quality to ensure against anything terrible happening, but Forest began the season in lacklustre fashion and were desperately short up front. They relied as much on Oliveira for goals as they had on Antonio, but there weren't as many. The autumn release of *I Believe in Miracles* only served to highlight how far the club had fallen from the heady European Cup days the film celebrated. And the casualties kept mounting: Pinillos ruptured his cruciate to end his season in December. Eerily like the previous campaign with the manager's job on the line, the highlight was another unexpected win over Derby. Freedman made Forest harder to beat and, with Cohen finally back but no sign of Fryatt, Reid or Assombalonga, they went on a 13-game unbeaten run and, in Bojan Jokic, even found a like for like loan replacement for Pinillos in the January window.

But still powder-puff up front, Forest were unable to turn draws into wins and Freedman was seen as a better talent scout than tactician. The football was dull and the crowds dwindled. The atmosphere? A subdued grumble. Overall, though, he was doing a solid job and said: "There has not been a strategy in place since the chairman has been here and we need to have one. I think I like to put things in place over the longer term." It was a fatal mistake – 'longer term' doesn't exist under Fawaz and, in another act of impetuosity that was depressingly familiar, Freedman was sacked on March 13th. And the managerial cycle would start all over again – or so we thought.

It was premature on two counts: Freedman deserved the chance to operate without an embargo, which was expected to be lifted in the summer, and Forest were not completely safe from the drop. And this time there was no replacement in the wings. The owner asked coach Paul Williams, with the assistance of Reid, to take over till the end of the season. They survived but four years since the takeover, Forest finished only three places higher than where Cotterill had left them.

In this second half of Forest's 150th anniversary season, Fawaz had not been able to get anything right – not even the anniversary. When it was announced that tables at the dinner were priced at a staggering £2,400, the European Cup-winning legends threatened a boycott. To Forest's acute embarrassment, the scandal even made the nationals and they had to lower the prices. The dinner went ahead but Fawaz didn't make it – flight delay from Kuwait, apparently.

It was one calamity after another and across a broad spectrum – some of them cringeworthy, all avoidable. Where Cloughie once claimed Wembley was the club's second home, Forest's new *pied-a-terre* in the capital was the High Court. Yet another unpaid tax bill saw yet another winding up order from HMRC – the fifth under this regime. Wages were also late, the delay put down to a public holiday in Kuwait. That excuse had been used before, too. They still owed Derby £90,000 for tickets for the game at the Ipro – the second consecutive season that 'the sheep' had a justifiable bleat. Normal practice is to settle such matters within a week. Perhaps it was because Forest had spent more than £450,000 on agents' fees in the four months between October 1, 2015 and February 1, 2016 – the fourth highest in the division and quite an achievement when under embargo.

Soon after he let Williams run the team, Fawaz was accused of picking it by *The Sun* who claimed the caretaker had threatened to quit in protest. Both owner and coach went into denial mode but it was known that Fawaz often grilled his managers on team selection. The paper's "sources" also revealed that staff members were being pressed to divulge the starting XI hours before kick-off.

All this led to European Cup winners Kenny Burns and Garry Birtles despairing of their former club in their columns in the *Nottingham Post*. Burns said "it should never have come to this", while Birtles felt Forest alternated between "shambles" and "turmoil". Warnock's words about "no one knowing the rules" came to mind over paperwork cock-ups involving loanees Ben Hamer and Kyle Ebecilio. The former had to go back to Leicester before dirtying his gloves – depriving Forest of a sound back-up keeper. But the latter would have more serious implications. Ebecilio had already been loaned back to Holland but a failure to read the small print prevented Freedman from bringing in a desperately-needed and already teed-up striker in January, 2016. That failure may even have led to him losing his job. Other clubs, including Venky's-owned Blackburn and Massimo Cellino-owned Leeds, managed to negotiate their release from embargo much earlier while QPR have seemingly dodged the sword of Damocles. But with no CEO, no one knowing the rules and Fawaz not there half the time, there was a sense that no one was batting on Forest's behalf.

So, four years since the owners breezed in full of optimism, the club were just three places higher and the biggest casualties of FFP; six managers had been sacked and, according to the accounts released for the 2014-15 season, a total of £67m had been spent. At least that is how much the Al Hasawis had put into the club in interest-free loans. Even if failing to make it to the Premier League's TV rights feast isn't mentioned, it is a record of staggering incompetence. No one doubts Fawaz's "passion" – but there's plenty of that in 'A' Block and no one there is trying to run the club. He seems a slow learner, repeats the same mistake and whatever passed for a 3-5 year plan, appears to have been written on the back of an envelope long since posted to nowhere. A theory which gained traction with each excruciating cock-up is that Fawaz is not the sharpest knife in the drawer and Forest were, it is alleged, bought as a toy to keep him amused. It is claimed that elder brother Abdulaziz, who presided so impressively over their unveiling, is the real brains of the family. The worry has always been what happens when his kid brother throws his favourite toy out of the pram.

Towards the end of the 2015-16 season, there were signs he might be getting rid of the pram. In May, Fawaz said: "I mentioned before that if the right people came and they wanted to pay the right money, something might be possible. I am still involved. Maybe in the future there will be some investment. But I want to be part of this; I want to be part of Forest. I do not want to leave Forest until the right time. I hope that we win promotion and I am the chairman."

But when the identity of the prospective buyer was revealed, frying pans and Dante's inferno immediately sprang to mind. No one has ever looked less 'fit and proper' than Greek shipping magnate and Olympiakos owner, Evangelos Marinakis. With a girth as wide as the Aegean Sea and a charge sheet that might have been penned by Homer, a quick Google search explained the delay. Olympiakos had won the Greek league six times in a row, the last one by a 28-point margin. Credit for that, however, is sullied somewhat by Marinakis's ban from any football activity. It was imposed when he was arrested in 2015 after a 173-page report by the public prosecutor alleged that he was "directing a criminal organisation" with the aim of achieving "absolute control of Greek football's fate by the methods of blackmailing and fraud". He was also accused of trying to change the outcome of a game by bribery, and arranging an explosion. That incident was believed to relate to an alleged bombing of an uncooperative referee's bakery business. No one was hurt but that morning's buns were on the burnt side.

An odyssey indeed but Marinakis has denied any wrongdoing. In a previous trial, he was acquitted of match-fixing and entering a referee's locker room at half-time to threaten him. But that case may be reopened after one of the three judges who let him off was found to be under investigation over his dealings with Emilios Kotsonis, a close Marinakis associate and former fellow director at Olympiakos FC.

If there's a smidgeon of truth in the allegations it would be consistent with the luck the Hasawis have experienced at Forest. They've been cursed by injuries, in particular, and suffered more than any club in the country from FFP. That was partly because they were advised it wouldn't happen and when it did, they had no one to fight their case. But the payment issues show both an ignorance of the culture and an unwillingness to change. Indeed, persistent defaulting over petty amounts raises questions about basic competence as well as judgment. When season tickets were late, it was allegedly because the printers were still owed and when the phones were on the blink, the suspicion was that bill hadn't been paid either. Fawaz did not seem to know how to run a football club and on the evidence of four exasperating years, he's none the wiser now.

Worst of all, though, was his treatment of senior staff, especially managers, as if they were undesirables on Big Brother. But even that dreaded cycle had stalled: by the time Euro 2016 got under way, 90 days after Freedman's sacking and three weeks before pre-season training was due to start, there was still no sign of a replacement. One by one, the candidates went elsewhere, mostly to rival Championship clubs: Villa, Derby, Leeds, Blackburn and Rotherham all announced new appointments. Gus Poyet had been keen but never got a proper answer from Forest and went to Real Betis instead. Martin O'Neill stayed with the Republic of Ireland, Nigel Clough with Burton Albion, Oscar Garcia with Rapid Vienna. Nottingham-born and bred Nigel Pearson was not pursued and went to the other end of Brian Clough Way. All had sniffed sizable rodents. When the waiting reached 100 days, you felt Godot himself would have been pinning up the team sheet before a manager was appointed.

So it was a shock when, three and a half months after Freedman's sacking, that Philippe Montanier was announced. There were inevitable cries of 'Philippe Who?' as few Forest fans had heard of him – or at least before they started to Google every available coach in Europe. And even though he might have been 17th choice and a late replacement at that, the 51-year-old Frenchman's CV was actually half-decent. He'd guided Boulogne to promotion to Ligue Un in his first year, taken Real Sociedad into the Champions League and also had success at Rennes. He was to be head coach following the appointment of Pedro Perreira as director of football. With the arrival of Apostolos Vellios for €1m from Iraklis and an impressive unveiling where Montanier spoke reasonable English, it suddenly seemed that after months of drift, things were falling into place. And the assumption was that the would-be owner was behind it. Victor Sanchez had been earmarked for the Reds' hot seat but Marinakis quickly diverted him to Olympiakos when his own boss resigned. It was shaping up like a continental structure but fans weren't fussed – any structure would be better than the ramshackle Cardboard City of recent years – and 'Philippe Who' wasn't such a bad appointment. There was even a spike in season ticket sales. But still there was no actual news of the takeover happening.

That was because the Football League were, quite understandably, stalling. Anxious to avoid a repeat of the embarrassing nutmeg that Cellino had pulled on them at Leeds, they were waiting for the Greek judicial process to take its course. After all, Forest's prospective new owner was accused of being the ringleader of systematic fixing – not just the odd dodgy offside. So the club's big, fat Greek wedding, which had been "imminent" for months, was shrouded in doubt. UEFA also announced they were looking into Marinakis and in September it was reported that Forest had finally distanced themselves from him and were talking to an American consortium instead. It had reached the point where almost anybody would do.

Forest had come close to kicking off the 2016-17 season in an empty ground. The local council refused to give the club a safety certificate for the City Ground because they did not have a safety officer. The previous occupant of that role was shifted in a restructuring exercise so the cert couldn't be issued until a replacement was named. A CEO can be given the responsibility but the club didn't have one of those either, of course. So the 30,500 capacity was reduced to a big, fat zero. It was almost a case of 'Come back Marthur, all is forgiven'.

This had been a landmark year for Forest with its 150th anniversary, but it was also when it officially became a laughing stock. After a slightly reduced capacity for the opening game, the problem was sorted, but there was still time for another piece of business that *'Dumb and Dumber'* would have rejected as too fanciful. It was the sale of Oliver Burke, the jewel of the academy, the best thing to happen to Forest in a decade, a youngster of such quality that a top-flight team could be built around him. He'd played only a handful of first team games but every top club in Europe had a scout watching him and at 19 he was already a Scottish international. He was one of the hottest properties in Europe. Even if claims he was the new Gareth Bale were a little over-egged, to let him go at all was criminal. To let him go with no sell-on clause was a decision that surely called for the men in white coats. At the very least, Burke's value was likely to increase between £5 and £10m a year, possibly much more, yet Forest had not asked for any slice of that in the deal with RB Leipizig. And it wasn't as if the German club didn't have the money – they were owned by Red Bull. Burke's sale could have funded players to take Forest up, an upgrade to 'A' status for the academy and even got HMRC off their backs for a few years. Talk of gift-horses, you had to seriously question the marbles of whoever sanctioned such a deal.

But then that was followed by yet another winding up petition from HMRC for non-payment – the sixth under the Al Hasawis. Forest said they were "disappointed" the matter had gone to court again as all debts had been paid – with the Burke money presumably. For the fans, "disappointment" didn't do it – the fall from European royalty to defaulting, zero capacity 'North Korean' pariahs had been hard to take and, like many when it comes to tragedy, they really didn't know their Greek from their Shakespearean.

To sum up, the first four years of the Al Hasawis had been the flipside of the Doughty era with its six decades of experience in the back office and when managers were given time – although in some cases, too much. Fawaz had backed Davies and Pearce initially but his enthusiasm was as unpredictable as the weather. Sometimes he was so hands-on he wanted to pick the team, yet he could be distant enough to allow Davies and Price to practically declare home rule. In short, he has been more cheerleader than chairman. You might say: "Nothing becomes him in his life at Forest like his attempt at leaving it." Would it have been better with the devil they didn't know? As one Forest supporter told me: "Being run by an alleged crook has got to be better than being run by a proven idiot." Fawaz had arrived because of the European Cup: it's still weighing Forest down.

Notts County

NOTTS COUNTY

1

Just what are Munto doing in a book about foreign owners? You may well ask. For a few torrid months in 2009, the owners of Notts County were not foreign at all – they just pretended to be. Or more accurately, a trio of Englishmen pretended there was a foreign Mr Big behind them. Coming amid the fool's gold rush of mystery takeovers from abroad, the shotgun marriage between the Magpies and Munto screams for inclusion. A year after Sheikh Mansour showed just how to transform a club at Manchester City, and before the Venky's at Blackburn and various at Portsmouth showed how not to, the fascination that filthy-rich foreigners had for British football clubs was at its height. As was the belief among fans that such people would be their saviours. The Munto Months – for that's all it lasted – the Qadbak Catastrophe or the Trillion Dollar Con (as Panorama called it), provides a crash course in how the sweetest of dreams can turn into a living nightmare. All the familiar ingredients are here from bucket rattlers to non-existent billionaires; Middle Eastern promise of Premier League football and fabulous riches, a fit and proper farce and an unpaid milk bill that led to a £7 million debt. The Notts County takeover ticked all the boxes and more. There was North Korea, the Serious Fraud Office, Sven and Sol and a try for Becks. Encapsulating all the hope, greed and despair of early 21ˢᵗ century football ownership, it was a parable of the times.

**

"The first few weeks were like a fairytale. Notts County were on everyone's lips and I was thinking I could end my career here."

Sven-Goran Eriksson.

No more than a hefty clearance north east of Notts County's home ground, livestock had been bought and sold on Saturday lunchtimes from 1886 until 1993. In farming circles, Meadow Lane was as well-known for its cattle market as its football and when downwind, as home fixtures often seemed to be, the crowd would be assailed by a pungent aroma. But never in more than 100 years had it approached the foul stench left by Munto Finance after a few acrid months in 2009.

The Augean Stables that Ray Trew stumbled into when he bought the club for £1 in February 2010 took more than the breath away. The Lincoln businessman might have been tempted to divert the nearby Trent to sluice Meadow Lane – such was the mess he found there. "We expected it to be bad, but probably not this bad," said Trew's chief executive, Jim Rodwell. "The club was living beyond its means," he added. "We all know you can live like a king on credit for six months but after that you hit problems."

Perhaps their predecessors had tried too literally to convince the Football League that the Bahrain royal family was behind them – for someone really had been living like a king. Trew told *Panorama* that close to £200,000 had been paid out of the club in cash apparently to a "fake prince". There were two payments made to the 'prince's' girlfriend, and $90,000 went on food and five-star hotels in Bahrain.

There was also a bill of £40,000 for chauffeur services, believed to be for driving Sven around. By the time Trew's staff had completed the fumigation process, the debt came to £6.9 million but they still had to hold their noses around the players on huge salaries. Top earner was Kasper Schmeichel on £1m a year for five years, which amounted to a third of the club's annual revenue.

But even more urgent than offloading the goalkeeper was a winding-up petition issued by Her Majesty's Revenue and Customs. Munto had neglected to pay a tax bill of more than £600,000 and only a one-off payment of £321,000 and the promise of a further £50,000 a month for the next year averted the threat. Administration still loomed but drastic economies by Trew's new regime managed to avoid that too. Bizarrely, in spite of all this, the club won promotion.

When Munto's big beasts Russell King and father and son Peter and Nathan Willett disappeared, they left their front man holding the battered baby. Believing there was still a pulse in what he called 'the project', chairman and chief executive, Peter Trembling, bought the club for £1. For two months he stumped up the players' wages out of his own pocket. When I asked if it were true that it cost him £500,000, he replied: "£499,994." I felt his pain. He had previously admitted to coming close to a nervous breakdown before selling to Trew – at least he got his £1 back. Chauffeur-driven Sven had also been taken for more than a ride. In the end, the Swede did the honorable thing and waived his last two months' salary. Notts made him life president. But it was the broken dreams and the sense the club had been well and truly had that was the real legacy of their erstwhile owners. It had been wham, bam and not even a note on the fridge door. A classic con but with several bewildering twists.

Vandalising an institution as venerable as the world's oldest league club felt like the mugging of a grand old lady – for they were well aware of who they were dealing with. "A wonderful strapline which we can market to football's global audience," was how Trembling had referred to it. Almost 150 years of history had come to this – a catchy phrase that might have been dreamt up over lunch in a trendy wine bar. Founder members of the Football League. Albert Iremonger. Tommy Lawton. Jimmy Sirrel. Tony Hateley. Jeff Astle. Don Masson. Les Bradd. All legends in Magpie lore. But now they amounted to no more than a slithery morsel of marketing jargon.

Notts County should be protected by Unesco. Pioneers of the planet's biggest sport, they're in the Columbus/Armstrong/Hillary and Tensing league – and have stayed the course. They were playing this game when Palmerston was dispatching gunboats and the Confederacy held the upper hand in the American Civil War. It was a generation before many of today's football giants were born, before Newton Heath was a twinkle, before anybody. They donated shirts to a fledgling Juventus and, a century later in a different football universe, missed being founder members of the Premier League by a season. But in 2009 they were down to their last few quid and fell victims to conmen. Not any old con, mind, but one that *Panorama* claimed stretched to eight time zones and 13 digits.

Between the few and the trillion is quite a tale. The cash discrepancy reflected the gulf in aspirations between the wide-eyed fans and their wide-boy 'saviours'. The fans were told that Premier League football was possible; for the conmen the goal was to get rich, of course, albeit at a rather curious pace. Notts County were a mere vehicle. How they came to meet could only have happened in these days of Tinder dating between football and greed. But even now, seven yo-yo years later, there is a mystery to it. Notts only just survived, no one has been brought to justice and we still ask why? Why Notts? Why a football club? And why one 87th among 92 in the pyramid?

If the years have brought no answers to these ever-pertinent questions, there has been no shortage of blame heaped upon the victims: the club, the supporters trust that ran it, the fans, Sven, Trembling and the Football League in particular all copped it. The wise-after-the-event brigade is still staggered by the apparent gullibility of the above. Such a conclusion is easy to reach with hindsight but fails to take into account just how elaborate, complex and convincing was the scam. Scratch the surface and the hoodwinked are not the suckers they appeared. Many had doubts and made discreet background checks. But the perpetrators always passed muster. There was a £5 million bank guarantee from First London Bank, approval from lawyers and assurances from Rothschilds and Deloittes; these were more than nods and winks.

The end of the 2008/09 season was Notts' lowest ebb – and there had been a few. In 1965 and 1987, they had had the last rites. Then at the turn of the millennium they'd been in administration and, even after the tireless efforts of fund-raisers, were saved only by the generosity of a lifelong fan who had wanted to remain anonymous. Businessman Haydn Green bought the lease of the ground from the Council and a substantial amount of shares in the new club. The club was then run by him, the trust and two other businessmen. No one shareholder had a majority. It was only later, when Green gave his shares to the trust that they ran the club. But Notts County were anything but an advert for the fan ownership model.

In-fighting drove Green to distraction. Steve Thompson, who had been Notts County FC chairman for two years and then became a director of both club and trust, remembers: "It was absolute civil war at one point. Haydn became a very bitter man. He got really ill, became stressed and had these rages on the phone to me about the club. I am absolutely convinced that this contributed to his death."

Green died of a heart attack in March 2007. He had just turned 60 and Notts County had lost their guardian angel. He had given his shares to the trust who became the majority shareholders in the club but the organisation continued to flounder. Says Thompson: "By 2009, it was apparent that we only had a few thousand pounds in the bank. It was pretty obvious the club was going to go bust." Then the so-called 'cavalry' appeared.

The first approach came from Trembling towards the end of the 2008-09 season. Club chairman John Armstrong-Holmes recalls: "Vice Chairman Roy Parker and I met with him once the season had ended. Trembling told us of his Middle Eastern colleagues and their interest in taking control of the club. It was a whirlwind two weeks culminating in Roy Parker and I flying out to Bahrain (at our own expense) to meet with Trembling and his colleagues. Our discussions mainly involved Trembling, Nathan Willett (whose father once worked for the Al Hani family) and a royal. *Panorama* featured the alleged royal involved but it wasn't the person we met. The connection with Al Hani also gave credibility. The visual presentation we were given during these discussions was VERY impressive too."

Didn't it sound too good to be true? I asked. "On the one hand, yes, on the other, no," he replied. "Over an intense three days we discussed matters in great detail. They were completely believable and everything was very plausible. The fact that Trembling lived locally, and had brought about the meeting was initially comforting. The bank guarantee was the deciding factor though. I was sceptical from the outset. But Munto's law firm confirmed their bona fides and then there was the Football League's take on the deal. It all pointed to being very genuine. In my opinion, under the trust the club would struggle forever. The club needed real investment." Once convinced, the chairman pushed for acceptance, uttering the fateful words: "We are talking about more money than this club has ever seen."

Thompson acknowledged: "It did sound like an unbelievable opportunity," but still urged caution: "I just wanted it [the takeover] to slow down and to do some investigations. Although the club recommended it, I voted against but was one of very few [55] who did [out of 869]. There was nothing known about them [Munto Finance]. I am always deeply suspicious when people don't show their face. It didn't make any sense. I remember ringing the *Nottingham Evening Post* and saying: 'I don't believe this is true' and being told to back off because they'd done the checks and said 'this is it'."

Trust secretary John Collin was similarly circumspect. 'Was it manna from heaven?' I asked him. "It looked that way," he said. "I did have doubts but was hoping against hope that I was wrong – like a few others. Over 93% voted in favour of Munto. On the face of it, it looked good. There was nothing you could put your finger on to say it was a sham. The most vocal opponents were those who felt you had to run a football club in the same sort of way as the Soviet Union. They didn't want football with money: they wanted it untainted and pure with no money."

What they got was more like Russia under Boris Yeltsin. On June 4, a deal was struck between Munto and the Magpies' shareholders, and Armstrong-Holmes said: "I firmly believe this is a momentous day for all those involved with Notts County." On June 30, the supporters trust approved, giving its majority stake to Munto and on July 14, the company completed the takeover with Trembling the new executive chairman. Suddenly the club was awash with money; it was out with the old, in with the new and no one could accuse the new regime of failing to hit the ground running. A week after taking over, Sven-Goran Eriksson was presented to the media.

The Swede had also needed convincing. For a man of his pedigree – Benfica, Sampdoria, Lazio, England, Mexico, Man City and more – the move smacked of the fallen prizefighter scuffling in the fairground booth. His star had waned after he'd been harshly sacked by Thaksin Shinawatra at City. He takes up the story in a coffee shop near his apartment in Guangzhou, southern China. It was during his first stint as coach in the Chinese Super League and he was more than happy to talk, especially about Nottingham to a Nottinghamian. I asked him how on earth he'd got involved. He smiled: "I had no job and was contacted by my agent at that time, Athole Still, who told me it was Notts County and I said 'no'. But he insisted, saying 'come and listen to these people'. Anyhow, he convinced me so I went [to the Dorchester hotel in London] and they presented a fantastic idea. Two English gentlemen – well, they were not gentlemen! [he laughs] – suggested that I take care of all the football side [as director of football] and do it exactly how I wanted to do it. From the bottom of League Two taking them to the Premier League in five years, that was the plan. So I signed a five-year contract with them. I was thinking it was like a dream that I could build a football club. Not my club but I could do it how I wanted. It was fantastic, to do all the things I'd dreamed about. And then, wham. Gone. It was very disappointing."

Eriksson's agent had checked out the Munto men through Deloitte Touche who confirmed the company's bank guarantee. Sven himself did his own due diligence by speaking to Sir David Richards, one of his former bosses at the FA, and was assured all was in order. So he embarked upon this chapter of his football odyssey in an upscale apartment on the leafy fringes of Nottingham. "It was a lovely place by the river, not far from the ground. Nottingham has lots of restaurants – I liked it very much and was driven around in a Volvo. There was some money as salaries were paid in the beginning. The first few weeks were like a fairytale. Notts County were on everyone's lips and I was thinking I could end my career here." 'At Notts County?' I blurted out. "Yes. I knew the fan base was not big enough and that Forest were a much bigger club. When I was there Forest had more fans, a better stadium and training ground. Everything was better. But the project at Notts County was to rebuild everything. The idea was to be bigger than Forest." Did you think that was possible? He did not blink: "With all the money they said they had, yes."

Even among the sceptics that was the dream. I asked Collin: 'Did you really sense that at long last Notts could become the city's premier club?' He said: "Yes, that was the hope among Notts supporters – we saw ourselves overtaking Forest [who were struggling at the time] and being *the* team again. Crowds went up. It created a lot of interest in Nottingham. When your team's doing well, all is well with the world." But Doubting Thompson was not so sure: "Even when Notts were in the old Division 1 the average gate was 11,000," he reminded me. "They were just not going to get big gates – the city is not big enough – and Forest are a well followed club. If you look at Notts, the history, the fan base and the money needed to get them into the Premier League, well, I wondered about it. If you've got the money, you can get out of League

Two. You need another £3m to get out of League One but to get out of the Championship, you're talking at least £25m. They would have to at least double what they were spending on players. But when Sven arrived, I was told they had hundreds of millions. There were so many high-level, right-thinking people sucked in by them. Money blinds you but I still had nagging doubts. All this talk about Sven's 'historic challenge', 'the oldest club' and 'very private people'… did they exist?"

NOTTS COUNTY

2

"Football is driven by financial investment (Man City/Chelsea) and so in the knowledge that Notts had £50m to invest I thought it a very solid opportunity."

Former Notts County CEO Peter Trembling.

No one was better placed to verify the existence of these 'private people' than Trembling who once said: "I had lunch with one of them recently and he was one of the nicest people I've ever met." But he did not divulge his identity. Lunch – or even coffee – was something that eluded Trembling and I in both London and Nottingham during August 2015 before he finally agreed to an e-mail exchange. I asked how he got involved. "[Nathan] Willett called me and asked me to come in as exec chairman/CEO," he explained. 'Were you, like Sven, attracted by the uniqueness of the challenge?' "Not really. It was the fact (or perhaps not) that they had a lot of money to spend on a famous old club and to restore it to its previous glories."

Trembling, a Derby County fan, had been in football as commercial director at Everton and when asked if he thought it a tall order, answered: "No. Football is driven by financial investment (Man City/Chelsea) and so in the knowledge that Notts had £50m to invest I thought it a very solid opportunity." I asked: 'Apart from your friendship with Nathan Willett, what was it that convinced you this was the real deal?' He replied: "My friendship with Willett acted as the introduction and nothing else. What convinced me was the public endorsement (*Daily Telegraph*) of their credibility from Meryck Cox the CEO of Rothschilds, the support from the likes of Tim Yeo, MP, the Bahraini royal family and SGE [Sven-Goran Eriksson]."

It was a persuasive line-up. And you could throw in other names too. Eminent investment banker Sergei Popov, ex MD of Russia and

Oil and Gas, and Air Chief Marshal Sir John Walker, former head of British Intelligence, were a couple more to conjure with. Both were on the advisory board of First London whose bank guarantee should have been enough to show the finances were in place. Also mentioned were a former Prime Minister of Pakistan, Moeen Qureshi, who had once been Vice-President of the World Bank, and Shakir Ullah Durrani, ex Governor of the Central Bank of Pakistan. Both were distinguished names; neither had any involvement whatsoever. Looking back, it's as if names were being plucked out of Wikipedia but at the time, and with endorsements from Rothschilds and Deloittes, it could hardly have looked more kosher.

On the football side there was the ex-England manager and *scudetto* winner, Eriksson. Like Armstrong-Holmes and Trembling, Collin and Thompson were swayed by the Swede's involvement. Collin said: "When they got Sven and Sol Campbell, you thought this must be the real deal." Ditto Thompson: "When Sven came in, Goodness me, I put my hands up and said 'OK, I got that wrong. But despite this I always felt there was something wrong with the deal."

Once the trust had ceded control, Munto, who were also in the throes of buying the BMW Sauber F1 team, were smartly off the grid. Eriksson brought along his perpetual sidekick, Tord Grip, and former Coventry and West Brom striker Lee Hughes arrived in a move that had already been in the pipeline. Hughes would score a hat-trick on his debut – a 5-0 win over Bradford. Midfielders Ben Davies and Johnnie Jackson also joined. Eriksson soon made his presence felt by going back to Manchester City to recruit Kasper Schmeichel for £1.4m. It looks a bargain now but it was easily a record fee for a League Two club – and certainly a record salary. These were heady days. The new season was barely under way, Notts were flying and everything looked possible – well, everything but the next signing.

Keen to maintain momentum, Eriksson said: "I felt we needed another spark." So, with that inimitable, quiet persuasion of his, he convinced Sol Campbell to join. "He was 34 and without a club, but I felt he had more left in him and he was the big name needed to give us a boost," said the Swede. The capture of the 73-cap England veteran and Arsenal Invincible looked a masterstroke. It was both an impressive statement that the owners were serious and a sign that good old Sven had not lost his touch. Campbell agreed a five-year, £10m contract which was some deal for a player three weeks short of his 35th birthday and a staggering coup for a League Two club. It would, however, turn out to be no more than a marriage made in Mammon.

In fact, it was barely consummated. Campbell had not had a proper pre-season since he'd left Portsmouth and was nowhere near match-fit. Then he complained about the training facilities where he was supposed to work himself into shape. As that was taking longer than expected, doubts grew about how he would cope among the hoi polloi of the lower leagues. He did not make his debut until September 19 at Morecambe. Still carrying a couple of layers of rust, Campbell was given the run-around by journeymen clearly relishing the task. Notts lost 2-1 before a crowd of 3,335. Already wondering what he'd let himself in for, this bitter taste of League Two football appeared to make up his mind. On the Monday, he asked to be excused training because of a sore hamstring; on the Tuesday he trudged off mid-session – for good.

Notts agreed to release him from his £40,000 a week contract and it went down as a big mistake by both parties. It was a bold try by the club but suggested they were trying to sprint before they could crawl. For Campbell it was simply not as it had looked in the brochure. "I was being a mug," he admitted, "for believing the promises." He told the *News of the World*: "I knew I would be the club's first big signing but was told I would be the first of many. Names like Roberto Carlos and Benjani were mentioned. But nothing materialised. The only thing I'm guilty of is taking people at their word. So I'm not embarrassed, not hurt or humbled or anything like that – I am just disappointed." Trembling immediately countered: "I'm a bit surprised by Sol's comments. Things have gone at an astronomical pace over the last few months. Signing nine players in three months is unheard of at our level and we've started work on a new training ground. We've been linked with about 88 players... But I've never talked about Benjani to anybody at all. Roberto Carlos? Sven, I understand, did talk about [him] but it never went beyond a conversation. Sven talks every day about four or five players we might be looking at, but most are more aligned to League Two." Campbell would eventually get himself fit and go on to play Premier League football again for Arsenal and Newcastle – Notts are further away than ever.

Campbell's departure had been the first bump on the road for 'the project'. Its suddenness and manner were the last things the new owners needed, especially as they were coming under increasing scrutiny from the Football League. More details about the Mr Big (or Bigs) were required before he (or they) could pass the fit and proper person's test. But Armstrong-Holmes had begun to smell a rat even earlier. "Soon after the trust agreed the deal, I felt something was badly wrong," he told me. "Some things they did were not ones associated with monied people. For instance, they removed all the crafted existing club logos from the stands including the apex on the Jimmy Sirrel stand and replaced them with a cheap PVC banner containing a new logo. Anyone seeking to re-brand would do it properly. It wouldn't have cost a lot of money. This perhaps simple thing sent worrying signals to me and I began asking, shall we say, very awkward questions. This culminated in Trembling issuing an exclusion order against me. I was banned from the ground, even though I rented office space there but this is another story. But the Sven effect and excellent start to the season meant no-one was going to listen. The fans were euphoric."

I asked Trembling if he felt Campbell was a turning point. He wrote: "My own view on Sol's walkout is that he actually didn't fancy Division Two. He may have felt the cash wasn't there; I'm not sure to be honest. He was a decent chap but, with hindsight, when he decided to go it probably suited all parties."

It was a measure of the Walter Mitty world in which Notts were then living that an even bigger name than Campbell had been targetted. Whatever his faults, Eriksson could never be accused of setting his sights too low and one of the countless calls he made was to the agent of the world's most hyped footballer. Then at LA Galaxy, David Beckham was still in the England squad and still the biggest brand in the game. Goldenballs at Meadow Lane would have been Beyonce at the Dog & Duck but Notts were serious – Munto's lawyers were in the advanced stages of drawing up a lengthy contract. Mercifully, the man himself wasn't. Back in England for a game with Croatia, Becks was asked if he would consider such an outlandish move. "No, not yet," he teased. "I haven't spoken to Sven for a while." He never did speak to him and that was as close as the ultimate fantasy signing went. But it had the desired effect – 'the world's oldest club' *were* now on everyone's lips.

Lips inside the club, however, were sealed when it came to another key man. Russell King, along with Nathan Willett, had outlined 'the project' to Eriksson and promised him shares in Swiss Commodity Holding. "I don't think anyone at the football club was in any doubt that he was pulling the strings," Trembling told *Panorama*. "But he did not want to be known publically." So he was nicknamed Lord Voldemort – He Who Cannot Be Named from *Harry Potter*. "I think he quite enjoyed that," added the CEO.

However, the Dark Lord did not prove a very able puppeteer. Following Campbell out of the door were finance director, Alex Clemence, and media officer, Matt Lorenzo, the latter having only just joined from Sky. The club found itself on the wrong end of no less than three county court judgments for unpaid bills. Sure signs that if the wheels were not coming off, the nuts were beginning to loosen.

Armstrong-Holmes was not surprised. He said: "Money which the club had in the bank was siphoned off (basically stolen) before the season had started. Apart from the players/staff no-one was getting paid. Prior to Trembling and Co., it was difficult to make ends meet but we did just that. Our suppliers were paid. HMRC was paid. Players and staff were paid. Come September, I began talking with the *Guardian* newspaper and provided them with evidence to substantiate their articles which lead to the demise of Tembling/Munto."

Things were no better on the field. Three successive defeats had them fifth in the table in early October, and King and Willett wanted manager Ian McParland sacked. The Scot had survived only because Eriksson "had not wanted my first move to be firing the coach". But now the Swede agreed a new man was needed and, typical Sven, was not going to settle for anybody. "I immediately thought of my friend Roberto Mancini," he told me. "He had been sacked by Inter at the same time I left Man City and had not worked since. Inter were still paying him his contract, but he was interested and came over. We – Russell, Nathan, myself, Mancio and his agent – all met and he wanted the job. By the end of the meeting I felt we had our next manager." Typically, King and Willett, who had not paid the tea lady, promised to match the six million euros Mancini was still getting from Inter.

As hard as it is to imagine a black and white scarf being immaculately furled around Mancini's neck at Meadow Lane, there was no reason he and Sven could not combine again – as long as the £50m materialised. After all, as player and manager, they'd landed the treble with Lazio. And Eriksson was sufficiently committed to Notts to dash a lifelong dream of managing his native Sweden. "A couple of months after I signed for Notts, I was approached by the Swedish FA," he wrote in his autobiography, *My Story: Sven-Goran Eriksson*. "I had always hoped I would one day get the job but the trouble was I'd just signed for Notts County. So I turned it down. It proved to be a huge mistake."

Then came what he called "the craziest thing that happened at Notts County." He said: "Nathan Willett asked me to go with them to North Korea. I had doubts about it from the beginning and I phoned a member of the British Government, a lady I knew there. She told me: 'You can't go.' But King and Willett insisted: 'Notts County depends on you going.' It was about the public listing of the shares for Swiss Commodity Holding, the company in which I held stock options. So I phoned the Swedish embassy and they said: 'Of course, you can go.' They had an ambassador there and I had lunch with him when I went."

On October 19, a delegation that included King, Willett, Eriksson, two mining experts, an unknown woman and a man named Khan, who Sven believed was a member of the Bahrain royal family, left London to do business with a prominent cog in 'the axis of evil'. The former Notts County director of football recalled: "I was not involved in any negotiations and while King and Nathan Willett were doing that I visited football grounds and gave advice on coaching. I was travelling with someone from the North Korean FA. I saw junior games, stadiums, lots of things for three or four days." I asked if he was offered the North Korean coaching job – as widely reported in the British media. He said: "No. The only thing they asked for was a favourable draw at the World Cup! They thought we could fix it for them. Oh, and footballs – there was a national shortage of footballs."

So what was the purpose of the trip? I asked. He sighed as if it was still painful to recall: "North Korea was the big, big thing whereby the company could make money. I think they thought they'd have so much money if the shares had come out – the whole idea was to take out all the minerals from the earth and help North Korea put them on the market." At a ceremony in the Mansudae Assembly Hall where the party met the Dear Leader's right-hand man Kim Yong-nam, Sven says: "I saw King handing over certificates worth not millions but billions. I tried a joke, saying that sort of money would buy a few players and was told: 'Take it easy, Sven – you'll get your players.'"

By the end of the trip, he wasn't so sure. "Something went wrong," he recalled. "Russell and Nathan became very agitated as we waited at the airport. I asked what the problem was but couldn't get a straight answer. It had something to do with an oil delivery from China to North Korea. From what I gathered, it was to be some kind of gift. The delivery was supposed to have taken place during our time in the country but had apparently not happened."

Eriksson remembered seeing King "screaming at some poor woman behind a counter and that was the last he saw of him". The Swede managed to get back to London but wasn't sure King did and what he'd seen had given him plenty to ponder on the long trip home via Beijing. He immediately phoned Mancini to tell him not to come. "I did not want Mancio to give up his big salary from Inter and not get paid," he said. But Notts still needed a manager and, having turned down the job himself, he brought in fellow Swede Hans Bakke – "a cheaper option" – with whom he'd worked at Man City.

With impeccable timing, the Football League announced that Notts' owners had passed the 'fit and proper person's' test the day after their delegation left for North Korea. But by now even Trembling was making cuts. To my question about the pivotal moment, he wrote: "There were a number of things that were causing concern but no one pivotal moment. I had no reason to doubt the money was going to arrive and particularly more so given that the lawyers had endorsed the guarantee from the owners. What I did ensure though [after Campbell's departure] was that we curtailed spending to a bare minimum. Despite inaccurate reports to the contrary, we never once failed to meet payment of players and staff wages, although I didn't take any salary towards the end." That was because the 'we' had suddenly become very personal – Trembling was paying the players out of his own pocket. The pivotal moment was not far away.

Eriksson, meanwhile, was worried he was not able to fulfill the promises he'd made to the North Koreans. "They wanted to bring the national team to Europe and for us to help with arrangements," he said. "But nothing happened so I wondered what was going on. I felt bad that we were letting them down." He would soon feel a lot worse. "Then I had a call from someone at BMW who warned me about Russell King. The deal he had with the Formula One team had collapsed as he had apparently lied about the finances."

Everyone's worst fears were confirmed on November 8 when *The Sun* revealed that King was a convicted fraudster. "County Powerbroker is an ex-con' was the headline for what the paper dubbed an 'in-depth probe into who the powerbrokers are behind the mystery company that owns the League 2 club, Munto Finance." King had served a two-year jail sentence for an insurance fraud in 1991. His business empire, Zodiac Toys, had been in ruins prompting him to fake the theft of his Aston Martin, which he'd hidden in a garage, claiming £600,000. Alarm bells may not have sounded in his house but they clanged all the way from the pit lane to the pitch. When asked for the moment he first smelled a rat, Trembling answered: "When The Sun ousted [sic] Russell King."

As Eriksson famously told *Panorama*, his first suspicions had been aroused "when the milk bill wasn't paid." But now the Munto project was in ruins, King fled to Bahrain and Willett disappeared. Bakke, sensing the deepening morass, also quit. Trembling and Eriksson were left wondering what to do. Both still believed Notts had potential and began a desperate search for backing. On December 12, Trembling bought the club for £1 from Munto whom he thanked for "the way they have conducted the sale of the football club. They have been responsible for changing the outlook of a club which has previously finished in the bottom six of the Football League for four times in the past five years. Now we cherish ambitions to secure promotion this year and deliver sustainable progress into the Championship and beyond." Like hundreds of his other statements, it was apparently written with a straight face.

With the team now back under assistant coach Dave Kevan, who had survived the entire saga, Trembling and Eriksson scoured Europe trying to raise money. Trembling insisted: "It is the best investment opportunity, pound for pound, in English football." But no one was convinced. 'How close did you come [to finding a backer]?' I asked. "Very" was his answer. When an insolvency expert, from the respected firm Begbies Traynor, called him, Trembling made the excuse that he was driving and never returned the call. In the end, he gave up and in February sold the club to Trew for £1. A pound for a pound but hardly what he had intended.

NOTTS COUNTY

3

"What the League did was rigorously apply the rules and regulations that existed at that time."

Football League chairman Brian Mawhinney on allowing Notts County's mystery owners to pass the fit and proper person's test.

So, what to make of this extraordinary episode? It was not your bog-standard descent of vultures onto the nearest available carcass. The slim pickings of Notts County were never going to satisfy the voracious appetites of people hoping to feast for life after making a killing in the real world. Their project was far more than a mere con: the planning was meticulous enough for a NASA probe into another galaxy, the cunning was Machiavellian, the expectation the biggest mining coup since Klondyke.

Goldman Sachs rated North Korea's mineral resources among the richest in the world and Munto had brought some pretty impressive coves on board. After all that, could the fizzle on the launch pad really have come down to the non-arrival of a train in north-east Asia? Was it signal failure? Leaves on the line or the wrong kind of snow? Couldn't they have waited? And why was there a Snafu at Pyongyang airport when it was time to go? Even now there are far more unanswered questions than zeros on the certificates that Sven had seen handed over.

Trembling confirmed the source of the anticipated cash when I asked if the money for 'the project' was supposed to have come from the Middle East or North Korea. "ME", he wrote. Not that there'd been much doubt. Sifting through the bewildering fusion sandwich of evidence and rumour, wondering who the "very private people" might be and why the very public ones chose to hide their co-conspirators' identities; and sorting the Muntos from the Qadbaks... we can only hazard a guess as to why Notts County were involved.

I put that to Armstrong-Holmes. "Good question," he said. "It may have been a credibility step as they were seeking to buy the F1 BMW team at the same time. Only the Premiership offers the 'pot of gold' so in many ways it is all quite mystifying. The sums we talked about were comparatively small and realistic – around £5-10 million to get from League 2 to the Championship. Not great sums in the scheme of things, but for little Notts County it was the pathway to a return to the Championship where in the seventies we resided for a good number of years."

However we look at it, the only logical reason for Notts having anything to do with whatever King and the Willetts had been cooking up was as a sweetener. The owners were certainly no Caesars – King's name was not on any document and "Dark Lord" was no sobriquet for an emperor. They very definitely weren't saviours and they were far too cunning to be suckers. The default setting of football fans is to defend the downtrodden club at the mercy of the ruthless predator, but we may underestimate the strength our clubs have. For a business deal ostensibly between the unlikely bedfellows of Bahrain and North Korea, it seems that football in general and Notts in particular were essential lubricants.

After all, Sven was told the Notts deal "depended" on his presence in Pyongyang after which he would have his players. And football was one of the few things the pariah state of North Korea did which was in sync with the rest of the world. They had even qualified for the 2010 World Cup finals. They might not have heard of Notts but 'the world's oldest club' would have resonated. And they had heard of Sven. The two together represented a valued asset, the owners of which would have stature and face. In a country where gestures – grand and small – count for a lot in negotiations, the football club would have ensured that Munto, Qadbak, Swiss Commodity Holding or whatever they called themselves, would have been taken more seriously. They even had something to give.

Owning Notts would also have appealed to the "Bahrainis". Not as much as if they'd owned Manchester United – or Newcastle whom they looked at – but Notts had that strapline. Munto's acquisition of the club for next to nothing and their ambitious plan to exploit its fabled heritage would have counted for something – as it already had with sections of both football and financial establishments. There were members of parliament and the media; the former head of British intelligence and a leading member of Italian football's intelligentsia; Deloittes, Rothschilds and First London, football managers and mineral consultants, Sven and Sol. The illustrious line-up was explained by Walker who admitted: "I was taken the same way Sven was taken. They just wanted names".

Paul Fallon, a lawyer who worked on the case and has since written an excellent book about it called *Political Football*, states that Notts County "would ensure the integrity of the investment." He adds: "Buying Notts was a small show of Bahrain's good faith. They hoped it would ease the way to the much larger announcement of investment in North Korea's silver reserves. Otherwise Bahrain's good name might be tainted by association with a pariah state. Buying an English football club can make you popular and generate headlines."

If Sven had gone on to coach the North Korean national team – even part-time in Europe – it would have been a huge publicity coup for the strange, faraway land of which he (and Notts) knew little. And the prestige of the world's oldest club would have been appreciated by the Bahrainis – well, that was Munto's thinking. But if it was going to take the best part of £50m to get Notts into the Premier League, that is an expensive lump of sugar. Certainly, there would be no money from the football club until the top flight was reached – which would take a minimum of three years and probably a few more. That seemed far too distant and iffy a prospect for such slick operators and, when I asked Sven if the riches of the Premier League might have been part of the overall attraction, the idea was pooh-poohed. "I think they thought they'd have so much money if the shares had come out, they could do whatever they wanted," he said.

As *Panorama* revealed, there were as many holes in the cover story as there had been in King's insurance claim. They had simply been adroitly camouflaged by a distinguished roll call and devious accounting. Things were not as they seemed and nor was the team sheet: people were not who they appeared to be. The 'Khan' who went to North Korea was not a member of the Bahrain royal family as claimed but Abid Hyat Khan, an English business associate of King's on the run from British authorities. Then there was "the investor" who had been introduced to Armstrong-

Holmes as "a royal prince of a family from the Middle East". The Notts chairman told me: "He was in all the meetings in Bahrain prior to the deal being completed but he did not say much. He talked about how wonderful it was to be doing this. He was talking about how we were the oldest club in the world and the fact that his son played football." *Panorama* claimed this individual had no royal connections. The Anwar Shafi mentioned turned out to be a man who ran a paving stone business in Peshawar and had absolutely nothing to do with Munto. He ran a small family operation and although he admits to having met King, he was never going to pave any streets with North Korean gold.

I asked Sven if he got paid. He said: "In the beginning I did but at the end I waived my cash. I could have stuck to my contract. Then they disappeared. Peter Trembling, myself, Tord Grip and others had all said 'OK' to this project but it must have been a con trick from the beginning. But even now I find it hard to believe they would cheat Notts County." The Swede, who was entitled to as much as £2.4m, was too trusting by half. Later that year he would discover that he'd been duped of many times that amount – by his own financial advisor.

At the end of the day – and certainly by the end of the season – the cheating was not confined to off the field activities. As several League Two managers pointed out, by blatantly exceeding the league's limit that wages should be no more than 60 percent of turnover, Notts had "cheated" the rest of the division – and got away with it. Although the Football League eventually imposed a ban on recruitment, the damage was done as far as their rivals were concerned: Notts held on to their high earners who helped them to promotion.

Strangely, it seemed scant consolation. It was time for the few doubters to say 'I told you so' and the supporters trust inevitably copped its share of blame. Nor did some Notts fans escape criticism. Some had even taken to waving wads of notes at visiting supporters while bills went unpaid in order to pay the wages. Collin remembers: "Success on the field seemed to anaesthetise the fans. There were one or two odd things like the eviction of the rugby club and the change in the logo... but the euphoria was reinforced by the acceptance of Munto's ownership by the football authorities. I think that removed a lot of any lingering doubt."

Indeed, any naivety on the part of the club or fans pales compared to that of the Football League who, incredibly, deemed the owners "fit and proper" without knowing who they were! When then chairman of the Football League, Brian Mawhinney, was asked why approval was granted, he said: "What the League did was rigorously apply the rules and regulations that existed at that time." They claim to have tightened up since, but to borrow Dennis Healey's famous description of an attack by Geoffrey Howe: "It was like being savaged by a dead sheep." Unfortunately for football, Notts County's were not the only wide eyes over which the wool was being pulled.

Portsmouth

PORTSMOUTH

1

"I maintain that during that period Portsmouth FC was in the most chaotic state that any English club has ever been in. The fact that a convicted fraudster was running the club's finances tells you all you need to know."

Portsmouth Trust's Colin Farmery.

"It was like pass the fucking hand grenade." That was the Portsmouth chairman's unambiguous riposte to a suggestion the club's ownership saga must have seemed like 'Pass the Parcel'. But Iain McInnes was just warming up: "Vlad the Impaler couldn't have done more damage," he chuckled. We'd only just met but the one-liners were already coming thick and fast. And after I'd outlined the book, he deadpanned: "Whether you'll get the Pulitzer Prize without it being posthumous, I don't know: but watch out for the poisoned umbrellas."

The avuncular electronics millionaire had launched into a witheringly satirical onslaught on his predecessors. "Of all the clowns our clubs have had among foreign owners, Portsmouth have had the worst," he claimed. "And 'clowns' is much too nice a word. The most plausible was Sacha Gaydamak, who said he was going to develop the ground. He dug enough holes to reach Australia but never did rebuild. He appeared to be a guy of substantial worth and there were rumours that his father Arkady was actually the beneficial owner. The story goes that when Arkady was running for mayor of Tel Aviv, he listed a Premier League football club among his assets." I remind McInnes that Arkady was on Amnesty International's wanted list for gun-running in Angola. "I'm forgetting that," he smiled. "Arkady got himself into trouble inside Israel and co-incidentally – although we were told categorically that Sacha's business had nothing to do with his father – we started selling players like it was auction time. Sacha just left it to [CEO] Peter Storrie and lots of players

283

went out and a few came in. Administration was being mooted at that time and we did end up being the first Premiership club to have that dubious honour. That's still our major claim to fame.

"Next came Sulaiman Al Fahim, the front man for the Manchester City deal but not as rich as we thought. He went public to say he was owed lots of money and sold on to the Fake Sheikh [Ali Al Faraj] who, to this day, we don't know if he existed. He was photographed in a head dress but, let's face it, he could have been Lawrence of Arabia for all we know. At this time we started hearing names like [Balram] Chainrai and [Levi] Kushnir. I'd had a business in Israel where I'd got seen off but had retained a relationship with a firm of prominent lawyers. They were able to tell me that Gaydamak Snr had had business dealings with Chainrai and Kushnir who had been to the High Court in Israel and got a win against him to the tune of £17m. That's the figure that kept recurring as what they wanted for the football club. They had an offshore company in Tortola, where my boat was recently, in the British Virgin Islands. I went looking for their address and the only place I could find was a chicken shack. It seemed appropriate – at least it was kosher.

"There was also a character called [Daniel] Azougi who got involved – an Israeli Mr Fixit who had convictions for fraud against his name back in Israel and came to Fratton Park on a regular basis. I tell you, this is *the* story – the others [about other clubs] might be murky but with this one you're going deeper than Jacques Cousteau would ever have dared. As I've often said, without a chauffeur or a GPS none could have found their way to the ground."

McInnes had reached the time there were four owners inside a year – and the hand grenade was being tossed around between them. He went on: "Chainrai came in and put us in administration so we were docked nine points. Then we get relegated and along comes Vladimir Antonov, a Russian businessman who was head of a bank. Rumour has it that he was partly funded by Chainrai on a 'you pay me, I pay you back' kind of basis. It got us out of administration and they were quite sensible about some of the things they did. But Chainrai wasn't getting his money and pretty soon put us back into it. Fraud had been discovered at Antonov's bank and he was put under house arrest. You only had to look at CSI [Convers Sports Initiatives] to have doubts. It looked like a group of businesses trying to run fast to go somewhere until someone found out what was really going on.

"To be fair to Chainrai, he had claimed right from the word go that he was a reluctant owner of the football club, never wanting to be or suggesting for one minute his £17m was in payment for the club. He basically said he lent it in the best interests of the club to people he thought would take the club forward and he didn't get it back. You can only speculate the link between him and Arkady Gaydamak has to be the main motivation. It's a helluva coincidence, isn't it? Who will ever know? There could be so many books and films about this – we need to get the film before Jack Nicholson dies because he's got to play a part." 'Who would he play?' I ask. "Probably Harry Redknapp!"

If that was the captivating trailer, there were several options for the opening scene. Portsmouth had been in deep trouble long before, having faced bankruptcy in 1976 when they were saved by the SOS campaign; and again in 1998 when they went into administration. Then it was a foreign owner – the ubiquitous Serb-American Milan Mandaric – who turned them around. But for the purposes of this story, it is the start of the more recent shenanigans where we kick off.

By far the most interesting of those who may or may not have owned the club is Arkady Gaydamak. A carrier of four passports – Russian, Israeli, Canadian and Angolan – he might have been invented by Frederick Forsyth. Having made his billions in arms and diamonds, in 2009 he was sentenced in absentia by a French court to six years for tax fraud, embezzlement, money laundering and arms trafficking in the Angolan civil war of the 1990s. He got it reduced to three years on appeal. And if the Pompey saga ever makes it to the big screen, no director worth a carat could miss a clip from *Blood Diamond* to kick it off. At a time (2012) tea ladies were being sacked, Gaydamak Snr lost a $2billion court case with the so-called king of diamonds, Lev Leviev. There was testimony from both a Russian rabbi and an Angolan general. Connecting all this with a medium-sized football club on England's south coast may be a stretch, but you can see where McInnes is coming from. If you believe Gaydamak Snr was the power behind his son's throne, you are beginning to link the dots – his own and the club's woes uncannily coincide. And according to whispers, he took a keen paternal interest.

Although a wanted man, it is alleged that Papa Gaydamak turned up at Sacha's birthday bash one year, flying by private jet into a local airport where checks are limited. Unlike his mild-mannered son, it is said that he can be quite terrifying and must have appeared that way to Redknapp if one eye-witness account is true. After the tightening of the transfer budget, Harry, in his inimitable way, had had a bit of a moan about Sacha and said he needed new players. According to sources – and the incident was seen by several people – Papa Gaydamak cornered Harry, grabbing him by the throat. He told him that if he badmouthed his son again, he'd be flying straight back. A couple of days later, there was a newspaper story about Harry praising his excellent chairman.

McInnes recalls it all starting to go wrong soon after the high-water mark of the 2008 FA Cup final victory. Portsmouth boasted the likes of Jermain Defoe, Peter Crouch, Lassana Diarra, Sulley Muntari, Sol Campbell and Glen Johnson, most of them bought during Sacha's early years of plenty. He had paid Mandaric £32 million for the club in July 2006 and, according to Colin Farmery, then of the Portsmouth Supporters Trust, "started throwing money around like Roman Abramovich did at Chelsea." The club was riding high back then with Redknapp the moggie with the bowl of Devonshire – open chequebook to sign who he liked by an out-to-lunch owner. Never one to let the cream curdle, he assembled an eclectic mix of internationals and got them to play as a team. Sacha sat back and basked in the glow. The spending was way beyond the means of a club pulling gates of 20,000, but for the first couple of years it was pocket money to Gaydamak Snr. Listed as the sixth richest man in Israel in 2006, this billionaire arms dealer-cum-philanthropist (yes, I know) was described by the *Boston Globe* thus: "Imagine Rupert Murdoch with a dash of George Soros and your favourite James Bond villain thrown in." His assets were not frozen until 2009 but he already knew that diamonds may no longer be forever. The scandal dubbed Angolagate had been brewing in France for years and he was aware of the direction of the wind. Sacha claimed it was the recession of 2008 that caused the cutback – and it was true he was owed millions and having trouble getting them back. That summer he began a fire sale of players and Redknapp, acutely aware of the shift in the breeze, left for Spurs in October. It took just two years for Portsmouth to go from Wembley triumph to winding-up petition.

Portsmouth Supporters Trust chairman Ashley Brown is another who feels the fall was not unconnected to Papa Gaydamak's legal woes. "All of a sudden there was more interest in selling players and less in buying them," he told me. "Undoubtedly that was when things started to go wrong for Sacha. I asked: 'When the club was spending like there was no tomorrow, did you fear that something like this could happen?' He said: "A few people did and I was one. We won the FA Cup, played in Europe. The trouble is that when the team is doing well many fans are unconcerned about anything else, you could say that people have their heads in the sand. But all you had to do was look at the annual accounts. You can look at the annual accounts of Chelsea and Man U and you can see it all going wrong but of course they'll always survive, and we did for a time because we had this supposedly generous benefactor who was obviously into loans and leveraging debt. It didn't take much research to see his dad was associated with African arms money. The fact that there was always this denial that his dad had any involvement with the football club whatsoever is an extremely doubtful position, let's face it."

For all that, Farmery maintains: "While I'm, relatively speaking, more sympathetic than many towards the [Sacha] Gaydamak position, the big question always was where the money came from. He always insisted it was his own. His dad? Well, he always, always denied it. Initially, he was perceived as a positive influence. Up until the summer of 2008 he was, dare I say it, the ideal owner. He was discreet and charming in private, didn't interfere with the football side of things and signed the cheques at the end of the month to cover the losses. He's French with a Russian surname, Jewish but culturally French. The Gaydamak project was the same as the Abramovich project in that it was to put some of the family wealth into a football club and found a dynasty. The conventional wisdom is that it was a money laundering exercise of some sort.

"At end of the day, we put out the best team we'd had in two generations, won the [FA] Cup and played AC Milan. But after the global financial crisis in September 2008 and the court case in France, the Pompey cash tap was turned off. We stayed in the Premier League but the problem was we had no cash – we'd used it all to pay off some of the more pressing debt. More importantly, Gaydamak proved unable to sell to an owner with either the necessary finance or desire to nurture the business. We had Sulaiman [Al Fahim], who we heard was backed by Thaksin Shinawatra, and a Saudi guy [Al Faraj], who was favoured by the CEO. Eventually, Sacha sold to Sulaiman because he'd got wind that behind the Saudi guy were Chainrai and Kushnir, who were in significant business conflict with his father at the time."

Forty-three hand-to-mouth days later Al Fahim, the founder of a UAE reality TV show, was begging for help from a man whose very existence was questioned. It turned out that the Arab *"Apprentice"* was not even an intern when it came to ownership – and couldn't pay the wages. When the alarm sounded he was at a chess tournament in Valencia. He vowed to come back and explain all to the fans but failed to turn up, and 'chessgate' soon became checkmate. Al Faraj – or someone who may or may not have been connected to him – took over. The *Daily Mail* called it 'not only the shortest but the most ill-fated tenure in Premier League history.'

Farmery continues the sorry tale: "Matters had come to a head in September, 2009 and within weeks we were being loaned money by Mr Chainrai and Mr Kushnir. Mark Jacob, a London solicitor, was *de facto* CEO, although Storrie remained in place and then came Daniel Azougi, a convicted fraudster, to run the finances. What a bloody mess! No one knew what money was coming in or who it was going out to. I maintain that during that period Portsmouth FC was in the most chaotic state that any English club has ever been in. The fact that a convicted fraudster was running the club's finances tells you all you need to know."

At this juncture, none of the hand grenade tossers had been detected by the 'fit and proper' person's test. There might have been an excuse for The One Who May Not Have Existed but there were others involved who wouldn't have eluded Inspector Clouseau. Gaydamak Snr was headline news in France and Israel, while Al Fahim had been hastily dropped by Manchester City. Azougy, who was effectively running the show at one point, had been outed by Israeli media as a debt collector for Shlomo (Shelley) Narkis. Rejoicing in the title 'King of the Grey Market', Narkis's methods, it was alleged, included firebombing and assassinations by machine-gun wielding motorcyclists. There is no suggestion that Azougy was involved in any of that but a report of a 2001 case in the Israeli newspaper *Yedioth Ahronoth* was hardly complimentary. It quoted the judge, David Rozen, describing Azougy as, "a sophisticated lawyer willing to do anything to reach his own personal goals. He lied, cheated, used a forged document and stole money from his clients." Yet the same Azougy was allowed to run a venerable English football club on a day-to-day basis. He even sold two of its prized assets, Younes Kaboul and Asmir Begovic, behind the back of then manager Avram Grant to Spurs and Stoke respectively. The FA? "We're aware of him," said a spokesman, "but were assured he was below director level."

While the FA was being assured, fan sites were able to dig up enough dirt on certain individuals to bury them alive. No one was more forensic than Pompey season-ticket holder Micah Hall, whose blog was published by Farmery. The latter told me: "We had all sorts of fly-by-nights and Micah used to check 'em out, demolish 'em and we'd move on." Hall's day job was in crisis management.

Brown agreed that "Sacha was certainly not this type of person – or involved in the same activities – as his dad," but added: "I don't know how much of a football person he is. I think he liked the idea of owning a football club. He was on the London social set of the Russians and at the time we were a Premier League club so owning a football club is quite a nice extra to have that would have been something for him to talk about."

Brown had taken me from the famous mock-Tudor entrance to Fratton Park to what he called the boardroom. It was mostly whitewash and frosted glass, and had all the ambience of a railway station loo. It was nothing like the hallowed sanctuary I'd expected. He explained: "This was once a classic football boardroom, wood panelling and with a boardroom table. In fact, the table was given to us by the Royal Navy and the chairs were from HMS Warrior. Sacha chucked them out and they were found in a skip. A painting of HMS Victory* once hung on the wall but that disappeared and he turned it into this more modern-looking room. You'll notice even the plug points were changed to fit Russian-sized plugs so all the Russians could come in and plug in their bits and pieces." Despite the name, HMS Warrior never saw action and the only time the chairs felt any heat was when the backsides of Churchill and Montgomery descended on them during World War II. Sacha wasn't to know the history but his Siberian khazi was another disconnect between a foreign owner and the heritage of a British institution – in this case, in more ways than one.

*The painting of HMS Victory was removed by Milan Mandaric but has since been returned.

PORTSMOUTH

2

"It is a feeling of relief, almost of pleasure, at knowing yourself at last genuinely down and out. You have talked so often of going to the dogs – and well, here are the dogs, and you have reached them, and you can stand it. It takes off a lot of anxiety."

George Orwell in Down and Out in London and Paris.

The boardroom was not the only place where Sacha Gaydamak rearranged the furniture. Says Brown: "Arguably he did some good for the club. But his time was also when they started to siphon off all the land around Fratton Park that the club had built up over a period of time, but then it got moved on into separate companies between Mandaric and Sacha selling up. One of the good things the city council did was to say that in the city plan that if that land was ever developed, there had to be benefit to the football club. And that's what has stopped a number of people coming in. I would suggest that if they had not done that Portsmouth FC might not be here now as in the period it was in administration, it would have been easy for someone to come in, buy the club, knock down the ground and build something else."

Al Faraj was never likely to do that – he never set foot in the place – but he did exist. It wasn't quite like finding the yeti, but the *Daily Mirror* called it an exclusive when they quoted him as saying: "When I bought Portsmouth I made it clear I would stay in the background and allow a management team to run the club headed up by chief executive Peter Storrie. This acquisition is entirely separate to my other businesses and I didn't purchase the club intent on having to justify my actions or fall under public scrutiny. I'm an intensely private man and I don't feel comfortable in the spotlight." Brown agreed that he did exist but felt he was "a junior clerk or something" whose name was being used. The question was: by whom?

Meanwhile, the manager's job was given to Paul Hart after he'd impressed as caretaker following the sacking of Redknapp's successor, Tony Adams. He was even given a few million to spend late in the summer window, but despite a last-minute trolley dash of signings, couldn't buy a win. After losing the first seven games of the 2009/2010 season and 10 of his first 13, the inevitable axe fell in November and none other than Avram Grant took over. The ex-Chelsea manager's time in charge was when it really hit home how desperate things were off the field. Cash dried up again and players' wages were paid late no less than four times. But they weren't the only ones not getting their dues. Highlighting the plight as only the internet can, the club's website went down for a few hours on January 28, 2010. The Bournemouth-based digital supplier, Juicy, literally pulled the plug on long-standing debts.

Of greater consequence, an even more critical provider, Balram Chainrai, who had financed Al Faraj's purchase of the club, had not been receiving his repayments. The Hong Kong businessman had "become aware" of Portsmouth FC after winning the case against Arkady Gaydamak. He now stepped in with his company, Portpin, taking over Al Faraj's 90 per cent shareholding. He reaffirmed that this was the only reason he assumed control. "Anybody who is ready to give me the money I put into the club and lent to the club in good faith, I'm ready to take it and walk," Chainrai told the *South China Morning Post*. "They can step straight into my shoes and I'll be happy. I'm sick of these accusations. People can say that I'm asset-stripping or doing this or that, but it simply isn't true. In the beginning I was asked to help out financially by the previous owner. The consideration I was offered to help out was attractive as a business proposition, but things began to snowball very quickly. It was obvious things were going downhill fast and before I knew it I was in this situation. Business is all about profit. If I had known it was going to end up like this I would never have got involved. I've always lead a low-profile life and I want to go back to it."

I asked Brown why he thought Chainrai's company had got involved. "They thought there was an opportunity to make a significant amount of money," he said. "But it was an incredibly poor decision by these supposedly astute guys. They thought they could loan this business money at a high rate but they were never able to get it back. And they've been chasing this £17m, which is what they thought they were owed, ever since. Or right up to the court decision anyway. That's the only reason they got involved. They lent money, the club couldn't pay them back and they inherited the club. They enjoyed a bit of success in going to the Cup final again and then we went down in the same year – and that was when it started to go horribly wrong."

Yes, it was only starting – and the owners were not the only ones to blame, according to Brown. He said: "When the writing was on the wall, not only for relegation but financially, the then chief executive was willing to sign players on 4-year deals at £68k a week. I don't think anyone should underestimate the damage Peter Storrie did to this football club. He had jumped on the gravy train and wasn't willing to get off it. Under Sacha, I think he could get away with what he wanted – either Sacha didn't care, didn't see or didn't want to get involved – but the CEO put himself on the team's win bonus. If we won, he'd get three grand, if we drew he'd get 500. Who's ever heard of that?" For his part, Storrie declined to be interviewed.

As dire as things were, it was almost a halcyon era for what was to come. Portsmouth were still in the Premier League but in the knacker's yard financially. After realising the true extent of the debt was £135m, Chainrai put the club into administration in February 2010 and a month later they were docked the inevitable nine points by the Premier League: it meant certain relegation but was the only way to avoid liquidation. Incredibly, Grant led the team to a second FA Cup final in three seasons and although they went down 1-0 to his old club Chelsea, he ended up a folk hero to the Pompey faithful. Only they appreciated just what he'd been up against as no less than 26 players left on permanent transfers and another 11 on loans: picking a team was an achievement. The lachrymose Israeli had somehow inspired a stirring, against-the-odds campaign. But in the overall picture of Portsmouth's demise, the return to Wembley proved no more use than grabbing the last deckchair on the Titanic, and they duly sank to the Championship at the end of the season.

Storrie had stepped down on March 12 with Adrian Adronikou of UHY Hacker Young appointed as administrator. A bit of a showman, he was soon perceived "as part of the problem" by some fans who felt he was acting to keep Portpin's £17m debt alive. The irony of having recruitment company, Jobsite, as shirt sponsors didn't stop him putting 85 per cent of the club's employees out of work. With all that and facing another HMRC bid to prevent them coming out of administration, the club endured an entire summer on football's death row.

When Mr Justice Mann finally sat down to deliberate on August 3, 2010 it took an agonising three days before the taxman's challenge was dismissed. Pompey fans celebrated wildly but the reprieve would be short-lived. On the field, performances belied the parlous state of affairs off it. Grant had resigned with a heavy heart but, after an indifferent start to the new campaign, the latest bearer of the poisoned chalice, Steve Cotterill, had Pompey winning again. He and striker Liam Lawrence were respectively nominated for Manager and Player of the Month awards in October during which Portsmouth stood just five places off the playoff positions. A swift return to the top flight was being whispered. As Farmery insisted: "The [match] atmosphere has been good: it's been off the field where we've had the problems."

On October 22, 2010 the end really did look nigh as the club issued its starkest statement yet: "It appears likely that the club will now be closed down and liquidated by the administrators as they are unable to support the continued trading of the club." The latest crisis had been caused by Sacha Gaydamak, still a creditor, demanding an upfront payment for one of his loans. Even Farmery was despondent, admitting at the time: "This is perhaps going to be the death knell of the club." But sanity prevailed yet again and Gaydamak softened his demands. Two days later an agreement was hammered out that allowed the club to continue trading and, at long last, come out of administration.

The upturn in form didn't last while off the field the mood was as sour as ever. Chainrai told the *South China Morning Post*: "There is a small group of fans – approximately a dozen – who are on their own planet and not the fans of the city of Portsmouth." Bob Beech, chairman of fans' group SOS Pompey, responded: "In terms of customer care, I think Mr Chainrai went to the Gerald Ratner school of business." Although it may not have been appreciated at the time, a 16th place finish with Cotterill surviving to start a new season, was the nearest thing to stability the club would see for a while. That daft notion would not last long.

On June 1, 2011, Chainrai sold the club to CSI, owned by London-based Russian businessman Vladimir Antonov. The problem here was that, in 2009, Antonov's Lithuanian bank Snoras had been barred from opening a UK branch. It had provided "misleading information" about its anti-fraud controls. The FSA ruled it was "part of an ongoing pattern of behaviour by institutions controlled by Mr Antonov". So had he cleaned up his act? Apparently not and in November, 2011 he was arrested and charged with misappropriating £200m. Snoras was put into administration.

Said Brown: "CSI started very positively and they were doing some things right. But only a few months in Antonov had his assets frozen by the Lithuanian Government and was the subject of a Europe-wide arrest warrant." According to the Baltic investigative journalism centre *Re: Baltica*, Antonov had "gambled with depositor money to fuel his business ambitions and desire for a luxurious lifestyle."

McInnes had not been the only one to have doubts about CSI. Brown said: "We had our suspicions at the trust and I did some digging. When Balram sold to CSI it was done on tick. There was a series of payments before Antonov had overall charge of the club in case they defaulted which they did. It was only a matter of time before the football club was put into administration for a second time and three or four months later it happened. There was also the realisation that the club had fallen back into the hands of Chainrai because he was still owed the money for the sale. That was really the start of what turned into an 18-month battle from when CSI first went into administration and us actually winning in 2013."

Another start, another battle. In October 2011, Cotterill left to join Nottingham Forest whose offer of a three and a half year contract must have seemed like a career in the civil service. Rookie Michael Appleton was appointed as the new boss on November 10. He would later say: "For 10 days the job was brilliant. Then the owner was arrested. From that day on, it's been carnage." Antonov appeared in court in London on November 24, along with his business partner Raimondas Baranauskas. Both were accused of asset-stripping and denied any wrong doing. Only the week before CSI had attempted to reassure everyone that it was "very much business as usual." For Portsmouth, it was.

CSI duly entered administration and on November 29, Antonov resigned as chairman of the club. It was the latest excruciating twist. Three years earlier, Portsmouth had been FA Cup winners, finished eighth in the Premier League and held AC Milan to a 2-2 draw in the UEFA Cup. But now, a precarious 19th in the second tier, they were looking at a 10-point docking that would send them to the bottom. They tried to put a brave face on it, declaring that "it is not in administration and continues to trade," but Farmery was not so confident. Mindful of the history, he told the BBC: "The worst-case outcome is that because the club is potentially going insolvent for the second time in 18 months, the Football League may take a dim view of that." He added: "The other side is the Football League approved these people as being 'fit and proper' to run a football club."

As a distressing autumn turned to a desperate winter, battle lines were again being drawn. Portpin filed a charge at Companies House over the parent company and became a secured creditor over CSI. HMRC issued a winding up petition for over £1.6 million in unpaid taxes. Money was also owed to other football clubs as well as utility companies. With the looming threat of power and points being cut, January 2012 was the darkest month yet. In a post on the Socialist Party's Portsmouth branch website, Ben Norman wrote: "If that tale of scoundrels, creditors and financial incompetence is confusing it all resulted in a press conference with new manager Michael Appleton announcing that the team could not afford to scan the injury of club captain Liam Lawrence. Nor could the club afford the coach to the away fixture at Burnley. The club's electricity was about to be cut off and angry suppliers had padlocked the groundsmen's sheds." Norman had prefaced his commentary with a quote from George Orwell's *Down and Out in London and Paris*.

"It is a feeling of relief, almost of pleasure, at knowing yourself at last genuinely down and out. You have talked so often of going to the dogs – and well, here are the dogs, and you have reached them, and you can stand it. It takes off a lot of anxiety."

Being down and out in Portsmouth and Southsea may not have had the same ring, and there was still anxiety. As Guy Thomas, a leading insolvency lawyer and football finance expert told the BBC: "This is as bad as it can get for Portsmouth without the club ceasing to exist."

3

"If you think of the mayhem they've been through, the club has been like a tortured soul for the past three years."

Portsmouth administrator Trevor Birch.

There was, however, a chink of light. Chainrai had wanted Adronikou, who was handling the same process with CSI, to return as the administrator but, after HMRC insisted there should be no conflict of interest, the court opted for PKF's Trevor Birch. An ex-player and a former CEO at Chelsea, Leeds, Everton and Sheffield United, Birch said: "The intention is to try and sell the club as a going concern. I'm used to dealing with clubs in crisis. You could say most of the Championship is in crisis, with 30 per cent of clubs paying wages in excess of 100 per cent of their turnover. You have to travel hopefully and confidently. Maybe the new appointment will encourage someone to come out of the woodwork and bid [for the club]."

Brown, whose supporters trust were very much in the woodwork even though the historic panelling had gone, told me: "We were very lucky when Trevor was appointed – of PKF as it was – as that gave us a free run at saving the club and wrestling it free from the people who were trying to milk it dry. We were fairly sure that the purpose of Balram keeping the club at that time was only to milk the last few parachute payments. They were trying to get back the money they loaned plus what they felt was additional."

McInnes noted: "We hadn't expected a battle royal with the previous owner [Chainrai]. He had said that he just wanted out. But as soon as someone else was in he wanted back in again. They really were the Hokey Cokey group. On a number of occasions we were very close to losing the club back to him or to people he'd introduced to the club. When he said they were people that weren't associated with him, my honest belief was, well, it was a case of 'you might think that but I couldn't possibly say it'. But the reality was we were up against someone who was prepared to go to any lengths and any cost to try and get the club back."

All that stood in Chainrai's way was the fit and proper person's test. Challenged by a Pompey fan to explain how CSI had been given a pass, the Football League was unusually candid in its reply. "The steps taken by the Football League were based upon evidence of proof of funding, together with related business plans," it wrote. "It appears that the evidence was at best misleading and possibly fraudulent with the league not being alone in accepting this evidence." Their honesty, although commendable, afforded scant comfort. Nor did Birch's first major move. After making 31 people, including new CEO Lampitt, redundant, the administrator admitted: "The cash available is worse than we first feared. We are struggling to make it to the end of the season."

As Birch sought in vain for a white knight, the trust stepped up their efforts to take over. Throughout the crisis years they had dreamed of doing so along the lines of the German model but initially it had seemed beyond their reach. However, encouraged by Birch who said their idea "was a sensible way forward," trust spokesman Ian Mclachlan announced a scheme where individuals could make a refundable deposit of £100 to a protected account. They were fully aware they would need some bigger hitters if they were ever going to be taken seriously as prospective buyers, but it was a start. And the fans needed a straw to clutch when relegation struck again. On April 21, 2012 a 2-1 home defeat to Derby consigned Pompey to the third tier for the first time in three decades. The 10-point deduction had proved decisive.

That summer, as the rest of Britain prepared for the London Olympics, Pompey fans could be forgiven for not embracing the mood. For them all that was going 'faster, higher and stronger' was the club's rush to oblivion. On July 12, the Football League imposed another 10-point penalty to make it a total of 29 points docked in four seasons. Twelve days later Birch announced that he would have no option but to close the club unless all senior players left by August 10. Second last to leave was Israeli defender Tal Ben Haim, the biggest earner who reached a compromise deal over his wages the day before the deadline. At least no one asked him to turn out the light.

But the fans had still not given up. By now, according to Farmery: "The trust were testing the waters to see if there was a fan appetite to raise the cash to survive. We did a pre-issue in 2011, the trust having been set up in 2009. It had taken a couple of years to be mature enough to ask fans to put up £100 with an option to put up another £900 to buy a share in Portsmouth FC. And we used that capital to eventually buy the club. We got about £1.5m raised in pledges which was the biggest amount raised of its kind. To be honest, Trevor probably didn't regard us as having enough, but we were a safety net if he had to liquidate the business. We would have set up a Phoenix club and started in the Southern League Premier or Conference South maybe. Some regarded this as the only way to break the link. We called it Plan B – we had a club ready to go if necessary – and we came close to liquidation on a number of occasions. And in midsummer, Trevor was flirting significantly with Portpin to sell the club back again because he could see no alternative.

"But the trust bid stalled as it wasn't enough. We had been talking to Iain McInnes in early summer. It was a flirting dance initially. The trust needed additional investment and additional credibility. Iain and the High Net Worth (HNW) investors he'd been working with weren't in a position to do it themselves either, so in the late summer of 2012 we came together in this amalgam of fans and High Net Worth people. He bought into the community club ethos and the trust recognised not only their investment but that they were credible business people who were very successful in their own right, and we created an alliance. The HNWs had between them raised about £1.5m and they had 40 per cent and the trust about 60 per cent. To begin with, there was significant scepticism among the fans but it was a breakthrough."

McInnes admits to being a reluctant commander-in-chief. He recalls: "I was asked to be involved as a High Net Worth – I hate the word – individual in going into an alliance with the supporters. I went to a couple of meetings and said – and this is public knowledge – I don't think this is for me. I don't want to be a part of a committee. I didn't mean I wouldn't invest but I didn't want to be responsible for leading it, as it were. A number of things happened: they had a rethink and needed someone with a bit of authority and money. Trevor came and saw me and said without you and people like you this isn't going to work. So I did it for the good of the club. Before the court case, four or five of us stood to lose in an excess of a million quid and get nothing back. Still nothing had come out of the individual supporters' accounts as we were funding the whole thing, and we've now got ownership. We formed a board that reflects the ownership of the HNWs and the fans. I always said winning the peace might be more difficult than winning the war."

As the fans became energised, the team suffered. With no players – all the pros having left – no money and the 10 point deficit with which they began the season, it said much for the faith and determination of both the trust and HNWs that they were getting their collective act together. And on October 17 the PST were named by Birch as 'preferred bidders'. Chainrai reacted by saying: "Whilst we note PKF's decision, we recognise that preferred bidder status has no basis in law. And we are confident that our bid offers both the best deal for creditors."

On November 7, Appleton, after a valiant 12-month battle, had had enough and left for Blackpool. Two days later Chanrai halted his attempt to buy the club. Doubts had emerged that he would pass the Football League's newly named and stiffened 'owners and directors test', one of the stipulations being that an owner or director cannot have been involved with a club that has twice gone into administration. Chainrai was in control of Pompey when they went into administration in 2010 and may have had some involvement as a shadow director when they were placed into it for a second time in February 2012. Portpin always denied this but PKF now turned to the PST as it looked to bring the club out of administration. "It was a real tipping point," said Farmery, "because fans looked at it and thought 'bloody hell, it could be them'. If not them, it could be curtains. It was a seminal moment and they came round to thinking it could be done." There were also those who felt Portpin's difficulties were a certain poetic justice.

Still defiant, Chainrai said: "We believe that the Football League has been put in an invidious position by the administrators – PKF. It is the administrators' job to manage the administration to a successful conclusion to the benefit of all creditors and yet PKF has off-loaded this responsibility to the Football League. First, Trevor Birch named Portpin as preferred bidder, then, before the Football League was given any time to actually assess our bid, Trevor Birch decided to suddenly withdraw our preferred bidder status the same day, without any credible reasoning. The PST was then named by Trevor Birch as the preferred bidder even though our bid remains with the Football League as they continued the process of evaluating our offer."

He added: "And Pompey fans should be in no doubt that in my opinion they are being manipulated here. Behind the PST bid are a number of property developers who now appear to be becoming the majority stakeholders rather than the PST themselves. I believe their interest in buying the club is to secure the land. The illusion of the trust owning Fratton Park is just that: an illusion. In reality, property developers will own the land, but they are using the veil of the trust's bid as a vehicle to obtain and develop land around the ground without having to spend any money on much needed improvements to Fratton Park."

On behalf of the trust, Farmery countered: "It's ridiculous for Portpin to suggest that this is underhand. We've been transparent in that we are working with a strategic property developer. As everyone knows, the long-term future of Portsmouth Football Club depends on doing a deal on the land around the ground in order to create a stadium that is fit for the 21st century."

Portpin's retreat appeared to leave the coast clear for the PST to eventually take over the club. The dire performances of the team – even a record winless streak of 23 games – seemed secondary to what would be a monumental victory for the fans after years of false hopes, misery and despair. But it wasn't over yet. In the best traditions of Hollywood blockbusters, there had to be one final, excruciating twist. At one minute to midnight, they learned they had been gazumped.

"It was the worst and most unforgettable moment of the whole saga," says McInnes. "Keith Harris reared his ugly head with a higher bid and tried to convince us that the deal was nothing whatsoever to do with the previous regime. Immediately, I pointed to those previous connections with Portpin and we refused to have anything to do with it. We were determined to return the club to people who care about it, and the local community."

Recalls Farmery: "Harris had been brought in by Portpin and was so confident he had it in the bag he was announcing his management team, his directors, and who his investors were, and there was a Football League board meeting the next day. We all believed at that point that we were screwed and that Harris was going to take over and the whole dirty process was to continue."

In 2010, Harris, then at Seymour Pierce, had worked on the sale of the club to CSI and admitted being paid £650,000 for his services. On his motives for the Portsmouth he said: "After 36 years in banking I was looking for a lifestyle change. I think I can run a football club pretty well, and Portsmouth is a very good prospect. There is the potential upside, with this supporter base, some investment from us and decent management, of competing for promotion to the Premier League. I'm not in it just to make money, but I'm not doing it to lose money."

Among his backers was Pascal Najadi, a Malaysian banker now based in Moscow, who I managed to contact via email. To my question why he got involved in Pompey, he answered: "Whilst we do not comment on internal business strategies I can sum it up for you as follows: 1. English Football is [the] world's best. 2. Football is the most active sports cash flow model. 3. PFC was in dire straits and we hoped to replicate a Chelsea success with expert banker, Keith Harris. 4. The expertise of Keith Harris was key to our involvement – he made Chelsea a success story unparalleled. 5. The PFC fan base is one of the most loyal in Great Britain, we wanted to include them to be part of a success." He ended the message by saying: "You might understand that I closed this chapter with the horrible assassination of my late father in KL 29/7/13." In a tragic and totally unrelated incident, Najadi's father Hussain, a renowned international banker, was assassinated by a lone gunman while walking with his wife and another companion to a parking lot in a back street of Kuala Lumpur. A hitman was arrested but the case has not been solved.

Harris's intervention was late but his counting of chickens premature. Recalls Farmery: "Then the Football League, bless 'em, came out the next day and said: 'No, we're only going to deal with the supporters trust. The elation was almost as great as actually getting it." No less than three times the League was to insist on the trust as the only bidder – a stand that had Chainrai and Harris crying foul. But still there was the small matter of the ground – acceptance of the trust's bid was dependent on the club being fully reunited with Fratton Park and Chainrai still had a charge over it. He wanted at least £7million; the trust were offering what they felt was a "realistic" £3million. No one was surprised that it was going to the wire.

Judgment day was April 10, 2013 but talks began the day before to settle this issue once and for all. They dragged on well past the witching hour and into the early afternoon of the next day. They actually delayed the court proceedings. The critical intervention came when Birch secured an order from the judge forcing Chainrai to sell the ground for £3m – despite the larger offer. The drama unfolded in Court 30 of the Rolls Building annex of the high court in London. McInnes takes up the story: "The judge [Justice Peter Smith] was known to be a maverick. A pal of mine told me he could be a good thing – or the worst thing. 'I'll give you an inkling,' he said. 'You'll find out early enough because he'll lay into the QC of who he thinks has got the weakest arguments to try and curtail the arguments.' So we're sitting in the offices trying to sign the deal with Chainrai. It kicked off at 2pm – it should have been 12 but the paperwork was still not signed. Their lawyer was next door. Some lads were getting tweets that the two QCs wanted to make opening statements. But the judge didn't want opening statements – he said he was a football fan and knew the arguments. One is offering £6.3m, one offering £3m – at that point, we're in trouble. Eventually they got the paperwork signed. Ironically, Chainrai's QC is a lifelong Pompey fan. The judge read [the arguments] for about 15 minutes then said: 'Would you two please approach the bench?' I thought 'Oh, we'll be back here tomorrow'. Then he said: 'I'm a Hull supporter – we passed you a long time ago.' And he added: A lot of ordinary supporters won't understand what's going on. I'm going to give the two QCs 20 minutes but before you adjourn you will likely be owners of your own football club.'

"Two minutes before we got the signed document," continues McInnes, Chainrai and his brother Deepak had given up. We were told Kushnir wanted someone to make a personal statement of intent, a gesture. It was like would you get your kiddie's piggy bank out so we've taken everything you have. I said: 'I'll transfer 10 grand and you'll have it within the hour.' So he came back and said: 'Levi said thanks, but declines your offer and wishes you well for the future of Portsmouth FC.' Bizarre."

When the judge finally signalled a trust victory, pandemonium broke out inside and outside the court. No Pompey goal has ever been greeted with such euphoria. The fans in court cheered wildly, fans back in Portsmouth danced in the streets and McInnes and Co were hugging each other and shedding tears. A chorus of Pompey Chimes broke out inside the court.

Portsmouth would become the largest club yet to be owned by fans with the trust taking a 51% shareholding. Chainrai accepted £3m plus a six-figure sum to cover costs and compensation. Brown declared it an "historic day", adding: "We're incredibly pleased. It's been a draining fight, but we've achieved what we set out to do. We now want to look to the future. We've got a clean break and we've now got a football club that is owned by the fans, owned by people who love it. We're going to have a football club that is run sustainably, transparently and in the proper manner."

The final word goes to McInnes who said: "I shed some tears in court because it's a fantastic day for the football club. I always believed we'd do it. It's been my job to hold everyone together. It's about the long-suffering fans of Portsmouth Football Club who hopefully don't have to suffer any longer. What everyone underestimated from the word go was the togetherness that has been forged. We've won the war, now we have to win the peace."

The chimes really were a-changin'.

PORTSMOUTH

4

"Of all the sagas, Portsmouth takes the cake – it personifies everything that can go wrong with owners who want to use a host vehicle, as it were, for pleasure and gain or whatever, and don't invest in infrastructure."

Administrator Trevor Birch.

I caught up with Trevor Birch at his London office a few months later. Looking back, he told me: "I came back into administration to get away from professional football and the first job I get is Portsmouth! You couldn't make it up. They [HMRC] came to me because of my experience in the football industry. They knew it was a difficult situation. Portpin had previous involvement and they weren't happy with Portpin bringing in their administrators to control the thing. They then suggested me.

"Of all the sagas, Portsmouth takes the cake – it personifies everything that can go wrong with owners who want to use a host vehicle, as it were, for pleasure and gain or whatever, and don't invest in infrastructure. Although huge amounts were spent – that's what I mean by pleasure – nothing went on infrastructure, the stadium. They don't have a training ground – they train in a public park! For a club that spent eight years in the Premier League and spent fortunes on players, it's sacrilege that they haven't got a decent stadium and a new training ground."

And the fans? "They're among the very best. The atmosphere in the ground pound for pound is as good as any I've been to in the world. When the band's playing it's incredible. It's a one-club city with its tradition. The capacity is 25,000 but they could get close to 40,000 in the right environment. I'm a big believer in these football clubs being community assets. In this day and age when people are fed up with politics, and there's not the same pull for religion, the football club is the main focal point of a community. When there's a very real risk of losing that and it effects people's lives. If Portsmouth had gone into liquidation and the ground had been lost it would have been very uncertain as to whether it would have reappeared. Space is at a premium in Portsmouth and they wouldn't have had anywhere to play. They couldn't have afforded to play at the old stadium if they'd dropped down a few [more] divisions."

Were they saved in nick of time then? "Yes. It was touch and go at many stages during administration; it could have gone but it didn't. They still survived, the decks have been cleared now and with a fair wind and a properly run club, they should be fine." I ask: 'Was it worse than you feared?' "Yes. They always are, aren't they? We were aware that there many complex issues not least of which was ownership of surrounding land because the club had been split from the land when the club was sold to [Sacha] Gaydamark who still had residual ownership of many parts of the land. The stadium had a debenture in place to Portpin. That was an issue we had to deal with but the first issue was player contracts, the residual liabilities to the players. In an insolvent situation in an English football club, you can't just get rid of them. You have to carry on paying them or they can leave if they want. But if they can't get that money elsewhere they'll stay. They know they will be guaranteed their money. I had to try and compromise with the players. What I was asking them to do was to take a compromise over monies due to them over the next two or three years."

It wasn't quite the equivalent of convincing turkeys to vote for Christmas but it was close. Outside of politicians, bankers and celeb entertainers, no one has a worse rep than footballers. Greedy, narcissistic, mercenary... and now Birch was trying to get them to take a pay cut. "They could have left without any money but just a promise that they'd be paid over a period of time by whoever takes over the club in the future," he explained. "There were a load of variables so you can understand why it took so long. But between February and August we got it done with 18 senior players. None started the following season. Some didn't have clubs to go to. You have to praise them for agreeing to take a compromise to save the club. If you're looking for heroes... well, Tal Ben Haim was a big earner and he took a cut."

Luke Varney was another who wrote off money to help keep the club in existence. Altogether there were 25 ex-players owed a total of £6.72m when the season ended in May 2013. As welcome as their removal from the payroll was, they had to be replaced and Birch remembers: "The Football League wouldn't let us sign players on long-term contracts. So everybody we signed was on a one-month contract and every single month we had to re-sign 20 players. They were heroes as well as they stuck with it. They had a belief in the club. It's a great club."

The settlement wasn't perfect. There were discrepancies between what players agreed and a gulf between what they received and what was left for local creditors. That's because of the much-criticised football creditor rule that protects its own – players and clubs being at the head of the queue. Other creditors, owed £24m, accepted the trust bid's offer of around £1m, although McInnes stressed they are paying small businesses and charities in full. The bid borrowed £1.6m from Portsmouth council, now repaid, and £1.2m from a local property developer, Stuart Robinson, to help pay Chainrai his £3m. Robinson bought the car park and adjoining land, which was subject to so many unrealised plans, and built a supermarket on it. The store opened in November 2015. McInnes summed it up when he said: "We must never forget what happened because we must never let it happen again. But all that has been exorcised. This is a proper football club again, and we're looking forward."

Brown agreed: "It's chalk and cheese from where we were, thoroughly enjoyable, a bit frustrating at times. It's probably the highest capital base that the club has had. We're back to where we were when I started watching. In my opinion this model which is not so very different from the German model that works for 18 out of 20 Bundesliga sides. If this model doesn't work I fear for the future of quite a lot of people in football. Yes, the players did compromise – most of them – Trevor might have his own opinion on that. But it went right down to the wire as a couple of players didn't believe that if we went into receivership they'd get anything because Chainrai was promising he would pay them every penny they were owed. My opinion is that he wasn't going to do that and he would pocket the money and bugger off."

To my question about getting back into the top flight, he says: "It's almost impossible. If we can get back into the Championship, it would be a really great achievement for us. We've signed a lot of players on salaries that are so low it would surprise the average man in the street. We've done it because we are a big club in this division and people love playing at Fratton Park because it's an old fashioned stadium with a great atmosphere. The only feelgood factor in Portsmouth right now is what's happening to the football club. We're in a far better financial position than we budgeted for. I think the most difficult thing has been the football side. We've had to change the manager more often than we wanted to do. I think the board would stand by every decision we made to hire and fire those managers. That's a learning curve in itself. The football itself is a learning curve."

Farmery put it this way: "We are well aware we are a laboratory experiment. We see ourselves as a pioneering club and whether we can make it all the way back to the Premier League, I'm not sure. We have now got this hybrid model that's unique. We're confident we can make it work and gradually the fans have begun to realise it might work." When I asked him later, as Head of Inclusion & Safeguarding at PFC, to sum up how the experiment has been going, he said: "In the two and a half years since the community bid was successful, both the fans and the club have been on a huge learning curve. It is fair to say I think a large number of people, both fans and those now running the club, under estimated how difficult it would prove to get a successful side on the field. Going through three managers (Whittingham, Barker and Awford) in two seasons was hardly indicative of bringing stability to the club some might argue, although there were genuine mitigating circumstances which justified each decision. Off the field however, the club has gone from strength to strength, increasing its season ticket base year on year, despite disappointing performances on the field. A number of long-overdue infrastructure issues have been addressed, including a new training ground in the city and significant investment in patching up Fratton Park. By and large I believe fans understand what the current Board and management team are trying to do and have given them the benefit of any doubt there might have been because they can see the intentions are honorable. There are significant challenges ahead, especially if the club is successful on the field and finds itself back in the Championship any time soon, but it is as well-placed as it can be to rise to these and after the past six or seven years it would be a much nicer 'problem' to have to be grappling with than wondering whether we'd even have a club at all. "If we had liquidated, nothing would have stopped Chainrai building houses or whatever at Fratton Park. There's no other land to build a stadium on and 20,000 people would have lost a football club, the life blood of a community. There was no certainty that, after liquidation, Portsmouth would have reappeared."

In an attempt to get his side of the story, I wrote to Balram Chainrai and offered to meet him in Hong Kong. I mentioned that I would be in Macao for the Manny Pacquiao-Brandon Rios fight and he suggested we meet there as he was also going to the fight. He was staying at the venue no less, at the exclusive 'Mansions' in The Venetian, but our meeting did not go as I had hoped. He answered neither his mobile nor the land line phone for 45 minutes – I got reception to try as well – so by the time I had been received by his butler (yes), he was ready to take his family to lunch. He was both apologetic and friendly, promising to meet later, the time dependent on his progress in an afternoon poker tournament. And he asked his driver to take me back to my hotel. The 'Mansions' really lived up to their name and I had a brief glimpse of another opulent world. In the evening, his Girl Friday (flunkies come with a mansion) was waiting at a neighbouring casino and ushered me to one of the inner sanctums where the real money is won and lost. Chainrai introduced me to a couple of his cronies and ordered whisky and champagne. If this was any kind of statement about Portsmouth, I was scratching my head. Perhaps he was reading my mind as when I took out my recorder, he said: "Oh, no, put that away. I don't want to do an interview." 'Then why did you agree...?' "The Portsmouth thing's over and I just want to show that we can be friends." I told him I had nothing to do with Portsmouth and he had wasted my time. As if to placate me, he asked if I wanted to join a card game. I declined. He stuck the TV on and the Merseyside derby was on. As I watched, supping his champagne, I told myself I had been in worse situations. About 15 minutes later, he came back to the bar and announced matter-of-factly that he'd won "220,000". I didn't bother to ask what currency. He then made a comment on the game. He even mentioned Portsmouth but only to say something about owners getting a raw deal. After asking again if he'd talk on the record, the firmness of his reply told me it was a lost cause. I thanked him for his

309

champagne and we parted amicably. To this day I'm unable to explain why he invited me.

But what he told the *South China Morning Post* in January 2013 seemed to come from the heart: "Running a club is a full-time job. You can't run it from Hong Kong. You have to be living in England and be hands-on every day." He added: "This was not my regular business, so it was all new to me. I'd be more vigilant and careful before investing my money into anything like this again. When things start to go bad they go downhill fast."

For heroes, there are too many to list here but all those who rattled buckets, Brown and Farmery of the trust, whose unstinting work and dogged determination were something to behold and, McInnes whose leadership and commitment, not to mention humour, held the whole thing together. No dog has ever gone after a bone with more determination than Micah Hall, and there is Birch, for being a football man with a genuine desire to keep the club afloat after years of slash and burn. Mick Williams, one of three fans on the board, spoke for many when he said: "They tried to take our history and our heritage away from us." Famous fan John Westwood said: "This club is the heartbeat of the city and a big part of people's lives. The foreign investors don't realise that communities survive on the identity of their football club." The city council did though and also played its part by agreeing to offer the club a bridging loan of £1.45m at a crucial time.

There was mutual admiration too. Birch said: "The PST has shown what can be achieved when fans unite together for the good of their community. The club has been through considerable turmoil over the last few years, and I hope it can now enjoy a period of stability and the chance to build solid foundations for a sustainable future based on hard work and honest endeavour.

"For some clubs it's definitely a model to look at very carefully. For a club like this that has been through so much, it almost needs to return to the fans for a bit of TLC." He said the club was "very close" to going bust throughout the 15 months of his tenure as administrator. In the early days, people got sick of me saying it might go into liquidation. And if it had and the stadium had been lost, it may never have reappeared."

What can be learned from this unfortunate saga? The overwhelming message is that no matter how ruthless, how predatory and how numerous(!), opportunist owners can be fended off and eventually overcome. But only if the fans unite as one. Portsmouth's fans showed an extraordinary unity and resolve, and with the authorities – Football League and Portsmouth Council – also rallying to their aid along with (second time round) a sympathetic administrator, the bad guys were eventually beaten. Bad guys? As Birch says, whatever it was they wanted – pleasure or gain – they were riding roughshod over a storied, century-old institution that was the focal point of an entire community. And of which they knew very little. Whether it was a vehicle for more gain, revenge or a turf war, they had no right to choose it as a battleground and if they wanted their money back, they had no right to destroy it – as they almost did – in the process. Even with all the help Pompey got, it was still a damned close thing.

As it was, according to Farmery, the whole mess stemmed from the Gaydamaks attempting to do an Abramovich-lite – and getting ambushed by a French court case and the global recession.

He says: "The thing that always pains me is when people think Portsmouth was a very simple case of boom to bust. That wasn't the case. Had Gaydamak Snr stayed out of trouble and the money kept flowing, we'd probably have a new stadium and be in the Premier League now. Not quite at the Man City/Chelsea level but in the top half. Fulham under Al Fayed were perhaps a better example. I'm not necessarily saying that is a good thing in itself, but by Premier League standards Pompey could have punched their financial weight. The primary reason Portsmouth imploded was not because of the FA Cup, not because we put all that money into it, but because we got into the grip of people who were fighting a business turf war by proxy and Portsmouth FC was the proxy."

I suggest to McInnes that when it comes to foreign owners, Portsmouth are the opposite end of the spectrum to Manchester City. Borrowing the title of David Conn's *magnum opus*, I ask: If they are *Richer than God*, what are you? It didn't take him long: "Poorer than Moses," he quipped. Both had found their way out of the wilderness.

Queens Park Rangers

QUEENS PARK RANGERS

1

"I was thinking of buying a pizzeria and someone mentioned QPR. I thought it was a barbecue restaurant."

Flavio Briatore.

"It's cost me 50 million quid to find the game's immoral," said Tony Fernandes after QPR were relegated in 2013. A clutch of over-priced and over-paid millionaires had taken the budget airline boss for a very expensive ride. *The Independent* called the club: "An El Dorado for aging mercenaries". A few years earlier, Flavio Briatore described their predecessors as "a load of shit".

The modern history of QPR sees players mostly in supporting roles to a star-studded board. As colourful as the stadium is drab, directors have included a Brazilian World Cup winning captain, Britain's richest man, the boss of Formula One, a wanted man, wheeler-dealers, fly-by-nights and a high flyer who was one of *Time Magazine's* 100 Most Influential People for 2015. Alas for Fernandes and the club, he has not been as influential when it comes to football.

This tale is essentially about two regimes: the Lakshmi Mittal/Bernie Ecclestone/Flavio Briatore trident – a veritable Messi, Suarez & Neymar among the extravagantly heeled – and their successors led by Fernandes. The first was immortalised in *The Four Year Plan*, the second is into its fourth year and as many discarded drawing boards. Throughout, QPR have shown that being richer than Croesus is no guarantee of getting a football club to function properly, let alone succeed on the pitch. In fact, building a world-famous brand or Asia's biggest budget airline from two planes must have seemed a doddle in comparison.

"For the real beginning of this saga," says the supporters trust's Neil Jackson, "you have to go back a bit further to when we were drifting after David Bulstrode's death." 'Drifting' would be blissful equanimity compared to what was to come. For decades, very rich men would try – and mostly fail – to make something of a modest club that is seldom a hospital pass from distraction. Property developer Bulstrode had wanted to merge it with Fulham and call the combined club, Fulham Park Rangers. The combined fury of the fans saw him off. Bulstrode died of a heart attack in the arms of his blonde mistress, according to the red tops.

Then there was a race horse owner who barely got under starter's orders, and a music tycoon who didn't always hit the right notes. After Ian Holloway had conjured an unlikely promotion from the third tier in 2004, only a dodgy loan from an unlikely place kept the club alive. Back then, Panama was better known for its canal than its "papers", but ABC, an off-shore company registered in the tax haven, lent QPR £10m – at 10% interest when the normal rate was 3%. Rangers were warned they'd better sign up or the team wouldn't be playing the following week. It would not be the last time a Rangers chairman had a gun pointed at his head.

The next came in the literal sense – or so Gianni Paladini claimed. The Italian-born former agent and interpreter was not in the Forbes league and had to mortgage his house to buy his shares, but somehow ended up as chairman. Minutes before the 2005-06 season kicked off, he claimed he was met by fellow director, David Morris, and led to his office where he was surrounded by thugs who told him: "Sign, sign the paper – or we'll kill you." Terrified, he said he signed over his 14.7% shares and survived to call the cops and have his day in court – but had his evidence shredded and lost the case.

Jackson's take on it is: "Something happened. Daniel Morris, David's brother, left the country before the trial and is still on the run. And Paladini wears a bullet-proof vest." Showing his survival instincts, Paladini would later instigate a boardroom reshuffle with none other than Dunga flying in to cast the deciding vote. Paladini was nothing if not well-connected – another board member was Antonio Caliendo, a one-time Mr Big of Italian agents. Caliendo's greatest claim to fame was that 12 of the 22 players in the 1990 World Cup semi-final between West Germany and Italy were on his books.

Journeymen on the field, jokers off it just about summed up Rangers back then. Holloway was put on gardening leave for having flirted with Leicester and in came former player Gary Waddock. It took a late penalty from Paul Furlong in the last game of the 2005-06 season to avoid the drop. That summer's pre-season tour seemed to sum up the state of the club. Clive Whittingham of the fanzine *Loft For Words*, described it as being what you might expect from "the Dog and Duck Second XI's summer tour of Ibiza." Fans called it one of the worst Rangers teams in memory. Paladini meanwhile managed to wheel and deal to ensure the players were paid and the club stayed out of administration. Often it was a close-run thing.

In 2007, QPR were pretty much back to where they were just over a decade earlier – in the second tier and heading south. But the desperate state of the team and the finances was just part of an overwhelming sense of despair. "We began to wonder if the club was cursed," says Jackson. "There was even a rumour that a *feng-shui* master's advice had been ignored back in 2005 and some believed we were now paying the price."

Rangers' youth team had failed to produce a top player since the last millennium but in Ray Jones, 18, a highly-rated England Under-19 striker, they thought they had someone who might buck the trend. In the early hours of August 25, Jones's VW Golf collided with a double-decker bus in East Ham and he was killed along with his two teenage passengers. It felt like the last straw. In the previous November, youth team players had been involved in an incident that saw a Vietnamese student fall to his death under a tube train. One young hopeful, Harry Smart, was seriously injured. Six months before that another starlet, Kiyan Price, was stabbed to death in a classroom. And in February 2007, a 'friendly' between the Chinese Olympic team and a fringe QPR side erupted in a 30-man melee. 'The Great Brawl of China' was the inevitable headline. Rangers were fined £40,000 and assistant coach, Richard Hill, was banned for three months. The game had been meant to help foster better international relations. But it was Jones' death that really devastated the club and was its darkest moment yet. Recalls Jackson: "Just when we thought something might happen [for the better], something would bring us down." Back then no one was saying the darkest hour is just before dawn.

"The next match was against Southampton and during the minute's silence for Ray Jones, I noticed Flavio Briatore," remembers Jackson. "The club was still in a state of shock and we got beat. Then we were taken over by Briatore and Bernie Ecclestone. If not for that, there was very little doubt the club would have folded. We hadn't paid the rent on the training ground, the gates were locked and the players couldn't use it. The people we owed money to were queuing up and the tax man pushed through the queue. But Paladini got us the deal. He was always one week away from a deal and this time he succeeded."

Whilst there was immense relief, fans wondered why a couple of F1 moguls were suddenly buying a football club, especially one stuck in the pits and in need of more than a tyre change. But in December they were joined by Lakshmi Mittal, then the world's fifth richest man. As Jackson recalls, "We were the richest club in the world in theory." In practice? "That would be an entirely different matter."

And so began *The Four Year Plan*, actual and cinematic. You only have to glimpse the trailer to Mat Hodgson's award-winning documentary to wonder how the powers that be agreed to this fly-on-the-wall account. And why they hadn't called for the insecticide at the first Briatore tantrum. The walls were almost knocked down in frustration but 'the flies' remained steadfast to produce a classic of its kind. *The Guardian's* Michael Hann called it "dynamite" and "possibly the most vivid insight into the running of a football club yet committed to film." Paladini kicks at the advertising boards as if he means to hurt them. Briatore is soon calling successive managers "that fucking hooligan" and "that prick in the dugout". Then he demands the names of fans who booed him.

The inevitable question that hung over him was: What's a multi-millionaire Casanova like you doing in a place like this? He seemed to have it all – the F1 team, the yacht, the women – but was spending wet Wednesday nights in Shepherd's Bush. Even when winning, it was far from the ultimate male fantasy existence to which he was accustomed. King of the pit lane with perma tan, silver hair and gold fly – he owned a men's couture company that flogged jeans with gold buttons for £500

– he was hardly a natural fit. Even after a forensic search, the only thing found to be remotely in sync with Rangers was the blue tint of his designer shades.

He hadn't always been loaded, though. Born in the small town of Verzuolo to primary school teachers, he did not shine academically and left school with a low-grade diploma. He became a ski instructor, then a restaurant manager and, when that closed with huge debts, he sold insurance door-to-door. His big break came when he bumped into Luciano Benetton in 1974. He somehow talked his way into getting hired and his radical approach to retail and advertising turned the clothing company into a giant – and made both of them a fortune. In 1989, the Benetton founder introduced Briatore to Formula One and though he was no petrol head, he was to have a similarly turbo-charged impact on team performance.

He was not supposed to be as hands-on at QPR but try telling that to the poor sods in the dugout. The plan was to reach the Premier League in four years and have some fun on the way. It could never be regarded as a purely business acquisition because – as Paladini noted – there was never a dull moment. And if promotion was the substance, there had to be plenty of style too – especially for a man who didn't feel properly dressed without a voluptuous babe on each arm. As he told Adrian Deevoy in *The Observer*, Briatore wanted to do what he'd done in Formula One at Benetton – make a modest name famous and reap the rewards. Upon taking over QPR, he said: "Football is more than just 11 players on a field – it's a brand as well." When they heard that fans knew they had to fasten their seatbelts.

It wasn't love at first sight with the football club and, compared to the electricity of the F1 track, South Africa Road must have seemed as if it were lit by gas lamps. He had a challenge on his hands but was not long in coming up with what he thought was a solution – turning QPR into a "boutique club" for the rich and famous.

If there was method in this wanton disregard for the die-hards and apparent marketing madness, it was in QPR's lack of a huge fan base. No matter how many gazillions were thrown at it, the club would never be an Arsenal, a Chelsea or a Spurs. But W12 is a short chauffeur drive from Kensington, Holland Park and Mayfair where a lot of zillionaires hang out. It was an even shorter hop in a chopper – the preferred mode of transport for Briatore and his mates. Bugger the loyal fans, attract the loaded ones. As he put it, "I'm not going to be told what to do by someone who pays twenty quid."

And so began the systematic gentrification of Loftus Road. Says Jackson: "He came up with the idea of a W12 club with gold, silver and bronze class seating." Long-term season ticket holders were turfed out of their ancient lairs and prices went through the tin roof. There was a special dining area – a branch of Cipriani's restaurant in which he was a shareholder – and, adds Jackson, "the whole experience of going to QPR would encompass a good meal, a comfortable seat with a blanket over you and, in the fullness of time, much more. In the front entrance there was a chandelier that cost £12,000 and the words 'QPR Boutique' were etched on the windows."

If this was 'doing a Benetton', he drove into the gravel on the first chicane. The 'blokes who pay 20 quid' were not impressed. They responded by bestowing upon Briatore his very own chant: "Bri-a-tore, he's a wanker, he's a wanker." Besides alienating the real fans he was taking the prawn sandwich brigade to a whole new level of conspicuously disinterested consumption. Where once there was half-time Bovril, there was now beef *carpaccio* behind Perspex. There would be few real fans left as most were priced out, while on chilly nights with the windows shut, even the clinking of wine glasses would be out of earshot. What next would he come up with for the millionaire with everything but a team? Scented candles in the directors' box? Saunas? On-demand massages? A rich man might need something to occupy him if Rangers were finding the opposing defence difficult to break down.

Briatore betrayed his ignorance of the club when he admitted: "I was thinking of buying a pizzeria and someone mentioned QPR. I thought it was a barbecue restaurant." But that was never going to restrain him once ensconced in the boardroom. The clay pigeon shoot of managers began when he replaced compatriot Luigi De Canio with Ian Dowie. A more rigorous fitness regime and direct style of play saw an encouraging start to the 2008/9 season. The highlight was Rangers' 1-0 win at Aston Villa in the third round of the League Cup that meant an away tie to reigning League champions, Manchester United. It did not look like a plan but for a few fleeting days in the autumn of 2008, with debts paid, new faces and the team climbing the table, things did seem to be looking up.

QUEENS PARK RANGERS

2

"If there was an idiot, we've found him."

QPR director Alejandro Agag speaking about managers in
The Four Year Plan.

The feelgood factor from Villa Park proved illusory. The next match was a 2-0 home defeat to Derby which Briatore missed as he was in Singapore leading the Renault team in Formula One's first ever night race. It was a no-brainer and he had no choice, but how he wished he'd endured that miserable loss instead of what would unfold in the Far East.

In the oppressive heat of the tropics, Briatore had been dismayed to see his No.1 driver and protégé, Fernando Alonso, eliminated from qualifying with a fuel problem before he could set a lap time. He had to start the race from 15th on the grid. According to Briatore's accusers almost a year later, that was when a devious plan was hatched. On the 14th lap, just after Alonso had pitted, Renault's No.2 driver Nelson Piquet Jr. crashed into the barriers. The safety car came out and all the leaders pitted. Alonso was first out, took the lead and ended up winning the historic race. It was September 28, 2008.

Upon returning to London, Briatore turned his attention back to his football club – and sacked Dowie. The Ulsterman had been in charge for just 15 games and won eight of them to take Rangers to ninth in the table, a point from the play-off places. Everyone was stunned. Briatore was not merely hands-on, he had them around his manager's throat. A heavy downpour at the fourth-round League Cup clash at Manchester United caused newly-installed caretaker, Gary Ainsworth, to leave his mobile phone in the dressing room. After a 1-0 defeat he trudged back to find there were 72 missed calls – all from Briatore.

Ainsworth's successor was Paolo Sousa, who Briatore dubbed 'the New Special One' but it didn't take long for the Portuguese to find he would not be getting special treatment. Instead, he was on the wrong end of what would be the *piece de resistance* of the Italian's interference. It came during a 0-0 draw with Crystal Palace when Briatore was 6,500 miles away at the Malaysian Grand Prix, but watching the match in Kuala Lumpur. Unimpressed, he called Sousa at half-time and ordered him to make a substitution. At the start of the second half, Lee Cook duly came on for Liam Miller.

But it was on the track where Briatore had gone completely feral. In August of the following F1 season after making a bitter exit from Renault, Nelson Piquet Jr. told a very different story about the Singapore Grand Prix. Granted immunity from punishment, the Brazilian admitted to the FIA that he'd been under orders from Briatore and chief engineer, Pat Symonds, to deliberately crash his car to help Alonso. After initially threatening legal action, Renault soon owned up and forced Briatore and Symonds to resign. A subsequent FIA investigation banned the Italian from F1 for life – the most severe sanction in the sport's history. Briatore appealed and got the ban overturned as well as €15,000 compensation.

He'd done it, he claimed, "to save the team", but couldn't get away from it being a form of race fixing and, to ensure he didn't fall foul of football's fit and proper person's test, he resigned as a director of QPR. He explained: "So as not to create embarrassment to the English Football Association after what happened in Singapore."

It was a rare moment of prudence amid a frenzied cull of managers – the tally reached six, including caretakers, in the 12 months since Sousa left in April, 2009. *The Four Year Plan* shows director Alejandro Agag shouting, "If there was an idiot, we've found him." Despite the chaos and a lowly league position, fans detected a more positive vibe. Alejandro Faurlin, an Argentine playmaker, and Adel Taraabt, a Spurs reject striker, arrived in July – both largely unheralded acquisitions made by Paladini. The chairman was by now dubbed the Teflon Man as no matter how much mud flew around the club, nothing stuck to him, while Mittal's son-in-law, Amit Bhatia, gave the board a much-needed voice of reason. When Rangers were drawn away to Chelsea in the FA Cup, fans took a banner to Stamford Bridge claiming: "We're richer than you." Many brandished £20 notes.

QPR fans had their gloat but the team did not live up to their new-found status. Chelsea won the tie and it was soon business as usual at Loftus Road – welcoming a new manager. It was a bit of a surprise to find the paths of Neil Warnock, 61, a man of many clubs, and Rangers, a club of countless managers, had not previously crossed. But from the outset in March 2010, it seemed a decent fit. Briatore, who retained his shares and a big influence, wanted "a strong man" to sort out an ever-changing dressing room. He agreed a 3½-year deal, buying out Warnock's contract with Crystal Palace. QPR were 20th in the Championship, three points off the relegation places, but Warnock said: "I am delighted to be joining a club with the history that QPR has. As a manager, Loftus Road is always a place I loved because of the fantastic atmosphere there. Looking from afar, I believe this is the perfect time to come in, with the new structure and chairman in place."

Armed with a sizable budget, he made some judicious signings and had Rangers moving safely up the table before the season ended. It was enough to fuel a degree of optimism for the following (2010/11) season but no one expected QPR to storm to the title – even when they were top. The threat of a points deduction loomed large for much of the season as the FA inquired into the transfer of Faurlin. In keeping with QPR's recent history, it was far from a straightforward matter with Rangers being accused of buying a player owned by a third party. With the Carlos Tevez affair still fresh in the memory, many felt the FA would throw the proverbial book at Rangers – hence their genuine fears that a points deduction might cost them promotion. Indeed, seven charges were laid at their door and it was against this background that the club had to continue its promotion push.

There was a very real prospect of the Promised Land being snatched away as Briatore faced a bleak future in his other sport. Prolonging the agony, the FA's tribunal did not reach a verdict on the case until the final day of the season – they found the club guilty of one charge and fined them £875,000 but there would be no points deduction. The fans heard the news on their way to the game and celebrated by doing congas on the tube.

It was vindication for Warnock and the board, and enabled the latter to say 'mission accomplished'. They had taken a team from the

Championship basement into the Premier League in three years although fans and anyone who saw *The Four Year Plan* would say the team did it in spite of, rather than because, of them. Briatore and Ecclestone quit while they were ahead – selling to Fernandes. "I believe we did it quite well but, I tell you, it was no fun at all," said Briatore. "You need to treat football like a full-time job and not like an investor. There were too many people. The manager, the assistant manager and, always, you were dealing with the agents. In the end, we sold it."

So how do we assess this reign that might have achieved its main objective but outraged supporters, terrorised managers, troubled the FA and was never anything less than tumultuous?

Unlike some owners featured in this book, Briatore (and to a lesser extent Ecclestone) are football fans. The Italian was a lifelong follower of Juventus while Ecclestone described himself as a Chelsea fan. So there was at least some feel for the game itself. Of Briatore's credentials, there was no doubt – he was even linked with the Juventus presidency. But an affinity with football at large only made his contempt for QPR's managers and supporters all the more inexcusable. Whether it was knee-jerk sackings or hiking the cost of admission, it was shocking in scale. Indeed, few of those owners who have confessed to blind ignorance of the mores of the game have treated managers and fans with such disdain. It was arrogant, demeaning, unnecessary and almost feudal. And for such so-called smart-arse businessmen, it was surprising – and counterproductive. No less than a dozen managers tested the ejector seat in less than four years and the number of caretakers tells us that often no successor was lined up. It was back-of-an-envelope stuff and the modus operandi of the madhouse.

During *The Four Year Plan*, captain of the day Mikele Leigertwood gives his verdict: "The last three years has been a nightmare to be honest." If their penny wise, pound foolish ways are anything to go by, you can see why. In a rare cameo, Ecclestone looks at the water bottles and says: "We need to cut down on this expenditure," while Ishan Saksena, then MD, explains: "The philosophy [in football] is if you are spending so much on players, what is another 10, 20 grand here or there? But when you add up those 10, 20 grand, it's like a few million which we can use to buy players." Mr Micawber might have approved but he wouldn't have travelled to matches by helicopter and Ferrari.

Officially, they have to go down as saviours and credit has to be given for clearing the debt, especially removing the Panamanian millstone. But these guys were loaded and gratitude is grudging. The boutique idea was nonsense – football without atmosphere isn't football. For a Juventus fan to come up with it is unforgivable – Briatore wouldn't try it on the ultras in Turin and he shouldn't have tried it in W12.

He expressed a wish for attractive football – they all do, don't they? – but how could any coherent style of play – attractive or otherwise – be implemented when the guy in the dugout had the career-expectancy of a bomb disposal officer? He did seem genuinely enthused by the opportunity to 'do a Benetton' all over again but chose the wrong vehicle to have any chance of repeating that success with the dreaded 'brand'. The word is to football fans what garlic is to the vampire and QPR's were repelled by the notion. But he should have known better than to equate a clothing company with a football club anyway. Once again, we have to conclude that football is not like any other business – and certainly not one where shock advertising could work. The best thing they did was getting Warnock. He had won six promotions in all and if there were doubts about him at the highest level, he was the man for this division. We have to give them that, but had they stayed to complete the transformation of Loftus Road... it does not bear thinking about.

QUEENS PARK RANGERS

3

*"I'm taking what I consider to be an unpolished diamond to become a
fully-fledged diamond over the next period of years."*

Tony Fernandes

A budget airline boss takes off on a flight of fancy to buy West Ham
– the club he's supported since he was a boy – only to land at no-frills
QPR with someone else's baggage. If that's a cheap shot at an entire
industry, it's how cynics might sum up Tony Fernandes' arrival in
football. The Malaysian, founder of a ground-breaking, award-winning
budget airline, tried hard to get the Hammers but endured a bumpy
ride. Karren Brady made fun of him: "He offered to buy half our club for
nothing, on the basis that it would be worth more with him running it.
We politely declined!" The two Davids (Gold and Sullivan) played hard
ball and although talks went on all through the summer of 2011, the
idea was eventually ditched. "He wants the whole club for two bob,"
complained David Sullivan. Fernandes hit back and after a bout of
twitter turbulence, he changed course. Messrs Briatore and Ecclestone
prepared the runway in another part of London, grateful their F1 crony
still had enough fuel.

Briatore had already sold his share to Ecclestone but still called the
shots. Fernandes bought the F1 supremo's 66 per cent for what *The
Guardian* said was "around £35 million". After the long and bitter wrangle
with Gold and Sullivan, the QPR deal was done with a haste befitting
the fast lane. Fernandes owned Lotus at the time and the cosiness of
the sale led many to assume a quid pro quo – in return for buying out a
disinterested Bernie, there was the promise of a bigger role in F1.

Mittal remained as a 33 per cent minority shareholder and Bhatia, who
had resigned in protest against the ticket price hike, would come back as
vice-chairman. One worry for Fernandes was that he'd made such a fuss

about being a Hammers' fan, it might look as if he was buying Rangers on the rebound. But Rangers' fans, although no lovers of West Ham, were impressed by how he fronted up on that. Indeed, the Malaysian came across as a refreshing change – similarly loaded but dynamic and with a deft, man-of-the-people touch. But there were plenty of items still on the carousel that had been left by his predecessors.

Even though they'd been promoted as champions, the team needed a lot spending on it. Of this he was made painfully aware watching the first game back in the top flight – a 4-0 home defeat to Bolton. Rangers finished with 10 men and, in Warnock's words, "committed suicide". Many cattle-class fans left early but not before aiming abuse at Briatore in the well-upholstered cockpit of the directors' box. "Seventy-two quid for this shit" was the gist.

The Briatore/Ecclestone decision to hike prices had been taken almost as soon as promotion had been won – and spoiled the party that was still going on. Many seats now cost £72 and the cheapest were £47. Season tickets were up by almost 40% from last term and the increases were met with dismay by Rangers fans. "It's an absolute disgrace and, yet again, underlines the total contempt the owners of QPR have for the fans," said Paul Finney of the *Independent Rs* website. "Flavio Briatore's dream is a 'boutique' club, which has an exclusive feel to it and is the place for wealthy people to be seen."

Fernandes was well aware that it was no bed of roses in W12, but once the deal had been finalised in the early hours of the morning on Thursday, August 18, he met the press to announce the takeover. Media-savvy in the worlds of F1 and aviation, he was never going to be caught out by a few football hacks, but the way he spoke still managed to impress. No new owner ever promises to park the bus, flog the best player and merge with hated neighbours on the first day – even if they try it on the second – but Fernandes looked as if he might be a different breed to the norm. And certainly from his predecessors.

He was humble enough to tell the media he would be relying on Bhatia's support "in taking what I consider to be an unpolished diamond to become a fully-fledged diamond over the next period of years." And on the vexed question of West Ham, he added: "Everyone knows I've followed West Ham all my life, but I've always had a soft spot for QPR. Rangers were one of the first teams I watched as a child at Loftus Road. The opportunity to get involved with the club was mentioned to me by the previous owners and here I am. I've always wanted to be involved in football and the appeal of a London Club, like QPR, was too good an opportunity to turn down. It's funny how life has a way of spinning things round. It goes full circle sometimes. I never imagined that one day I would become chairman."

He hit just the right notes to give rise to a degree of optimism and came across as the polar opposite of Briatore and Ecclestone. "The fans pay good money and are stakeholders, so whatever we do, I want the fans to be proud. We'll do it in style and with integrity." How different to Briatore's contempt for "the man who pays 20 quid"!

Born in Kuala Lumpur, Fernandes inherited his entrepreneurial spirit from his mother who took him to Tupperware parties as a small boy. At 12, he was sent to Epsom College boarding school then studied at the London School of Economics, where he qualified as an accountant. Passionate about music – he plays the guitar and piano – he worked in the music industry for 14 years, becoming financial controller for Richard Branson's Virgin Records, then returned to Malaysia as the youngest managing director of Warner Music where he would become regional vice president.

But the move that earned him fame and fortune was buying debt-laden AirAsia, with three partners, for one Malaysian ringgit (20p) in 2001. He had to remortgage his home and had only £250,000 initially to invest but within a decade turned it into a low-cost airline flying 18 million passengers to 65 cities in Asia and around the world. On a turnover of £790m, it made a pre-tax profit of £200m, according to its most recent annual report before he bought QPR.

If Fernandes' arrival lifted spirits, he was quick to play down hopes of a massive splurge on players. "I philosophically don't believe that's the way to build a football club," he said. "It's important to build deep structures and to build from the bottom up." Even AirAsia's tagline 'Now Everyone Can Fly' hinted at a more egalitarian persona than had been seen for a long time although he was not averse to using the word 'branding'. When asked by *CNN* if, as a businessman focusing on building brands, he might lose sight of his sporting interests and, in turn, the supporters, he said: "Oh no, absolutely not. They're integrated. You need to build brands to get the budgets for the fans to be able to get the players for them to have success. So they're very interlinked. Unless you have a big 'sugar daddy'. I'm not a sugar daddy, or a sugar mummy. Maybe a sugar baby."

A favourable first impression was badly needed as the summer had been soured by both the admission price hike and the boardroom in-fighting it triggered. Bhatia, more in tune with the fans than his partners, had tried to buy out Ecclestone, but with their row rumbling, little was spent on the team. Prior to Fernandes' arrival five players had come in but only DJ Campbell at £1.25m had cost a fee.

With only a few days of the transfer window remaining, Warnock convinced him of the need to bolster an inadequate squad. 'Sugar baby' was an apt description as the manager admitted the pair were "like kids in a sweet shop" as they discussed new additions. They signed six players in five days for just about the £10m budget Fernandes had indicated would be available. In came Shaun Wright- Phillips, Luke Young, Joey Barton, Armand Traore and Anton Ferdinand. A fair bit of Premier League experience was brought in for not a huge amount in transfer fees, but the wages and agents' fees would be another story. So, too, would the commitment of some of them.

The full magnitude of the task facing Warnock and Fernandes to keep Rangers in the top flight was rammed home by neighbours Fulham on October 2. And the 6-0 scoreline was not the full story – the surrender was abject with a disinterested Taraabt, subbed at half-time, walking out of the ground during the second half and allegedly catching a bus. Redemption would come three weeks later in the infamous match with Chelsea when Anton Ferdinand alleged that John Terry had called him "a fucking black cunt". It kick-started a racial furore, but not QPR's season. With Rangers 17th on January 8, Fernandes decided a change was necessary to ensure safety. He liked Warnock and hit it off with him – but the prospect of losing the coveted place in the top flight in the first season was something the board felt they wanted to avoid at all costs. Fernandes said: "It was one of the toughest decisions I've ever made."

The sacking smacked of panic and many feel it was his first big mistake. He immediately compounded it by making his second – appointing Mark Hughes. As often happens when a popular manager is sacked, the fans did not take to his successor. Known as a draw specialist, Hughes' best work had come with Wales and Blackburn. He doesn't take any nonsense from his players, but lacked Warnock's humour – and fire: Sparky would be slow to ignite the team.

He would buy three players in the January window – Djibril Cisse, Nedum Onuoha and Bobby Zamora, spending more than Warnock had in the previous summer – but it didn't work. "It was difficult when I walked in," Hughes would say later. "The atmosphere wasn't easy, there was a bit of resentment around the place." Along with the threat of relegation, it lingered until the dying embers of the season. Rangers' escape was a mere footnote to the drama of those final moments when Manchester City won the League. But grateful for the lifeline, Hughes and Fernandes wanted to ensure they wouldn't have to endure such agony again. The 2012-13 season would be crucial for both – Hughes was anxious to restore his reputation after an acrimonious time at Fulham while Fernandes was eager to establish QPR as a Premier League club. "We made big decisions," Hughes said. "I felt at the end of the season the squad wasn't strong enough to stay in the league. We had the opportunity to change that." Again Rangers opted for experience and landed Ryan Nelsen, Robert Green, Park Ji-sung, Andrew Johnson, Fabio, Junior Hoilett and Samba Diakite. But in a start eerily reminiscent of the previous season, they were thumped 5-0 at home by Swansea in the first match. Hughes called it "embarrassing" and promptly bought three more seasoned pros in Julio Cesar, Jose Bosingwa and Esteban Granero.

As early as mid-September, it looked like they'd been chucking good money after bad. The bigger names were just not delivering and concern was mounting. The fans, who had never warmed to Hughes, were becoming more vocal and, after a chastening 3-2 defeat at West Brom on October 6, took to twitter calling for Harry Redknapp. On November 23, the Welshman was put out of his misery. "This is a club where the chairman and shareholders look at all things in a long term view," Fernandes tweeted. "But also take the views of the fans who are the most important constituents of the club. To us fans come first."

Hughes has admitted his time at QPR was 'without a shadow of a doubt' his toughest in management but insisted he has 'no cross to bear' over the manner of his departure. There was certainly no sympathy for R's fans. Michael Hann summed him up as: "The man who named a Premier League squad with only three forwards, two of whom promptly got injured. The man who led the club with all the charisma of a black bin bag, caught in the breeze." An even more sobering epitaph came with the news that QPR had paid the third highest amount (£6.8m) in agents' fees in the Premier League for the 2011/12 season. It was behind only Manchester City (£10.5m) and Liverpool (£8.6m), and almost treble the £2.5m they'd spent in 2010/11.

QUEENS PARK RANGERS

4

"This has been a tragic season in many ways. It is a Shakespearean play in the making."

Tony Fernandes after relegation at the end of the
2012-13 season.

Fifteen months after taking over things could hardly have gone worse for Fernandes. QPR were in dire straits without a win and had just four points from 12 games. A fortune had been spent. Far from being polished, the diamond was still in the ground and the miners were working to rule. It was not a time for tinkering and the owner knew it: what was needed was an escapologist and none had a better rep than Harry 'Houdini' Redknapp. An arch wheeler-dealer and deadpan dispenser of Cockney wit, he was the Arthur Daley of football, and Fernandes had been "in awe of meeting" him. His first 17 matches yielded 19 points. The escape was on.

But Redknapp soon realised that he was being paid to get blood out of reluctant mercenaries. In his autobiography, *Always Managing*, published early the following season, 'Arry, as he's universally known, reserved a chapter for the squad he'd inherited: "The attitude stank," he wrote. "Attitude towards the game, attitude towards training. I can't remember a worse one – and behaviour like that cannot be altered overnight." It wouldn't have been Fernandes' favourite bedtime reading. Redknapp went on: "The directors and owners were nice people but they were naive in football terms and I think certain people they had trusted – agents and advisers – had let them down quite badly."

Redknapp was relatively restrained in the January transfer window, bringing in only five players, the most notable being Loic Remy, an excellent buy for £8m from Marseilles, and Chris Samba for £12.5m. Rangers had become such a magnate for the mediocre that West Brom's

Peter Odemwingie made his famous deadline day drive to Loftus Road and sat in the car park hoping for a contract. *Sky Sports* had also expected more activity and had studio pundits primed. Ex Crystal Palace owner Simon Jordan suggested "lunatics were running the asylum", while Niall Quinn, when asked if Rangers' policy was financial suicide, said: "It's heading that way."

The stick with which critics most frequently beat Rangers was Samba – a signing that Anzhi Makhachkala director, Leonid Tchachenko, said QPR were "out of their minds" to make. The Samba that 'Arry remembered was a warrior, but after a year of riding the Dagestan gravy train, he wasn't even match-fit. They managed to return him in the summer for half a million less than what they paid, but wages of £100,000 a week still made for a significant loss.

Relegation was confirmed with three games to go – to the apparent amusement of Jose Bosingwa. The defender was booed off after the decisive match at Reading but was one of many who had taken Rangers to the cleaners. After the tame surrender, Fernandes tweeted: "Sorry to all QPR fans. But the plan goes on. Now more than ever. We owe it to you. Took 3 years to get Caterham right. No quitting". He added: "Planning starts tomorrow. Meeting harry at 11 to discuss squad. Going to be tough but we will come back stronger".

Redknapp noted: "Nobody is trying harder than him to put right what's gone wrong. He loves the club and they're very fortunate to have a chairman like him I think. The only advice I would give Tony is: get off Twitter." When it was suggested the owners might not be ruthless enough for a dirty business like football, Redknapp said: "I'm sure he is ruthless. You don't become a successful business man if you're a fool." But football was a well-known graveyard for successful businessmen becoming fools.

There followed one of the most honest admissions ever made by a football club chairman. Seated on the pitch at Loftus Road surrounded by the press, Fernandes opened his heart, saying: "I've seen all of the parts that make football quite ... maybe immoral is a strong word but they would sell their grandmother to do something. It's all parts of the football ecosystem. I don't want to go down that route [of naming people] as we have to work with them. But what I am saying is there are people in the business where money comes first. Passion is just something that comes naturally to me. If I was a player, I'd go out every week and give it 150%. I don't know if every player in the Premier League feels hurt when they lose a game. The right sort is very important. I was naive in thinking that everyone was like me. I think I allowed myself to be exploited but that's my choice. I don't think I will be exploited any more. Agents are trying to get the best contracts and there's no two ways about it, I had to pay premiums. It wasn't easy persuading Jose Bosingwa to come. It wasn't easy convincing Julio César, Brazil's No1 goalkeeper, to come. This has been a tragic season in many ways. It is a Shakespearean play in the making."

When Fernandes spoke of how "ethics and principles should come first", *The Guardian's* David Hytner admitted the thought occurred that "Fernandes is maybe too nice, too sensitive for this gig." The owner said: "The music and airlines businesses are tough but I've been successful in them. There's a manner in how you have to be a tough bastard and I don't think I have to be an asshole to be successful in football. I have to be smarter and learn from the experiences, although nobody can train you for relegation or for a player refusing to play [like Bosingwa] because he is a substitute."

Almost two years after he'd taken over, it was not looking as it had in the brochure – *his* brochure. Lots of money had been spent but the team had got worse, there was little evidence of youth development, plans had been ripped up, managers changed but the diamond was deeper in the ground. The budget airline boss had been taken for a flight of fancy. When asked how much he had spent on QPR, he replied: "I don't actually know, but it would be around the £50million mark."

It was the same, raw honesty that fans had heard in Shepherd Bush pubs when the owner drank pints with them, and what appears on his twitter account. I asked Neil Jackson about the owner's *mea culpa*? He said: "He's great at populist gestures. He does podcasts, he's not invisible. He does talk. He's got a lot of time for the fans. He did our fans forum and the majority of fans are on side – absolutely. We're not convinced about 'Arry though. We didn't like the way he was playing. We got impression Tony Fernandes was getting fed up with him too."

There was a time in June 2013 that they were fed up with each other. Redknapp wanted to sign Wayne Bridge but Fernandes blocked the deal. He told *Sky Sports News*: "We have had no row at all... We just want to do things properly and we have learnt a lot from last season. We want players who want to play for us and we want to protect ourselves against players who may get injured or who may not be fit enough." Contrary to certain opinions, it sounded like sanity *was* being restored.

Although desperate to bounce straight back, QPR spent little in the 2013 summer transfer window: just six additions with a wealth of experience for circa £10m between them. Many of the high earners were shipped out but Rangers struggled to get much of their money back... In a clear demonstration of the new policy, the high-earning Remy, who might have banged them in for fun in the Championship, was loaned to Newcastle. At last the owner was able to say: "Now we're in a position where we can trade." The penny – or more precisely, £50m – had dropped.

After the third game of the 2013-14 season, Rangers were never outside the top four. And there was ambitious talk of a long-term plan to build a new 40,000-seater stadium as part of a massive redevelopment project at Old Oak, a couple of miles from Loftus Road but still QPR territory. But in March the accounts for the previous season were announced: Rangers had spent more in wages than Atletico Madrid and Borussia Dortmund. QPR had spent £78m, which was 128% of turnover, compared to Atletico's £54m. Rangers went down to the second tier of English football, Borussia reached the final of the Champions League. Atletico won La Liga and would reach the Champions League final the following year. *The Independent* wrote: "Doing a QPR could soon be added to the lexicon of football disasters the way Leeds and Portsmouth have." Rangers' debt now stood at £177m and the loss for that year was £68m. The permitted maximum under Financial Fair Play rules was £8m.

To tide them over, Fernandes arranged a loan of £27m from Barclay's Bank in Hong Kong. To put it in perspective, it was the third largest loss in English football history with only Chelsea and Manchester City, respectively owned by an oligarch and a sheikh, having recorded higher figures. They hadn't just broken the rules: they'd pretended they didn't exist. And they hadn't inserted relegation clauses in the players' contracts either. But there was still a way out – promotion would mean they didn't have to face the music as they would no longer be under the Football League's jurisdiction. It was Shit or Bust 2.0.

The football was dire but Charlie Austin's goals ensured a final playoff spot against Derby. For years, it has been the world's richest single sporting event – worth circa £120m to the winner in 2014. But to Rangers it would be worth even more. Put another way, defeat would be far more costly to Rangers than their opponents for they would then have to face whatever fines the Football League had in store for them. But almost from the kickoff, Rangers were simply not at the races and Derby dominated. Somehow it remained level at half-time but when Gary O'Neil was sent off on the hour, it looked curtains for QPR. But as often happens, the 10 men regrouped and provided even stiffer resistance. But with extra-time looming and a man advantage, Derby were still favourites. Then in the 90th minute, substitute Bobby Zamora seized on a Derby error and, to the disbelief of both sets of fans, rammed home the winner. It was QPR's very own Michael Thomas/Kun Aguero moment. It took half a second, but delirium broke out in the blue and white ranks. Rangers had done it and 'Arry had escaped again. There would be no fine and Rangers were back where they started under the Malaysian owners. A second chance when all seemed lost. It was larceny for which there is no logic and certainly no legislation. The Damoclean sword the Football League held over them was removed. For now.

QUEENS PARK RANGERS

5

"They've got to learn it's a religion not a business."

Neil Jackson, Rangers' Supporters Trust.

Zamora's goal had given the owners more than a lifeline. Redknapp was seen to punch the air before disappearing in a scrum of delirious players and coaches at the whistle, but it was Fernandes for whom the joy was unconfined. He was carried by Joey Barton around the Wembley turf and walked through the corridors at Wembley, trophy in one hand, bottle of beer in the other, saying: "I am just going to enjoy today, we've got to let the players enjoy it." The fans certainly did – they were dancing in the streets of Shepherd's Bush that night. It hadn't happened very often.

The morning after he knew how lucky he had been – and how much work there was to be done. Even more sobering stats than Derby's domination of possession included a wage bill of £13m to Rangers' £72m; just 170 Premier League appearances to Rangers' 4,264, and Derby were debt-free while Rangers' debt was £177m. On top of all that, Derby had played attractive football ever since Steve McClaren, who had a brief coaching stint at QPR earlier in the season, had taken over; Rangers' football had barely been worth watching. "We are not perfect," said Fernandes, "but we are smarter and wiser this time round." Were they? Fans had heard all this before. Whilst they admired honesty, a few did wonder if they'd be better off under an 'asshole'.

By July 2014, the euphoria had subsided and fans did not know what to expect in the summer transfer window. Before any signings were made, Fernandes sold his F1 team to a Swiss and Middle Eastern consortium. Caterham had not won a single point since launching in 2010, and their best finish was 11th. Compared to them, Rangers were Barcelona. But as Jackson recalls: "Selling off his F1 team gave us a fright. It showed Fernandes's vulnerability and that his patience can run out – it was a fair warning to the fans."

As for recruitment, it looked like the same mistakes were being made. Seven seasoned pros came in for a total of over £30m including Rio Ferdinand on a free, and the net spend was just over £20m. It was a fair bit and salaries were again high, but they were now back on the gravy train. Much would depend on Austin's goals and 'Arry's nous. But was this being 'smarter and wiser'?

Rangers started the new season where they would finish it – in the relegation zone. But an even bigger threat emerged – the drop might not just be to the Championship but to the Conference! In September, the Football League confirmed that if QPR refused to pay the fine incurred for breaching the FFP rules – which they'd said they'd fight – they could be chucked out of the League altogether.

With the signings not having the desired effect, they were unable to grab a single point from their first 11 away games. In October, Ferdinand, who was not even a shadow of his Manchester United self, announced he would retire at the end of the season. Sandro was injured half the time and Redknapp accused Taarabt, who had come back from a loan spell at Milan, of being "three stone overweight". As another dire season wore on, 'Arry, burdened by dodgy knees and results that were even more crippling, appeared to lose his appetite for the fray. Rangers' fan Toby Young put it like this in *The Spectator*: "Imagine Arthur Daley taking on Garry Kasparov at chess and you'll have some idea of what it's been like watching QPR this season." Then came news that put the woes of the football club into perspective.

It was 8.30am on Sunday, December 28 and the QPR owner was leaving his house in Kuala Lumpur with his children. The AirAsia founder's mobile phone rang. He sensed something was amiss when he saw the call was from Bo Lingam, chief of operations at the airline. Lingam told him that flight QZ8501 had gone missing over the Java Sea en route from Surabaya in Indonesia to Singapore. "When you hear the words 'we've lost contact with an aircraft' it's never a good thing, is it?" Fernandes would say. He added: "My world changed. I just felt shock really, and a sense of helplessness. It's every airline chief executive's worst nightmare."

What he called 'the worst 50 days of my life' had started. It was the third Malaysian-owned plane to go down in nine months, a coincidence that made some wonder if the country was jinxed. But QZ8501 had not been shot down; nor had it 'disappeared'. It looked a more straightforward affair – but it was Fernandes' plane. Nothing that happens on a football pitch could compare with the shock and horror. Fernandes, unlike Malaysia Airlines officials who had behaved like rabbits in headlights in the aftermath of MH370, acted swiftly and decisively. He fronted up immediately, spoke clearly, flew to Surabaya, assisted with the search, comforted grieving relatives and attended funerals. He handled an extremely difficult situation with care and aplomb.

In such genuinely tragic circumstances, the club understood they could not be his first priority. He remembers "turning on to watch the Sheffield United game [in the FA Cup] — and turning it off pretty quickly. No, it wasn't top of my list. I remember there was a draw with Crystal Palace. I still wanted QPR to win and had one eye on Twitter hoping to see a goal. Your life becomes split in two: you have to deal with the pain but you also have to make sure you deal with the people who are still alive and provide their livelihoods, and QPR is one of those."

But both eyes were back on the club when it came to the transfer window. He tweeted: "No more cheque book. We have good players. Bought all the players manager asked for in sunmer [sic]. Our players not mercenaries. Good guys. If something intresting comes up we would look at it. But I'm not optimistic. Given the right motivation, tactics and coaching we can achieve much more."

Fernandes held firm and although in the bottom three, QPR allowed January to pass without making an addition. Redknapp resigned the next day. It was 5.30am when he called the chairman. He said it was because of his wonky knees. "I just felt it right that I didn't try and persuade him," said Fernandes, who added: "So I put the phone down and thought 'Mmm, what am I going to do?' I was brushing my teeth – so I finished doing that." He asked Chris Ramsey to take over and teased the fans, tweeting: "I've found the dream manager."

If there had been no change on the field, there was plenty off it with Les Ferdinand's appointment as director of football prompting CEO

Phil Beard to quit after three and a half difficult years. Form picked up a little but relegation, with all its consequences, looked inevitable. But Fernandes said: "If we go down, it's not the end of the world because we are still going to be on a disciplined course and doing the right thing. And hopefully becoming a Southampton or a Swansea. Or one of those clubs, who have done the right thing and invested in the right ways." They did go down but Ramsey was still given the job on a permanent basis and Fernandes remained defiant: "This time we go down in a much stronger position," he said, "with a better structure in place and better solutions to pursue with what we want to do in the long term."

To many, he sounded like a broken record at a broken club. A post on a QPR message board ruefully stated: 'Fernandes took over the team in the Premier League with debts of around £20m and could this summer preside over one heading for the Championship with debts of more than £200m.' It was also pointed out that since Fernandes took over, the Hoops had spent just short of £120m – more than stable Premier League clubs such as Everton, Swansea, West Bromwich Albion and Stoke City. Michael Hann wrote: "The obvious conclusion from the last few years is that there is a deep-seated problem within the culture, whereby failure is tolerated. Possibly the reason, in many fans' eyes, is that the club doesn't seem to be central to the ambitions of Tony Fernandes and the consortium that owns Rangers."

To be fair, Fernandes has never pretended he doesn't have a lot on his plate. During Redknapp's time, he said: "My job is AirAsia, it's going well and it's what I'm focused on. I am focused on effective communication with the senior management [at QPR], with Phil [Beard] and Harry [Redknapp]. We get together by video conferencing. But nothing beats being here." Nor could his financial commitment be faulted. In November, 2015, he converted £180m of loans into equity.

"It feels like I have been doing turnarounds all my life and this is one hell of a turnaround," he added. Like most turnaround experts, he insisted the key lies with getting the right people on board. But to begin with, he didn't even do that. Beard has an enviable record in events management and turned around The Dome. But he's not a football man. Hughes and Redknapp have been successful at most of their other clubs, but at QPR they were not the right fit. Ditto a whole host of players who had done the business elsewhere. As Hann put it: "The club has taken good managers and players, and turned them into dross, giving them the footballing anti-Midas touch."

One view of events at Loftus Road over the last five years paints Fernandes as the latest in a line of astute businessmen to have misplaced their astuteness once they get the keys to a football club. On football's new breed of owners, Jackson feels: "They've got to learn it's a religion not a business. He [Fernandes] can see the opportunities out there. It's now about cross-fertilising the brand. He likes the publicity, he likes doing it but we always take it with a bit of cynicism. The club seems settled, we're not worried about the club's future. We want the club back again. Anything that could happen to this club did happen."

In February, 2016, Fernandes gave a revealingly frank interview to *Loft For Words'* Clive Whittingham who noted he had recently been defending his record and asked him to name his main successes and failures? Fernandes said: "I wouldn't say I was defending my position, because there's not a lot to defend truth be told – numbers are numbers, positions are positions. I was trying to say that it's not as bad as it's made out to be. If you're a QPR fan sometimes it feels like apocalypse has arrived, and I was saying it's not the end of the world. We're committed and we have a good team in place – though there's no guarantee that will fix everything. That's what I was trying to say, rather than defend my record, which cannot be defended… We didn't buy properly, but we backed our managers. Hindsight is wonderful, when we signed a lot of those players people were enthusiastic. We didn't get criticised at the time."

Whittingham asked: "After five tough years, and the money spent, why carry on?" Fernandes replied: "I still love it. Why are you still writing the way you do about QPR? It gets into your blood for better or worse. I get depressed when we lose now, even though it doesn't make much difference this season. I've had some of the happiest days of my life here. Wembley… If I get hit by a bus tomorrow, I've had an amazing life and Wembley is one of those things that not many people can experience. Being carried around by Joey Barton, hugging Charlie Austin, seeing 40,000 ecstatic QPR fans. It's a wonderful feeling, and it doesn't change. Winning against Ipswich last week was as good as any other victory. The dream lives on that we can make this little club something bigger."

When Whittingham says, "You'll never be able to sell this club for the amount you've converted to equity," he says: "No I don't think so. But we would never have been paid back that debt anyway, so we may as well. Never say never, who would have thought Southampton would grow to the size they have in such a short space of time? It's a long term project, there will be hairy moments, but in a strange way by being down here, being in midtable, maybe it gives us time to do what we always wanted to do and there's less pressure. It might take two, three or four seasons but we want to get it right. As a competitive person you always want to go up, but we're not taking short cuts."

Five years is an awful long time to keep repeating mistakes and admitting naivety – as Fernandes has done. There have been two relegations and a huge turnover in players while the owners have been on the job but not learning. Indeed, the greatest achievement of his reign has been to keep the majority of fans onside. His honesty and openness have gone a long way and his passion for the game is undiminished. Asked to explain why he hasn't packed up, he says: "Winning is an amazing feeling. You don't get that in business, you don't get that in many things. Listen, there'll be more downs than ups but the ups balance out the downs." That said, his misadventures in the transfer market were memorably compared by Barry Glendenning on the *Football Weekly* podcast to "a hunk of fresh meat being lowered into a tank of piranhas".

Fernandes' ownership is a unique and intriguing case. The "diamond" is still to be extracted, the building of the club has been mostly from the top down, the new stadium looks a non-starter, the training ground is yet to be completed and last season was the first time youth was given a chance. By his own admission he's been naive yet his public relations and people skills are world-class. Even with AirAsia, he has been called a showman in a Richard Branson sort of way and his lapping up of the Wembley glory reveals Caesar traits. But his enduring determination to get the club out of the hole he's dug for it suggests he could yet become a saviour of sorts. You hope he succeeds. He has spoken of the tragedy being "Shakespearean", and when you look at his first love's rise to Olympic stadium, Europe and 50,000 season ticket holders on the other side of London, the irony cannot be ignored. The money Fernandes has wasted at QPR would have been enough to buy a bigger club – even West Ham.

Wolverhampton Wanderers

WOLVERHAMPTON WANDERERS

1

"The headlines belonged to my favourite team, Wolves. Even then kids liked to follow the successful team: they always appear more glamorous for that reason.

George Best

Molineux in the early fifties: misty nights in the Black Country, floodlights that might have been installed by Thomas Edison, 'Soviet' opponents who looked like they'd been trained by Josef Stalin. Home fans weren't worried though – Wolves were trained by Stan Cullis. It was the Iron Curtain versus the Iron Manager. Wolves, champions of England, old gold shirts glistening under four clusters of what seemed no more than 40 watt bulbs on stilts, had the nation glued to nine-inch black and white screens. Long before the Champions League was even a twinkle, these were big 'European nights'. Dynamo and Spartak of Moscow, and Honved, with half the Hungarians who had bewitched England at Wembley and Budapest, were vanquished: Cullis hailed Wolves as 'champions of the world'.

The claim was unverifiable but far from outrageous: Real Madrid, Racing Club of Argentina and 'a South African XI' would also fall to Wolves' long-ball game. Devised by Cullis, it was an 'up and at 'em' approach from a side with skill and dash as well as sinew. If General Patton had been a football manager, it was how he'd have set up a team. And as Patton did with his troops, Cullis put the fear of God into his players. They, in turn, would 'die' for him. They won the League in 1954, 1958 and 1959, were runners-up in 1950, 1955 and 1960, and came third in 1953 and 1956. 'World champions' might have been a stretch, but in England, with respect to the Busby Babes, Wolves were the team of the decade.

Cullis's proclamation of top dog status – gleefully fanned by a jingoistic Fleet Street – was greeted with predictable cynicism on the continent, not least by the French. But it would convince *L'Equipe* editor, Gabriel Hanot, of the need for a proper European club championship. Hanot had been persuaded of the merits of such a tournament by journalist, Jacques Ferran, who had covered South America's already established Copa Libertadores. Hanot vowed to press UEFA for an equivalent. It's not just in using shaving cream at free-kicks where that continent has led the football world.

Hanot wrote: "Before we declare that Wolverhampton are invincible, let them go to Moscow and Budapest. And there are other internationally renowned clubs: AC Milan and Real Madrid to name but two. A club world championship or at least a European one – larger, more meaningful and more prestigious than the Mitropa Cup and more original than a competition for national teams – should be launched."

The Mitropa Cup was the Johnstone's Paint trophy of the old Austro-Hungarian Empire and Hanot's proposal was put to the UEFA congress of March 1955. It was approved a month later. But when the inaugural European Cup kicked off the following season, there was no Wolves nor any other English representative. Ted Drake's Chelsea had pipped Cullis's men to the title and the tournament was for champions only in those days, second and third really being nowhere. But – and this is where the irony is cruellest – after all Wolves' epic trailblazing, English clubs were banned from taking part by the Football League's secretary Alan Hardaker. The notorious Little Englander's explanation, as told to *The Times*, was: "Too many wogs and dagoes."

It is a football tragedy that Wolves, at their rampaging Honved peak, were never unleashed on the other big beasts in a proper continental championship. As it was prior to the emergence of Manchester United's 'Busby Babes', the West Midlanders were *the* team to follow. Among their admirers was a wide-eyed youngster who would become the most iconic footballer of the next decade. None other than George Best told *Hard Tackles and Dirty Baths: The inside story of football's golden era*: "The headlines belonged to my favourite team, Wolves. Even then kids liked to follow the successful team: they always appear more glamorous for that reason. It was reading those reports of the Wolves games that got me hooked. I became aware of the great traditions of the Wolves team and their exploits domestically and internationally. Wolves were one of the first clubs to play under lights, and there was an extra-special feeling about a game being played in the evening. It was sheer theatre."

Back in those austere, post ration-book days, there had not been much competition – the magical Magyars apart. In club football, Real Madrid were yet to establish their aristocratic hegemony over Europe, Eusebio was still playing barefoot in Mozambique and Ferenc Puskas had yet to gallop through the Iron Curtain. There were quibbles about the style – "kick and rush" said some – but Cullis was fiercely proud of it.

Yet purists point to how Honved had passed Wolves off their own park to build a 2-0 lead. It had the makings of a magical encore to the Magyars' humbling of England but for one precaution that Cullis had taken. Ron Atkinson was on the Molineux groundstaff at the time and remembers: "It rained cats and dogs that day, only stopping in the late afternoon. Around 4.30 Cullis summoned the groundsman and told him: 'Put the hosepipes on'." By half-time, the pitch had become a quagmire and in the second half, Honved's slick passes congealed in the Molineux mud. As fit as the army side were, they tired and Wolves, who trained like commandos and had an unbeaten home record to protect, seized the initiative. Long balls flew unhindered over the cloying surface and three second half goals sent the crowd into delirium. The amphibious comeback sparked Cullis's claim for supremacy and went some way to redeeming the reputation of English football. Ditto skipper, Billy Wright, who, in chasing the ghostly Nandor Hidegkuti at Wembley, had been described by *The Times'* Geoffrey Green as 'a fire engine looking for the wrong fire'. Wright had a better sense of direction in a flood.

There was much more to Wolves than their Route 1 tactics. They were pioneers of sports science and took fitness to a new level. They were among the first to invest in floodlights and sticklers for detail – even wearing special satin shirts that shone more lustrously under the glow. It's a bar-room discussion double 'if', but their pioneering efforts might have been rewarded by a Real Madrid-like dominance had the European Cup been established five years earlier. And if English clubs had not been at the mercy of a racist autocrat.

Prior to the Spaniards snaring Hungary's Puskas and Argentina's Alfredo di Stefano, the marauders in old gold might well have been the dominant force. With Bert Williams in goal and Wright marshalling the defence alongside Ron Flowers and Eddie Clamp, they had no weakness at the back. The creative mastermind was Peter Broadbent, who could ping long balls with laser accuracy to the fleet feet of wingers, Jimmy Mullen and Johnny Hancocks, the latter known as 'Dynamite' in size 2 boots. Roy Swinburne and Dennis Wilshaw were the fangs of an irresistible pack.

Another of the pub imponderables is just how good Wolves may have been had they shown Madrid's ruthlessness in player recruitment. The crown jewel they missed was not a foreign mercenary but from their own backyard, a lad who seemed destined for the same stratosphere as Real's fabled foreign duo. Duncan Edwards, from nearby Dudley, was already a legend in his school lunch hour when Cullis got to hear of him. The manager, duly impressed by the outrageous gifts and strength of this man-child, would sit in his car outside the Edwards house waiting for Big Dunc to come home. He never imagined him not signing for his local club, especially when they were 'champions of the world'.

But Manchester United were also on the trail and alas for Cullis, for England, but most of all for Edwards, it would be the Busby Babes that the boy joined. Cullis was to lament: "I knew they'd got him when I saw a brand new washing machine in his mum's kitchen." Oh, fate's fickle finger – but for the gift of that humble appliance, the greatest unfulfilled talent in English football history may not have been on board the plane that crashed in the Munich snow – he'd have been playing for Wolves instead!

Just a reminder of the company Wolves have kept and to provide some necessary perspective on the plight the club found itself in during the summer of 1982.

WOLVERHAMPTON WANDERERS

2

"It really was an amazing period. The whole of the country seemed to be talking about what was happening at Wolves. We even replaced the Falklands War as the main item on some news bulletins."

Former Wolves director Doug Hope.

It is the afternoon of July 30, 1982, a Friday, 'D-Day' as many inevitably called it for one of England's greatest clubs. Wolverhampton Wanderers, founder members of the Football League and almost permanently domiciled in the First Division, are facing extinction. In the five previous decades, the club had spent just three seasons outside the top flight, were league champions three times and runners-up on five occasions. In that time, they'd also won both the FA Cup and League Cup twice and been finalists in the UEFA Cup. But having done the hard yards to perpetuity, they were now deeply in debt and at the door of the knacker's yard. Already in receivership, they would go under if no bids came in.

Five o'clock was the deadline and Dave Harrison, who was covering Wolves for the Wolverhampton *Express & Star*, will never forget the suspense of that fateful afternoon. "I was in the office. I'd written two stories – one that Wolves had gone to the wall and another that Wolves can play on. We held the paper back. I could either have been in Birmingham, where negotiations were going on, or in the office making phone calls. My link with it was the Football League press officer, Andy Williamson, who was keeping me up to speed. I was ringing him on the hour. It got to about twenty to five and I rang again. He said: 'We've heard nothing.' I said: 'It looks like they're going to go.'

"It got to ten to five and I rang the Football League again but there was no answer. Here we were trying to run a special edition of the paper and I couldn't get the news. I thought 'blimey, they've gone home. How am I going to find out now?' I tried again at five to and then at three minutes to, and Andy answers. 'Where were you?' I ask. He says: 'I've got my coat on – I've been in another part of the building. But Wolves have been saved.'

"'Who by?' I ask. 'I can't tell you – there's a confidentiality agreement. I can't say who it is.' I said: 'I've got the story ready to go – if it's Dougan's lot put the phone down.' It went dead. That was his way of telling me. We sold 20,000 copies in the town and 'Dougan's lot' were the new owners of Wolves. The only other bids were from Ken Wheldon of Walsall and a joint one from Doug Ellis, of Villa fame, and ex-Wolves keeper, Malcolm Finlayson, who were trying to pick it up on the cheap. I don't think the Official Receiver would have gone for them anyway."

The rescue had been totally unexpected. The Football League had even omitted Wolves from the pools coupon for the first day of the coming season. They'd taken the precaution of 'promoting' Lincoln City from the Third Division to replace them while Peterboro were moved up to the Third. No one knew who was behind it yet more than three decades later their names still resonate. Mohamed Al Hassan Bhatti and Mohamed Akbar Bhatti were among the first foreign owners of a British football club. Their four-year reign would be a disaster – the template of how not to run one – yet they had saved the club when no one else would. And got no thanks – Derek Dougan, the club's legendary former striker and the Bhattis' front man, got it all.

Wolves had got into this mess because of what became known as "Marshall's Folly" – the decision by chairman, Harry Marshall, to replace the much-loved Molineux Street stand with an anonymous carbuncle. It cost a then eye-watering £2m. Symbolic of the brutalism of the day, it was meant to show that Wolves were marching with the times – providing sponsors' boxes and comfortable seating. It was just phase one of a wrecking/rebuilding programme and the sense the club was coming off its axis was heightened by a plan to turn the pitch around.

Fans were furious long before the bill came in. It was as if Wolves' very soul was having a Caesarian: the distinctive 'Tudor' gables that had gazed approvingly at the long ball, bowed meekly to the wrecking ball. And as if that were not callous enough, the unloved replacement was set back 30 yards from the playing surface. Patrons compared it to the turf where binoculars are required for viewing the distant furlongs. With the atmosphere more disgruntled morgue than roaring cauldron, home advantage was surrendered. But what brought Wolves to the brink was the financial millstone. In less than three years after the stand's official opening, the club had, by Marshall's own admission, debts of £2m and was losing £5,000 a week.

It led to open rebellion against the so-called "Marshall Law". Local insurance broker and lifelong Wolves fan, Roger Hipkiss, led a revolt among shareholders and the chairman was eventually toppled. But "Marshall's Folly" remained: a broken club and a ground with a concrete blot on a once-proud but crumbling landscape.

As rescues go, they don't come more left-field than the one Harrison announced to his readers. "Mysterious from Day 1", is how he describes 'Dougan's lot'. The mystery men were the two Bhatti brothers, who were seldom seen but still haunt true believers of a Wolverine persuasion today. Almost three decades after the takeover, a poster on a Wolves fan site, who had the temerity to mention their names, immediately slammed the brakes to write: "There, I have uttered the dreaded words..."

But there was no sense of dread as the fans celebrated that Friday night. Their beloved club was still alive and 'Dougan's lot' were good enough for them. And the man leading the rescue was their hero – a Messianic figure and this was his second coming. "The Doog had been idolised as a player," says Harrison. "And it was great for the fans to have him back in the fold. They thought these new owners were going to spend a fortune before they knew who they were. There was a meeting at the Civic Hall to announce this great new era for the club and, at the first home game, the Doog stood with the fans behind the goal and called them 'my people'."

Dougan had not lost his common touch since he'd left Molineux as a player. Or his charisma. The shock of hair, which had been a respectable prototype for Carlos Valderrama, was long-since tamed and bore an autumnal grey. But he still had the gift of the Irish gab. In the intervening 17 years, he had been part of a charismatic trio with Brian Clough and Malcolm Allison that gave television its golden age of outspoken punditry. And as PFA leader, he'd proved an able and caring administrator. With this impressive body of work embellishing a playing career as an old gold-plated Molineux legend, he seemed the ideal man to lift the gloom and lead Wolves back to their glory days.

The Doog became chairman with local property developer and car dealer, Doug Hope, also a Wolves fan, as vice-chairman. Hope explains how it all came about. "It started rather obscurely when I put an advert in the *Express & Star* for a Rolls-Royce I had for sale. A guy rang up and we ended up doing a swap deal for a property and the Rolls-Royce." One thing led to another and through various contacts in the property world, Hope ended up getting in touch with Allied Properties. He says: "The whole deal was put together within three weeks and a lot was taken on trust. It was clear to me that there was development potential at Molineux and that could be used to fund the club, with the key factor being that a supermarket could be built at the rear of one of the stands. Derek and I had meetings with the leaders of the council and were given to understand that if the club's future was secured, we would have their support."

Meanwhile, the Bhattis kept very much to themselves, did nothing to help their cause and a fair bit to hinder it. Harrison recalls: "They used to slide in at the last minute. We [the paper] managed to snap a picture of them once in the directors' box. But I never saw them and I was there every single day." Asked why they were so secretive, Hope says: "That was just their way. They naively thought the press wouldn't dig into where the money had come from to 'save the Wolves', and wanted Derek and I to front it. That lasted about a week before the press identified them."

They'd reckoned without Derek Tucker, chief news reporter at the *Express & Star*, who, according to Harrison, "was a good, old-fashioned Rottweiler of a reporter who did some digging at Companies House. Essentially the company was Allied Properties but it was he who found out the main men were the Bhattis. Mohamed was 30 and Akbar barely 20." As to where they were from, Hope says: "My understanding was that they were brought up in Manchester, but may not have been born there. I believe they were of Pakistani origin. I seem to remember someone saying the elder one had studied at Manchester Business School. There was an implied inference of Arab links and they seem to have international connections. The only time I saw them dressed in Arab attire was when Derek and I were first introduced to them by the MD of Allied Properties, Mike Rowland. Allied had done quite significant residential developments in the South of England prior to buying Wolves. The business was run from the Hertford Street office in Mayfair which we all visited frequently."

With a Rolls-Royce ostentatiously parked outside, pictures of King Faisal on the walls and various opulent Arabian trappings, it was a far cry from where Dougan had first met the Bhattis – in a Portakabin at Manchester airport. But even that was plush enough to have been from Babylon, according to the Doog. "They were lucky to get him," says Dave Harrison. "They needed a front man to carry it through as they were totally unknown." And it was on his every word of blarney and football nous that the brothers hung. Never one to waste a soliloquy when a syllable would do, the Doog did not just tick every box, he filled them with emeralds.

He told Peter Lansley in *Running with Wolves:* "When you see Mahmoud Al Hassan Bhatti drive up in a Rolls-Royce, at his own aviation company, and know of his luxurious offices in London, you can't help but feel impressed. And when Peat Marwick & Co, the accountants dealing with the receivership, show you a bank draft for £2,050,000, you have reason to think the club can be saved and built up again." The extra £50,000 had been for the Football League who had demanded it as a guarantee Wolves would fulfil their fixtures.

However, it soon became apparent that the owners' football knowledge was less than encyclopaedic. Says Hope: "The Bhattis' company, Allied Properties, was primarily a property development company, but they were initially very enthusiastic about the club. Up until Christmas everything went well. In the early days they tried to arrange friendly games via their international contacts. I remember returning to Molineux one afternoon to be met by one of the girls in the office who was in something of a flap. She said could I phone London straight away as Mr Bhatti needed to ask me something urgently. I duly did so and the voice on the end of the line said words to the effect 'thank goodness you've phoned. How do you spell Juventus?'"

In *The Doog,* that Harrison wrote with former *Express & Star* sports editor Steve Gordos, they tell of the Wolves-Bhattis story being front page news all over Britain. Hope is quoted as saying: "It really was an amazing period. The whole of the country seemed to be talking about what was happening at Wolves. We even replaced the Falklands War as the main item on some news bulletins."

Wolves was another kind of reclamation job but Dougan did not need a task force – he simply breezed through the club in time-honored, new broom fashion. Manager, Ian Greaves, often acclaimed the best since Cullis, was sacked along with commercial manager, Jack Taylor, the former World Cup referee, and secretary, Phil Shaw, who had served the club for 33 years. Two of the replacements, according to Harrison, were Dougan's "only good moves": ex-Aston Villa official, Eric Woodward, and manager, Graham Hawkins. Woodward was the calming yin to Dougan's excitable yang while Hawkins, yanked out of Shrewsbury Town, belied the 'Graham Who?' headlines to mould a winning blend of youth and astute signings.

The mood was helped by the good start Wolves made to the season. Says Harrison: "They bought a couple of players on the cheap but basically used a load of kids – four teenagers on the opening day. The fans were happy but winning matches camouflaged the truth. It was seat of the pants stuff as essentially there were no funds. They couldn't even pay the staff wages. There was one tale of a suitcase full of fivers arriving on a Friday so they could pay up. The next day the police called the club secretary and said: 'Would you mind not broadcasting a story that a suitcase full of money was floating around Wolverhampton?'"

To the question of when he first smelled a rat, Harrison answers: "They started to fall away toward the end of the first season but had points on the board, having brought a few players in. In that respect, fans thought 'Hey, this is alright'. When we won promotion, Graham Hawkins was told he'd have a transfer budget to strengthen the side and he'd lined up David Seaman, Mick McCarthy and Gary Lineker. But they never materialised and the Doog went in over the head of Hawkins and bought Tony Towner, a winger from Rotherham, who he tried to say was another Waggy [Dave Wagstaffe]. Towner cost £80,000 but didn't deliver. It turned out the whole transfer budget had been blown on this guy. We'd gone up but were out of our depth and didn't win for 14 matches."

3

"The Bhatti brothers were given hints that they'd get planning permission but the council took a dislike to them. There were echoes of Enoch Powell, it was the 80s and they didn't get permission."

Dave Harrison, *Express & Star*.

Promotion in that first season proved a false dawn that masked an unravelling behind the scenes. The owners secured an overdraft from Lloyd's Bank but then fell out with them. Dougan was not alone in feeling they would have been better off not going up. Talking to the Bhattis "20 times a day" offered scant reassurance. The chairman admitted to getting "bad vibes" as early as the first Christmas and soon found himself having to give personal guarantees for an overdraft so the players could be paid. Hipkiss and Hope were also putting their own money in. Besides subsidising the club, the Doog was practically living at the ground. "I spent more time with the cleaning lady than anyone else," he said, describing the task as "swimming against the tide."

It had turned when the council refused the planning permission for the supermarket. In *The Doog*, Hope said: "When things started to turn against us, the Bhattis pulled their money out. They felt the council had reneged on the agreement. They stood to make a lot of money out of the development. When permission was eventually granted [to another group] I am led to believe the development company, the Gallaghers, made millions out of it. That sort of money would have enabled us to build Wolves into a real force."

Hipkiss feels strongly that it was nothing short of a betrayal by the council and that devious forces came into play. He said in *The Doog*: "It wasn't obvious and, of course, no-one would admit it, but I reckon there were racist undertones. Don't forget Wolverhampton was the constituency of Enoch Powell, author of the infamous 'Rivers of Blood' speech, and I believe there was still an element of those sentiments prevailing through the town. They were dark-skinned outsiders and a lot of people in the community didn't like that. The Bhattis had a raw deal – no question about it. They had been promised everything and ended up with nothing. They couldn't keep putting their own money in and getting nothing in return. To this day Allied Properties have never been paid money held and owed to them by Wolverhampton Council. I believe with compound interest this amounts to £3 million plus." That was in 2011.

Hope adds: "It didn't help the Bhattis' cause that they refused to speak to anyone. On a personal level they were fine, but they didn't want a public profile and you couldn't get away with that in football." Not even in those pre social media/camera phone days could you hope to slink in and out of the directors' box without arousing suspicion. As saviours of the club they had been entitled to considerable gratitude, but their surreptitious manner aroused inevitable doubts. Harrison remembers saying: 'We'll do a nice piece on you and tell the world how great you are', but 'oh, no', they'd say, 'we're very private people'. You were suspicious and that suspicion magnified a million fold when you found out they hadn't got any money." Well, at least money they were prepared to invest.

Nor did their Mayfair office avoid the notion it might be an Aladdin's Cave. Harrison says: "The chairman of the supporters club took a detour to their offices on a trip to London as he wanted to hand in a petition. He got as far as the intercom and as soon as he said who he was it went dead." Even in their honeymoon period, they were never going to do 'a Doog' and milk the adulation of the terraces. But they made a crucial mistake in thinking they could act like Howard Hughes and it wouldn't matter.

By the second season, Harrison's relationship with the Doog had deteriorated. "As a businessman he had no idea," he told me. "He was ahead of his time in a way for things like sponsored shirts but he never made any real money. And I fell out with him. You could have a conversation and you'd be his best friend, then you'd say something and he'd turn – just like that. He was such a complex character – a Jekyll and Hyde." In fairness to Dougan, he was working under great strain for a club he genuinely loved and for no monetary reward – his promised five-year contract never materialising. He had defended the indefensible with the Bhattis, but eventually he would turn against them.

It was hard to say whether things were worse on the field or off it during the season after promotion. The winless start coincided with a fire sale of players. Prized asset Andy Gray, who had been valued at £1m the previous year, was sold to Everton for just £180,000 and promising goalkeeper Tim Flowers ended up being sold by the receiver to Southampton for £80,000. Then Hawkins was sacked – and Dougan was unable to help his friend. As a sign of his waning power, the Ulsterman also couldn't prevent old nemesis, Tommy Docherty, from taking over. The board were desperate for someone to lift the gloom and felt the Doc's renowned sense of humour might do the trick. His opening gambit was: 'Derek Dougan is to football what King Herod is to babysitting'.

The Scot, who had lost his early powers to mould a team but not his wit, developed a genuine affection for Wolves and battled gamely. But it was the botched attempt to upgrade the ground – now a dilapidated shell – that would lead the club to receivership. In 2011, John Lalley looked back and wrote a lament in the *Express & Star*: "Molineux remarkably had descended into a shambolic and ugly eyesore, the stadium, if such a word was even remotely applicable, had been allowed to degenerate into a virtual slum dwelling. It was a neglected, decaying relic, crumbling on its foundations and a gaping architectural insult to a remarkable club and to the scores of great players who had proudly worn a gold shirt. It was a betrayal of a special heritage and the darkest period in the club's existence. Looking back now, the entire ghastly scenario simply beggars belief. As stunning visual evidence of this harrowing demise, there stood the remains of the North Bank, bleached of all colour, reduced to a dilapidated ruin, standing pitifully like a discarded doll's house stuck in its own time warp."

One by one, the three old stands were closed for safety reasons and, talk about smelling rats, the dressing room was overrun by the things as the players were to discover to their horror. But perhaps the most pitiful, almost Dickensian, tale of how close to the poor house the erstwhile 'champions of the world' came was when Neville Hamilton collapsed in training with a suspected heart attack. Docherty recalled: "They were just carrying him into the ambulance when Greg Fellows, my assistant, ran towards him and started taking the lad's boots off. It was a very grave situation for the boy so I said to Greg, 'What the hell do you think you are doing?' He replied, 'Gaffer, we have only got 14 pairs of boots in the whole club and can't afford to lose these'."

The Doc was sacked after a run of 21 games without a win and Wolves were in Division Three – worse off than when the Bhattis had taken over and Dougan was coming to the end of his tether. As his drinking worsened, his behaviour became erratic. Finally, in January 1986, he jumped before he was pushed. In *The Doog*, Hipkiss says: "In the end he did resign, but it was under pressure. Eventually there was a unanimous board vote inviting him to step down. It affected him when he left. He was disappointed and for a long time didn't want anything to do with any of us. The problem was that he did not really have a good business brain."

Dougan blamed everyone else and in an interview with *Running with Wolves* claimed he was owed between £150,000 and £200,000. In a desperate attempt to stop the plunge through the divisions, Bill McGarry, the hard taskmaster who had led them to glory in the 1970s, returned as Docherty's successor in 1985. But, unhappy about the way the club was being run, McGarry quit after just 61 days. He said solemnly: "I don't want to preside over the death of a great club."

Wolves duly dropped into Division 4 for the first time in their history but stayed alive. On 2 July, 1986 the Bhatti brothers' era came to an end when the official receiver was called in. But the club was saved from extinction when Wolverhampton Council purchased Molineux for £1.12 million, along with the surrounding land. Gallagher Estates Limited, in conjunction with the Asda Superstore chain, agreed to pay off the club's outstanding debts, subject to building and planning permission for an Asda superstore on land adjacent to the stadium being granted by the Council.

It is not difficult to imagine how the Bhatti brothers felt. "They did feel cheated," says Hipkiss who denies they were simply naïve. The assumption has been among many that theirs was a classic 'nod and wink' arrangement but Hipkiss, who also joined the board, insists it was not and that there was a letter of commitment from Wolverhampton City Council. He maintains: "It is quite clear – the council reneged on the agreement. Ten years later they [the council] wouldn't have got away with it.

"It was a very good idea and a few years later a local businessman does exactly the same thing and gets approval – for exactly the same site. Tony Gallagher, of Gallagher Estates, told me it was up to that point, the most profitable deal he'd ever done. Asda came in and they're still there to this day. Gallagher could have developed Molineux had he wanted to but he was a rugby man, not a football man, so the chance was missed. The Bhattis got a very raw deal which goes a long way to explaining what happened afterwards."

Adds Hope: "It became clear that the council support for the supermarket was not forthcoming and the Bhattis dug their heels in and wouldn't, or couldn't, provide money to fund the club. There was huge opposition [to the plans] from the local 'establishment', most notably the operators of the main shopping centre, Manders. Whether there was a racist dimension to it I can't say for certain. There was certainly a lot of ill-feeling and it was the view of many locals, that a couple of upstarts, Derek and myself, had brought in some outsiders and taken over the town's prize asset. They were collectively kicking themselves for allowing such a situation to happen." Harrison also feels it may well have been down to racism. He said: "The Bhatti brothers were given hints that they'd get planning permission but the council took a dislike to them. There were echoes of Enoch Powell, it was the 80s and they didn't get permission."

Wolverhampton would not be the first council to get cold feet after pressure from local businesses. And with unknown outsiders, it would have been that much easier to pull the rug. The Bhattis had a sound business plan as has been shown by the subsequent and continuing success of the supermarket on the same footprint – it is the most profitable in the area – and the killing the developer made. Nor has the supermarket infringed upon the hallowed turf. Alarmists had feared shopping trolleys cluttering the channels down which Hancocks and Mullen had chased. Molineux has now been impressively rebuilt with the Asda store hidden away behind the towering Stan Cullis stand.

After more than three decades of inching towards (and occasionally beyond) political correctness, those original questions have to be posed once again: were the Bhattis that bad? Or just unlucky? Were they ahead of their time? Will history view them more kindly?

Bhatti is still a forbidden name in many a Black Country household: one synonymous with abject failure in running a football club. Even after the chaos wrought by certain owners of recent times elsewhere, the perception is that the Bhatti brothers remain in the pantheon of dishonour among their kind. Bhatti by name and batty by... was an irresistible gift to the local wags.

In summing up, the Bhattis were probably 10 years ahead of their time in planning and 10 years behind in public relations. That said, the local community was similarly tardy when it came to race relations. A decade later, as Hipkiss suggests, the Bhattis would not have been treated like that. Their visionary plan – totally acceptable now as clubs try to suck the marrow from every square inch they own – may have indeed financed a Wolves revival and instead of being pilloried, they might have been regarded rather differently. As it was, they presided over the darkest days in Wolves' history. Their allergy to appearing in public compounded their cluelessness about the actual running of a football club, its place in the community and their relationship with the fans. And it negated any sympathy they may have been due. Yes, they saved the club from one abyss – only to dump it in another.